The Palgrave Lacan Series

Jacques Lacan is one of the most important and influential thinkers of the 20th century. The reach of this influence continues to grow as we settle into the 21st century, the resonance of Lacan's thought arguably only beginning now to be properly felt, both in terms of its application to clinical matters and in its application to a range of human activities and interests. The Palgrave Lacan Series is a book series for the best new writing in the Lacanian field, giving voice to the leading writers of a new generation of Lacanian thought. The series will comprise original monographs and thematic, multi-authored collections. The books in the series will explore aspects of Lacan's theory from new perspectives and with original insights. There will be books focused on particular areas of or issues in clinical work. There will be books focused on applying Lacanian theory to areas and issues beyond the clinic, to matters of society, politics, the arts and culture. Each book, whatever its particular concern, will work to expand our understanding of Lacan's theory and its value in the 21st century.

Luca Di Gregorio

Lacan in Italy

Clinic, Politics, Aesthetics

palgrave
macmillan

Luca Di Gregorio
University of Southampton
Southampton, UK

ISSN 2946-4196 ISSN 2946-420X (electronic)
The Palgrave Lacan Series
ISBN 978-3-031-91527-7 ISBN 978-3-031-91528-4 (eBook)
https://doi.org/10.1007/978-3-031-91528-4

Cover illustration: ©Karyn R. Millet/Getty Images

This Palgrave Macmillan imprint is published by the registered company Springer Nature Switzerland AG.
The registered company address is: Gewerbestrasse 11, 6330 Cham, Switzerland

For Andrea Di Gregorio (1954–2013)

Psychoanalysis gives us a chance, a chance to start again
Jacques Lacan, *My Teaching*

Che l'eredità abbia bisogno della distanza per realizzarsi?
Massimo Recalcati, private conversation

Acknowledgements

This book is the result of multiple journeys I have undertaken over the past two decades, each sparked by special encounters with remarkable individuals.

If psychoanalysis offered me *a chance to start again*, this was only made possible by my life-changing relationship with Maurizio Cottone, with whom I began my psychoanalytic journey all the way back in February 2005. This journey made all others possible. For this and much more, I owe him an enormous debt of gratitude.

My own migration journey took me from being a small-town Italian boy, unable to speak English, to settling in the UK. I moved abroad with the hope, as Freud once said, of loving and working freely. This would never have been possible without Lisa Ugolini, who believed in me against all odds and gave me the confidence to take my first step towards learning English.

My academic journey began with my MA, supervised by Giovanni Bottiroli, whom I would like to thank for his incredible intellectual generosity. It then continued with my PhD at the University of Kent, where I had the privilege to be supervised by Alvise Sforza Tarabochia, to whom I extend my warmest thanks for his invaluable support (if only my superego could speak with his calm and caring voice!). This book grew out of my doctoral dissertation and is, in many ways, a homage to the unforgettable years I spent in Canterbury, surrounded by wonderful people:

Wissia Fiorucci, a very special friend and a great mentor, Fran Beaton, Francesco Capello, Marine Ganofsky, Alex Marlow-Man, and Silvia Pulinas. I would also like to thank Fabio Vighi, the external examiner of my PhD viva, for supporting this project in its early stages. Special thanks also go to Massimo Recalcati for believing in me as a young scholar and for accepting my invitation to deliver his first talk in the UK for the conference I co-organised at Kent in 2015. Our conversation during an evening walk back from Canterbury Cathedral is a fond memory I cherish dearly.

My tumultuous academic journey continued at the University of Winchester, where Thomas Nørgaard provided me with invaluable opportunities to develop my teaching career. It eventually led me to the University of Southampton, where I was fortunate enough to secure my first full-time, permanent academic position. At Southampton, I am privileged to be surrounded by exceptional, supportive, and lovely colleagues, including Pritti Aggarwal, Daniela Bisci, Jo Culpin, Polly Hardy-Johnson, Kathy Kendall, Clare Polack, and Linda Turner from the Faculty of Medicine, as well as Aude Campmas and Joan Tumblety from the Southampton Centre for Medical and Health Humanities.

Throughout these years, my students have all taught me a great deal about myself, allowing me to discover and nurture my deep and enduring passion for teaching.

I would not have embarked on these journeys without the love, unwavering patience, and endless encouragements of my mother Laura, my siblings, Valentina and Matteo, and my beloved late *nonna* Erminia.

I would be completely lost without my irreplaceable and amazing friends, whom I would like to wholeheartedly thank for their constant support: Giacomo Bartolucci, Donato Capitella, Callum Dixon, Dave Chivers, Rima Eshkal, Felix Felbermayer, Francesca Ferraro, Iris Huang, Elisabetta Montebelli, Karwan Moutasim, Sara Silvestri, and Andrew Vaughan.

I am also grateful to Victoria Weavil for her expert assistance in editing and refining the language of my book.

Thank you to Ian Morton, Nick Morton, Anne Nicholson, and Mike Nicholson, for welcoming and teaching me so much about British people and culture.

Finally, my deepest and most heartfelt thanks are owed to my lifelong partner, Stuart Duncan Morton, for loving me in a way I have never experienced before and for stopping me from endlessly floating in outer space. He is—along with our lovely cat Polpy—my family and my homeland.

Praise for *Lacan in Italy*

"Di Gregorio's book offers a fascinating panorama of Lacan in Italy, exploring not only Lacan's own special link to Italian culture but also the development and dissemination of his ideas in Italy. This book will appeal to analysts and students of Lacanian psychoanalysis, as well as to anyone interested in how psychoanalytic ideas take root and crystalize in particular cultural environments, and the light this sheds on intellectual history more generally."

—Darian Leader, *Psychoanalyst and member of the Centre for Freudian Analysis and Research, UK*

"At the heart of this book lies the singular relationship that connects Lacan to Italy. For Italian culture, Lacan not only elicited a renewal of psychoanalytic practice but also embodied a brilliant crossroads between the languages of philosophy, politics, and art. Di Gregorio masterfully reconstructs this story, identifying key themes, moments, and contexts through which it came to life. Despite their profound differences, Italian Lacanians have produced research that goes beyond analytical semantics, establishing a profound relationship with contemporaneity. In their research, terms such as real and symbolic, desire and enjoyment, unconscious and subjectivation have found a meaning that goes beyond Lacan's letter, addressing the traumas and questions of our time. Among those who opened up this area of research, the figure of Massimo Recalcati stands out for his extraordinary ability to renew the Lacanian word, combining scholarly thought and clinical experience."

—Roberto Esposito, *Professor Emeritus at Scuola Normale Superiore di Pisa, Italy*, and author of *Bios* (2008), *Communitas* (2010), and *Immunitas* (2011)

"Di Gregorio's book transcends the mere categorizing of Italian interpretations of Lacan. Rather, the work is fuelled by the author's passionate engagement with Lacan's ideas, highlighting their universal significance. This is a scholarly rigorous and intellectually sophisticated journey through one of the most stimulating intellectual pursuits of modern times."

—Fabio Vighi, *Professor of Critical Theory, Cardiff University, UK*

"Does being Lacanian today mean endorsing the materialistic cynicism of the drive, promoted by the capitalist discourse, which suppresses the singular experience of desire? Or is it more about integrating—rather than opposing—the classic Lacan of the symbolic (desire) with the late Lacan of the real (*jouissance*)? How might we deal with the traumatic excess of the subject's real, without taming or domesticating it? Do affirmative modalities of the real exist? These are the crucial questions raised by *Lacan in Italy*. Di Gregorio not only helpfully traces the history of Italian Lacanianism but also skilfully examines how Italian Lacanians have inherited and renewed Lacanian theory and practice through a unique engagement with the real in the clinical, sociopolitical, and artistic domains. This outstanding book bridges the gap between Italian and Anglophone Lacanianism, opening up a rich and promising dialogue with far-reaching transnational implications."

—Massimo Recalcati, *Psychoanalyst, Italy*, and author of *The Telemachus Complex* (2019) and *The Temptation of the Wall* (2022)

"*Lacan in Italy* is a truly significant achievement. The book provides a rich and accessible overview of Lacan's reception in Italy, both in and beyond the clinic, and a unique guide to the inventive, critical work of Italian psychoanalytic thinkers. The volume will be indispensable for anyone exploring the impact of Lacanian psychoanalysis on our understanding of contemporary politics and culture."

—James Martin, *Professor of Politics, Goldsmiths, University of London, UK*, and author of *Psychopolitics of Speech* (2019)

"A fantastic book – well-written, informative, clear, conceptually rich – which takes the reader on a journey through the clinical, cultural and historical developments of Lacanian psychoanalysis in the Italian context. Novel articulations of key Lacanian concepts – drive, jouissance, extimacy, the decline of paternal authority, etc. – are detailed, just as new clinical and diagnostic priorities are illuminated, all with Di Gregorio's characteristic conceptual flair."

—Derek Hook, *Professor of Psychology at Duquesne University, USA, and Extraordinary Professor of Psychology at the University of Pretoria, South Africa*

"Throughout its history psychoanalysis has taken root in different locations in subtly but significantly different ways. This is very much the case with Lacan's reception in Italy, where the understanding of a particular Lacanian practice has, while remaining distinctly Lacanian, taken on a flavour of its own, shaped by the education system, local requirements, and the schools and strong personalities which make up the Italian Lacanian scene. This much-needed book functions not just as guide to this vital field but, moreover, helps us to appreciate the unique contributions of Italian Lacanianism and how this can feed productively into our understanding of Lacan and his teaching in the English-speaking world."

—Calum Neill, *Professor of Psychoanalysis and Continental Philosophy, Edinburgh Napier University, UK*, and director of Lacan in Scotland

Contents

1

Introduction: Lacan and Italy

In her controversial biography *Jacques Lacan: Outline of a Life, History of a System of Thought*, Élisabeth Roudinesco recounts a time when, during a dinner conversation with his close friend Maria Antonietta Macciocchi, an Italian writer and politician, Lacan enthusiastically revealed:

> The Italians are so intelligent, my dear! If I could choose where to die, I would like to end my days in Rome. I know every corner of Rome, every fountain, every church …. And if it couldn't be Rome, I would be happy with Venice or Florence: Italy is the sign I was born under. (1997, p. 408)

Lacan's passionate declaration is hardly surprising given his unwavering fondness for the country of *la dolce vita* throughout his life. He loved spending his leisure time exploring Italy, from the north, where he played winter sports in the Alps (Contri 1978), to the south, where the Amalfi coast and the island of Capri provided the perfect setting for his boat trips (Roudinesco 1997). Although Lacan treasured many Italian cities, he was particularly fond of Rome, which he first visited in 1934 during his honeymoon with his first wife, Marie-Louise Blondin (Roudinesco 1997). Unlike Freud, who was mainly fascinated by ancient Roman

L. Di Gregorio, *Lacan in Italy*, The Palgrave Lacan Series,
https://doi.org/10.1007/978-3-031-91528-4_1

archaeological sites, Lacan was more drawn to the baroque churches and sculptures scattered throughout the Eternal City (Mehlman 1990).

Italian culture permeates Lacan's *Écrits* and seminars, as evidenced by his numerous references to Italian masters (Da Vinci, Tiepolo, Palladio, Dante, Galilei, Fellini), artworks (Bernini's *Ecstasy of Saint Teresa*, Caravaggio's *Bacchus*, Palladio's Neoclassical architecture), and iconic cities (Venice, Vicenza, Florence, Turin, Naples), which testify to his lifelong passion for the country. Even the expression *Che vuoi?* from his graph of desire and the Borromean knot from his topology are linked to Italy. The former is the Italian translation of the question 'what do you want?'—a question Lacan encountered in the Italian original in Jacques Cazotte's short story 'Le Diable amoureux', set in Naples—while the latter comes from the coat of arms of the Italian noble family Borromeo.

Lacan's deep affinity for Italy was not limited to his vacations and cultural passions but also extended to his professional life. It is also intertwined with the dissemination of his work. Lacan's 'public debut' (Miller 2013, p. vi) took place in Italy in 1953, when he delivered his legendary 'Rome discourse' at the University of Rome. In 1967, a year after the publication of the *Écrits* in France, he embarked on his first lecture tour across Italy, stopping in Milan, Pisa, Rome, and Naples. From then until the 1970s, Lacan made an increasing number of visits to the country to participate in academic symposia, psychoanalytic congresses, and press conferences.[1] These include his renowned talks *On the Psychoanalytic Discourse*, delivered in Milan in 1972, as well as the *Triumph of Religion* and *The Third*, both presented in Rome in 1974. During these years, he also developed connections with prominent Italian intellectuals, such as

[1] The bilingual volume *Lacan in Italia/En Italie Lacan*, edited by Giacomo Contri and published in 1978, includes Lacan's key interventions delivered in Italy between 1953 and 1974. It also provides a tripartite periodisation of the reception of Lacan's thought in the country. According to Contri, while there were only a few Italian supporters of Lacan in the 1950s, by the 1960s, small groups of followers had begun to emerge, laying the groundwork for a cohesive Italian Lacanian movement, which finally surged in popularity during the 1970s. However, this peak was followed by a period of latency, during which Italian Lacanianism garnered a negative reputation and receded from prominence. While Chap. 2, 'History of Italian Lacanianism', aligns with Contri's periodisation to some extent, it diverges in certain respects and extends the analysis of the Italian reception of Lacan's thought to the present day.

the semiotician Umberto Eco, and leading Italian psychoanalysts, including Elvio Fachinelli, Franco Fornari, and Cesare Musatti.

Lacan's numerous visits to Italy in the 1960s and 1970s were also intended to lay the groundwork for establishing a Lacanian movement in the country. During these visits, he openly voiced his expectations of his Italian followers. This culminated in *Note to the Italians*, dated 1 April 1974, in which he publicly addressed a small group of key pupils—Giacomo Contri, Muriel Drazien, and Armando Verdiglione—whom he referred to as 'the tripod' (Contri 1978). The trio were tasked with founding an Italian Lacanian school modelled after the *École Freudienne de Paris*.

Despite the eventual failure of this project, Lacan anticipated the growing influence his work would have on Italian culture and society. During a press conference with Italian journalists in Rome on 29 October 1974, Lacan affirmed:

> In ten years, my Écrits, even in Italy, even translated as they are, will strike you as small potatoes, as commonplace. For there is something that is rather odd, which is that even very serious writing eventually becomes commonplace. In very short order, you will see, you will encounter Lacan on every corner. Just like Freud! Everyone imagines he has read Freud because Freud is everywhere, in the newspapers, etc. That will happen to me too, you'll see. (2013, p. 71)

Lacan's prediction proved remarkably accurate. In Italy today, Lacan's legacy extends well beyond academic and psychoanalytic circles, permeating newspaper and magazine articles and radio and television programmes, and even serving as an inspiration for Italian rock stars (Todesco 2021). Concepts such as *godimento* (enjoyment), *desiderio* (desire), *discorso del capitalista* (discourse of the capitalist), *evaporazione del padre* (evaporation of the father), and *soggettivazione* (subjectivation) have become part of everyday language in Italy and are frequently invoked in public debates.

Considering the close ties between Lacan and Italy, it should come as no surprise that his teaching found fertile ground in the country. However, the prominent role of Lacanian psychoanalysis in Italy today is the result of a gradual and lengthy process—marked by setbacks and still unfolding—driven by the dedication of several Italian Lacanians, which lies at the centre of this monograph.

In this book, I will trace the history of the reception of Lacan's thought and explore its development in Italy, providing the first comprehensive account of the relevance and contributions of Italian Lacanians. I will critically examine Lacan's influence in the country and discuss his legacy, introducing Italian Lacanianism—its key themes, clinical applications, sociopolitical criticism, and aesthetic developments—to an English-speaking readership for the first time. While I do not intend to argue for the existence of an 'Italian Lacan', as this could imply a unified and homogeneous national framework—diluting the internal differences that contribute to its dynamism and plurality and isolating it from international developments—I will nonetheless contend that there has been a distinct Italian appropriation of Lacan. This reception is shaped by specific historical circumstances, intertwined with the trajectory of Italian psychoanalysis, and deeply influenced by Italian culture and politics. These distinctive features are reflected in the unique way in which Lacan's teaching has been received, applied, and developed in Italy. However, just as the notion of a 'national philosophy' has become outdated (Esposito 2012), confining psychoanalysis within national boundaries oversimplifies its complexity and overlooks the transnational exchange that has driven its evolution. The aim of this book is thus twofold: to firmly place Italian Lacanianism on the map, highlighting its significance and uniqueness, while also building a bridge for dialogue and connection with Lacanian traditions and receptions across different countries and languages.

The timeliness of this book is underscored by several factors. Firstly, Lacanianism is increasingly transcending national boundaries, becoming a transnational phenomenon that is no longer confined to a particular country, linguistic tradition, or cultural geography. It has become deterritorialised, with English serving as its lingua franca. Yet any Lacanian reception is profoundly shaped by the linguistic, cultural, and sociopolitical context in which it first emerged and developed, rendering the analysis of the Italian milieu and the historical developments of the Italian Lacanian movement particularly relevant. Secondly, in recent years, Italian Lacanians have garnered growing attention beyond Italy. An increasing number of articles and books by Italian Lacanian psychoanalysts, such as Sergio Benvenuto, Domenico Cosenza, Marco Focchi,

Silvia Lippi, Franco Lolli, and Massimo Recalcati, have been translated into, published, or cited in English (Aguirre 2011; Benvenuto 2020, 2024; Busiol 2022; Chiesa 2011; Cosenza, 2023; Hook and Vanheule 2023; Lippi 2020; Recalcati 2019, 2020b, 2021, 2022; Rousselle 2024; Turner 2023). Lastly, as a consequence of these developments, Anglophone scholarship has begun to pay more attention to Italian Lacanianism, although such an interest has remained limited and sporadic, lacking a comprehensive critical and historical analysis of the broader phenomenon.

For instance, in the seminal article 'The Italian Turn: A Certain Tendency in Contemporary Psychoanalytic Aesthetics', cinema and media scholar Mauro Resmini argues that a 'new and unique tendency' has emerged in the field of psychoanalytic aesthetics, one that is distinctively Italian in origin and Lacanian in orientation (2013, p. 271). Resmini acknowledges, however, that the existence of this Italian Lacanian trend 'remains to be argued for and demonstrated' (2013, p. 271). Additionally, his analysis of Italian Lacanianism and its influence is still confined to the aesthetic domain, without expanding into other fields, such as the clinic and politics.

More recently, in *Lacanian Psychoanalysis in Practice*, Diego Busiol (2022), an Italian Lacanian analyst based in Hong Kong, presents several contributions by and interviews with Italian and French Lacanian clinicians, preceded by a brief timeline of Lacan's reception in Italy. This offers a valuable glimpse into the Italian Lacanian tradition, which, as Busiol notes, 'is largely unknown outside national borders' (2022, p. 5). Nonetheless, Busiol's remarkable work does not provide a contextualisation of Lacan's Italian reception beyond the late 1980s, overlooking the Lacanian *renaissance* in postmillennial Italy. It also lacks a critical framework and a comprehensive analysis of the broader cultural, philosophical, and sociopolitical context, both of which are necessary to fully situate Italian Lacanianism and its profound influence on these fields.

In this book, I will not enter into the details of the vicissitudes of the various Italian Lacanian groups, schools, and organisations, or indeed their divisions and rivalries, as such information falls outside the scope of this study and there is a risk of the broader perspective being lost in overly intricate points. Instead, I will focus primarily on the most significant Lacanian clinicians working in Italy, those who have not simply explained or historicised Lacan's thought, but made original contributions, with a particular emphasis on Massimo Recalcati. My decision to grant Recalcati such a prominent position in this study is based on his prolific body of work, which includes several articles and books translated into English, his role in transmitting Lacan's teaching to new generations, and his leadership in establishing and directing Lacanian associations and training institutions in Italy. His influence also extends beyond the clinical field, reaching into broader cultural contexts and resonating with the general public. For over two decades, Recalcati has been a key figure among contemporary Italian Lacanians and a prominent public intellectual, serving as the most visible representative of Italian Lacanianism and one of the main contributors to Lacan's renaissance in Italy today. In addition to Lacanian psychoanalysts, I will also discuss the contributions of those Italian scholars who, albeit not clinicians, have engaged extensively with Lacan's work and explored its intersections with fields such as philosophy, politics, cinema, and literature. At the end of the book, a selection of key works by Italian Lacanians, in both Italian and English, will provide a preliminary, though not exhaustive, bibliography of their major contributions.

In order to examine Lacan's reception in Italy, contentious issues of genealogy, legitimacy, and transmission also need to be addressed—issues that, not exclusively to the Italian context, have frequently sparked controversies, frictions, and heated debates among Lacanians, often leading to disagreements and ruptures. Indeed, the lingering influence of Lacan's charisma and the tendency to fetishise his texts still have a significant bearing on how both clinicians and scholars engage with Lacan's legacy. In *Conversations with Lacan*, Benvenuto identifies the 'militant exegesis' as the most popular, and potentially risky, approach to reading Lacan today. The danger comes from treating Lacan's body of works as a 'sacred text that contains the core of all truths [...] which the exegesis of today has the task of clarifying' (2020, p. ix). Benvenuto believes this approach is mainly aimed at preserving and asserting the 'correct' interpretation of Lacan by 'enact[ing] a militancy similar to political, ethical, or religious ones' (2020, p. ix). There is a clear risk here of stifling the vitality of Lacan's legacy, and severely undermining its potential. Another significant danger here is dogmatism. While Recalcati acknowledges the remarkable clarity and philological accuracy of Jacques-Alain Miller's commentary of Lacan, he critiques it for establishing a Lacanian orthodoxy that leaves little room for alternative interpretations (Recalcati 2009, 2013).[2]

On the contrary, Italian Lacanianism is characterised by a 'dynamic', 'secular' reading of Lacan, which is 'inherently plural and naturally prone to contamination' (Resmini 2013, p. 273). Italian Lacanians have moved towards a creative and subjective engagement with Lacan's legacy, rather than adhering strictly to orthodoxy (Bottiroli 2002). For instance, Cosenza highlights the importance of engaging in a personal response to Lacan's text, one that navigates the initial alienation and disorientation, passing through a 'separative passage', where readers are prompted to assert their own interpretation rather than resorting to pre-established readings, ultimately leading to a 'subjective outcome' (2010, p. 55).[3] Similarly, Recalcati emphasises that Lacan's legacy must be subjectivised and, therefore, 'demands invention up to the limit of heresy' (Recalcati 2020a, p. 14). After all, Lacan himself repeatedly urged his followers to develop their own thought independently, famously asserting 'don't imitate me!' (2019, p. 88).[4]

I will contend that Italian Lacanianism is characterised by the primacy of the register of the real, through which key psychoanalytic notions—such as the unconscious, symptom, and subjectivity—have been entirely reframed. The prominence of the real is a feature shared by several national appropriations of Lacan (Irwin and Motoh 2014; Jaanus and Stewart 2004; Laclau 1989), which can be partly attributed to Miller's *orientation lacanienne* and his leading role in the transmission of Lacan's teaching. According to Miller, Lacan's thought shows a progressive

[2] Although in the past, Miller has seemingly encouraged plural and heterogenous readings of Lacan's text, arguing that fully engaging with Lacan's teaching necessarily involves maximising 'its contradictions, its antinomies, its deadlocks, its difficulties' (1994, p. 75), he has increasingly opposed what he perceives as overly personal interpretations of Lacan, such as those put forward by Slavoj Žižek and Alain Badiou (Miller-Rose and Roy 2017, p. 10).

[3] All translations from the Italian are mine, unless sourced from an existing translation.

[4] Interestingly, some of the most prominent Italian Lacanians identify either as post-Lacanians (Recalcati in Lingiardi 2016) or, hyperbolically, as not Lacanian at all (Benvenuto 2020, p. 155), arguably to distance themselves from those ideological and dogmatic readings of Lacan.

emphasis on the real, which constitutes its fundamental trajectory[5] (Miller 2008). Lacan himself describes his teaching as an 'orientation of the real' (2016, p. 102), referring to this concept as something distinctly his own, a notion that he invented (2016, pp. 110 and 113). Lacan conceptualises the real as fundamentally negative: it is 'the impossible' (1998, p. 167), 'what does not work' (2013, p. 61), 'that which resists symbolization absolutely' (1988, p. 66), and 'something that lies on the fringes of our experience' (2020, p. 24). Unsurprisingly, this notion has mainly been associated with trauma, horror, monstrosity, formlessness, abjection, unbounded enjoyment, and death. However, Lacan also acknowledges that 'the real carries more than one meaning' (2020, p. 24).

The central argument of this book is that Italian Lacanianism advances an affirmative conceptualisation of the real, regarding it not only as disruptive, traumatic, and deadly for the subject, but also as potentially generative. In doing so, Italian Lacanianism bridges the 'classic' Lacan, centred on the primacy of the symbolic (and desire), and the 'new' Lacan, focused on the primacy of the real (and *jouissance*). It also avoids endorsing mystical or metaphysical interpretations of the real by grounding it firmly within the clinical context. Indeed, another crucial argument is that the hallmark of Italian Lacanianism is the prominence of the clinic. It is from this clinical basis that Italian Lacanians engage with sociological, political, and aesthetic domains. In contrast to the trend in Anglophone receptions of Lacan, which have historically employed a declinicalised Lacan (Roudinesco 1997) in the humanities and social sciences to explore a wide range of topics—from electronic music to ecological crises, and from chemsex practices to Pixar movies—Italian Lacanians' engagements with other disciplines remain firmly anchored in clinical concerns.

I will thus analyse how Italian Lacanianism adopts, emphasises, and problematises the notion of the real from three key perspectives: the clinic, politics, and aesthetics. This will centre on a discussion of three key areas: the so-called new symptoms—such as anorexia, bulimia, depression, panic attacks, and addictions—which are viewed as psychopathological

[5] This teleological perspective, however, is challenged by several Italian and international Lacanians (Bottiroli 2023; Eyers 2012; Recalcati 2013).

manifestations of the discourse of capitalism and the erosion of the symbolic in contemporary society; Italian Lacanians' sociopolitical critique of capitalism, nationalism, and populism; and Italian Lacanian psychoanalytic aesthetics, which explores new realist trends in the arts and media.

Chapter 2, 'The History of Italian Lacanianism', traces the reception of Lacan's thought in Italy through its various stages of development, situating it within both the national and transnational cultural and sociopolitical context. Beginning in the mid-1960s, after the success of the *Écrits*, interest in Lacan grew despite some early opposition from academics and psychoanalysts. In the 1970s, Lacan's ideas began to permeate the Italian cultural landscape, influencing feminism, the gay rights movement, Marxist thought, and the arts. The chapter also identifies this period, which was characterised by the pioneering application of psychoanalysis to social criticism, antipsychiatry, and community therapy, as the foundation for the sociopolitical commitment of postmillennial Italian Lacanianism. The chapter then moves on to a discussion of the 1980s and 1990s, when the rise of Lacanianism was unexpectedly stalled by the scandal involving Armando Verdiglione, an Italian pupil of Lacan whose criminal actions severely damaged the reputation of Lacanian psychoanalysis. From the 2000s to the present, however, Lacanianism has shed its negative reputation, experiencing a renaissance in Italy that has largely been driven by its most prolific and charismatic figures—a new generation of Italian Lacanians trained and analysed by Jacques-Alain Miller—with a strong focus on the real.

Chapter 3, 'Clinic', argues that Italian Lacanians promote a 'clinical turn' in the postmillennial reception of Lacan's theory, historically dominated by academic appropriations in fields outside the clinical domain. It also argues that Italian Lacanians place the primacy of the real at the centre of their clinical practice, regarding it as crucial for understanding contemporary forms of psychopathology where the drive and *jouissance* come to the forefront. The chapter examines Italian Lacanians' take on the *new symptoms*, which are situated at the intersection of psychopathology and the dominant social discourse, and explores Recalcati's concept of the *subject without unconscious*—severed from the symbolic Other and disconnected from desire. In this chapter, I also discuss the Lacanian clinics established by Recalcati and other Lacanians across Italy, which are characterised by social commitment, including low-cost psychoanalytic psychotherapies, and community engagement. The discussion then turns to the unique intertwining of sublimation and subjectivation that could be seen to characterise Italian Lacanianism, emphasising the dialectic between desire and *jouissance* and the more generative aspects of the real. The chapter ends with an analysis of *In Treatment*—the Italian adaptation of the American TV series based on the Israeli format *Be Tipul*—exploring how the show portrays the real in a clinical setting.

Chapter 4, 'Politics', explores how Italian Lacanianism extends into political and social spheres beyond the clinic by examining the libidinal dimension of politics, dominant societal discourses, the evaporation of the father, and the role of Silvio Berlusconi in epitomising the shift from a politics of desire to one of *jouissance*, foreshadowing contemporary populist nationalism. The chapter also addresses Italian Lacanians' critique of capitalist discourse, which de-subjectifies individuals, fosters subjects without unconscious, and perpetuates the fantasy that structural dependence on the Other can be bypassed. Italian Lacanianism views the foreclosure of the (subject of the) unconscious as the greatest threat posed by capitalist discourse. The chapter then investigates the interplay between Italian Theory and Lacanianism, discussing concepts developed by Italian Lacanians, such as Recalcati's *securitarian drive* and *fascist unconscious* and Lolli's *unconshow*, as well as contributions from Italian philosophers, like Tarizzo's *collective subjectivation*, Ferraris' *realitism*, and Berardi's *third unconscious*. It concludes with an examination of the documentary *Videocracy*, arguing that, rather than merely a critique of Berlusconi's media-driven ideology, it presents an exemplary documentation of the Italian postmillennial subject's relationship to *jouissance*.

Chapter 5, 'Aesthetics', explores Italian Lacanian aesthetics, which centres on the real, with a view to moving beyond pathographic models and hermeneutic interpretations. This aesthetic approach, effectively an *aesthetics of the real*, seeks to understand how the extra-symbolic dimension of the real can be integrated into the symbolic representational framework of artistic practices. The real in art is ultimately irreducible to meaning or interpretation—what can be considered as the *unconscious of art*. Italian Lacanian aesthetics also rethinks the concept of realism in the arts. The notion of the *return of the real* reflects a shift away from traditional aesthetic qualities—such as beauty and harmony—towards abjection, formlessness, and degradation. This realism is often described as extreme, traumatic, or psychotic because the real disrupts the imaginary-symbolic fabric of the artwork. The chapter closes by examining the film *Reality*, arguing that it transcends the binary of everyday reality versus the fake reality presented by the media, instead revealing the fictional fabric of reality itself.

Chapter 6, 'Conclusion: Towards an Affirmative Real', summarises the novelty and specificity of Italian Lacanian thought. It contends that Lacan's legacy in postmillennial Italy is marked by an affirmative conception of the real. Italian Lacanians conceive of sublimation and subjectivation—beyond the aesthetic and clinical realms—as the capacity to engage with, channel, and make the real of *jouissance* fecund in a dialectical relationship with desire. The chapter also opens up pathways for further research and situates the book within broader scholarly and cultural contexts.

Bibliography

Aguirre, Maria-Cristina. 2011. Bulimia, Anxiety and the Demand of the Other. In *Lacan and Addiction. An Antology*, ed. Yael Goldman Baldwin, Kareen Malone, and Thomas Svolos, 177–185. London: Karnac.

Benvenuto, Sergio. 2020. *Conversations with Lacan: Seven Lectures for Understanding Lacan*. London: Routledge.

Benvenuto, Sergio. 2024. *Lacan, Kris and the Psychoanalytic Legacy: The Brain Eater*. London: Routledge.

Bottiroli, Giovanni. 2002. *Jacques Lacan. Arte, linguaggio, desiderio*. Bergamo: Bergamo University Press.

Bottiroli, Giovanni. 2023. *Jacques Lacan. Oltre la scolastica*. Verona: Ombre Corte.

Busiol, Diego, ed. 2022. *Lacanian Psychoanalysis in Practice. Insights from Fourteen Psychoanalysts*. London: Routledge.

Chiesa, Lorenzo. 2011. Biopolitics in Early Twenty-First-Century Italian Theory. *Angelaki* 16 (3): 1–5.

Contri, Giacomo, ed. 1978. *Lacan in Italia/En Italie Lacan: 1953–1978*. Milan: La Salamandra.

Cosenza, Domenico. 2010. L'inconscio tra matema e reale. In *L'inconscio dopo Lacan. Il problema del soggetto contemporaneo tra psicoanalisi e filosofia*, ed. Domenico Cosenza and Paolo D'Alessandro, 43–58. Milan: Edizioni Universitarie di Lettere Economia Diritto.

Cosenza, Domenico. 2023. *A Lacanian Reading of Anorexia*. London: Routledge.

Esposito, Roberto. 2012. *Living Thought. The Origins and Actuality of Italian Philosophy.* Translated by Zakiya Hanafi. Stanford, CA: Stanford University Press.

Eyers, Tom. 2012. *Lacan and the Concept of the 'Real'*. Basingstoke: Palgrave Macmillan.

Hook, Derek, and Stijn Vanheule. 2023. *Lacan on Depression and Melancholia*. London: Routledge.

Irwin, Jones, and Helena Motoh. 2014. *ŽiŽek and his Contemporaries: On the Emergence of the Slovenian Lacan*. London: Bloomsbury.

Jaanus, Maire, and Elizabeth Stewart. 2004. General Introduction. In *Lacan in the German-Speaking World*, ed. Maire Jaanus, Elizabeth Stewart, and Richard Feldstein, 1–3. Albany, NY: State University of New York Press.

Lacan, Jacques. 1988. *Freud's Papers on Technique. The Seminar of Jacques Lacan, Book IV, 1953=1954*. Translated by John Forrester. London and New York: W.W. Norton.

Lacan, Jacques. 1998. *The Four Fundamental Concepts of Psychoanalysis. The Seminar of Jacques Lacan, Book XI, 1963–1964*. Translated by Alan Sheridan and ed. Jacques-Alain Miller. London and New York: W.W. Norton.

Lacan, Jacques. 2013. *The Triumph of Religion*. Translated by Bruce Fink. Cambridge: Polity Press.

Lacan, Jacques. 2016. *The Sinthome. The Seminar of Jacques Lacan, Book XXIII, 1975–1976*. Translated by Adrian Price. Cambridge: Polity Press.

Lacan, Jacques. 2019. The Third. Translated by Philip Dravers. *The Lacanian Review* 9: 83–109.

Lacan, Jacques. 2020. *The Object Relation. The Seminar of Jacques Lacan, Book IV, 1956–1957*. Translated by Adrian Price. Cambridge: Polity Press.

Laclau, Ernesto. 1989. Preface. In *The Sublime Object of Ideology*, ed. Slavoj ŽiŽek, ix–xv. London: Verso.

Lingiardi, Vittorio. 2016. https://www.repubblica.it/venerdi/libri/2016/03/02/news/lacan_il_criptico_spiegato_ai_mortali_in_due_volumi-134633929/. Accessed 20 December 2022.

Lippi, Silvia. 2020. *The decision of desire*. Translated by Peter Skafish. Minneapolis: University of Minnesota Press.

Mehlman, Jeffrey. 1990. Translator's Foreword. In Élizabeth Roudinesco, Jacques Lacan & Co. *A History of Psychoanalysis in France, 1925–1985*, xi–xvi. London: Free Association Books.

Miller, Jacques-Alain. 1994. ÉximitÉ. In *Lacanian Theory of Discourse*, ed. M. Bracher, M. Alcorn, R. Corthell, and F. Massardier-Kenny, 74–87. New York: New York University Press.

Miller, Jacques-Alain. 2008. The Other Side of Lacan. Translated by Barbara P. Fulks. *Lacanian Ink* 32: 60-71.

Miller, Jacques-Alain. 2013. Foreword. In: Jacques Lacan, ed., *On the Names-of-the-Father*, vi–viii. Translated by Bruce Fink. Cambridge: Polity Press.

Miller-Rose, Eve, and Roy, Daniel. 2017. Entretien nocturne avec Jacques-Alain Miller. *Lacan Quotidien* 698. http://www.lacanquotidien.fr/blog/wp-content/uploads/2017/05/LQ-698-2.pdf. Accessed 1 November 2020.

Recalcati, Massimo. 2009. Letture di Lacan. *aut aut.* 343:19–29.

Recalcati, Massimo. 2019. *The Telemachus Complex. Parents and Children after the Decline of the Father.* Translated by Alice Kilgarriff. Cambridge: Polity Press.

Recalcati, Massimo. 2020a. *Convertire la pulsione. Sul processo di soggettivazione nell'esperienza dell'analisi.* Trento: Paginaotto.

Recalcati, Massimo. 2020b. *The Son's Secret. From Oedipus to the Prodigal Son.* Translated by Alice Kilgarriff. Cambridge: Polity Press.

Recalcati, Massimo. 2021. *The Enduring Kiss. Seven Short Lessons on Love.* Translated by Alice Kilgarriff. Cambridge: Polity Press.

Recalcati, Massimo. 2022. *The Temptation of the Wall. Five Short Lessons on Civil Life.* Translated by Alice Kilgarriff. Cambridge: Polity Press.

Resmini, Mauro. 2013. The Italian Turn: A Certain Tendency in Contemporary Psychoanalytic Aesthetics. *American Imago* 68 (2): 271–297.

Roudinesco, Élisabeth. 1997. *Jacques Lacan: Outline of a Life, History of a System of Thought.* Translated by Barbara Bray. Cambridge: Polity Press.

Rousselle, Duane. 2024. *Psychoanalytic Sociology. A New Theory of the Social Bond.* London: Bloomsbury.

Todesco, Claudio. 2021. La saggezza di Vasco. *Rolling Stone.* https://www.rollingstone.it/musica/interviste-musica/la-saggezza-di-vasco/596219/?fbclid=IwAR28Kl4xTWUFHpwxM2x36NPNPimwK4CrJDjmbKkpua5foU-p9LwMwrJvlZRU Accessed 17 March 2022.

Turner, Kirk. 2023. *Lacanian Fantasy. The Image, Language and Uncertainty.* London: Routledge.

2
The History of Italian Lacanianism

National and Transnational Lacan

In Italy today, Lacanian psychoanalysis holds a prominent role, enjoying an excellent reputation that has recently expanded beyond national borders. This was not always the case, however. The current situation is the outcome of a gradual process, not devoid of setbacks, which is deeply entwined with the national context, the wider historical developments of Italian psychoanalysis, and the international vicissitudes of the Lacanian movement. In fact, in his 1997 article 'Italy and Psychoanalysis', the Italian Lacanian analyst Sergio Benvenuto openly questioned the relevance and influence of Italian psychoanalysis, acknowledging its narrow international reception, especially in the Anglophone world. Benvenuto bluntly asserted that:

> very few are interested in Italian psychoanalysis: up until now, Italy has not produced as many famous 'masters' in this field as have Austria, Germany, Switzerland, France, Great Britain, the US, and other countries. Hence the widespread - and partly unjust - belief that Italian psychoanalysis is insignificant. Unjust, because I believe the average level of Italian analysts is high enough; but we lack charismatic and internationally well-known personalities. In psychoanalysis, we weren't so lucky to have someone like

L. Di Gregorio, *Lacan in Italy*, The Palgrave Lacan Series,
https://doi.org/10.1007/978-3-031-91528-4_2

De Chirico, Gramsci, Fellini, Primo Levi, Italo Calvino, Pasolini, Eco, Armani, Agamben and others. (1997, para. 1)

The reasons for this are rooted in the historical, cultural, and geopolitical context of twentieth-century Italy, which at first hindered the national reception and circulation of Freud's ideas and, subsequently, delayed the international dissemination of Italian psychoanalysis. Indeed, from its very inception, Italian psychoanalysis encountered fierce resistance from all the major cultural and political powers. The Catholic Church rejected the supposedly atheistic and pansexual materialism of Freud's metapsychology, while philosophical idealism—inherently anti-metaphysical and anti-positivistic—accused Freud of biological determinism. The Fascist regime denunciated psychoanalysis as Jewish and Italian Marxism later condemned it as fundamentally bourgeois. Moreover, since Freud's theory was introduced in Italy through the Austro-Hungarian liminal city of Trieste, psychoanalysis was persistently regarded, usually with some suspicion, as foreign. Psychoanalysis was perceived as Teutonic after World War I, Jewish under the Fascist regime, American in the aftermath of World War II (David 1990), and Parisian when Lacanianism reached Italy (Roudinesco 1990).

For most of the last century, Italians remained predominantly 'consumers rather than producers of psychoanalysis' (Civitarese 2016, p. 215), translating and importing foreign psychoanalysts, such as Jung, Winnicott, Klein, Bion, and, later, Lacan. Italian xenophilia was, however, counterbalanced by a lack of internationalisation in local psychoanalysis. The very limited reach of the Italian language, along with the tendency of Italian psychoanalysts to speak and publish predominantly in their native tongue,[1] inevitably excluded international readerships and

[1] A few notable exceptions are the first Italian psychoanalyst, Edoardo Weiss, a pupil of Freud's and the founder of the *Società Psicoanalitica Italiana*, who published some of his books in English after moving to the USA as a refugee in the late 1930s; Ignatio Matte Blanco, a Chilean psychoanalyst who spent most of his life in Italy and published his most renowned book, *The Unconscious as Infinite Set* first in English in 1975 and only subsequently in Italian in 1981; Eugenio Gaddini, who published extensively in the *International Journal of Psychoanalysis* in the 1970s and 1980s; and Franco Fornari, the pioneer of the Kleinian school in Italy, whose popular books, including *Psychoanalysis of the Atomic War* and *Psychoanalysis of War*, were translated into English during the 1970s.

further confined Italian psychoanalysis to within its national borders. Therefore, despite its worth, the isolation and provincialism of Italian psychoanalysis hindered the emergence of internationally prominent analysts. For several decades, Italy was thus regarded as a psychoanalytically underdeveloped country lacking its own original and independent psychoanalytic thought (Conci 2008).

After a long process of assimilation, this trend gradually shifted and the peculiar 'isolation and openness' (Borgogno and Luchetti 2016, p. 4) of Italian psychoanalysis proved to be instrumental in the autonomous and creative development of those psychoanalytic orientations coming from abroad. From the 1990s, the number of Italian contributions translated into other languages steadily increased, leading to the international acknowledgement of Italian psychoanalysis as a creative, pluralist, and cross-disciplinary school of thought (Bollas 2007). Additionally, since Italian psychoanalytic centres developed in a capillary way, rather than being centralised in a single capital city (as was the case in both Paris and London), hierarchical and monolithic drifts were limited. This contributed to a diversified psychoanalytic landscape. At the turn of the century, the internationalisation of Italian psychoanalysis increased exponentially, leading to a wider appreciation of its contributions: from the post-Bionian field theory advanced by Antonino Ferro and Giuseppe Civitarese to international collaborations, such as those of Vittorio Lingiardi and Nancy McWilliams, editors of the 2017 *Psychodynamic Diagnostic Manual (PDM-2)*. It also led to prominent leadership roles, for example, for Stefano Bolognini, who in 2010 became the first Italian president of the International Psychoanalytic Association (IPA).

The 2016 edited book *Reading Italian Psychoanalysis*, whose contributors are analysts affiliated with the IPA, marks a key milestone in the official recognition of Italian psychoanalytic thought in the Anglophone world. The book nonetheless lacks any overt reference to Italian Lacanianism in its tracing of the history and themes of Italian psychoanalysis. Not only does this lacuna signal the enduring ostracism of Lacanian psychoanalysis from the IPA, which was still largely perceived as a heretic and thus illegitimate version of Freudianism; it also dismisses one of the most significant developments in Italian psychoanalysis to take place in recent years. Nonetheless, in postmillennial Italy, Lacanians successfully brought psychoanalysis back to the public sphere and contributed significantly to its 'international turn' (Conci 2008, p. 70) by eliciting a growing appreciation for their theoretical and clinical contributions, as the many English translations of Sergio Benvenuto's and Massimo Recalcati's books prove.

This mounting interest in Italian Lacanianism, both within and outside of Italy, is part both of a national tendency in which Lacanian psychoanalysis shifted from being marginalised to becoming hegemonic, and of a transnational context, with the Lacanian orientation having now become widespread in many countries, making Lacan's legacy more prominent than ever before. Hence, it is crucial to address the historical and cultural circumstances of the Italian context within which Lacanian psychoanalysis was first coldly received and later thrived, while also taking into account its transnational dissemination. As Visacovsky aptly points out,

> psychoanalytical ideas are not received, appropriated and applied in a historical, social and cultural void, but established according to pre-existing particular conditions. Undeniably, the contextual peculiarities can explain theoretical and therapeutic acceptances and resistances. (2009, p. 228)

The responsiveness to the national context has held particular importance for the affirmation or demise of Lacanian psychoanalysis. This is clearly the case in the early inception of Lacanianism in France, where Lacan successfully filtered Freud's thought through the French intellectual tradition and cultural milieu. In *Psychoanalytic Politics: Freud's French Revolution*, Turkle (1978) contends that the French remained relatively resistant to psychoanalysis until Jacques Lacan gained prominence as an 'indigenous heretic whose structuralism and linguistic emphasis were resonant with the French Cartesian tradition' (p. 48). Lacan's ability to engage with the cultural and political environment, along with his affiliation with Marxist circles at the *École Normale Supérieure*, played a pivotal role in promoting his ideas as a 'distinctly French reading of Freud' (p. 10). According to Turkle:

> Most intellectual movements undergo some form of cultural adaptation to different national settings. But psychoanalysis is not just an intellectual

> position: its extension as a therapeutic strategy makes it especially sensitive to its environment. In order to be effective, therapies must be relevant to a culture's prevailing modes of making sense of experience. (1978, p. 49)

When Lacanianism began to be disseminated outside of France, it partially lost its originally national connotations and became a complex transnational phenomenon. A few years after Lacan's death, in the preface to Žižek's *The Sublime Object to Ideology*, Laclau signals that distinctive receptions of Lacan had already emerged, which 'varied from country to country' (1989, p. ix). In *Lacan in the German-Speaking World*, Jaanus and Stewart further acknowledge that these diverging acquisitions of Lacan, developed in different countries, arose from adapting 'Lacan's ideas to their own specific historical, cultural, and geographic-linguistic experiences, and their own traumas' (2004, p. 1). For instance, in Latin American countries, the reception of Lacan was greatly affected by political vicissitudes, as in the case of Argentina (Russo 2009), where Lacanian psychoanalysis was the driving force promoting social change against the oppression of the military dictatorship, despite which Lacanianism flourished to such an extent that nowadays 'Lacan is more alive in Argentina than in France' (Gherovici 2019, p. 119). The reception of Lacan also carries a strong political connotation in Spain, where it coincided with a breaking away from Franco's dictatorship and from the totalitarian political past (Visacovsky 2009). Predictably, in these countries Lacanianism is part of the national identity, being associated with militancy and activism, as opposed to the medicalisation and depoliticisation predominant in the North American and Australian receptions of Lacan (Ellingsen 2013).

As a transnational phenomenon, Lacanianism 'can only be understood as a historical process that occurs as a result of movements between sites, places and cultures but that, at the same time, is linked to local conditions' (Damousi and Plotkin 2009, p. 8). Although an authentically Italian, American, or Slovene Lacan may never exist, it is undeniable that different versions of Lacanianism are forged by the sociopolitical, philosophical, and historical frameworks through which Lacan is received in each individual country. Unsurprisingly, given that the unconscious is primarily a linguistic phenomenon, Lacan's ideas have been received and interpreted differently across various linguistic regions, each of which has developed its own unique conception of psychoanalysis (Benvenuto 1997; Rabaté 2000). Linguistic and cultural differences are indeed at the root of the variations that exist among the many receptions of Lacan, which can be broadly divided into two distinct paradigms: the Continental/Latin Lacan and the Anglophone Lacan (Rabaté 2000; Damousi and Plotkin 2009). These two paradigms not only reflect cultural differences but also stem from profoundly distinct philosophical traditions, with one being rooted in idealism, intellectualism, and continental philosophy, and the other in empiricism, anti-intellectualism, and analytic philosophy.

Lacan himself had reservations about the Anglophone world, lamenting that the English language obstructs the unconscious (Rosman 2020), habitually scorning the 'American way of life' (1992, p. 219, 1998, p. 127, 2006, p. 685), and complaining about the 'cold objectivity' of the English people (2006, p. 512). These remarks, which reveal much about Lacan's style and preferences, nonetheless highlight the gap between the Romance-language countries and the Anglophone world. As André Green put it, 'French psychoanalysts belong to a different cultural tradition from that of the Anglo-Saxon world, where empiricism and pragmatism are considered to be qualities; where intellectualism and abstraction count as vices rather than as virtues' (1996, p. 4). In this respect, Lacan's idea that healing is merely a supplementary benefit of the analysis may be bewildering in a goal-oriented and evidence-based context like the Anglophone one (Fink 2014).

This explains why, initially, Lacan's thought spread mainly throughout Romance-language countries during the 1960s and 1970s, and only subsequently moved to North America during the 1980s and 1990s (Rabaté 2003). Clearly, the Italian reception falls within the Continental/Latin paradigm, in which Lacan's thought was generally particularly well-received by artists and associated with social movements, and where Lacanian psychoanalysis was regarded as belonging more to the realm of the humanities, detached from psychology and medicine. Overall, in these Romance-language countries, especially in the 1970s, Lacanianism intertwined with Marxism, feminism, antipsychiatry, and intellectual culture, and was frequently stigmatised by doctors. Moreover, at the time it was fairly common for Lacanian psychoanalysts like Jacques-Alain

Miller and Massimo Recalcati, who had graduated in philosophy, to be trained in the humanities. This background often manifests itself among Lacanians in their resistance to life sciences and analytic philosophy (Johnston 2013).

Interestingly, despite its association with the humanities, in France and other Romance-language countries, the acquisition of Lacan's ideas retained a clinical connotation, remaining closely tied to psychoanalytic practice. In contrast, in the English-speaking clinical world, Lacanian psychoanalysis was initially marginalised (Parker 2004). However, academic institutions in the UK and USA first received Lacan as a representative of French Theory, primarily influencing literary criticism, cinema, and feminist thought (Benvenuto and Kennedy 1986; Laclau 1989). As Evans points out, 'the distinction between theory and practice is so much part and parcel of the Anglo-American tradition that an author such as Lacan, who refuses this division, is simply assigned to the category of "theory"' (1998, p. 14). This distinction lies at the heart of the separation of the clinical from the cultural acquisition and transmission of Lacan's thought. This overtly clashes with Lacan's own stance, however, according to which psychoanalytic theory and praxis are inseparable (Lacan 2013a).

After Lacan's death, the Anglophone reception of his work reinforced this separation between theory and clinical practice. Lacan's ideas were confined to the humanities, which became the main channel of their transmission and dissemination, leading to a 'systematic omission of the clinical dimension', as Rabaté contends in *Lacan in America* (2000, p. xxv).[2] At the turn of the decade from the 1980s into the 1990s, Lacanianism became an extremely popular theoretical trend that was well-established in universities, particularly in the USA. The application of Lacan's theories broadened to a wider range of fields, such as cultural studies, visual studies, social sciences, as well as 'to issues of race, gender, and class' (Feldstein 1996, p. xi). In the Anglophone world, the 1990s were characterised by a versatile use of Lacan's thought. This trend was

[2] A few notable exceptions to this de-clinicised Lacan in Anglophone literature in the late 1990s and early 2000s are *The Lacanian Clinical Field Series* (from 1998 to 2004), *The Subject of Lacan* (2000), *After Lacan* (2002), *The Later Lacan* (2007), and Bruce Fink's books. These publications appeared at the turn of the century when questions about the future and survival of psychoanalysis itself were particularly pressing.

promoted by those Lacanian scholars who pioneered fruitful and innovative connections between Lacanian theory and other disciplines—above all Slavoj Žižek and the other representatives of the Slovenian school, who significantly expanded Lacan's audience. This confirms the 'illuminating effects' of Lacan's theory (Laclau 1989, p. ix), demonstrating its applicability across diverse fields, which is even more evident today.

Due to this wide and popular use of Lacan's theory, however, the clinical roots of his thought were often overlooked and its more strictly clinical aspects displaced by those theoretical notions that could be applied to the analysis of ideology and contemporary sociopolitical issues. According to Gurewich,

> Lacan's contribution has been derailed from its original trajectory. No longer perceived as a theory meant to enlighten the practice of psychoanalysis, his brilliant formulations have been both adapted and criticized so as to conform to the needs of purely intellectual endeavors far removed from clinical reality. (2000, p. xi)

Roudinesco calls this approach the 'secularized reading of Lacan', which was also taking place at a point at which, in France, 'Lacan's work ha[d] become an object of thought, detached from any clinical implications' (1997, p. 434). Secularised readings of Lacan can be found not only in the Anglo-American reception of Lacan's theory (Evans 1998; Laclau 1989) but also, to a significant extent, in the use of Lacan by the representatives of the Slovenian Lacanian School (Hughes and Malone 2002).

In *Žižek and His Contemporaries: On the Emergence of the Slovene Lacan*, Irwin and Motoh argue that the Slovenian school is fundamentally 'theoretical' and 'non-clinical' (2014, p. 49). The Slovenian Lacanian orientation, whose main representatives are Slavoj Žižek, Alenka Zupančič, and Mladen Dolar, is primarily philosophical in nature and is influenced mainly by Marx, Hegel, and German idealism. It is also characterised by a political reading that revolves around ideology and political resistance (Irwin and Motoh 2014). Slovene Lacanian thought, which is undoubtedly one of the most original appropriations of Lacan, contributed extensively to the dissemination of Lacan's theory on a global scale in

English-speaking academia. Slovenian Lacanians are extremely de-territorialised: Žižek[3] admits that they do not even exist in Ljubljana (Žižek and Daly 2004); rather, they are international and transnational theorists who use English as their lingua franca and engage in global issues.

A new generation of Lacanian scholars is now following in their footsteps. Consequently, today's Lacanianism is more de-territorialised. This is exemplified by the ever-growing number of edited books, monographs, and journals in which Lacanian psychoanalysts and scholars from around the globe provide their contributions to the Lacanian field and engage in fruitful exchanges. They bring their national perspectives into a transnational setting through the medium of the English language, thereby opening up the dialogue among national receptions of Lacan. The 2023 edited book *Capitalism and the New Political Unconscious* is another case in point here (Panattoni and Vighi 2023). The volume includes contributions from Italian Lacanian analysts and scholars, such as Massimo Recalcati and Fabio Vighi, alongside Lacanian philosophers from other national contexts, including Slavoj Žižek, Todd McGowan, and Samo Tomšič, discussing contemporary politics through the lens of Lacanian psychoanalysis. The ever-evolving landscape of Lacanian studies is thus a complex one, where national and transnational paradigms intertwine, and despite the common use of English, the ideas remain deeply rooted in and influenced by local and national contexts.

Similarly to the French Freud—who is not simply 'a person but a complex social and cultural phenomenon' (Turkle 1978, p. 15)—the Italian Lacan cannot be associated with a single individual, but rather results

[3] Žižek's own reception is deeply intertwined with the specificities of national and intellectual contexts. While his education and early career were based in his native country, Slovenia (Irwin and Motoh 2014), he subsequently moved to France to undertake a PhD, supervised by Jacques-Alain Miller, and to become one of his analysands. Žižek's philosophical orientation, which innovatively combined French and German philosophers and placed Lacan outside of the clinical practice, was not well received by French Lacanians or intellectuals (Bar-El 2023). A different linguistic and national context, however, gave Žižek a platform to launch his international career. Indeed, by adopting the English language and thanks to the support of Ernesto Laclau and Chantal Mouffe, Žižek found success in England. In the UK, he was initially invited to the Essex School of Discourse Analysis for talks, lectures, and seminars along with other international scholars, including Judith Butler, Alain Badiou, and Yannis Stavrakakis (Robinson 2004; Townshend 2003). Žižek then became extremely popular, especially in the US, and eventually reached the status of a global public intellectual.

from the national context, with its cultural traditions and sociopolitical events. In the next sections, I will outline the vicissitudes of the Italian Lacanian movement and contextualise Lacanianism in twenty-first-century Italy. In order to better understand the particular trajectory of Lacanianism towards our contemporary moment, I will trace the history of the Italian reception of Lacan further back through the different periods in which it developed and evolved, while also providing an overview of the Italian sociopolitical and cultural context.

The Reception of Lacan in the 1960s

In the early 1950s, Lacan was not yet the popular, albeit controversial, French master who initiated a new psychoanalytic movement and he therefore did not attract many Italian followers. However, over the years the number of local loyal supporters steadily grew thanks to Lacan's official visits to Italy, the most significant of which took place on 26 and 27 September 1953 at the Institute of Psychology of the University of Rome. On that occasion, Lacan delivered the paper *The Function and Field of Speech and Language in Psychoanalysis* in the presence of several renowned Italian psychoanalysts, including Nicola Perrotti, one of the founding members of Italian psychoanalysis. The Rome discourse was a 'veritable manifesto' (Rabaté 2003, p. xxiii) of Lacan's doctrine, which, for the first time, introduced key concepts of his theory in a coherent and systematic way.

Later on, his exclusion from the IPA in 1963 and the publication of the *Écrits* in 1966 earned Lacan wide recognition beyond psychoanalytic circles but also polarised his public image as either a heretical psychoanalyst or an absolute master. In the 1960s, Lacan's fame also grew in Italy, which was one of the first European countries to be particularly receptive to Lacanian psychoanalysis. The reasons for this are manifold. In 1966, the first complete translation of Freud's works began, reigniting interest in Freudian psychoanalysis among intellectuals and scholars. This interest was further fuelled by the Oedipal imagery associated with the student protests and worker unrest of the late 1960s. Given Lacan's innovative reading of Freud as well as his anti-establishment attitude, this context created the ideal conditions for his thought to infiltrate Italy. Although a full Italian translation of the *Écrits* was not available at this time, interest in Lacan began to increase among his Italian audience, as proven by several invitations he received from prominent Italian psychoanalysts such as Franco Fornari, as well as from academics.[4] At this stage, however, talking of an Italian Lacanian movement would have been anachronistic since there was not yet a well-established network of Italian Lacanians, but only a few isolated individuals interested in his work.

When Lacan's name began to circulate among small Italian psychoanalytic and intellectual groups, it was mainly associated with structuralism and linguistics, the key theoretical framework for his return to Freud, which also earned him popularity in France and a reputation as a renowned intellectual in other countries. In his first ever interview released to an Italian audience, in 1966,[5] Lacan underlines the crucial role played by linguistics in his work. 'The basic structures of language', he posits, 'are the very coordinates that enable me to comprehend what occurs at the level of the unconscious' (Caruso 1969, p. 163). Lacan insists on the linguistic foundation of psychoanalysis, something Freud did not make explicit, concluding that 'the only difference between his position and mine lies in the fact that, opening one of his books, I immediately say: this is linguistics' (p. 164). Nevertheless, Lacan emphasises his

[4] In 1964, Enrico Castelli invited Lacan to deliver a talk on ethics and science at the colloquium 'Technique and Casuistry' held at the University of Rome from 7 to 12 January. The essay *On Freud's "Trieb" and the Psychoanalyst's Desire* provides a summary of the main issues addressed by Lacan on that occasion. In 1967, Lacan travelled to Italy on several occasions to deliver lectures: *The misapprehending of the subject supposed to know* on 14 December at the Institut Culturel Français in Naples; *From Rome '53 to Rome '67: psychoanalysis. Reason for a defeat* on 15 December at the University of Rome; an unpublished paper on 16 December at the Scuola Normale Superiore of Pisa where he was invited by Jean Roudaut, a professor of French literature; and *On psychoanalysis in its relationships to reality* on 18 December at the Istituto Milanese di Psicoanalisi. In 1968, Lacan also held public talks in Italy: *Incomprehensible to someone normally constituted* on 6 November at the Centre Culturel Français in Turin and *Social conference of Doctor Lacan* on 7 November at the Institut Culturel Français in Florence. See Contri (1978) and Lacan (2001).

[5] Lacan was interviewed in Paris in November 1966. Subsequently, part of the interview was published in *Fiera letteraria* (16 November 1967); the interview was then published in its entirety in *Psicoterapia e scienze umane* (April–June 1968), and finally in the book *Lévi-Strauss, Foucault, Lacan* (Caruso 1969), which introduced Lacan to a broad Italian audience as one of the main representatives of structuralism.

fidelity to Freud throughout the entire interview as he repeatedly, and humbly, reiterates that there is nothing in his *Écrits* that goes against, or even beyond, Freud, leaving it entirely to other people to establish whether he is a mere exegete of Freud or rather an innovator of psychoanalysis.

The close relationship between Lacanian theory and linguistic structuralism will always remain a distinguishing trademark, but it is particularly notable in the Italian reception of Lacan during the 1960s and 1970s. In *La struttura assente*, the Italian semiotician Umberto Eco negatively[6] regards Lacanian structuralism as ontological, claiming that, according to Lacan, 'the symbolic order is not constituted by the individuals but, rather, is what constitutes them' (1968, p. 325). For this reason, 'the symbolic, the signifying chain, are nothing but the manifestations of the unconscious, through which what constitutes us is revealed' inasmuch as 'the signifier prevails over the subjects' (1968, p. 325). According to Recalcati (2009, p. 20), Eco's account is the epitome of the semiotic reading of Lacan's work, which is predominant at this stage of his reception. For Eco, Lacan should be approached through the lens of structuralist linguistics, which emphasises the autonomy of the symbolic and the constituting power of the signifier, positing the overdetermination by linguistic structures and language almost as a reified essence. At this point, the Italian reception of Lacan exclusively stresses the language-like dimension of the unconscious to the detriment of the real, the Lacanian register beyond language and signification, which are barely mentioned by Italian scholars at the time. This would remain the predominant interpretation of Lacan for several years (and not only in Italy). A decade later, the close association with the linguistic turn continued to dominate the prevalent approach to Lacan's thought, as confirmed by the Italian philosopher Franco Rella. The Lacanian unconscious, Rella contends, relies entirely on language. Hence, 'everything is played out within language itself, within the signifying order' (1980, p. 88). This perspective can, in fact, still be found today. In postmillennial times, Esposito

[6] Eco would later acknowledge that, at the time, he did not fully grasp the specificity of psychoanalytic discourse (Tarizzo 2003, p. 120). For a more detailed discussion about Eco and psychoanalysis, see Smith (2006, 2010).

continues to lay the emphasis on Lacan's logocentrism, positing the sovereignty of language as the 'epicentre' of Lacan's theory *tout court* (2012, p. 6).

In its infancy, Italian Lacanianism was somewhat culturally isolated, facing scepticism and, at times, overt rejection—unlike in France, where Lacan's groundbreaking approach provoked far-reaching debate (Vegetti Finzi 1986). This difference in reception was partly fuelled by the cultural rivalry between Italy and France (Benvenuto 1987a), as Lacanianism was mainly 'received as "Parisian" by the whole of the Italian intellectual community' (Roudinesco 1990, p. 543). For instance, it was attacked by members of the Italian Psychoanalytic Society (SPI), including Cesare Musatti, who fiercely opposed the development of Lacanian psychoanalysis in Italy (Vegetti Finzi 1986). Despite this aggressive opposition, Lacan captured the interest of a loyal, albeit restricted, group of Italians, including Giacomo Contri, the first Italian member of the *École Freudienne de Paris* (EFP), Armando Verdiglione, the most controversial figure of the Italian Lacanian movement, and Muriel Drazien, who moved from Paris to Rome to promote Lacanian psychoanalysis.

At the time, there was also another prominent Italian psychoanalyst who was particularly fascinated by Lacan. Despite his training and affiliation with the SPI, Elvio Fachinelli was attracted by Lacan's unconventional attitude and soon became one of the first promoters of Lacan in Italy (Benvenuto 1997). On a theoretical level, Fachinelli considered post-Freudian psychoanalysis to be guilty of either dismissing or overtly rejecting Freud's most crucial notion of the unconscious. In Lacan, he found an ally against some psychoanalysts' defensive attempts to downplay the radical Otherness of the unconscious in their clinical practice. On an institutional level, Fachinelli, like Lacan, was critical of the psychoanalytic establishment and profoundly distrusted institutionalised psychoanalysis—a stance that gained him the reputation of a dissident psychoanalyst. A glaring example of this can be found in the counter-congress Fachinelli co-organised in 1969 with other European analysts and trainees during the IPA's international congress in Rome (Herzog 2017). The aim was to voice dissent against the hierarchical and dogmatic management of the IPA, which was accused of being unresponsive to social struggle and of promoting an elitist form of psychoanalysis. Despite initially declining his official invitation, Lacan eventually decided to witness the protest in person, maintaining a neutral position for the entire duration of the counter-congress (Contri 1978). This was one of the first steps towards establishing what Roudinesco defined as 'a curious Italian Lacanianism, both sectarian and picturesque, rooted in the margins of an official psychoanalytic society in crisis' (1990, p. 543).

The Inception of the Lacanian Movement in the 1970s

During the 1970s, Italian psychoanalysis attained an unprecedentedly prominent position in the public sphere, similar to the psychoanalytic boom of the 1940s in the USA (Benvenuto 1997; Fachinelli 2011). This was an epochal turnaround from the pervasive resistance it had endured in pre-war times. Over the course of this decade, the popularity of Lacanian psychoanalysis in Italy also grew substantially thanks to the influence of the official and newly established Italian Lacanian movement. Italian Lacanianism made a significant contribution to the popularisation of psychoanalysis not only by engaging in public debates around mental health and psychiatric reform but also by influencing artists and academics, reforming psychoanalysis and its settings, and remaining politically engaged (Contri 1978; Vegetti Finzi 1986). In many ways, these characteristics anticipated and paved the way for the major traits of Italian postmillennial Lacanianism, with some of the key notions of the latter—desire, subjectivity, political commitment, and the role of psychoanalysis in the *polis*, for instance—being rooted in the debates and events of this decade.

In the 1970s, a profound change took place in the very fabric of the Italian nation due to the country's sudden modernisation. In brief, during the years of the 'economic miracle', Italy went from being primarily agricultural, relatively poor, country to becoming a prosperous, industrialised nation characterised by a predominantly urban and consumeristic society. The shift from an archaic social system to a neo-capitalist mass society triggered the rapid disappearance of small rural communities, religious traditions, and the sub-proletariat, which ultimately generated a widespread profound alienation (Diazzi and Sforza Tarabochia 2019). The far-reaching implications of industrialisation did not escape Lacan who, in the late 1960s, acutely observed that 'there is a lot of this alienation about nowadays [...] whether in economics, politics, psychopathology, aesthetics, and so on' (1998, p. 210). According to the Italian versatile artist and public intellectual Pier Paolo Pasolini, during this process of modernisation, Italy was alienating its past while undergoing an irreversible 'anthropological mutation' (1999, p. 307). Pasolini's expression effectively conveys how these sudden, yet profound, changes deeply affected the values and customs of Italians, bringing about radical and unprecedented psychosocial transformations. Echoing the renowned discourse of the capitalist delivered by Lacan in his 1972 keynote speech in Milan,[7] Pasolini contended that a new power escaping any definition, and no longer coinciding with a specific political or religious ideology, was colonising the unconscious of the Italians. Furthermore, he argued that this new unstoppable power manipulating Italian society was the most violent and totalitarian there had ever been (1999, p. 327). Pasolini regarded this as a new and more powerful form of fascism, responsible for turning Italians from vassals into consumers:

> Consumer anxiety is an anxiety of obedience to an unspoken order. Everyone in Italy feels degrading anxiety from the pressure to be equal to others in consuming: in being happy, in being free: because this is the order that he has unconsciously received, and which he "must" obey. (1999, p. 330)

Given its position between the realms of medicine and philosophy's humanistic inquiry, psychoanalysis was particularly well-suited to the Italian milieu of the time and was bolstered by a widespread demand for

[7] In the 1970s, Lacan travelled to Italy on several occasions to deliver keynote lectures and public remarks: on 12 May 1972 at the University of Milan he delivered the paper *On the Psychoanalytic Discourse*; on 3 February 1973 in Milan at the Museum of Science and Technology he delivered the paper *Psychoanalysis in its reference to the sexual relationship*; on 22 March 1974 he delivered *Logic and Love* at the Clinic of nervous and mental diseases in Rome; on 30 March 1974 in Milan delivered a speech entitled *To the Freudian School*; on 29 October 1974, at the Centre culturel français in Rome, Lacan held a press conference to present the 7th Congress of the *École freudienne de Paris* and the transcription became *The Triumph of Religion*; on 1 November 1974 he gave the address *The Third*. See Contri (1978) and Lacan (2013b).

care and knowledge, becoming the privileged interpretative framework for the discontent of the Italians (Vegetti Finzi 1986).

The political commotion and social unrest of the 1960s and 1970s promoted a 'movement of extroversion' in Italian psychoanalysis (Benvenuto 1997), which resulted in the emergence of a socially and politically committed psychoanalysis and new settings for its interventions. Resembling militant Marxist intellectuals and social activists, some pioneering psychoanalysts pushed their sphere of intervention beyond the consulting rooms, which had thus far been affordable only for the upper class. The *clinica del lavoro* (labour clinic) and the Niguarda counselling service in the suburbs of Milan were successful, yet short-lived, examples of a working-class psychoanalysis, for instance, which from 1969 to 1974 provided free psychoanalytic evening sessions to workers, both in individual and small group settings. These were set up independently by the psychiatrist and psychoanalyst Enzo Morpurgo, supported neither by the city council nor by the communist party (Diazzi 2021). As Barbetta contends, 'factories, schools, public spaces, hospitals, family homes, and even streets, became an enclave where psychotherapy could work, empowering the so-called patients in the process of enabling them to reshape their own lives within the community' (2019, p. 156). This is why for many Italians, psychoanalysis 'remains intimately bound to the radical and visionary epoch of the leftist dissident' (Benvenuto 1997, para. 5), epitomised by Fachinelli's groundbreaking reformist efforts.

Similarly to Lacan, Fachinelli contested the psychoanalytic mainstream, which he regarded as authoritarian on both the institutional and clinical levels. Fachinelli conceived of psychoanalysis not simply as a cure for the individual but also as a powerful tool for political criticism and social change, thus pushing the boundaries of the standard psychoanalytic setting and disseminating psychoanalytic practice among the working class through innovative community projects. This was the case, for instance, with *L'erba voglio*, a self-run nursery school in Milan experimenting with non-authoritarian pedagogies, which Fachinelli established in 1970 alongside leading feminists Lea Melandri and Luisa Muraro (Gutherz 2019). The anti-authoritarian approach, the notion of desire, and the relationship between the individual and society were key concepts and concerns for Fachinelli. In *Dissident desire*, published in 1968,

Fachinelli addressed the student movement's focus on anti-authoritarianism. Engaging with the Frankfurt school, which was influential in Italy at the time, Fachinelli acknowledged the crisis of patriarchy and paternal authority. However, unlike many other analysts and academics, rather than simply dismissing the youth dissident movement as merely revolting against parental authority and sexual repression, Fachinelli regarded the kernel of the movement as mainly standing against the 'renunciation of desire' (2019, p. 297). Drawing inspiration from Lacan, Fachinelli exhorted the younger generations to preserve their radical desire, contending that what ultimately matters is not the actual object of desire but keeping desire alive, that is, being in a desiring state. Fachinelli evoked the image of a 'dissident desire' in opposition to the mere 'satisfaction of need' promoted by society (2019, p. 299). In so doing, as Barbetta argues, Fachinelli 'proposed a new setting for the psychoanalytic encounter, where desire is connected to the social world and the subject is seen as part of a collective being rather than as a monadic individual independent from social structures' (2019, p. 156).

Desire was one of the principal reasons for the ambivalence of feminist and gay rights movements towards psychoanalysis during this decade. This ambivalence arose because psychoanalysis was seen as both a practice directed at liberating the subject's desire and, at the same time, as a bourgeois and patriarchal tool to oppress and regulate desire. The Marxist topic of the liberation of labour from capitalist exploitation overlapped with the post-Freudian stance of freeing the sexual drives from social repression. The feminist and gay rights movements, along with Fachinelli, anticipated the emphasis that twenty-first-century Italian Lacanianism would place on the Lacanian notion of desire and the concept of the evaporation of the father (see Chaps. 3 and 4). It is noteworthy that, although the concept of desire was widely debated even outside Lacanian circles during that period (Rovatti 2003, p. 28), the discourse on enjoyment, the Lacanian notion often juxtaposed with that of desire, remained largely absent in the 1970s. However, enjoyment has emerged as a pivotal concept in contemporary transnational Lacanianism, particularly in its political and psychosocial applications.

The alliance between feminist and gay activist groups rests on the call for sexual liberation, subverting gender roles, and challenging stereotypes. Italian feminism operated a political appropriation of psychoanalysis 'more for activist than for academic reasons' (Malagreca 2007, p. 62), which contributed to the *pratica dell'inconscio* (the practice of the unconscious) and to protests calling for the recognition of abortion as a right. Italian feminists adopted strategies such as the use of personal experience to analyse and question mechanisms of oppression, as well as consciousness-raising groups and self-help practices, 'which sought to explore the unconscious and saw in psychoanalysis an essential kind of knowing that could avoid lapsing into ideology' (Melandri 2019, p. 80). Italian feminist thought investigated the relationship between subjectivity, the political realm, and social change, bridging the gap between the psychic and the political spheres and borrowing extensively from psychoanalytic thinkers to challenge patriarchal ideology. The Italian feminist movement brought to the fore categories that had previously been considered apolitical, such as the body, sexuality, desire, and the unconscious, infiltrating the public discourse and the political lexicon with a stronger emphasis on the individual. It thus shifted 'the boundaries between private life and political life' (Melandri 2019, p. 22). Italian feminists delivered a critique of the Oedipal and patriarchal symbolic structure and offered a rehabilitation of marginalised subjects, through the reappropriation of the body in biological/physical and psychical terms, alongside the foregrounding of the personal story and lived experience.

The Italian gay rights movement addressed further the connection between the political and the psychical against the backdrop of the social construction of gender roles and sexuality. Psychoanalysis was thus a key point of reference, but it was not beyond critique. In *Towards a Gay Communism: Elements of Homosexual Critique* (1977), Mario Mieli, a Freudo-Marxist thinker and one of the founders of the Italian gay rights movement, contends that psychoanalysis was not immune from the 'deadly domination of capital' (2018, p. xxxviii), joking about the increasing popularisation of psychoanalysis, due to which nowadays 'the unconscious is sold in slices over the butcher's counter' (2018, p. 224). In the wake of Pasolini's anthropological mutation and Marcuse's desublimation, Mieli argues that:

> capital seeks to take possession of even the unconscious […]. It may be successful, either because it is more difficult today for the unconscious to

explode in an uncontrolled fashion, given the efficiency of conditioning, or because, by way of repressive desublimation, capital enables the unconscious to 'emerge' in alienated forms, in order to subsume it, to deprive men and women of it, and to deprive women and men of themselves. (2018, p. 107)

Although Mieli favours Deleuze and Guattari's critique of Lacanianism (Dean 2018), his work bears the mark of Lacanian theory. Similarly to Lacan, Mieli blames post-Freudian analysts for shying away from the subversive potential of psychoanalysis and from Freud's radical conception of sexuality.[8] Mieli's perspective, according to which all individuals are equally inhabited by a constitutive lack (Malagreca 2007), emphasises the notions of desire and the subject, which are so pivotal in contemporary Italian Lacanianism. However, in Mieli's account, the notion of the desiring subject is rooted in a 'liberationist model of queer sexuality' (Dean 2018, p. viii), which differs radically from the standpoint of post-millennial Italian Lacanians, who instead emphasise the intrinsic positivity of lack, and caution against the idea of total liberation. According to Mieli, desire is originally transsexual, perverse, polymorphous, and, as such, not univocally oriented towards a specific object. Later on in life, however, desire is constrained and repressed by the hetero-capitalist apparatus that, by means of 'educastration', creates 'erotically mutilated' subjects (Mieli 2018, p. 4). Hence, the desiring subject suffers from these superimposed restrictions which are also determined by class, gender, sexual orientation, and ethnicity; Mieli advocates, accordingly, for breaking free and liberating eros.

The antipsychiatry movement itself exhibited a notable combination of philosophical thought, particularly in its phenomenological-existentialist strand, and psychoanalytic principles. This amalgamation played a significant role in emancipating mental illness from its purely organic framework, paving the way for psychiatric reform rooted in

[8] In his book, Mieli calls those psychoanalysts holding repressive and dogmatic views on sexuality 'psychonazis' and fiercely attacks Franco Fornari, head of the Italian Psychoanalytic Society at the time, and Elvio Fachinelli, for their homophobic remarks (2018, pp. 216–239). Mieli also regarded the anti-psychiatry movement with suspicion, sarcastically claiming that anti-psychiatrists are 'better at making sense of Lacan than they are at understanding homosexuality' (p. 25).

social, non-medical perspectives drawn from sociology, anthropology, and a philosophical understanding of subjectivity. In those years, the conceptual framework for understanding mental suffering underwent a transformation, shifting from a focus solely on psychiatric diagnoses and medical aetiology towards a more holistic perspective centred on the individual suffering subject, viewed within the context of broader sociopolitical and economic dynamics. Consequently, subjectivity became intertwined with broader historical and socioeconomic factors affecting the wider community, and came to be understood in terms of intersubjectivity. However, the antipsychiatry movement largely perceived psychoanalysis as a tool of social control for the upper class and as an elitist therapy for wealthy people.

The main representative of Italian anti-institutional psychiatry is Franco Basaglia, a psychiatrist with a philosophical inclination, who spearheaded the reform of Italian psychiatry. His efforts culminated in the passing of Law 180 in 1978, which mandated the closure of asylums in Italy, regulated the provision of psychiatric treatment, and established local psychiatric healthcare. In Italy, as in other countries, there existed an 'alliance between Lacanian clinical practice and the psychiatric reform' (Russo 2009, p. 218). This convergence underscores Basaglia's criticism of psychoanalysis, which aligns with Lacan's perspective. Basaglia viewed psychoanalysis as overly deterministic; accessible only to the wealthy; excessively fixated on the patient's desires rather than on their needs; dismissive of the social aspect; and overtly dogmatic and normalising. Moreover, although Basaglia never directly references Lacan, his thought resonates with Lacan's teaching, particularly in terms of subjectivity and its intrinsic connection with Otherness, a central tenet shared by both (Recalcati 2009, 2010; Sforza Tarabochia 2014). In short, therefore, in a manner akin to the Lacanian subject who is always-already alienated in the Other, the Basaglian subject exists only in relation to, and as an integral part of, the world. In his account of Basaglia's theory of the subject, Sforza Tarabochia (2014) asserts that, as in Lacan, subjectivity is marked by a constitutional lack. Basaglia emphasises the importance of restoring the focus on the subject and their social bonds, as well as advocating for the reconstruction of a sense of community and countering the trend towards reducing human existence to merely organic functions (Sforza

Tarabochia 2011). Basaglia's later texts veer towards sociopolitical criticism to foster political interventions aimed at improving the lives of people with a mental illness (Sforza Tarabochia 2014, p. 234). Finally, Basaglia also shares with Lacan a belief in the necessity of subverting, or at least challenging, any position of power and authority in the treatment.

In the wake of the linguistic turn, psychoanalytic literary studies increased in popularity within academic circles during the 1970s, being characterised by a 'strong focus on language and the rhetorical features of texts' (Caldwell and Capello 2010, p. 3). This can be seen, for example, in the work of the French studies scholars Francesco Orlando and Stefano Agosti. However, this Lacanian influence also encountered strong persistent resistance from within the humanities. In *The Freudian Slip*, published in 1974, the philologist and literary critic Sebastiano Timpanaro accused Lacan of charlatanism, exhibitionism, and an 'erroneous and confused knowledge' of linguistics (2011, p. 58). Despite this resistance, Lacan's thought also inspired the work of Italian artists, including that of the poet Andrea Zanzotto (Johnson 2000) and the unconventional actor Carmelo Bene (Chiesa 2016). The psychoanalytic wave of the 1970s influenced culture and the arts and, in turn, its portrayal became widespread in the media. Marco Bellocchio's cinema, for example, bears the mark of the new range of approaches that appeared in Italy after the economic boom, including gestalt theory, family therapy, group therapy, and Lacanian psychoanalysis (Brook 2010).

During the 1970s, a number of translations of key Lacanian texts furthered the growing interest in Lacan's thought. These include the *Écrits*, translated in full in 1974 by Contri;[9] the ongoing publication of Lacan's seminars, begun in 1978; and several works by renowned representatives of French Lacanianism, including Maud Mannoni and Serge Leclaire. Additionally, a number of Lacanian journals and reviews were launched (e.g., *Sic*, *Il piccolo Hans*, *Spirali*), enhancing the interdisciplinary approach and the public engagement that Lacan had promoted throughout his life, and which is now the trademark of Lacanians worldwide. By

[9] It is noteworthy that the complete Italian translation of the *Écrits* was released some years after the first French edition was published in 1966. In contrast, apart from a selection of essays translated into English in 1977, the English-speaking audience had to wait 40 years before the first complete English translation by Bruce Fink appeared in 2006.

the mid-1970s, Lacanianism had thus became a widespread, yet fragmented, movement in Italy—as testified by several Lacanian institutions, associations, and schools established across the country (Contri 1978; Roudinesco 1990; Vegetti Finzi 1986). In Milan, a key hub for the development of Italian Lacanianism, Contri founded the *Scuola Freudiana* (1972), while Verdiglione established *Semiotica e Psicoanalisi* (1973). In Rome, Drazien founded *La Cosa Freudiana* (1973), which she maintained over the subsequent decades with the help of her pupils Antonello Sciacchitano and Marisa Fiumanò.

To counter the fragmentation of the Italian groups and coordinate their leaders, Lacan felt it necessary to unify the movement by creating a Lacanian association in Italy (Contri 1978). At first, Lacan asked Fachinelli to take the lead on this project as he regarded the Italian psychoanalyst as '[his] first reader in Italy on whom [his] work has had an effect' (Contri 1978, p. 123). After Fachinelli declined the appointment, Lacan wrote *Note to the Italians* to encourage Verdiglione, Contri, and Drazien to take up this role, referring to them anonymously as the 'tripod', the 'three-legged' Italian group (Contri 1978). After several meetings held in Italy between March and December 1974, the Italian section of the *École freudienne de Paris* (EFP) was finally established under the name of *La Cosa Freudiana* (Busiol 2022). Conscious of the institutional disputes already tormenting his school in France, Lacan was well aware of the challenges that would be involved in establishing his school in Italy. In a 1974 interview for the Italian magazine *Panorama*, when asked to discuss the main characteristics of Lacanianism, Lacan cautiously answered that 'it's a little early to say, doesn't exist yet. We're beginning to get a slight whiff of it, like a presentiment' (2015, p. 17). This presentiment was unfortunately short-lived. Already in 1975, ignited by mutual accusations and rivalries, misunderstandings and clashes exploded between the three Italians, who would soon abandon the project to pursue independent careers (Roudinesco 1990, p. 543).

Due to this institutional failure and despite the increasing interest among academics, artists, and intellectuals, Lacanianism had a much weaker impact in Italy than in other Romance-language countries and was still comparatively marginalised. In fact, the 1970s were effectively 'a lost opportunity' for Italian Lacanians (Benvenuto 1997, para. 8). In

Lacan in Italia/En Italie Lacan (1978), Contri reviews the state of Lacanianism in Italy in the late 1970s, outlining the main issues and future challenges of the incipient Italian Lacanian movement. For Contri, Lacanianism was predominantly affected by what he terms 'obscurantism' (1978, p. 14), namely, the cynical exploitation and deliberate misconception of Lacan's teaching by certain Italian Lacanians for personal profit. This further damaged the credibility of Lacanian psychoanalysis, which had already been tarnished by the excessive eclecticism and intellectualism that had overshadowed the clinical practice. To counterbalance these mystifications and misappropriations, frequently disguised by jargon and overcomplicated language, Contri maintains that rigorous exegetic work is necessary, especially for the purpose of emphasising the ethical and scientific aspects of Lacanian psychoanalysis (1978, p. 15). Moreover, to legitimise the Lacanian field, Contri repeatedly emphasises that Lacanianism is not a deviation from Freudianism but rather its radicalisation, extensively arguing that the Lacanian method stems from, and remains firmly rooted in, Freud's psychoanalysis (1978, p. 18).

The sectarianism and rivalry among Italian groups, however, hindered the further development of a cohesive movement. In the span of just a few years from its inception, Lacanianism faced all the historical problems Freudianism had already experienced, such as in its efforts to ensure the Lacanian community remained cohesive but at the same time open to fruitful exchanges with other orientations, and in managing Lacanian institutions and schools, regulating psychoanalytic training and, most compellingly, guaranteeing the effective transmission of Lacan's body of knowledge to future generations. The latter issue was a particular source of concern for Lacanian communities, both in Italy and abroad, with conflicts and schisms emerging in relation to the movement's lineage and the recognition of its authentic descendants. Who was the real heir of Lacan, bearing the true meaning of his thought? Was there more than one? It would take several decades—a temporal distance required to mitigate the powerful influence of Lacan's charisma—for the 'proper' Lacanian legacy to emerge in Italy. The close proximity to Lacan himself prevented the first generation of Italian Lacanians from developing an original take on his teaching. In this decade, the most prevalent approach to Lacan's work among his pupils and followers was 'mocking Lacan, mimicking his style, maintaining the charismatic and inspired atmosphere that distinguished him' (Di Ciaccia and Recalcati 2000, p. 3). As already pointed out by Contri, this was particularly damaging for Italian Lacanianism, which was often associated with the charlatanism of some of its representatives, among whom Armando Verdiglione—infamous for his farcical imitation of Lacan's style—was the most notable. Although he has never been a member of the EFP (Miller in Benvenuto 1987b, p. 45), Verdiglione shamefully exploited Lacan's name to unscrupulously promote himself, an attitude that eventually led him to face legal trials and criminal convictions.

The Downfall of Lacanianism in the 1980s and 1990s

The philosopher Pier Aldo Rovatti was one of the first Italian philosophers to systematically extend Lacanianism beyond its clinical dimension while at the same time pressing Lacanian theory to prove its effectiveness in the clinical domain. Rovatti devotes a chapter to Lacan in the book *The Weak Thought* (1983), edited with Giovanni Vattimo, where he discusses necessity and impossibility, the real, and the subject. According to Rovatti, Lacan's thought revolves mainly around the notion of lack and, for this reason, is to be regarded as 'weak' in the sense that it is anti-authoritarian, non-normative, and anti-dogmatic. Rovatti's *lettura debolista* of Lacan engages with Lacan's text in unexpected ways—'contaminating it, using it, making it an instrument' (Recalcati 2009, p. 22). *A partire da Lacan*, the 1980 special issue of *Aut aut*,[10] edited by Rovatti, focuses on Lacan's

[10] *Aut aut* is one of the most renowned and well-established philosophical academic journals in Italy, underpinned by a phenomenological and existentialist approach. Since its inception in 1951, thanks to the Italian phenomenologist Enzo Paci, the journal has been advocating for the fruitful intersection of philosophy and psychoanalysis, which promoted a return of interest in the philosophical notion of the subject (Sinigaglia 2009). Since the notion of subjectivity is crucial in Lacan, it is unsurprising that *Aut aut* has been particularly keen to discuss the philosophical scope of Lacan's theory and practice throughout the years. After the 1980 special issue, *Aut aut* published two other special issues on Lacan: the 2009 *Leggere Lacan oggi*, which assesses the legacy and significance of Lacan in postmillennial Italy, and the 2020 *Ripartire con Lacan*, which explores those fruitful cross-disciplinary connections between Lacan's thought and other philosophies or fields.

legacy and the future developments of his thought in Italy. Rovatti's intention was to prevent Lacanianism from, on the one hand, dissolving into a socio-culturally trendy phenomenon completely detached from its clinical aspects, and, on the other, from being a sterile, at times grotesque, repetition of Lacan's main ideas by his pupils. For this reason, the contributors to the *Aut aut* special issue were Lacanian scholars and clinicians invited to discuss and assess their field. The issue comprises two distinct sections: one dedicated to philosophical contributions and the other featuring clinical ones. This thus marks the first Italian attempt to integrate the theoretical and philosophical aspects of Lacan's teaching within its clinical framework and to apply Lacanian theory to different disciplines without losing its clinical roots. In the *Aut aut* special issue, the Lacanian psychoanalyst Marisa Fiumanò argues that the reception of Lacanian theory was still very new in Italy and that Italian Lacanianism was hampered by the lack of a master officially and univocally recognised by the Italian Lacanian community (1980, pp. 243–244). This led, according to the Italian philosopher Franco Rella (1980, p. 91), to a peculiar situation in which Italian Lacanians either defended or exalted Lacan without properly engaging with his work. The most fruitful way to engage with Lacan is indeed forward-looking—oriented towards what his teaching can still generate, rather than backward-looking and focusing on replicating Lacan's slogans. This is precisely the trajectory developed in postmillennial Italy, where Lacan's Italian legacy is no longer confined to a mere repetition of his jargon but is instead originally and creatively deployed.

In the early 1980s, however, the more prominent Lacan employed in cultural studies, film theory, and feminist studies had already overshadowed the figure of Lacan as a practising analyst, regarded particularly in the Anglophone reception more as the 'Other Lacan' (Schneiderman 1980, pp. 9–16). It is noteworthy that, when editing one of the first introductory books on the Lacanian clinic for an English-speaking audience, Stuart Schneiderman worried that Lacan's clinical notions would be mainly received as 'abstract theoretical considerations' (1980, p. 9) disengaged from any practical application. Anglophone readers at the time were already more accustomed 'to see[ing] Lacan as a thinker, a master of hermeneutics, or even a self-indulgent metaphysician' (1980, p. 9) than as a rigorous and innovative clinician. After Lacan's death in 1981, the issue of his 'dialectic of theory and clinic' (Hughes and Malone 2002, p. 1) became exacerbated, particularly in the Anglophone world (Roudinesco 1997). After that point, the 'secularization of Lacan's work by philosophers and academics' (Roudinesco 1997, p. 435) progressed exponentially. Nevertheless, the *Aut aut* special issue sparked other initiatives centred on developing a rigorous study of Lacanian texts, with a particular focus on the clinic. In 1987, with Jacques-Alain Miller's support and approval, Antonio Di Ciaccia established the journal *La Psicoanalisi*, which has since published several translations of Lacan's unpublished papers as well as the *Lettres de L'École freudienne de Paris* and countless contributions by Lacanian psychoanalysts. Having trained with Lacan in the 1970s and attended his seminar in Paris, Di Ciaccia is the Italian editor and translator of several of Lacan's seminars and *Autres Écrits*. He joined the *École Freudienne de Paris* in 1976 and later became a member of the *École de la Cause Freudienne* when it was established in 1980.

The rise of Italian Lacanianism was unexpectedly halted by the scandal that struck Verdiglione, which made the headlines of Italian newspapers, throwing not only Lacanian but Italian psychoanalysis in general into a deep crisis. Verdiglione's ascent began in Milan in 1973, when he organised the conference *Psychoanalysis and Politics*, which was attended by renowned psychoanalysts, writers, and philosophers, including Fachinelli, Ionesco, Borges, Kristeva, and Guattari. His rise continued unrelentingly into the early 1980s (Roudinesco 1990, p. 544). During this time, Verdiglione's entrepreneurial attitude contributed significantly to the spread of Lacanianism in Italy and extended its reach beyond psychoanalytic circles, reinforcing cross-disciplinary connections. Thanks to his persuasiveness and entrepreneurial activity, Verdiglione successfully promoted Lacan's thought by several means, ranging from his publishing house and namesake cultural foundation to opulent conferences held around the world. In particular, Verdiglione's lavish cultural events contributed to the dissemination of Lacanianism in Italy while also attracting the attention of the media. Lacan never attended any of these events, even if his presence was announced on many occasions (Vegetti Finzi 1986). Retrospectively, Lacan's attitude, which 'neither expressed disavowal nor support for Verdiglione' (Roudinesco 1990, p. 544), can clearly be recognised as a 'disastrous policy' (Roudinesco 1997, p. 434) that profoundly damaged the Italian Lacanian movement. In Verdiglione's debatable appropriation of Lacan's theory, Lacanian psychoanalysis lost its specificity and clinical rigour, instead becoming a mere cultural, and at times distasteful, phenomenon. Verdiglione's questionable Lacanianism, flooded with jargon and exaggerated mannerisms, along with his shameless self-promotion, were often scrutinised and ridiculed by the media,[11] which—on several occasions over the years—reported rumours of Verdiglione's abusive and illicit behaviour towards patients, collaborators, and devoted followers (Armando 1997).

The fall of Verdiglione began in July 1985, when the police investigated him for the misappropriation of funds (Roudinesco 1990, p. 546), and ended in June 1986, when he was convicted of fraud and extortion (Armando 1997). The verdict fuelled an already extremely heated debate in the Italian media on the accountability of those Lacanian circles that, even if they did not actively encourage it, did nothing to stop the rise of Verdiglione. Inevitably, this cast suspicion on Lacan himself, reviving the controversies around his charisma and his own alleged abuse of power. Lacan's clinical work was discredited to such an extent that, for the Italian media, the criminal actions perpetuated by Verdiglione were seen as a direct consequence of Lacanian psychoanalysis, training in which was regarded more as an esoteric initiation than as a rigorous process (Contri 1978, p. 146). Moreover, Lacan's refusal to follow the standard psychoanalytic technique, instead employing variable-length sessions, his controversial procedure of the pass, and his announcement of the self-authorisation of the analyst deepened those concerns, fuelling the misconception that Lacanian theory was deeply flawed and lacked any scientific clinical rigour. Verdiglione's imprisonment fostered an exceptionally negative perception of psychoanalytic practice as potentially abusive and unregulated by the law, which brought the whole world of

[11] Verdiglione acquired a very poor reputation and the following are just a few examples of how the Italian press and some analysts referred to him: 'Jehovah's Witness', 'comic-opera "godfather"', 'mafioso of culture' (Roudinesco 1990, pp. 544, 546); 'wild', 'trickster' (Armando 1997, pp. 345, 346, 384); 'preacher-bewitcher', 'guru', and 'alchemist' (Aspesi 1986). Several newspaper articles depicted him as the main representative of 'wild psychoanalysis' (Armando 1997) and in 1987–1988 the television programme *Drive-In* aired a parody of Verdiglione by the comedian Ezio Greggio (*Curiosando*, online). More recently, Bruce Fink also referred to Verdiglione as a negative example (2014).

psychoanalysis into disrepute. In its public perception, Lacanianism became synonymous with an unorthodox, illicit clinical practice lacking any regulation and ultimately responsible for putting the patient at the mercy of unethical analysts.[12] To counter these mounting accusations, several Lacanians pointed out that it was actually Lacan who had first warned the public about the misuse of transference and who had extensively addressed the ethics of psychoanalysis in his seminar of the same name (Armando 1997, p. 441).

Nevertheless, Verdiglione's scandal promoted constructive debates on the ethical boundaries in the psychoanalytic relationship; the admission criteria for psychoanalytic training; and the regulation of psychoanalytic institutions. Hence, both the unconscious and transference became a juridical matter to be legislated by the Italian parliament which, in order to regulate the practice of psychotherapy and restrain criminal deviations, approved the Ossicini Law in 1989 (Busiol 2022). Although the Ossicini Law did not mention psychoanalysis explicitly, it led to psychoanalytic training being restricted exclusively to psychologists and medical doctors and prevented graduates from the humanities and social sciences from becoming psychoanalysts. In fact, the Ossicini Law made it compulsory for all psychotherapists practising in Italy to hold a postgraduate degree in either psychology or medicine, and allowed only those institutes sanctioned by the state to provide training in psychotherapy.

By the end of the 1980s, Italian Lacanianism had already entered a later phase of its reception. As in other countries where 'Lacanian ideas have stealthily yet steadily penetrated the social sciences, the arts and the humanities' (Nobus 1998, p. ix), by this time Italian Lacanianism too had become an intellectual trend that had permeated popular culture (more negatively than positively). The discredit cast upon the clinical aspect by Verdiglione and the heterogeneous uses of Lacan's theory among

[12] The following excerpt from Aspesi's newspaper article, which compares Verdiglione to Ron Hubbard, the controversial founder of Scientology, epitomises the growing mistrust toward Lacanian psychoanalysts: 'Perhaps the era of these preacher-charmers ends with the Italian guru, who, promising the happiness of the heart, of intelligence, of culture, of the senses, of power, have enriched themselves by taking advantage of the needs of so many people [...] so many people, above all the youngsters, need these new religions which exalt the individual, remove them from their emptiness to place them in an organised group, giving them a father figure to believe in to the point of adoration' (1986, online).

academics reduced Lacanianism to a mere fashionable phenomenon, more useful for philosophical appropriations than for rigorous clinical practice (Focchi 2008, p. 9). Lacanianism was thus detached from clinical matters and plagued by a sterile intellectualism. The aftermath of the *Verdiglione affair*, along with the persistent fragmentation of Lacanian factions across the country, exacerbated the unresolved issues around the legacy and transmission of Lacan's thought. In 1989, after residing in Belgium for several years, where he set up the institute *Antenne 110* for children with autism and psychosis, Di Ciaccia returned to Italy and, with the support of Miller, founded the *Istituto freudiano per la clinica, la terapia e la scienza* with central hubs in Milan and Rome. In the same year, Renata Miletto and other Lacanian psychoanalysts established the *Associazione freudiana*, inspired by the *Association freudienne* founded by Charles Melman in 1982, with headquarters in Milan, Turin, Rome, and Naples. Additionally, the *Sezione Italiana della Scuola Europea di Psicoanalisi* emerged from the *École européenne de psychanalyse* (EEP) established in 1990.

In the 1990s, the factions that made up the pluralistic world of Italian Lacanianism became even more fragmented and disempowered than in the previous decade and the prominence of Italian Lacanianism diminished drastically to the point that it almost disappeared completely from the limelight. Although this can be attributed mainly to the defamation caused by Verdiglione, Lacan's unpopularity in this decade was also partly due to the first generation of Italian Lacanians who had missed the opportunity to develop a truly original contribution and failed to make Lacan less elitist and more palatable to the Italian audience. Outside Italy, the reputation and expansion of Lacanianism took a different path as some Lacanians, such as Juan-Davis Nasio and Slavoj Žižek, succeeded in popularising Lacan's theory for the non-specialists and established themselves as media stars. The success of Lacanian thought abroad, in particular in its North American reception, did not foster a revival of Lacan's popularity in Italy, as Benvenuto had wrongly anticipated (1997, para. 8). Arguably, this resistance reflects the reluctance of Italian academic circles at the time to embrace the cross-disciplinary approach adopted by cultural studies and film studies. This hostility was also directed towards gender studies and queer studies, along with scepticism towards the Lacano-Žižekian model of discourse and culture analysis.

On the occasion of the ten-year anniversary of Lacan's death, Rovatti's 1991 newspaper article 'Lo scandaloso signor Lacan' thoroughly assessed Lacan's legacy in Italy, which was depicted as gloomy and declining. Rovatti drew a clear distinction between Lacan, whose multifaceted and innovative thought could present a possibility for re-launching psychoanalysis, and Lacanianism, which was stuck in the past, losing relevance, and consumed by internal fratricidal wars. Rovatti claimed that the usual vices afflicting Lacanianism—which include excessive jargon, intellectualisation, superiority complex, and dogmatism—as well as the issues affecting the transmission of Lacan's thought and the survival of Lacanian schools, all revolved around the 'difficult legacy' left by Lacan and the inability of Lacanians to put it to good use. If the 'signifier Lacan' could help restore the reputation of Italian psychoanalysis and the Lacanian movement in Italy, this could only happen, according to Rovatti, by moving away from the image of the absolute master and the overshadowing seductive power of his personality. Instead, he proposed putting Lacan's thought to the test and thereby prove that it is possible to create psychoanalytic culture through Lacan. For Rovatti, the solution lies in a different reappropriation of Lacan's thought: 'not repeated but rethought originally and rigorously from the perspective of the analytical practice' (Rovatti 1991, online). This is precisely the nature of Italian postmillennial Lacanianism, which has finally moved beyond Lacan's charisma and away from dogmatic readings. In the 2000s, Italian Lacanians dealt with several challenges revolving around the transmission of Lacan's thought, the development of a specific Lacanian clinic, and the centrifugal and destructive forces internal to the Lacanian movement. They also managed to restore the reputation of psychoanalysis in Italy, which had been so badly damaged by the scandals of the 1980s. In the 2000s, Lacanianism regained its popularity thanks to the work of a new generation of Italian Lacanians trained and analysed by Miller, including Domenico Cosenza, Marco Focchi, Massimo Recalcati, and Uberto Zuccardi Merli, who distanced themselves, to various degrees, from a mere philological reading of Lacan and from his dogmatic cult.

Lacan's Renaissance in Postmillennial Italy

On 12 February 2012, *Il Sole 24 ORE*, one of the most influential newspapers in Italy, published a controversial and scathing article about Lacanian psychoanalysis, written by Gilberto Corbellini, an Italian philosopher of science. In the article, entitled 'L'autismo dei lacaniani', Corbellini vehemently criticised Lacanian psychoanalysis for its 'damaging influence' (2012, p. 29), which he deemed to be not only cultural but also political in nature, and accused Lacanians of being exponents of one of the most insidious psychoanalytic sects, whilst describing Lacan as a 'questionable individual' (2012, p. 29). Ultimately, Corbellini reiterated the familiar criticism that psychoanalysis is unscientific. The publication of the article provoked numerous heated responses on the part of renowned Italian psychoanalysts. Such figures included the two Lacanians Di Ciaccia and Recalcati, who engaged in a lively public debate on the pages of Italian newspapers, including *La Repubblica* and *Il manifesto.* This controversy led to the publication of *In difesa della psicoanalisi* in 2013, a book written by four prominent Italian psychoanalysts (Simona Argentieri, Stefano Bolognini, Antonio Di Ciaccia, and Luigi Zoja), each of whom belongs to different psychoanalytic schools. Among other prominent events, Corbellini's article and the subsequent debate it provoked demonstrate the popularity of Lacan's theories in postmillennial Italy. Indeed, Corbellini's specific targeting of Lacanians is evidence that Lacanianism, more than any other psychoanalytic orientations, had successfully relaunched psychoanalysis in the Italian public sphere.

After its apparent demise during the 1980s and 1990s, a new wave of Lacanianism has been flourishing since the turn of the century, bringing about a Lacanian renaissance in postmillennial Italy. The 2000s were characterised by a vibrant phase marked by the emergence of new Lacanian schools, organisations, and journals. Among these were the *Scuola Lacaniana di Psicoanalisi,* founded by Miller in 2002 in Milan and affiliated with the World Association of Psychoanalysis (WAP), and its related journal, *Attualità Lacaniana,* published from 2004. Today, Lacanian psychoanalysis has become a fashionable and extremely influential trend, which corroborates Voruz and Wolf's account of Italy as a 'Lacanian country' (2007, p. xvi). The widespread interest in Lacanian psychoanalysis in Italy today proves that, although often regarded as 'sophisticated and hermetic', Lacan's theory is 'surprisingly suited [...] to popularization' (Benvenuto 1997, para. 8).

The postmillennial wave of Lacanianism is one of the most relevant trends in twenty-first-century Italian psychoanalysis, which succeeded, as Rovatti had hoped for in the 1990s, in bringing psychoanalysis back to the public sphere. This achievement is owed to a new generation of Italian Lacanians, spearheaded by Massimo Recalcati, who managed to take Lacanian psychoanalysis out of the margins and into a hegemonic position. This was possible because Italian Lacanians worked hard to tackle those issues that for decades had beset Lacanianism in Italy, and which had given rise to preconceptions and stereotypes in the Italian public perception. Firstly, they reinstated the clinic as the focal point of Lacanianism in their approach to contemporary psychopathologies. This prevented Lacanian psychoanalysis from being perceived solely as a philosophical theory among others and evidenced instead its efficacy in the clinic. Secondly, they avoided hermeticism and intellectualism in their reading of Lacan's works and in their application of Lacan's theory to other disciplines. Thirdly, they developed an ethical stance in connecting clinical practice with social justice and political commitment. For the first time since the pioneering, albeit short-lived, projects directed at establishing a working-class psychoanalysis in the 1970s, Italian Lacanians have successfully broadened access to psychoanalysis in a twofold way: by making psychoanalysis affordable thanks to low-cost Lacanian clinics dotted around Italy, and by bringing psychoanalysis out of the consulting room into the *polis*, reaching schools, universities, hospitals, prisons, and even courtrooms (Focchi 2008). These Lacanians ultimately succeeded in '"Italianizing" psychoanalysis, in making it enter into the blood and bones of the Italian way of thinking' (Benvenuto 1997, para. 8), as demonstrated by the significant presence of certain Italian Lacanians in the media and by their impact on university students across different fields (Benvenuto 2020). Therefore, in today's Italy, Lacanianism can provoke and inform public debates while remaining firmly rooted in clinical work—which always underpins more theoretical considerations, whether they concern politics, philosophy, or aesthetics. The Lacanian orientation thus regained prestige and Lacan's reputation was restored, reaching an unprecedently vast audience.

Massimo Recalcati is the key representative of contemporary Italian Lacanians, the public face of Italian Lacanianism and the main contributor to Lacan's renaissance in today's Italy. No other contemporary Italian Lacanian has contributed more extensively to the field of Lacanian studies in Italy than he has. Arguably, without Recalcati's strenuous scholarly commitment and his active efforts at public engagement through the media, Lacan would probably have been forgotten by the young generations of Italian psychoanalysts (Lingiardi 2016). Recalcati is also one of the most translated Italian Lacanians, whose works are receiving steadily increasing attention in English-speaking academia (Chiesa 2011; Mura 2015; Di Martino 2016; Sforza Tarabochia 2016; Di Martino and Verdicchio 2017; Busiol 2022; Lewis and Rose 2022). This is demonstrated, for example, by an entry for Recalcati in the recent *Bloomsbury Italian Philosophy Reader*, where he features among other renowned Italian thinkers. In light of this, his contributions will be more extensively discussed in the following chapters than those of other Italian Lacanians.

Recalcati's success gained wider reach among lay people after the publication of his 2010 work *L'uomo senza inconscio*, which brought Lacanian theory to new audiences beyond psychoanalytic circles (see Chaps. 3 and 4). This book offered a sociopolitical analysis of Italian society, which led to his first television interview, where he was invited to discuss the then prime minister Silvio Berlusconi. *L'uomo senza inconscio* is effectively a milestone in the Italian reception of Lacanianism. The book epitomises the Italian popularisation of Lacanian theory and its fruitful hybridisation with fields outside of the clinical domain, while remaining deeply rooted in clinical work and categories. Recalcati made Lacan popular among Italians by framing Lacan's thought through humanistic culture (philosophy, literature, visual art), with reference to Italian artists and public intellectuals (Pier Paolo Pasolini, Alberto Burri, Giorgio Morandi), and to Classical antiquity (Oedipus, Antigone, Telemachus), as well as by discussing Italian society (the evaporation of the father, patriarchal society, violence against women), and even by taking into account the Christian tradition in his psychoanalytic-oriented works. He also engaged with Italian historical events (e.g., 1968) and politicians (Silvio Berlusconi, Matteo Renzi, Beppe Grillo, Matteo Salvini, and Giorgia Meloni) through the lens of Lacanian psychoanalysis. As Pietro Bianchi contends,

> This operation should not be understood simply as a superficial application of a ready-made conceptual apparatus, but as a real re-appropriation of Lacan's text. Recalcati, through a process not extraneous to that of the analyst in the session, apparently limits himself to using Lacan's words and concepts, but in reality "detaches" them from Lacan's original statement and makes them his own, re-signifying them and taking them – sometimes audaciously – in an unprecedented direction. (2014, online)

Since the late 1990s, Recalcati has been incessantly promoting Lacan's work in the media, including in left-wing newspapers, such as *Il Manifesto*, *La Repubblica*, *La Stampa*; in interviews on the radio; on his own television show; and even in a pop song co-written with an Italian singer who was inspired by one of Recalcati's books and is now regarded as an Italian public intellectual.[13] Between 2018 and 2020, three television series (*Lessico familiare*, *Lessico amoroso*, *Lessico civile*) of Recalcati's late-night lectures were broadcast on the Italian national channel Rai3.[14] However, this media exposure, with its popularisation of Lacan's ideas, provoked outright disdain and distrust from some quarters. As a media phenomenon, Recalcati's Lacanianism was parodied by Italian comedians and even fiercely accused of commodification, vulgarisation, and indoctrination by some Italian Lacanians (Lolli 2019; Sciacchitano 2019). Recalcati

[13] In Italy, the term 'intellectual' holds a positive connotation which, to some extent, still carries the social and cultural prestige from the tradition of Italian intellectuals such as Antonio Gramsci, Benedetto Croce, Pier Paolo Pasolini, and Umberto Eco. In the Italian context, intellectuals typically come from a humanistic background and, in postmillennial Italy, they are seen as creators of new meanings and perspectives essential for understanding the contemporary world (Collini 2006). Although less emphatically than in the past, there is a continuity in the Italian public intellectual between the philosophical and political spheres (Antonello 2009). This politically committed and engaged intellectual is what Benvenuto regards as '[a]nother reason for the relatively low development of psychoanalysis in Italy': 'the fact that the highest model for an Italian intellectual was and is, even today, political commitment in the agora' (Benvenuto 1997, para. 2). Recalcati fits within the tradition of the Italian intellectual as an interpreter of contemporary society capable of making sense of the complexities and contradictions of today's global world.

[14] The 16 episodes of the television show centre on issues around family, love, and society, which Recalcati discusses from a psychoanalytic perspective by referring mainly to Freud and Lacan, answering questions from the audience, and hosting contributions by renowned Italian artists and intellectuals, including the Academy-award winner Roberto Benigni and the philosopher Roberto Esposito. The television series, and its edited clips posted on social media, furthered the dissemination of Lacan's thought in Italy, which became pervasive while Recalcati's media presence conferred on him the status of intellectual celebrity.

embodies the commitment of the Italian leftist Marxist intellectual of the 1960s to 1970s, shares Fachinelli's critical stance towards dogmatic psychoanalysis, believes in changing the institution from the inside like Basaglia, and promotes an accessible and affordable psychoanalysis for all classes. Over the last two decades, Recalcati has also created Lacanian psychoanalytic clinics and associations (Jonas Onlus, ALIPSI, Società di Psicoanalisi) as well as a school for psychoanalytic training (IRPA).

This postmillennial Italian phenomenon is not simply a 'revival of Lacanianism' (Benvenuto 2020, p. 31) that popularised Lacan and brought him back into the limelight. Rather, it is a new phase of Lacan's reception in Italy, which is no longer overshadowed by issues of lineage and orthodoxy. As Recalcati fittingly remarks:

> In Italy, many of us have fought to confer citizenship upon Lacan's work, which was surrounded by prejudices and misunderstandings largely due to the fact that its Italian reception, which took place during the seventies, was strongly influenced by the "Verdiglione phenomenon" and everything that it has produced. We are no longer in that time. Lacan's work is recognized as a classic [...]. Now we are in a subsequent phase. The problem is not that of conferring citizenship upon Lacan, but the conflict of interpretations. Which Lacan? Which Lacan are we talking about when we talk about Lacan? What interests us about his teaching? Today is no longer the time of citizenship, but of the [different] readings of Lacan. (2013, p. 260)

Despite Lacan's having reached Italy in the late 1950s, his body of work is only now displaying the extent of its potential.[15] In the twentieth century, Lacan's work was overshadowed at first by his charisma and, after

[15] Many seminars, however, remain unpublished and untranslated, including seminar 9, seminars 12–15, and seminars 21–27, with the exception of seminar 23. As a result, these missing pivotal works form significant lacunae that hinder a comprehensive assessment of Lacan's thought. According to Cima, these unpublished seminars can be grouped into three main blind spots, termed 'Lacanian obscurantism' (2020). Unfortunately, Lacanian obscurantism has led to a 'dangerously reactionary effect' (Cima 2020, p. 15), as Lacanian scholars have generally overlooked these unpublished works and downplayed their theses in favour of the more conventional arguments found in the published seminars. This tendency has also fostered the erroneous association of the final stage of Lacan's teaching with seminar 23, despite this being only a late phase rather than the final one. Examples include Thurston's *Re-inventing the Symptom. Essays on the Final Lacan* (2002), Voruz's and Wolf's edited volume *The Later Lacan* (2007), and Svolos' *The Aims of Analysis. Miami Seminar on the Late Lacan* (2020).

his death, by the conflicts and rivalries of the various litigious fractions. In Italy today, on the other hand, for the first time, the conditions are in place both for an innovative interpretation of Lacan beyond the 'ideology of Lacanian dogmatism' (Roudinesco 2014; Tupinambá 2021) and for putting his thought to good use. It was not until the third millennium, therefore, that Lacan was properly received in Italy, and his legacy put into motion to create something original, emancipated from a sterile and orthodox reading of his text. The postmillennial Lacanian renaissance has been marked and furthered by the publication of key monographs on Lacan authored by some of the representatives of mainstream Italian Lacanianism. The following texts are all secular readings: not exegetic, apologetic, or messianic. They centre on the real, a concept that had barely registered in the Italian reception of Lacan throughout the 1970s and 1980s (Recalcati 1994), and are partly influenced by Miller's *Orientation Lacanienne*.

Di Ciaccia's and Recalcati's *Jacques Lacan: Un insegnamento sul sapere dell'inconscio* (2000) represents a turning point in the Italian reception of Lacan, insofar as this introduction to Lacan for a lay audience departs from the obscure commentaries issued in the 1970s and 1980s, whose exoteric and elitist readings ultimately put off a wider Italian audience. Without diminishing Lacan's complexity and without adopting an apologetic or dogmatic approach, Di Ciaccia and Recalcati's book conveys the vitality and density of Lacan's constantly evolving thought by providing a rigorous theoretical and philosophical reading. More importantly, however, the book marks a discontinuity in the Italian reception of Lacan which, up until that point, had mainly revolved around the signifier and the language-like unconscious. Conversely, Di Ciaccia and Recalcati focus in particular on the Lacan who increasingly emphasised the register of the real, and view seminar 7 as a milestone in foregrounding the notion of the real. In their view, this seminar marks a significant shift, wherein Lacan underscores the centrality of the category of the real, not only theoretically but also clinically. From this seminar onwards, Lacan commits to 'going more deeply into the notion of the real' (1992, p. 11), which is also Di Ciaccia's and Recalcati's trajectory in their monograph. According to them, Lacan's purpose is to

> lead the ethics of psychoanalysis to the extreme point of an encounter with the real, with that "worse" that human beings try in every possible way to avoid. For, admittedly, there is no worse encounter – this is what psychoanalysis teaches – than the encounter with oneself, with one's own real. (Di Ciaccia and Recalcati 2000, p. 5)

In this respect, the book bears the mark of Miller's reading of the late Lacan. Di Ciaccia, who collaborates with Miller on the Italian translation of Lacan's works, and Recalcati, one of Miller's pupils, draw upon Miller extensively to articulate the 'Lacan contra Lacan'–namely, Lacan's shift from the transcendental logic of the signifier and the field of desire to the predominance of the drive and the field of the real. In *Jacques Lacan e il problema della tecnica in psicoanalisi* (2003), Domenico Cosenza, another pupil of Miller's, addresses the clinical facets of Lacan's theory. He also emphasises the primacy of the real and similarly pinpoints seminar 7 as a turning point in Lacan's thought. According to Cosenza, in this seminar Lacan positions this register at the core of the analytic experience, no longer merely as an operation of symbolisation of the imaginary, but rather as a radical attempt to apprehend something of the real within the symbolic. In line with the trend at the time, Cosenza's account of the notion of the real is rooted in negativity as it regards this Lacanian register exclusively as impossible, unrepresentable, and closely intertwined with the libidinal body. From this standpoint, the real thus represents the ultimate barrier that language, interpretations, and even understanding cannot cross. Similarly, Cosenza conceptualises *jouissance* negatively, primarily defining it as 'self-destructive satisfaction, malignant – an irresistible libidinal drive towards something that causes the subject, a suffering that brings pleasure' (2003, p. 29).

Although Recalcati's work is characterised by a focus on the register of the real, he increasingly departs from Miller. In the 1990s, Recalcati was particularly influenced by the Millerian tripartite periodisation of Lacan's teaching and Miller's reading of Lacan's works. In this decade, Recalcati conceived of the real through the void and the remainder, which are coterminous with, respectively, *das Ding* and *objet petit a* (1996), strongly emphasising Lacan's association of the real with causation. Recalcati's early works exhibit a strong clinical inflection as he argues that the real as such is predominantly the real of a subject, extimate to them, and that which cannot be mastered. Keeping the real firmly at the core of the psychoanalytic practice allows us, according to Recalcati, to avoid any reduction of psychoanalysis to a hermeneutic practice or a mere theory of interpretations. Rather, psychoanalysis is a theory of the limits of interpreting, insofar as its object is not simply meaning but that which escapes it. The crucial question thus strictly intertwines with ethics and clinical practice: 'how to subjectively embrace the real as the foreigner within us, as impossible, as irreducible to meaning, or, if you prefer, as destiny?' (Recalcati 2001, p. 10). Recalcati's reading of Lacan is fully laid out in the three remarkable books of the same name, *Jacques Lacan* (2012, 2016, 2023). In these works, Recalcati moves away from Miller's Lacanian orientation and instead focuses on the interplay between the notions of desire (*desiderio*) and *jouissance* (*godimento*).[16] For Recalcati, Lacan's most clinically valuable phase of teaching developed between the end of the 1950s and the early 1960s—'Lacan's existential phase' (Zupančič 2000, p. 170)—because in those seminars, Lacan discusses the concepts of desire and enjoyment in tandem (Recalcati 2012, p. 54). Recalcati contends that Miller's and Žižek's readings of Lacan tend to oppose the two, while prioritising *jouissance* over desire. On the contrary, taking his cue from the Argentine-Mexican Lacanian analyst Néstor Braunstein, who strongly advocates for taking these two concepts together, against 'Manichean formulations' (2003, p. 114), Recalcati investigates the fruitful combination of desire and *jouissance* in subjectivation, love, and sublimation—all of which, for him, represent affirmative ways to deal with the real, making it a harbinger of life rather than of death.

Giovanni Bottiroli foregrounds the relationship between the real and the symbolic in his book *Jacques Lacan: Arte, Linguaggio, Desiderio* (2002). In this non-clinical book, Bottiroli investigates Lacan's legacy in the fields of semiotics, linguistics, and aesthetics. Bottiroli argues that,

[16] *Desiderio* comes from the Latin *desiderare*, meaning 'to await what the stars will bring'. It is closely connected to a sense of a lack of satisfaction and implies a patient act of waiting, as well as a certain degree of uncertainty. *Godimento*, which derives from the Latin *gaudere*, is commonly associated with sexual pleasure in modern Italian and relates to a subjective feeling of satisfaction, varying from person to person. However, in the Italian linguistic tradition, *godimento* primarily has a legal meaning, referring to the right to enjoy a property or benefit, even if it is not directly owned but held in usufruct.

despite the emphasis on the symbolic and semiotics, the connection between psychoanalysis and linguistics has been insufficiently addressed in previous commentaries, leaving the full potential of Lacan's innovative thinking partially unexplored. According to Bottiroli, one of Lacan's main contributions was to show that psychic functioning is not simply factual—that is, reducible to and determined merely by a series of events—but also semantic, shaped by meaning. Hence, for Bottiroli, the Freudo-Lacanian unconscious is primarily a 'mode of thinking' (p. 52). Bottiroli identifies three main styles of thought or logic, that is, ways in which meaning is produced and experienced: firstly, the 'separative' style of thought—a disjunctive way of thinking that regards reality as homogeneous and merely factual; secondly, the 'distinctive' approach—a conjunctive logic, which is the most important style of thought for Bottiroli because it constitutes a flexible rationality that avoids the strict barriers of the separative, but does not fall into the third style, that of the 'confusive', which is a disjunctive way of thinking dominated by overlapping and reversibility, where similarities become identities, and which is thus the opposite of the separative. Bottiroli contends that approaching the paradoxical register of the real with the distinctive logic allows us to overcome some of its deadlocks and to fully grasp its philosophical novelty. As Bottiroli puts it,

> The *réel* digs a hole also on the side of the subject: whenever one encounters the impossible within possibility, and is attracted to something from which one is simultaneously excluded [...] one experiences the Real. (2002, p. 98)

Bottiroli claims that approaching the real with a disjunctive logic makes it impossible to fully grasp the real as that which is both beyond language and, at the same time, a hole within the symbolic. However, from the perspective of a conjunctive logic, this could make perfect sense as the real is indeed extimacy: external and internal at the same time. In his subsequent works, Bottiroli contends that the primacy of the real in Lacanian studies has resulted in a rather impoverished and rigid conception of the symbolic. In *Jacques Lacan: Oltre la scolastica lacaniana* (2023), Bottiroli challenges Miller's conventional chronological (and almost teleological) periodisation of Lacan's thought, which posits the real as the ultimate—most developed and mature—stage. Instead, he argues that the emphasis should be on the Borromean interconnection among the registers—a concept discerned since the early stages of Lacan's teachings.

Another non-clinical commentary on Lacan from an entirely philosophical perspective can be found in Davide Tarizzo's *Introduzione a Lacan* (2003), which provides an outline of the main texts by Lacan available in Italian and addresses the connection between subjectivity and meaning from a (rather covert) existentialist standpoint. When examining Lacan's divided subject, Tarizzo argues that the locus of the subject resides precisely within this split between thought and existence. Psychoanalysis has unveiled this division between knowledge and meaning—a division that essentially constitutes the subject. For Tarizzo, this leads to the philosophical problem of contingency—in his words, a 'fault, opening between knowledge and sense or between thought and being' (p. 103)—which coincides with the subject's own outlook on life. According to Tarizzo, Lacan's teaching invites us to embrace contingency, inhabiting it in a positive life-affirming way, rather than viewing it as a deficiency or adversity. Thus, in Tarizzo's view, Lacan's stance on ethics revolves around the encounter with, and acceptance of, the unpredictable. Tarizzo contends that, ultimately, the kernel of Lacan's teaching is that human beings cannot be healed and, therefore, should not persist in wanting to be cured. *Introduzione a Lacan* anticipates the later fruitful research of Tarizzo's biopolitical thought at the crossroads of psychoanalysis and political theory, where he investigates the political subject in modern democracy (Tarizzo 2021).

The category of the real is pivotal in Benvenuto's *Conversations with Lacan* (2020), which is the first monograph on Lacan written by an Italian Lacanian in English. Benvenuto, who has a propensity for engaging with other national and linguistic Lacanian traditions,[17] assesses the

[17] In 1995, Benvenuto established the *Journal of European Psychoanalysis* (since 2007, the *European Journal of Psychoanalysis*) with the aim of disseminating psychoanalytic ideas and contributions of European psychoanalysts and researchers through the English-speaking world. Over the years, the journal gained prominence due to its cross-disciplinarity and its independence from any psychoanalytic school or orientation, although there is a particular focus on Lacan. This English-language journal, which hosts sections in Italian and Russian, has been pivotal in overcoming linguistic barriers by connecting diverse psychoanalytic perspectives developed in different parts of the world (https://www.journal-psychoanalysis.eu/). Some interviews featured in the *Journal of European*

legacy of Lacan in today's psychoanalysis around the pivotal question: 'does Lacan belong to the declining psychoanalysis or can he announce its rebirth?' (p. 31). Avoiding despair and messianic declarations, Benvenuto deems Lacan to be a credible stronghold of psychoanalysis today insofar as he equally avoids cognitivist or humanist ideological drifts. The real and the subject are at the centre of Benvenuto's reading. As Benvenuto hyperbolically puts it, if Lacan is still worth reading today, it is because he addresses the real.

Benvenuto signals the prominence of the real in today's Lacanian studies in Italy and abroad and claims that 'all the young enterprising Lacanians of today have done away with the classic Lacanian themes of desire and lack. Instead, they place all their bets on jouissance' (p. 54). Nevertheless, Benvenuto refrains from defining the real as this would mean 'betraying its sense' (p. 90). This is not, however, an admission of defeat on Benvenuto's part, but rather his opportunity to emphasise that what is crucial is the use of the real, that it only 'acquires sense' (p. 90) in relation to the other two registers, the imaginary and the symbolic and, as such, only in relation to subjectivity *tout court*. If today is the time for different readings of Lacan's work, as Recalcati suggests, the field in which these diverging interpretations challenge each other is that of the real. Herein lies the innovative contribution of Italian Lacanian thought.

Italian Lacanian Thought

The real is one of the most slippery and multifaceted conceptual categories of Lacan's theory, which is renowned for being difficult to understand since Lacan does not provide a coherent and unambiguous definition of this category. As he openly admits, the notion is permeated by a persisting polysemy and 'ambiguity' (Lacan 1998, p. 41), which will never disappear as the different definitions of it vary depending on the context and their correlation with other notions (Evans 1996; Eyers 2012). Lacan

Psychoanalysis were published by Benvenuto and Molino in their 2009 co-edited book *In Freud's Tracks*, whose international contributors include leading Lacanians, such as Élisabeth Roudinesco and Françoise Dolto, and key representatives of other psychoanalytic orientations, including Christopher Bollas, Otto F. Kernberg, and Jean Laplanche.

variously refers to the real, for instance, as the 'death drive' (2016), the 'unconscious' (1998, 2018), the 'object of science' (2013b), and 'life' (2019). Thus, as Lacan puts it, '[i]f there is a notion of the real, it is extremely complex and in that sense it is not graspable, not graspable in a way that would constitute a whole' (2013b, p. 80). In addition to this indeterminacy, the difficulty of understanding the Lacanian real lies in the way in which he conceives it, since for Lacan, the real is neither an empirical nor a metaphysical entity: it is 'unimaginable' (Lacan 2013b, p. 76) and 'what doesn't work' (Lacan 2013b, p. 61). The real exceeds the other two Lacanian registers: there is no image capable of adequately representing it, nor can it be reduced to the semantic dimension of language. This is why Lacan labels the real 'impossible'.

The transnational reception of Lacan at the turn of the century is characterised by an increasing 'emphasis on the Real' (Laclau 1989, p. xiii). Over this time, the real attained the status of a 'central, determining concept' (Eyers 2012, p. 1), coming to the fore in many national Lacanian appropriations, for instance, in France (Laclau 1989), Germany (Jaanus and Stewart 2004), and Slovenia (Irwin and Motoh 2014). Nowadays, Renov's statement that 'the Real remains the most neglected term' (2004, p. 123) in Lacan's theory is thus utterly erroneous. The real has become so popular that not only does 'contemporary psychoanalysis as a whole bear the mark of [it]' (Voruz and Wolf 2007, p. xvi), but it is also 'already entering everyday discourse' (Fink 2014, p. 221), as had previously occurred with several Freudian concepts.

The emphasis on the real is also a defining feature of the postmillennial Italian reception of Lacan. Although it preserves the importance of the imaginary and the symbolic, Italian Lacanian thought is distinguished by its focus on the real. As the Italian Lacanian analyst Alex Pagliardini remarks:

> From philosophy to politics, from science to the clinic, from the arts to the media, a real passion for the real has spread everywhere, a rampant need to express it, define it, modify it, love it, burn it, torture it, eliminate it, affirm it. (2016, p. 9)

Instead of referring to an Italian Lacanian movement, which implies unity and homogeneity, I prefer to use the term Italian Lacanian thought, to reflect the 'inherently plural' and 'a-systematic' (Resmini 2013, p. 283) nature of this heterogeneous group of Italian Lacanians. These thinkers do not subscribe to a specific Lacanian school nor do they converge in a univocal and systematic movement. Their main representatives include psychoanalysts working in Italy and academics (such as film theorists, philosophers, and literary theorists).[18]

Despite this common emphasis on the primacy of the real, their interpretations of Lacan vary in terms of their theoretical and clinical perspectives on this category, as I will discuss in subsequent chapters. These differences among Italian Lacanians particularly pertain to concepts of desire (*desiderio*) and enjoyment (*godimento*) in relation to the real. Consequently, some analysts remain Millerian, both in the sense of following Miller's reading of Lacan and staying within the WAP, such as Domenico Cosenza, Antonio Di Ciaccia, and Marco Focchi. Others, like Massimo Recalcati, diverge from Miller in their interpretation of Lacan and have left the WAP; while others still, like Franco Lolli, were initially part of the WAP, then joined Recalcati's institutions and groups before moving in another direction. The younger generation of Italian Lacanians is particularly influenced by Recalcati, who has significantly shaped the reception of Lacan in Italy. However, even among these younger analysts, there are theoretical differences and differences in positioning. For instance, Nicolò Terminio remains closer to Recalcati's reading of Lacan and associated groups, while Alex Pagliardini distances himself from Recalcati's Lacan.

Italian Lacanian thought is deeply indebted to Jacques-Alain Miller (2005, 2008, 2022) for the primacy he accorded to the register of the real, and to Colette Soler's conceptualisation of the real unconscious (2014). Both perspectives predominantly focus on the late phase of Lacan's thought. Miller's reading of Lacan identified a progressive emphasis on the real as the

[18] I have called this group heterogeneous since it includes both psychoanalytic practitioners and academics working in Italy. It is noteworthy that there are also several Italian Lacanian scholars working in English-speaking academia, including Lorenzo Chiesa and Fabio Vighi, who have extensively engaged with Lacanian theory, and others who have occasionally written on Lacan, including Pietro Bianchi, Diego Busiol, Gioele Cima, Yuri Di Liberto, Andrea Mura, Mauro Resmini, and Alvise Sforza Tarabochia. In this book, I will focus mainly on the work of Lacanian scholars and clinicians working in Italy, although I will at times draw upon some of these Italian Lacanian scholars who write in English, some of whom are based in the UK and the USA.

fundamental direction of Lacan's teaching, which also resulted in the shift from conceiving of psychoanalysis as a practice of symbolisation of the real to seeing it as a practice of the real, centred less on interpretations and more on *jouissance*. It was when Lacan encountered the failure of the structuralist formalisation of the analytic experience that he started to devote increasing attention to the real and the mathemes. This is the 'Lacan who thinks against Lacan' that Miller has been discussing since the early 1980s (2022, p. 117). Similarly, Soler outlines the trajectory of Lacan's teaching in relation to the real as a 'redefinition of the unconscious itself' (2014, p. xiii), moving from a symbolic unconscious to a real unconscious.

In order to clarify this trajectory in his teaching, let us briefly turn back to Lacan's writings. Lacan shifted from the conception of a language-like unconscious in the 1950s, where symptoms are symbolic formations, to the conception of a real-like unconscious in the 1960s and 1970s, when symptoms are the kernel of the real, which resists symbolisation. More specifically, in his later phase, Lacan shifts from an 'historical-dialectical practice of progressive symbolization of the real' (Lacan 2006, p. 43) to a praxis based on the limit of interpretation, and resting on the dimension of the real. In *The Function and Field of Speech and Language in Psychoanalysis*, Lacan stated that 'symptoms can be entirely resolved in an analysis of language, because a symptom is itself structured like a language: a symptom is language from which speech must be delivered' (2006 [1953], p. 223). In *The Third* on the other hand, Lacan claimed that a 'symptom [...] comes from the real' (Lacan 2019 [1974], p. 91).

The unconscious structured like a language is a semiotic and transferential unconscious. It carries meaning awaiting interpretation from the analyst and, as such, revolves around the signifying chain and maintains a relation with the Other. On the contrary, the real unconscious is structured like a *lalangue,* a neologism Lacan coined to indicate the fragmented, chaotic, infantile speech. Its primacy rests on the drive and the body and it is discontinuous from the discourse of the Other (Miller 2008, 2021). This '*lalangue*-unconscious' (Soler 2014) carries the material connotation of the real, bearing the marks of drives and *jouissance* on the body. This shift holds 'immense practical and clinical consequences' (Soler 2014, p. xv), all revolving around how the real is conceptualised in clinical theory and how analyses are conducted in clinical practice, including the use of variable-length sessions. As Pagliardini claims,

> for Lacan, insisting on questioning and handling the real corresponds to a fundamental need, carried out with a rare constancy, to bend the analytic dispositive and process, as well as the technique, the ethics and the position of the analyst, to the immanence and the vehemence of the real. (2016, p. 10)

In Seminar 17, Lacan refers to *The Interpretation of Dreams* and *Beyond the Pleasure Principle* as the two main turning points in Freud's oeuvre (2007, p. 45). The first text establishes the importance of desire in the unconscious formations, while the second points to repetition as the indestructible force dominating unconscious behaviours, which Lacan connects to *jouissance.* From being primarily conceived as a signifying and symbolic apparatus revolving around desire, the classic Freudian unconscious is reconceptualised as an apparatus dominated by enjoyment. Taking their cue from this passage, Italian Lacanians consider this reconceptualisation to be particularly useful for understanding contemporary psychopathologies (see Chap. 3). Nicolò Terminio (2009), another Italian Lacanian analyst, further contends that in the language-like unconscious, the emphasis is more on its being structured by language, signifiers, and desire; while in the real-like unconscious, it is the drive-related aspect which comes to the fore, as the primary emphases are on enjoyment, the death drive, and repetition: the unconscious as '*tyche* of the Real' (2009, p. 25). As the Italian scholars Matteo Bonazzi and Daniele Tonazzo assert,

> More than the symbolic, for us the decisive question is the real; and therefore not the symbolic, transferential unconscious of the representations discovered by Freud, but the unconscious of the traces of jouissance [*godimento*], the traces of feeling that are produced beyond meaning and representation. (2015, p. 160)

Consequently, the perspective of current Italian Lacanianism conceives of the unconscious with a focus on the real, leading to a conception of the subject that is no longer exclusively understood through the lens of the symbolic. According to Terminio, 'the subject finds a new location, it is no longer identified in the laws of language, but when these laws falter' (2009, p. 21). Philosophically and, more importantly, clinically speaking, the subject is reframed through the lens of the real. As Terminio further argues, 'we are witnessing a new centering of the subject on the level of the drive. The drive side of experience is called jouissance' (2009, p. 25).

This move from a 'structuralist unconscious' (Guattari 2011 [1979], p. 9) to the view that 'the unconscious is the Real' (Lacan 2010, p. 156) stands as a pivotal tenet in postmillennial Italian Lacanianism. However, this shift informs not only the conceptualisation of contemporary symptoms and clinical practice but also the psychosocial analysis of Italy, with far-reaching implications for aesthetics (see Chaps. 3, 4, and 5).

In the transnational reception of Lacan, the notion of the real has garnered significant interest beyond the clinical domain and has thus been widely applied beyond the clinic.[19] Throughout this process, the real has frequently been abstracted from its original clinical context as articulated by Lacan or, at the very least, its clinical dimension has receded. The use of the real by representatives of the Slovenian school is an effective example of these 'de-clinicized' and 'secularized' readings of Lacan (Roudinesco 1997, pp. 434–435), since the real removed from its clinical context 'becomes the lever for philosophical and political intervention in the symbolic sphere' (Irwin and Motoh 2014, p. 185). Žižek bears particular responsibility for introducing the notion of the real into the humanities and social sciences without grounding it in the clinic (Hughes and Malone 2002), by replacing the specifically clinical aspects with theories of the subject and of ideological formations (Eyers 2012). This decontextualisation could be regarded as symptomatic of the splitting of Lacan's thought, particularly in its Anglo-American reception, where the philosophical side of Lacan has tended to overshadow the clinical side.[20]

Overall, common transnational readings of the Lacanian real mostly revolve around trauma and excess, something from which the subject needs to be protected and shielded, emphasising the disruptiveness and unbearability of this Lacanian register (Rousselle 2017). Firstly, given that the real presents itself in the form of 'trauma' (Lacan 1998, p. 55), it is deployed to discuss collective traumatic events, such as terrorist attacks

[19] In English-speaking scholarship, these publications range from philosophy (Zupančič 2000; Žižek 2002) and queer theory (Dean 2000; Edelman 2004) to film studies (Vighi 2006; McGowan 2007; Cowie 2007, 2011), visual studies (Ronen 2002; Adams 2003; Iversen 2007), and music (Wilson 2015). This proves the fruitfulness of applications of the real in investigating other fields beyond psychoanalysis.

[20] Recently, there has been a rising trend of Anglo-American clinicians engaging with Lacan's body of knowledge (Osserman and Wallerstein 2021).

or natural disasters (Žižek 2002) or those abject and traumatic aspects of contemporary visual art (Hal Foster 1996, 2017). Secondly, the real as *jouissance* is often related to an excess to be dealt with. Considering that *jouissance* is the Lacanian way of rethinking the death drive clinically, anthropologically, and in terms of the social bond, it is employed in a wide range of psychosocial and political analyses (Hook 2022). The real as *jouissance* has become a pervasive concept representing 'either the diagnosis, response, or solution for a wide range of contemporary discontents' (Rosman 2020, p. 3). Thirdly, another instance of the real associated with the death drive is that of the 'undead' (Žižek 1999). This incarnation of the real relates to a form of vitalism in living matter, not necessarily human, whose drive propels it endlessly. While the first two modalities are relatively pervasive in Italian Lacanianism, the latter is almost entirely absent from Italian Lacanian thought.

These modalities perpetuate the common reading of the real, interpreting it predominantly in negative terms, thus downplaying its generative potential and emphasising its inherent negativity (Dean 2000; Stavrakakis 2007). However, is it possible to envision the real not negatively, but rather in a more affirmative light? Could the real be seen not only as that which disrupts the subject, but also as a harbinger of life? In the Anglophone sphere of Lacanian reception, a few scholars have suggested the 'generative effects' (Dean 2000, p. 51) of the real and its 'more positive modalities' (Stavrakakis 2007, p. 16), especially as regards the process of subjectivation (McGowan and Kunkle 2004). As Tim Dean notes:

> the real nonetheless has a positive role to play in subject formation, since it represents not only a barrier to subjective or symbolic realization, but also the impossibility against which symbolization is constantly being elaborated. In other words, the real is generative, not simply constraining. (2000 p. 51)

This affirmative approach, I contend, is precisely the direction pursued by Italian Lacanianism. Although as subjects we experience the real primarily in traumatic encounters with what cannot be fully symbolised, these do not always necessarily produce negative effects. According to Recalcati, along with the 'oppressive modalities' in which the real manifests itself, such as the death drive and the compulsion to repeat, there are also 'affirmative modalities', which include love, the encounter with an artwork, and the desire of the analyst (Recalcati 2023). Therefore, Italian Lacanian thought sheds light on a different conception of the real—going beyond the view that it is primarily impossible, unimaginable, or disruptive, that which antagonises the subject and unsettles their life or derails analysis. Instead, as we shall see in the subsequent chapters, Italian Lacanians conceive the real as a life-affirming force that could also contribute to existence, to some extent generative. This conceptualisation of the real has clinical implications, fostering more affirmative ways of theorising and practising psychoanalysis. As Silvia Lippi aptly puts it, 'Psychoanalysis can be practiced in the affirmative rather than the negative, and can create joy out of the tribulations of the patient' (2020, p. XII). However, the idea of an affirmative approach is itself controversial among Italian Lacanians, some of whom use the adjective *affermativo* positively (Leoni 2016; Pagliardini 2020; Ronchi 2012), while others consider the affirmative reading promoted by 'neo-Lacanians'—to use Miller's expression (2021)—to be detrimental (Recalcati 2019, 2023). Nevertheless, I believe that both factions move in the same direction of affirming the real, despite profound differences. What, therefore, is the real of Italian Lacanian thought? First and foremost, it is the real of the clinic, so often dismissed in the reception of Lacan in Italy and other countries. Far from secluding psychoanalysis behind the closed door of the consulting room, however, Italian Lacanians operate clinically only in relation to the contemporary Other, as will be discussed in the next chapter, establishing a close connection between their clinical practice and contemporary society.

Bibliography

Adams, Parveen. 2003. Preface: Way Beyond the Pleasure Principle. In *Art: Sublimation or Symptom*, ed. Parveen Adams, xi–xvii. London: Karnac.

Antonello, Pierpaolo. 2009. Politics of (Dis)Engagement: Italians and British Intellectuals. In *Creative Intervention. The Role of Intellectuals in Contemporary Italy*, ed. Eugenio Bolongaro, Mark Epstein, and Rita Gagliano, 363–382. Newcastle upon Tyne: Cambridge Scholar Publishing.

Armando, Luigi. 1997. *Storia della psicoanalisi in Italia dal 1971 al 1996*. Rome: Nuove Edizioni Romane.

Aspesi, Natalia. 1986. Il tramonto del guru Armando. *La Repubblica*. https://ricerca.repubblica.it/repubblica/archivio/repubblica/1986/02/06/il-tramonto-del-guru-armando.html. June 2. Accessed 1 November 2020.

Barbetta, Pietro. 2019. Psychoanalysis in Milan in the Age of Dis-alienation: The Case of Elvio Fachinelli. In *The Year of Alienation in Italy: Factory and Asylum Between the Economic Miracle and the Years of Lead*, ed. Alessandra Diazzi and Alvise Sforza Tarabochia, 155–172. Basingstoke: Palgrave Macmillan.

Bar-El, Eliran. 2023. *How Slavoj Became Zizek. The Digital Making of a Public Intellectual*. Chicago: University of Chicago Press.

Benvenuto, Bice, and Roger Kennedy. 1986. *The Works of Jacques Lacan: An Introduction*. London: Free Association Books.

Benvenuto, Sergio. 1987a. Contro le ragioni del cuore. *L'Indice dei libri del mese*, 44–45.

Benvenuto, Sergio. 1987b. Ma non siamo una setta. Jacques-Alain Miller risponde a Sergio Benvenuto. *L'Indice dei libri del mese*, 44–45.

Benvenuto, Sergio. 1997. Italy and Psychoanalysis. *Journal of European Psychoanalysis*. http://www.psychomedia.it/jep/number5/benvenuto.htm. Accessed 18 October 2020.

Benvenuto, Sergio. 2020. *Conversations with Lacan: Seven Lectures for Understanding Lacan*. London: Routledge.

Bianchi, Pietro. 2014. Massimo Recalcati. Il vuoto e il resto. *Doppio Zero*, 28 February. https://www.doppiozero.com/massimorecalcati-il-vuoto-e-il-resto. Accessed 25 September 2022.

Bollas, Christopher. 2007. *The Freudian Moment*. London: Karnak.

Bonazzi, Matteo, and Daniele Tonazzo. 2015. *Lacan e l'estetica*. Milan: Mimesis.

Borgogno, Franco, and Alberto Luchetti. 2016. General Introduction. In *Reading Italian Psychoanalysis*, ed. Franco Borgogno, Alberto Luchetti, and Luisa Marino Coe, 1–6. London: Routledge.

Bottiroli, Giovanni. 2002. *Jacques Lacan. Arte, linguaggio, desiderio*. Bergamo: Bergamo University Press.

Bottiroli, Giovanni. 2023. *Jacques Lacan. Oltre la scolastica*. Verona: Ombre Corte.

Braunstein, Néstor. 2003. Desire and Jouissance in the teachings of Lacan. In *The Cambridge Companion to Lacan*, ed. Jean-Michel Rabaté, 102–115. Cambridge: Cambridge University Press.

Brook, Clodagh. 2010. *Marco Bellocchio: The Cinematic I in the Political Sphere*. Toronto: University of Toronto Press.

Busiol, Diego, ed. 2022. *Lacanian Psychoanalysis in Practice: Insights from Fourteen Psychoanalysts*. London: Routledge.
Caldwell, Lesley, and Francesco Capello. 2010. Introduction. *Journal of Romance Studies*. 10 (3): 1–9.
Caruso, Paolo, ed. 1969. *Conversazioni con Claude Lévi-Strauss, Michel Foucault, Jacques Lacan*. Milan: Mursia.
Chiesa, Lorenzo. 2011. Biopolitics in Early Twenty-First-Century Italian Theory. *Angelaki: Journal of the Theoretical Humanities* 16 (3): 1–5.
Chiesa, Lorenzo. 2016. *The Virtual Point of Freedom. Essays on Politics, Aesthetics, and Religion*. Evanston, IL: Northwestern University Press.
Cima, Gioele. 2020. *Il Seminario Perpetuo. Il tardo e l'ultimo Lacan*. Napoli and Salerno: Orthotes.
Civitarese, Giuseppe. 2016. *Truth and Unconscious in Psychoanalysis*. London: Routledge.
Collini, Stefano. 2006. *Absent Minds. Intellectuals in Britain*. Oxford: Oxford University Press.
Conci, Marco. 2008. Italian Themes in Psychoanalysis – International Dialogue and Psychoanalytic Identity. *International Forum of Psychoanalysis* 17 (2): 65–70.
Contri, Giacomo, ed. 1978. *Lacan in Italia/En Italie Lacan: 1953-1978*. Milano: La Salamandra.
Corbellini, Gilberto. 2012. L'autismo dei lacaniani. *Il Sole 24 ORE*, 12 January. 29.
Cosenza, Domenico. 2003. *Jacques Lacan e il problema della tecnica in psicoanalisi*. Rome: Astrolabio.
Cowie, Elizabeth. 2007. Specters of the Real: Documentary Time and Art. *Differences: A Journal of Feminist Cultural Studies* 18 (1): 87–127.
Cowie, Elizabeth. 2011. *Recording Reality, Desiring the Real*. Minneapolis: University of Minnesota Press.
Curiosando. https://curiosando708090.altervista.org/drive-in-19831988/. Accessed 2 September 2020.
Damousi, Joy, and Mariano Ben Plotkin. 2009. Introduction. In *The Transnational Unconscious. Essays in the History of Psychoanalysis and Transnationalism*, ed. Joy Damousi and Mariano Ben Plotkin. Basingstoke: Palgrave Macmillan.
David, Michel. 1990. *La psicoanalisi nella cultura italiana*. Turin: Bollati Boringhieri.
Dean, Tim. 2000. *Beyond Sexuality*. Chicago: University of Chicago Press.

Dean, Tim. 2018. Foreword 'I Keep My Treasure in My Arse'. In Mario Mieli. *Towards a Gay Communism. Elements of a Homosexual Critique*, trans. David Fernbach and Evan Calder Williams, vi–xiv. London: Pluto Press.

Di Ciaccia, Antonio, and Massimo Recalcati. 2000. *Jacques Lacan. Un insegnamento sul sapere dell'inconscio*. Milan: Bruno Mondadori.

Di Martino, Loredana. 2016. Rebuilding Ethical Desire in the Era of Narcissistic Jouissance: The Reinvention of Fatherhood in Antonio Scurati's *Il padre infedele*. *Italian Studies* 71 (1): 128–147.

Di Martino, Loredana, and Pasquale Verdicchio, eds. 2017. *Encounters with the Real in Contemporary Italian Cinema and Literature*. Newcastle upon Tyne: Cambridge Scholars Publishing.

Diazzi, Alessandra. 2021. Care or Control? Psychology and Psychoanalysis in Italian Factories. In *Italian Industrial Literature and Film. Perspectives on the Representation of Postwar Labor*, ed. Carlo Baghetti, Jim Carter, and Lorenzo Marmo, 119–135. Oxford: Peter Lang.

Diazzi, Alessandra, and Alvise Sforza Tarabochia. 2019. Introduction: Social and Mental Alienation in Italy Between the Economic Miracle and the Years of Lead. In *The Years of Alienation in Italy: Factory and Asylum Between the Economic Miracle and the Years of Lead*, ed. Alessandra Diazzi and Alvise Sforza Tarabochia, 1–40. Basingstoke: Palgrave Macmillan.

Eco, Umberto. 1968. *La struttura assente*. Milan: Bompiani.

Edelman, Lee. 2004. *No Future. Queer Theory and the Death Drive*. Durham: Duke University Press.

Ellingsen, Peter. 2013. *A History of Psychoanalysis in Australia: From Freud to Lacan*. Melbourne: PsychOz Publications.

Esposito, Roberto. 2012. *Living Thought. The Origins and Actuality of Italian Philosophy*. Translated by Zakiya Hanafi. Stanford, CA: Stanford University Press.

Evans, Dylan. 1996. *An Introductory Dictionary of Lacanian Psychoanalysis*. London: Routledge.

Evans, Dylan. 1998. From Kantian Ethics to Mystical Experience: an Exploration of Jouissance. In *Key Concepts of Lacanian Psychoanalysis*, ed. Dany Nobus, 1–28. New York: Other Press.

Eyers, Tom. 2012. *Lacan and the Concept of the Real*. London: Palgrave Macmillan.

Fachinelli, Elvio. 2011 [1970]. Lo psicoanalista deve definire la sua posizione nella società. *aut aut* 352:11–20.

Fachinelli, Elvio. 2019 [1968]. Dissident Desire. Translated by David Gutherz. *Psychoanalysis and History* 21 (3): 293–300.

Feldstein, Richard. 1996. Introduction I. In *Lacan, Politics, Aesthetics*, ed. Willy Apollon and Richard Feldstein, xixviii. Albany: SUNY Press.
Fink, Bruce. 2014. *Against Understanding, Volume 1. Commentary and Critique in a Lacanian Key*. London: Routledge.
Fiumanò, Marisa. 1980. La trasmissione di una teoria dell'inconscio. Il "caso Lacan". *aut aut* 177–178:243–255.
Focchi, Marco. 2008. Introduzione. In Jacques-Alain Miller, *Delucidazioni su Lacan*. Turin: Antigone Edizioni.
Foster, Hal. 1996. *The Return of the Real: The Avant-garde at the End of the Century*. Cambridge, MA: MIT Press.
Foster, Hal. 2017. *Bad New Days: Art, Criticism, Emergency*. London: Verso.
Gherovici, Patricia. 2019. The Argentinian Exception Proves the Rule. *Crisis and Critique* 6 (1): 115–129.
Green, André. 1996 [1986]. *On Private Madness*. London: Karnac.
Gurewich, Judith Feher. 2000. The Lacanian Clinical Field: Series Overview. In *Lacan in America*, ed. Jean-Michel Rabaté, ix–xv. New York: Other Press.
Guattari, Félix. 2011 [1979]. *The Machinic Unconscious. Essays in Schizoanalysis*. Translated by Taylor Adkin. Cambridge, MA: Semiotext(e).
Gutherz, David. 2019. On Not Getting What You Want: Elvio Fachinelli's Anti-authoritarianism. *Psychoanalysis and History* 21 (3): 267–291.
Herzog, Dagmar. 2017. *Cold War Freud. Psychoanalysis in an Age of Catastrophes*. Cambridge: Cambridge University Press.
Hook, Derek. 2022. Jouissance as Tool of Psychosocial Analysis. In *The Palgrave Handbook of Psychosocial Studies*, ed. Stephen Frosh et al. Springer Nature.
Hughes, Robert, and Kareen Ror Malone. 2002. Introduction: the Dialectic of Theory and Clinic. In *After Lacan. Clinical Practice and the Subject of the Unconscious*, ed. Willy Apollon, Danielle Bergeron, and Lucie Cantin, 1–34. Albany: SUNY Press.
Irwin, Jones, and Helena Motoh. 2014. *ŽiŽek and his Contemporaries: on the Emergence of the Slovenian Lacan*. London: Bloomsbury.
Iversen, Margaret. 2007. *Beyond Pleasure: Freud, Lacan, Barthes*. Pennsylvania: Pennsylvania State University Press.
Jaanus, Maire, and Elizabeth Stewart. 2004. General Introduction. In *Lacan in the German-Speaking World*, ed. Maire Jaanus, Elizabeth Stewart, and Richard Feldstein, 1–3. Albany, NY: State University of New York Press.
Johnston, Adrian. 2013. *Prologomena to Any Future Materialism. Volume One: The Outcome of Contemporary French Philosophy*. Evanston, IL: Northwestern University Press.

Johnson, John. 2000. The Problem of Theory in the Poetics of Andrea Zanzotto. *The Modern Language Review* 95 (1): 92–106.

Lacan, Jacques. 1938. *The Family Complexes in the Formation of the Individual.* Translated by Cormac Gallagher. Unpublished.

Lacan, Jacques. 1992. *The Ethics of Psychoanalysis. The Seminar of Jacques Lacan, Book VII, 1959–1960*. Translated by Dennis Porter and Edited by Jacques-Alain Miller. London: Routledge.

Lacan, Jacques. 1998. *The Four Fundamental Concepts of Psychoanalysis. The Seminar of Jacques Lacan, Book XI, 1963–1964*. Translated by Alan Sheridan and Edited by Jacques-Alain Miller. London/New York: W.W. Norton.

Lacan, Jacques. 2001. *Autres Écrits*. Paris: Seuil.

Lacan, Jacques. 2006. *Écrits. The First Complete Edition in English*. Translated by Bruce Fink in collaboration with Héloïse Fink and Russell Grigg. London/New York: W.W. Norton.

Lacan, Jacques. 2008. *My teaching*. Translated by David Macey. London: Verso.

Lacan, Jacques. 2010. *RSI. The Seminar of Jacques Lacan, Book XXII*. Translated by Cormac Gallagher. Unpublished.

Lacan, Jacques. 2013a. *On the Names-of-the-Father*. Translated by Bruce Fink. Cambridge: Polity Press.

Lacan, Jacques. 2013b. *The Triumph of Religion*. Translated by Bruce Fink. Cambridge: Polity Press.

Lacan, Jacques. 2015 [1974]. Freud Forever: An Interview with Panorama. Translated by Philip Dravers. *Hurly-Burly* 12:13–21.

Lacan, Jacques. 2016. *The Sinthome. The Seminar of Jacques Lacan, Book XXIII*. Translated by Adrian Price. Cambridge: Polity Press.

Lacan, Jacques. 2019. The Third. Translated by Philip Dravers. *The Lacanian Review* 9:83–109.

Lacan, Jacques. 2020. The Lacanian Phenomenon. Translated by Dan Collins. *The Lacanian Review* 9:16–43.

Laclau, Ernesto. 1989. Preface. In *The Sublime Object of Ideology*, ed. Slavoj ŽiŽek, ix–xv. London: Verso.

Leoni, Federico. 2016. *Jacques Lacan. L'economia dell'assoluto*. Naples: Orthotes.

Lewis, Michael, and David Edward Rose, eds. 2022. *The Bloomsbury Italian Philosophy Reader*. London: Bloomsbury.

Lingiardi, Vittorio. 2016. https://www.repubblica.it/venerdi/libri/2016/03/02/news/lacan_il_criptico_spiegato_ai_mortali_in_due_volumi-134633929/. Accessed 20 December 2022.

Lippi, Silvia. 2020. *The Decision of Desire*. Translated by Peter Skafish. Minneapolis: University of Minnesota Press.

Lolli, Franco. 2019. *Inattualità della psicoanalisi. L'analista e i nuovi domandanti*. Alberobello: Poiesis.

Malagreca, Miguel Andrés. 2007. *Queer Italy. Contexts, Antecedents and Representation*. New York: Peter Lang.

McGowan, Todd. 2007. *The Real Gaze: Film Theory After Lacan*. New York: Other Press.

McGowan, Todd, and Sheila Kunkle, eds. 2004. *Lacan and Contemporary Film*. New York: Other Press.

Melandri, Lea. 2019. *Love and Violence. The Vexatious Factors of Civilization*. Translated by Antonio Calcagno. Albany: SUNY Press.

Mieli, Mario. 2018. *Towards a Gay Communism. Elements of a Homosexual Critique*. Translated by David Fernbach and Evan Calder Williams. London: Pluto Press.

Miller, Jacques-Alain. 2005. Linee di lettura. In Jacques Lacan. *I complessi familiari nella formazione dell'individuo*, trans. Antonio Di Ciaccia, 85–102. Turin: Einaudi.

Miller, Jacques-Alain. 2008. The Other Side of Lacan. Translated by Barbara P. Fulks. *Lacanian Ink* 32:60–71.

Miller, Jacques-Alain. 2021. The One is Letter. Translated by Alasdair Duncan. *Psychoanalytical Notebooks* 37 (38): 13–44.

Miller, Jacques-Alain. 2022. Lacan Clinician. Translated by Anthony Stavrianakis. *The Lacanian Review* 12:100–137.

Mura, Andrea. 2015. Lacan and Debt: The Discourse of the Capitalist in Times of Austerity. *Philosophy Today* 59 (2): 155–174.

Nobus, Dany. 1998. *Key Concepts of Lacanian Psychoanalysis*. New York: Other Press.

Osserman, Jordan, and Hannah Wallerstein. 2021. Transgender Children: From Controversy to Dialogue. *The Psychoanalytic Study of the Child.* 75 (1): 159–172.

Pagliardini, Alex. 2016. *Il sintomo di Lacan. Dieci incontri con il reale*. Rende: Gaaland Edizioni.

Pagliardini, Alex. 2020. *Lacan al presente. Per una clinica del reale*. Rende: Gaaland Edizioni.

Panattoni, Riccardo, and Fabio Vighi, eds. 2023. *Capitalism and the New Political Unconscious. A Philosophy of Immanence*. London: Bloomsbury.

Parker, Ian. 2004. *Slavoj ŽiŽek: A Critical Introduction*. London: Pluto Press.

Pasolini, Pier Paolo. 1999. *Saggi sulla politica e sulla società*. Milan: Mondadori.

Rabaté, Jean-Michel, ed. 2000. *Lacan in America*. New York: Other Press.
Rabaté, Jean-Michel. 2003. Lacan's Turn to Freud. In *The Cambridge Companion to Lacan*, ed. Jean-Michel Rabaté, 1–24. Cambridge: Cambridge University Press.
Recalcati, Massimo. 1994. Letture di Lacan. *aut aut* 260–261:173–194.
Recalcati, Massimo. 1996. *L'universale e il singolare. Lacan e l'al di là del principio di piacere*. Milan: Marcos y Marcos.
Recalcati, Massimo. 2001. *Il vuoto e il resto. Il problema del reale in Lacan*. Milan: CUEM.
Recalcati, Massimo. 2009. Letture di Lacan. *aut aut* 343:19–29.
Recalcati, Massimo. 2010. Lo snodo Sartre, Basaglia e Lacan. In *Franco Basaglia e la filosofia del 900*, 11–22. Milan: Bema.
Recalcati, Massimo. 2012. La parola desiderio. In *Comunicare Lacan. Attualità del pensiero lacaniano per le scienze sociali*, ed. Mimmo Pesare, 53–63. Milan and Udine: Mimesis.
Recalcati, Massimo. 2013. Intervista a Recalcati. *LETTERa* 3:259–264.
Recalcati, Massimo. 2016. *Jacques Lacan. La clinica psicoanalitica: struttura e soggetto*. Milan: Raffaello Cortina.
Recalcati, Massimo. 2019. *Le nuove melanconie. Destini del desiderio nel tempo ipermoderno*. Milan: Raffaello Cortina.
Recalcati, Massimo. 2023. *Jacques Lacan. Ereditare il reale?* Milan: Feltrinelli.
Rella, Franco. 1980. Corpo e linguaggio. Nota sulla filosofia di Lacan. *aut aut* 177–178:71–93.
Renov, Michael. 2004. *The Subject of Documentary*. Minneapolis: University of Minnesota Press.
Resmini, Mauro. 2013. The Italian Turn: A Certain Tendency in Contemporary Psychoanalytic Aesthetics. *American Imago* 68 (2): 271–297.
Robinson, Andrew. 2004. The Politics of Lack. *The British Journal of Politics and International Relations*. 6 (2): 259–269.
Ronen, Ruth. 2002. *Representing the Real*. Amsterdam: Rodopi.
Ronchi, Rocco. 2012. *Come Fare*. Milan: Feltrinelli.
Rosman, Silvia. 2020. Introduction Translating *Jouissance*. In *Jouissance. A Lacanian Concept*, ed. Néstor A. Braunstein, 1–9. Albany: SUNY Press.
Roudinesco, Élisabeth. 1990. *Jacques Lacan & Co. A History of Psychoanalysis in France, 1925-1985*. London: Free Association Books.
Roudinesco, Elisabeth. 1997. *Jacques Lacan. An Outline of a Life and History of a System of Thought*. Cambridge: Polity Press.
Roudinesco, Élisabeth. 2014. *Lacan: In Spite of Everything*. Translated by Gregory Elliott. London: Verso.

Rousselle, Duane. 2017. *Lacanian Realism. Political and Clinical Psychoanalysis.* London: Bloomsbury.

Rovatti, Pier Aldo. 1983. Trasformazioni nel corso dell'esperienza. In *Il pensiero debole*, ed. Gianni Vattimo and Pier Aldo Rovatti, 29–51. Milan: Feltrinelli.

Rovatti, Pier Aldo. 1991. Lo scandaloso signor Lacan. https://ricerca.repubblica.it/repubblica/archivio/repubblica/1991/10/30/lo-scandaloso-signor-lacan.html. Accessed 28 December 2022.

Rovatti, Pier Aldo. 2003. Discussione su godimento e desiderio. *aut aut* 315:4–28.

Russo, Jane. 2009. The Lacanian Movement in Argentina and Brazil: The Periphery Becomes the Center. In *The Transnational Unconscious: Essays in the History of Psychoanalysis and Transnationalism*, ed. Joy Damousi and Mariano Ben Plotkin, 199–226. Basingstoke: Palgrave Macmillan.

Schneiderman, Stuart. 1980. *Returning to Freud. Clinical Psychoanalysis in the School of Lacan.* New Haven: Yale University Press.

Sciacchitano, Antonello. 2019. Lessico amoroso su RAI 3: a scuola serale di desiderio. http://www.psychiatryonline.it/node/7850. Accessed 28 December 2022.

Sforza Tarabochia, Alvise. 2011. Affirmative Biopolitics and Human Nature in Franco Basaglia's Thought. *Angelaki: Journal of the Theoretical Humanities* 16 (3): 85–99.

Sforza Tarabochia, Alvise. 2014. Lacking Subjects and the Subject of Lack: Basaglia and Lacan. In *Lacan and Philosophy: the New Generation*, ed. Lorenzo Chiesa, 221–237. Melbourne: re.press.

Sforza Tarabochia, Alvise. 2016. From the Obligation of Birth to the Obligation of Care: Esposito's Biophilosophy and Recalcati's "New Symptoms". *Culture, Theory and Critique.* 58:33–47.

Sinigaglia, Corrado. 2009. Back to Freud: Psychoanalysis and Phenomenology in Enzo Paci. In *Freud and Italian Culture*, ed. Pierluigi Barrotta, Laura Lepschy, and Emma Bond, 171–180. Oxford: Peter Lang.

Smith, Jonathan. 2006. De Te Fabula Narratur: Narrativity, Ethics and Psychoanalysis in the Critical Thought of Umberto Eco. *Forum for Modern Languages Studies* 42 (2): 168–182.

Smith, Jonathan. 2010. His Problem or Ours?: Notes on Eco and Psychoanalysis. *Journal of Romance Studies.* 10 (3): 75–88.

Soler, Colette. 2014. *Lacan: The Unconscious Reinvented.* Translated by Esther Faye and Susan Schwartz. London: Karnac.

Stavrakakis, Yannis. 2007. *The Lacanian Left: Psychoanalysis, Theory, Politics.* Edinburgh: Edinburgh University Press.

Tarizzo, Davide. 2003. *Introduzione a Lacan*. Bari: Laterza.
Tarizzo, Davide. 2021. *Political Grammars. The Unconscious Foundations of Modern Democracy*. Stanford: Stanford University Press.
Terminio, Nicolò. 2009. *Misurare l'inconscio? Coordinate psicoanalitiche nella ricerca in psicoterapia*. Milan: Bruno Mondadori.
Townshend, Jules. 2003. Discourse Theory and Political Analysis: A New Paradigm from the Essex School? *British Journal of Politics and International Relations* 5 (1): 129–142.
Tupinambá, Gabriel. 2021. *The Desire of Psychoanalysis. Exercises in Lacanian Thinking*. Evanston: Northwestern University Press.
Turkle, Sherry. 1978. *Psychoanalytic Politics. Freud's French Revolution*. New York: Basic Books.
Vegetti Finzi, Cinzia. 1986. *Storia della psicoanalisi. Autori, opera, teorie. 1895-1985*. Milan: Arnoldo Mondadori.
Vighi, Fabio. 2006. *Traumatic Encounters in Italian Film. Locating the Cinematic Unconscious*. Bristol: Intellect.
Visacovsky, Sergio Eduardo. 2009. Origin Stories, Invention of Genealogies and the Early Diffusion of Lacanian Psychoanalysis in Argentina and Spain (1960–1980). In *The Transnational Unconscious: Essays in the History of Psychoanalysis and Transnationalism*, ed. Joy Damousi and Mariano Ben Plotkin, 227–256. Basingstoke: Palgrave Macmillan.
Voruz, Veronique, and Bogdan Wolf, eds. 2007. *The Later Lacan. An Introduction*. Albany: SUNY Press.
Wilson, Scott. 2015. *Stop Making Sense: Music from the Perspective of the Real*. London: Karnac.
Žižek, Slavoj. 1999. *The Ticklish Subject. The Absent Centre of Political Ontology*. London: Verso.
Žižek, Slavoj. 2002. *Welcome to the Desert of the Real*. London: Verso.
Žižek, Slavoj, and Glyn Daly. 2004. *Conversations with Žižek*. Cambridge: Polity Press.
Zupančič, Alenka. 2000. *Ethics of the Real: Kant, Lacan*. London: Verso.

3

Clinic

The Clinical Turn

During a press conference held on 29 October 1974 at the Centre culturel français in Rome, the proceedings of which are transcribed and published in *The Triumph of Religion*, Lacan tenaciously steered away from the philosophical speculations prompted by Italian journalists. He made it very clear to his audience that, far from being mere abstractions, his theoretical notions were deeply rooted in his clinical practice and constituted a 'rigorous conceptual apparatus' that helps analysts to operate in a 'sober', 'serious', and 'effective way' (2013, p. 84). This is particularly true for his notoriously enigmatic concept of the real which, as Lacan reiterates later on in the text, should not be seen as a diversion into the realm of philosophy. On the contrary, this concept holds practical implications insofar as the real, along with the imaginary and the symbolic, is what enables psychoanalysts to 'remain afloat' in clinical matters (2013, p. 85). More crucially, Lacan regards the real as the main concern of psychoanalysis and the kernel of all clinical practice (2013, pp. 61, 62, 84) since analysts and analysands 'are forced to submit to it – that is, to brace themselves all the time' (2013, p. 62). A few weeks later, in the interview

L. Di Gregorio, *Lacan in Italy*, The Palgrave Lacan Series,
https://doi.org/10.1007/978-3-031-91528-4_3

Freud Forever, published in the Italian magazine *Panorama* on 21 November, Lacan emphasised the ethical considerations underpinning his notion by claiming that the real must remain the backbone of analytic treatment in order to avoid the risk of psychoanalysis degenerating into 're-adapting the individual to his social surroundings', which might ultimately derail into a 'comfort psychoanalysis for the salon' (2015, p. 14). This was a pivotal point for Lacan who, in criticising ego psychology and object-relation theory, often underlined that psychoanalysis should not be understood as a 'psychological orthopedics' (2006, p. 251) aimed at adapting the analysand to a reality 'measured against the ego' (p. 353).

In contemporary Italian Lacanianism, the value of Lacan's legacy lies first and foremost in the primacy of the real and its operational uses in the clinical context (Di Ciaccia and Recalcati 2000). With a focus on the notion of the real, Italian Lacanians since the 1990s have systematically sought to demonstrate the close link between Lacanian theory and clinical practice, countering the long-standing criticism, both in Italy and abroad, that Lacanian psychoanalysis lacks clinical validity, and is merely an intellectual endeavour. This marked the beginning of the clinical turn in the Italian reception of Lacan, which focused on bridging the gap between Lacanian concepts and clinical work. The goal was to demonstrate clinically oriented applications of Lacanian theory and restore its value in the Italian psychoanalytic community. First of all, Italian Lacanian thought extensively explores the connection between the real and the drive. Some Italian Lacanians, especially former pupils of Jacques-Alain Miller, associate the real with the drive, and thus also, albeit implicitly and not unanimously, with *jouissance*, the death drive, and repetition (Cosenza 2003; Recalcati 2020a). As such, Italian Lacanians have highlighted that psychoanalytic treatment is primarily concerned with the subject's libidinal economy, rather than with their external environment (Di Ciaccia and Fasoli 2013; Benvenuto 2020). As Massimo Recalcati notes:

> [...] what counts when beginning an analysis is not so much an evaluation of the reality (familial, social, intersubjective, etc.) surrounding the subject, but rather an evaluation of the *relationship* that the subject has built with the reality surrounding them. More precisely, the distinction between

reality and the real must be taken in the sense that the real – unlike reality – has to do exclusively with the subject. It is always the real of the subject. (2008, p. 248)[1]

Contemporary Italian Lacanians thus reiterate the value of this notion for the ethics of psychoanalysis to prevent clinical practice from degenerating into normative forms of psychotherapy aimed at making patients conform with social norms and expectations (Pagliardini 2016; Benvenuto 2020). The real of the drive sets Lacanian psychoanalysis apart from those psychoanalytic approaches that emphasise an intersubjective or relational approach, as well as from those that reduce psychoanalysis to a mere storytelling of the patient's traumas, since they both overlook the notion of the drive (Pagliardini and Ronchi 2014; Benvenuto 2020). According to Domenico Cosenza:

> Placing the encounter with the real of the drive and the transformation of that which self-destructively regulates its economy of enjoyment at the heart of the psychoanalytic endeavour is an operation that goes beyond psychoanalysis understood as hermeneutics, a narrative, or deconstruction. (2003, p. 169)

Most importantly, the primacy of the real in Italian Lacanian thought must be situated in relation to Miller's reading of Lacan and in the context of contemporary psychopathology (Ramaioli et al. 2003). Postmillennial Italian Lacanians employ the category of the real to make sense of contemporary symptoms, wherein the real dimension of the drive comes to the fore to the detriment of the symbolic component, demonstrating the limits of the symbolic. The emphasis of Italian

[1] In the essay *Direction of the Treatment*, Lacan identifies the 'subjective rectification' as the very first step of any psychoanalytic journey, followed by transference and interpretation, since it gives the subject the opportunity to discover their implication with the paradoxically painful pleasure of the symptom. 'Look at your own involvement', says Lacan, 'in the mess you complain of' (2006, p. 179). Interestingly, in the English edition, this passage on subjective rectification reads 'rectification of the subject's relations with reality [*le réel*]' (Lacan 2006, p. 500). As Thomas Svolos notes, *le reél* is translated in English as 'reality' rather than 'the Real' probably referring to 'the use of *le reél* Lacan made in the 1950s' (2017, p. 74). As the translator Bruce Fink points out, '*le réel* (the real) and *la réalité* (reality) are often indistinguishable in ordinary French usage as well as in this stage of Lacan's work' (2013, p. 98)

Lacanians on the real can thus be traced back to the challenges faced in contemporary clinical practice. Indeed, Italian Lacanians employ the real and its related notions of the real unconscious, enjoyment, and the death drive to shed light on clinical problems. From their perspective, in contemporary psychopathology the real of the drive imposes itself as an irrepressible alterity which resists any assimilation to the symbolic signifying chain. As Recalcati put it, the real 'imposes itself in its acephalous dimension as a pure thrust to enjoy, as a death drive' (2010, p. 160). This explains why psychoanalysts increasingly frequently experience the limitations of classical psychoanalysis based on symbolic interpretations (Di Ciaccia and Fasoli 2013). The clinical work conducted by Italian Lacanians in the 1990s and early 2000s not only changed the reception of Lacan in Italy but also initiated a clinical turn, where Lacanian clinical theory was rehabilitated in psychoanalytic circles and entered the broader social discourse. Although several Italian Lacanians contributed to this shift, Recalcati's work is particularly notable for its innovation as well as its ability to systematise theoretical issues, prove clinical validity, and achieve a broader impact. For this reason, his contributions will be discussed more extensively here than those of other Italian Lacanians.

In the 1990s, when Italian Lacanianism was still largely perceived as a philosophical trend with little clinical relevance, Recalcati's *L'ultima cena: anoressia e bulimia* (1997) helped establish Lacanian psychoanalysis as a relevant approach in the treatment of eating disorders, a pressing social epidemic during that period.[2] The publication of this book contributed to the clinical turn in the reception of Lacan in Italy since it led to a significant shift in the Italian understanding of Lacan's clinical approach, prompting a reassessment of his contribution to psychoanalytic practice

[2] Other Lacanian works that contributed to the discussion on eating disorders in Italy include Antonello Sciacchitano's *Anoressia, Sintomo, Angoscia*, published in 1994, and Gabriella Ripa di Meana's *Figure della leggerezza: Anoressia, Bulimia, Psicoanalisi*, published in 1995 and translated into English in 1997. While the former resembles the typically convoluted Lacanian style without providing much valuable clinical insight, the latter anticipates several key themes developed by Recalcati and postmillennial Lacanianism. Ripa di Meana discusses a 'defect of symbolization' (p. 38) in patients suffering from eating disorders and notes that their 'image becomes crystallized as pure or fetishistic enjoyment which is neither imaginary nor symbolic, but real. It emerges from the mirror and persecutes the subject' (p. 38).

and generating unexpected interest from a broad audience. In this seminal book, which consolidated the private and institutional work of several Lacanian psychoanalysts,[3] Recalcati developed a Lacanian framework to work psychoanalytically with monosymptomatic groups of anorexic and bulimic patients as an alternative to cognitive-behavioural therapies, the most common treatment for eating disorders at the time. In contrast to the descriptive psychiatry of the Diagnostic and Statistical Manual of Mental Disorders (DSM), which focuses on symptomatic manifestations, and unlike the medical approach directed at restoring healthy eating behaviour, as well as the sociological discourse that blames the media and the fashion industry for promoting unrealistic beauty standards, Recalcati's approach centres on the uniqueness of the individual subject and emphasises the distinct function of each person's individual symptoms. From his Lacanian perspective, anorexia and bulimia are not regarded as mere disturbances of the appetite but as subjective positions deeply intertwined with the person's history and their relationship with the Other.

In Italy, the Lacanian approach adopted by Recalcati and his colleagues in the ABA centres introduced the importance of differential diagnosis to identify the clinical structure underlying the symptomatic manifestations of anorexic and bulimic subjects. Lacan's clinical conceptual framework is based on subjective structures (neurosis, psychosis, and perversion) rather than on illnesses or disorders. According to this perspective, anorexia and bulimia cannot be considered as standalone structures;

[3] During the 1990s and the early 2000s, several Italian Lacanians cited in this book, and affiliated at the time with the World Association of Psychoanalysis (WAP)—including Domenico Cosenza, Franco Lolli, Massimo Recalcati, and Uberto Zuccardi Merli—worked at the *Associazione per la ricerca della bulimia e dell'anoressia* (ABA) (Association for the Study and Research on Anorexia, Bulimia, and Eating Disorders) (https://www.bulimianoressia.it/). This monosymptomatic therapeutic institution, with several centres across Italy, played a significant role in the early careers of these Italian Lacanians and was pivotal in inspiring Recalcati's idea to develop Lacanian clinical centres in postmillennial Italy, as will be discussed later on in this chapter. From 1994 to 2002, Recalcati served as the scientific director of this institution. During this period, he developed a pioneering application of Lacanian psychoanalysis to group settings, a practice previously explored in Italy only by Paul and Gennie Lemoine in the 1970s (Recalcati 2001). In this context, he also elaborated his theoretical and clinical contributions to understanding anorexia and bulimia (Cosenza 2023, pp. 79–81).

therefore, a diagnosis of anorexia or bulimia per se is not particularly significant unless it is placed within the context of a neurotic, psychotic, or perverse structure.

Moreover, in Freudo-Lacanian psychoanalysis, the subject is viewed as inherently divided, with classic neurotic symptoms representing the metaphorical and symbolic expression of an internal conflict between conscious will and repressed (sexual or aggressive) unconscious desire. However, Recalcati argues that anorexia and bulimia[4] are pathological 'solutions' that aim to abolish this division and therefore do not function as classic symptoms in the Freudian sense. These eating disorders are non-metaphorical and anti-symbolic. Rather than being a linguistic-symbolic manifestation of the unconscious representing the repressed truth of a subject, they identify the subject with a master signifier ('anorexia', 'bulimia') that guarantees no inner conflict. As a result, patients may find it difficult to appreciate the subjective meaning of their symptoms and the link with their own personal history, leading to a so-called holophrastic[5] petrification of their subjectivity (Recalcati 2008, pp. 190–286). Such solidified subjects are not split between their symptoms and the wish to understand them, and so typically do not seek out psychoanalysis. Instead, they are usually brought into treatment by concerned family members. The primary clinical challenge is thus to facilitate the subject's division, allowing the subject to appreciate their implication in their own symptoms.

Another merit of Recalcati's book is that it expands upon the sparse Lacanian remarks on anorexia and bulimia,[6] focusing on the interplay of

[4] Recalcati uses the hyphenated form 'anorexia-bulimia' to account for their interconnectedness. In his words, 'Anorexia is [...] a virtual bulimia, while bulimia is the destitution of the anorexic's endeavor to dominate the drives' (Recalcati 2011, p. 35). Some patients often sway between anorexia and bulimia. According to Terminio, this oscillation between the two concerns 'the dialectic between the dimension of the Ideal and that of the drive as Real' (2018, p. 109). According to Cosenza, 'Among the authors of Lacanian orientation, Recalcati is the one who has most valued Bernard Brusset's thesis on anorexia-bulimia as a unitary circuit of functioning oriented by the same logic' (2023, p. 14).

[5] In *Seminar XI*, Lacan refers to the 'holophrase' in terms of 'solidity' and a 'mass seizure of the primitive signifying chain' (1998, p. 238). He contends that the holophrase underpins the clinical manifestations of psychosomatic disorders, mental deficiency, and psychosis (1998, pp. 237–238).

[6] In *Family Complexes in the Formation of the Individual*, Lacan defines anorexia as an 'appetite for death' (1938, p. 21), highlighting the deadly enjoyment at play. In *The Direction of the Treatment*,

need, demand, and desire along with the role of enjoyment in the development of human subjectivity. Hunger is a basic biological need that infants express through crying, prompting their Other, represented by caregivers, to respond by providing nourishment. Since infants are entirely dependent on the Other for help, the latter's role extends beyond the mere satisfaction of primary needs as they also embody love. The demand, therefore, encompasses not only a request to fulfil a specific need and provide care but also a desire for the Other's love. As a result, for Lacan, desire transcends the satisfaction of a mere biological need.

Anorexic and bulimic behaviour, which involves either food refusal or excessive consumption, reflects the fundamental incompatibility of need and desire. In other words, desire cannot be quenched by simply satisfying one's needs. Thus, the true issue at hand in anorexia and bulimia is the relationship with the Other—an Other who may overwhelm through their demand or who merely meets needs without providing love. Recalcati's analysis is consistent with Lacan's concept of lack as a constitutive component of human subjectivity that gives rise to desire. The lack enables the subject to establish a relationship with the Other and access desire. This is because the subject is not a being but rather a lack of being (Di Ciaccia and Recalcati 2000, p. 63).[7] Bluntly put, in the anorexic

---

he states 'It is the child who is the most lovingly fed who refuses food and employs his refusal as if it were a desire' (2006, p. 524), suggesting that anorexia serves as a way to preserve the subject's desire against the Other's demand, implying a rejection of the Other. Miller emphasises this radical 'refusal of the Other' as a manoeuvre of separation (Miller and Laurent 1997). Recalcati extends Miller's perspective, arguing that, when this refusal is not an appeal to the Other, it becomes a strategy for the subject to separate themselves from the Other without undergoing alienation (2008). Another passing reference to anorexia appears in *Seminar XI*, where Lacan states 'In anorexia nervosa, what the child eats is the nothing' (1998, p. 104), emphasising that anorexia is ultimately a desire for nothing, an 'ascetic enjoyment', as Sergio Benvenuto describes it (2020, p. 62). This insight is particularly striking, as it highlights that the anorexic subject is not simply refusing food but eats the nothing. Additionally, in *Seminar IV*, Lacan depicts bulimia as a strategy to compensate for a love frustration through the satisfaction of primary needs (2020, pp. 166–167). For a detailed analysis of Lacan's scattered remarks on anorexia and bulimia, see Cosenza (2023).

[7] Benvenuto claims that Lacan provides an 'anorexic-like theory of human beings' (2020, p. 62). Similarly, McGowan regards the anorexic subject as 'the model for all desiring subjectivity' (2013, p. 29). As McGowan writes: 'The logic of anorexia lays bare the hidden workings of desire that operate within every subject. Subjects believe that they pursue various objects of desire (a new car, a new house, a new romantic partner, and so on) and that these objects have an intrinsic attraction, but the real engine for their desire resides in the nothing that the subject has given up and that every object tries and fails to represent. Objects of desire are desirable only insofar as they attempt to represent the impossible lost object, which is what the anorexic reveals. Still, the anorexic is

subject, the imaginary ideal of a skinny body becomes a prosthesis that covers up the lack of being, while in the bulimic subject the lack is displaced in the actual absence of the object-food, which can be easily made available to be devoured. The crucial point for Recalcati is therefore that anorexia and bulimia reveal the heterogeneity between lack and void. They demonstrate how the enjoyment of the void can annihilate the dialectic of desire that arises from lack.

Recalcati's theoretical and clinical work with anorexic and bulimic patients laid the foundation for his conceptualisation of the 'clinic of the void', which has gained significant traction amongst Italian Lacanians since the early 2000s and has been acknowledged in the English-speaking world (Benvenuto and Molino 2009, Busiol 2022, Cosenza 2023).[8] In *Clinica del vuoto: Anoressie, dipendenze, psicosi*, Recalcati (2002) builds on the work of the French Lacanian psychoanalyst Serge Cottet, who distinguished the clinic of lack from the clinic of emptiness (1997). The book is intended to provide a broader Lacanian theoretical framework for those contemporary pathologies that, in Recalcati's view, manifest a dissociation between the constitutive lack and the annihilating void and that foreclose desire by nullifying it in the pure enjoyment of the death drive. According to Recalcati, the clinic of the void is no longer a clinic of the lack, that is, 'a clinic of unconscious desire, repression and the return of the repressed, of the symptom and the subject's division' (2002, p. 9). Recalcati argues that the main trait of contemporary psychopathologies is the replacement of lack by a void.[9] This void can be a way for the subject to separate themselves from the overwhelming demand of the Other (anorexia), but it can also prompt the subject to engage in a compulsive

---

exceptional; most nonanorexic subjects imagine that their lost object can be found in something rather than nothing' (2013, p. 30).

[8] In the 2000s, Recalcati's pioneering work on eating disorders, which helped shape the paradigm of a 'new' clinic, was introduced to Anglophone Lacanianism through translations of his articles published in *Lacanian Ink* (see Appendix). These writings have since been cited in various English-language Lacanian publications (Aguirre 2011; Eyers 2012; Rousselle 2017). Additionally, Cosenza's work has also been referenced in English (Svolos 2011, 2017) and his monograph *A Lacanian Reading of Anorexia* was translated for the English readership in 2023.

[9] Similarly, Darian Leader distinguishes between a 'literal' and a 'metaphorical' emptiness (2002, p. 93) when discussing the mourning process and artistic creation.

consumption of food (bulimia) or substances (addiction). Clearly, this void has nothing to do with the symbolic and generative lack that, according to Lacan, is constitutive of human subjectivity and gives rise to the desiring subject of the unconscious. These 'empty subjects' (Recalcati 2002) are no longer beings defined by lack, but are instead inhabited by a void that is neither symbolised nor subjectivised, and which is ultimately dissociated from desire. Recalcati clarifies that the clinic of the void 'is not intended to define a new structure but is a crucial aspect of the contemporary psychoanalytic clinic' (2022b, p. 240).

In the article 'The Empty Subject: Un-Triggered Psychoses in the New Forms of the Symptom', Recalcati discusses the transition in contemporary clinic from the symbolic lack to the 'pure real emptiness unrelated to desire' (2005b, p. 86), noticing a shift from the symbolic to the real. He argues that:

> [...] the subject does not work on the lack to probe its value in the Other's desire, but rather "nothingifies", if we may say so, the lack itself by reducing it to a localized emptiness, to the stomach's emptiness. The anorexic rejection allows the survival not of desire as such, but of a kind of pseudo lack. "Pseudo" because it ends the relationship with the desire of the Other in order to be united with a radical thrust of auto-mortification. The by-product of the disconnection between lack and desire is a kind of reduction—of ossification—of lack itself to a reified emptiness, not vitalized by phallic signification, not signified, not metaphorical. An emptiness that could decline into nirvanization of the subject—anorexia —, or as compulsive avidity—bulimia. (2005b, pp. 85–86)

Recalcati's clinical and theoretical work on anorexia and bulimia not only contributed to the pioneering development of a new clinic for treating eating disorders in Italy but also paved the way for a fruitful analysis of the intersection of psychopathology and social discourse. Recalcati insists on the importance of taking into account the 'historico-social dimension of the clinic' (2001, p. 107). Anorexia and bulimia represent the pathological degeneration of two contemporary societal myths: the narcissistic, self-interested, and antisocial cult for the image (anorexic subject), and the cult for endless consumption[10] (bulimic subject) (Recalcati and Zuccardi Merli 2006).

In the article 'Hunger, Repletion, and Anxiety', Recalcati (2011) explicitly states that his clinical work with anorexic and bulimic patients enabled him to explore the interplay between psychopathology and social discourse, a hallmark of postmillennial Italian Lacanianism and a key factor in its relevance in Italy today (see Chap. 4). Not coincidentally, the article was published in *Angelaki*'s special issue *Italian Thought Today: Bio-economy, Human Nature, Christianity*, among articles by renowned exponents of Italian biopolitical theory, such as Roberto Esposito, Davide Tarizzo, and Giorgio Agamben. Recalcati holds the capitalist discourse accountable for transforming lack into void—no longer a symbolic hole produced by the signifier but an empty space that can be easily filled up by objects. The commodification of needs and the compulsion of consumption are indeed defining traits of late capitalist societies. The discourse of the capitalist takes advantage of unfulfilled demands and unsatisfied needs, exploiting the market's unlimited availability of objects. The illusion promoted by the capitalist discourse is that it conflates desire with need on the one hand, and the object of desire with the object of enjoyment on the other.

Anorexia and bulimia epitomise the new relationship that the subject establishes with the Other, fundamentally characterised by detachment or rejection. As such, anorexia and bulimia represent 'two exemplary declinations [...] of this new (post-human; monadic) version of the social bond' (Recalcati 2011, p. 34) in postmillennial society. As Recalcati puts it,

[10] In *Capitalist Bulimia: Lacan on Marx and Crisis*, Fabio Vighi's account of the deadlock of contemporary capitalism aligns with Recalcati's analysis. Vighi defines 'the specific pathology of contemporary capitalism' as bulimic (2016, p. 430) since 'the voracious oral drive of capital continues to *ingest* but is increasingly unable to *digest*, i.e., to turn the valorisation process into substantial wealth' (2016, p. 428). Vighi also implicitly refers to the new symptoms when he writes: 'As with the smoker, the gambler, the drug-addict or [...] the bulimic, the capitalist's accumulation-related enjoyment is always partial, or else it coincides with the constant, compulsive deferral of full and complete satisfaction. Capital, in other words, coincides with its own movement of expansion' (2016, p. 427).

> The bond with the Other and the dimension of the erotic-amorous exchange that it entails is substituted by the unilateral relationship with an unlimited series of inhuman partners (drugs, food, alcohol, psychotropic drugs, the fetishized imaged of one's body, virtual realities, and so on). (2011, p. 33)

The contemporary Other, embodied by the market, like the Other of anorexic and bulimic subjects, systematically confuses need with desire and inundates subjects with tempting, unlimited offers of commodities that claim to fulfil their lack and satisfy their needs. It is within this contemporary social discourse that the new psychopathologies emerge. Unlike in the past, these are

> [...] defined less by the metaphorical, enigmatic, coded nature that the return of the repressed takes as the agent of the subject's division, and more by a problem that radically affects the narcissistic constitution of the subject [...] and by practices of enjoyment [...] that seem to exclude the very existence of the unconscious, in the sense that enjoyment is not inscribed in the exchange with the Other [...] but is configured as [...] a product [...] that is readily available on the market. (Recalcati 2002, p. 10)

For Italian Lacanians in the 1990s, anorexic and bulimic subjects posed a significant challenge to the classical psychoanalytic clinic by presenting a 'desubjectivized symptom, disjointed from the unconscious, without demand and disconnected from the dynamics of transference' (Cosenza 2023, pp. 21–22). The clinic of anorexia and bulimia thus became a gateway for the theoretical and clinical advancements of post-millennial Italian Lacanianism, enabling a better understanding and more effective treatment of other pervasive contemporary pathologies, such as addictions, depression, and panic attacks. It also facilitated the development of a more appropriate metapsychological framework. These 'new forms of the symptom' (Cosenza 2023) reflect a shift from the classic symptom, as a symbolic and metaphorical expression of the unconscious, to a symptom that encapsulates a form of *jouissance* without meaning. Italian Lacanians thus argue that contemporary psychopathologies reveal a disconnection between symptoms and the unconscious, necessitating a radical rethinking and reframing of analytic practice.

New Symptoms and Subjects Without Unconscious

In the 1990s, the analytic work with anorexic and bulimic patients conducted in institutional and private settings played a crucial role in the clinical turn of Italian Lacanianism. The focus on eating disorders significantly enhanced the reputation of Lacanian psychoanalysis in Italy, which shifted from being perceived as an intellectual trend with dubious practical applicability to a rigorous and fruitful clinical approach. The connection of the theoretical and clinical work with contemporary societal issues also enabled Italian Lacanianism to become more firmly entrenched in public discourse and thus to gain prominence.

At the turn of the century, Italian Lacanians achieved even more recognition both in the broader psychoanalytic community and among the general public for expanding their focus on eating disorders to encompass the ongoing 'pandemic proliferation' of the so-called new symptoms (Mura 2015, p. 165). These include anorexia, bulimia, panic attacks, addictions, and depression (Cosenza et al. 2006). Since then, these new symptoms[11] have served as a testing ground for Italian Lacanians to demonstrate the efficacy of the Lacanian clinic in dealing with twenty-first-century psychopathologies and, more broadly, reha-

[11] Lacanians worldwide have sought to conceptualise this evolving clinical landscape. In *New Maladies of the Soul*, Julia Kristeva discusses the psychic life of modern individuals, arguing that 'new maladies', as she calls them, 'go beyond traditional classification systems' (1995, p. 9). Although they are 'not necessarily psychoses', she notes that 'they evoke the psychotic patient's inability to symbolize his unbearable traumas' thus wondering whether it would be more appropriate to refer to those people who suffer from them as 'new patients' (1995, p. 9). Some Lacanians employ terms such as 'new disorders of the unconscious' (Feher Gurewich 1999), 'contemporary symptoms' (Porcheret 2000; Britton 2004), 'new symptoms' (Freda 2001; Svolos 2011, 2017), and 'new psychic economy' (Melman 1999, 2018). In Anglophone Lacanianism, however, these expressions mainly refer to addictions (food, alcohol, drugs, work, etc.). Charles Melman's *Essay in Clinical Psychoanalysis: the Alcoholic* (1980) is one of the first French Lacanian works translated into English to address the sociogenesis of new symptoms by discussing the challenges of establishing a transferential relationship with the analyst, *jouissance*, and the disavowal of castration when working with acholic patients. More recently, the edited book *Lacan and Addiction* further exemplifies this trend (Goldman-Baldwin, Malone, Svolos 2011). Other English-speaking Lacanians have also recently established a direct link between these 'new' pathologies and the category of the real by claiming that contemporary symptoms are no longer metaphorical manifestations of the unconscious but rather a manifestation of 'the real of the body' (Dean 2000; Verhaeghe 2008; Gherovici 2011).

bilitating psychoanalysis at a time dominated by cognitive-behavioural therapies and pharmaceutical approaches. Italian Lacanians regard these symptoms as 'new' not because they are unprecedented in history but because they have emerged in a radically novel social context, one that demands a new metapsychological framework for their clinical understanding and psychoanalytic treatment (Cosenza 2003; Cosenza et al. 2006; Benvenuto 2009; Terminio 2009; Recalcati 2010; Busiol 2022). For instance, cases of drug use in antiquity and anorexia in the Middle Ages are well documented; however, these occurred within specific symbolic spaces and ritual contexts that are radically different from today's (Busiol 2022).

The new symptoms also represented the perfect opportunity for Italian Lacanians to deploy the reading of the 'contemporary symbolic' put forward by Jacques-Alain Miller and Éric Laurent in their 1997 seminar *The Other Who Doesn't Exist and His Ethical Committees*. This work had a profound influence on Italian Lacanians, offering a theoretical foundation for the development of their clinic of the new symptoms (Ramaioli et al. 2003). Miller and Laurent's work discusses the decline of the symbolic Other in contemporary society, reflected in the degradation of traditional symbolic institutions (family, church, nation), and addresses its clinical and social repercussions. Another influential aspect for Italian Lacanians, developed within the context of French Lacanianism, is the link between the crisis of the symbolic and the demise of the Name of the Father in our contemporary post-Oedipal society (Miller 1997; Lebrun 1997; Maleval 2000; Melman 2002).[12] According to this perspective, the Oedipus—the symbolic device that in the neurotic structure deals with the real of *jouissance*—has diminished in significance in contemporary society. Hence, to understand today's social dynamics, there is a greater need to focus on the psychotic structure, which is marked by the return of non-symbolised, unregulated *jouissance*. In the late 1990s, Miller and

[12] In relation to the decline of the paternal function, Italian Lacanians develop different, and at times conflicting, stances. For instance, Recalcati (2010), rather than insisting on the 'beyond' or 'decline' of the Oedipus, emphasises Lacan's expression 'evaporation of the Father'; Di Ciaccia and Fasoli (1) equate the crisis of the symbolic with the crises of the patriarchy; and Lolli (2019) strongly disagrees with the latter perspective and argues that the crisis of the Oedipus does not coincide with the crisis of the symbolic *tout court* (see Chap. 4).

the analysts of the *École de la cause Freudienne* expanded this concept of psychosis to include subjects whose structural functioning manifests a *jouissance* not grounded in the functioning of the paternal metaphor (Cosenza 2023; Greenshields 2021; Svolos 2017).[13]

Drawing from French Lacanianism, since the 2000s Italian Lacanians have developed their own specific contributions to the new symptoms, focusing particularly on the intersection between clinical and societal dimensions. While these symptoms are deeply intertwined with the history of the subject, they also represent pathological manifestations of broader social maladies. In their work, Italian Lacanians also focus on the clinical implications of the contemporary Other, who—as a result of the specific characteristics of contemporary society—suffers from a weakened symbolic network that fails to provide guidance and meaning. This results in an absence of limits or restrictions on the real of *jouissance*. The prevailing forces of capitalism and neoliberal ideologies have contributed extensively to this radical change. In the view of Italian Lacanians, the new symptoms are thus bounded to the specificity of contemporary societies, which are characterised by individualism, precarity, and self-realisation. For instance, anxiety and panic attacks manifest the widespread precarity of today's world, which is dominated by a lack of symbolic landmarks and a general sense of disorientation (Focchi 2022); depression reveals the exclusion of loss, failure, and death in a world that promotes never-ending success, achievement, and enjoyment (Lolli 2022); and addictions indicate the constant focus on consumption, ego-strengthening, and the fantasy of mastery (Busiol 2022).

Marco Focchi (Cosenza et al. 2006) and Franco Lolli (2012) argue that the real, unfiltered by the symbolic, emerges as an unbearable and traumatic existential experience in the contemporary clinic. This excessive and deadly dimension of the real, stripped of every symbolic garment, invades and threatens the subject. For Italian Lacanian analysts, the erosion of the symbolic grounding of the subject and the influence of

[13] Greenshields argues that, in the Millerian school, the emphasis on the clinical structure of psychosis was determined by 'a requirement on the part of Lacanians to respond […] to an American research program, the impetus for which was established by Otto Kernberg's observation in the mid-1960s' (2021, p. 14), which then led to establishing the category of borderline personality disorder.

the contemporary Other encourage a problematic relationship between the subject and the countless objects of enjoyment, which has led to a 'pure emergence of the dimension of the drive' (Focchi 2022, p. 157).

Considering this generalised drift of enjoyment, Miller's focus on the real has been particularly significant for Italian Lacanians. Bluntly put, in light of Lacan's late teaching, Miller regards symptoms more as an 'event of the body' than as an 'advent of signification' (2000, p. 43), shifting the emphasis from meaning to *jouissance*. As such, he contends that the clinical practice has entered a post-interpretative era in which the focus is no longer on deciphering the inner meaning of the symptom (Miller 1996). Consequently, the notion of *jouissance* has attained a central place in the Lacanian metapsychology of the new symptoms advanced by Italian Lacanians. The study *Civiltà e disagio. Forme contemporanee della psicopatologia* clearly outlines the connection between the new symptoms and enjoyment by stating that:

> The most widespread symptomatic forms of the discontent of civilization are today closely related to enjoyment, they are real practices of enjoyment (perversions, drug addiction, bulimia, obesity, alcoholism), or manifestations of a narcissistic closure of the subject that produces a stagnation of enjoyment in the body (anorexia, depression, panic). (Cosenza et al. 2006, p. vii)

In the clinic of the new symptoms, Italian Lacanians signal a fundamental transition from a clinic based on the symbolic, which is primarily focused on neurosis as formulated by Freud, to one centred on the real (Cosenza et al. 2006; Recalcati 2010; Terminio 2009; Pagliardini 2020), which is derived from the clinic of psychosis as theorised by Lacan and built on the key notions of the real unconscious and *jouissance* as 'irreducible to the signifier' (Cosenza 2023, p. 31). The clinic of the new symptoms marks a shift from a clinical framework that views the neurotic symptom as a metaphorical expression of the unconscious to one in which the symptom is detached from any symbolic unconscious dynamics, instead constituting a pure expression of *jouissance* in the body. Classic Freudian clinical practice was born from the encounter with hysterical patients whose symptoms manifested as bodily expressions (a 'conversion', as Freud called it) of their inner conflicts and traumas. According to Freud, a neurotic symptom is a compromise formation resulting from an unresolved conflict between repressed unconscious desires or traumas and is viewed as a coded message, or metaphor. Hence, the clinic of neurosis is primarily a clinic of the symbolic since the return of the repressed involves a symbolic return of the real. The new symptoms thus no longer present themselves as symbolic expressions of unconscious conflicts, the index of the repressed truth of a subject, which can be decoded through interpretation. Moreover, unlike neurotic symptoms, which Freud conceived of as metaphorical messages from the unconscious, the new symptoms lack a linguistic-metaphorical structure and do not represent a return of the repressed in symbolic form (a dream, slip of the tongue, or bungled action). This makes them resistant to psychoanalytic treatment, which relies on interpretation and the power of speech.

The clinic of the new symptoms centres around the subject's problematic relationship with their *jouissance* and involves elements derived from the clinic of psychosis and perversion (Busiol 2022). Italian Lacanianism emphasises that the paradigm for understanding the new symptoms and their functioning must shift from neurosis to psychosis because the clinic of psychosis is predominantly a clinic of unregulated *jouissance*. In the clinical structure of neurosis, there is a symbolic return of the real through unconscious compromise formations, while in the clinical structure of psychosis, there is a collapse of the symbolic and a return of the real (Lacan 1997). Drawing from French Lacanianism, Italian Lacanians contend that the new symptoms are characterised by a psychotic functioning. This clearly does not mean that all patients are to be considered psychotic, however, nor does it imply that Italian Lacanians equate new symptoms with psychoses. Additionally, the clinic of the new symptoms entails the clinic of perversion, understood as a disavowal of symbolic castration—an experience that typically marks a limit. This disavowal leads to an enjoyment without the Other, which disrupts the social bond by creating 'a tear between the self-destructive real where the patient finds themselves locked up and the word of the Other, the order of the symbolic' (Cosenza 2023, p. 30). The solid identification with the symptom reinforces the ego, forming a 'social mask' (Recalcati 2010, p. xi) or, in other words, a 'social label' (Focchi 2022, p. 157)—'I am anorexic', 'I am an addict', etc. This mask serves as a shield, protecting the subject from their inherent division and questions regarding their personal implication in their own suffering, and ultimately sustaining the illusion of an undivided subject, or a subject beyond castration. The new symptoms are thus a way to compensate for the crisis of the symbolic Other since they fulfil an 'identifying role' (Focchi 2022, p. 157).

Italian Lacanians thus view the new symptoms as manifestations of the real qua *jouissance*, which resist interpretation and symbolisation, rendering interpretations less efficient in clinical settings (Benvenuto 2009). While symptoms are typically seen as 'illnesses that speak', as the early Lacan suggests (2006 [1951], p. 177), the new symptoms tend to silence the unconscious. This has led Italian Lacanians to speak of a transition from the symbolic unconscious to the real unconscious. Lacan's take on the Freudian notion of the unconscious emphasises its role as the discourse of the Other; a symbolic domain of language and culture that is both transindividual and historical but nonetheless subject to transformations (Dean 2000; McGowan 2004). However, this raises the question of what happens when the contemporary Other debilitates the function of the unconscious, when the unconscious, at least as Freud theorises it, disappears in today's world (Žižek 2006; Svolos 2017; Melman 2018).

Recalcati's groundbreaking work *L'uomo senza inconscio: Figure della nuova clinica psicoanalitica*[14] (2010) investigates the vicissitudes of the unconscious in the new clinic and contemporary society, hyperbolically arguing that both are characterised by its disappearance. The book provides the first and most comprehensive account of the new symptoms in Italian Lacanianism, promoting a Lacanian interpretation of contemporary psychopathologies and examining the social discourse within which they emerged. Recalcati's work draws from a diverse range of

[14] The title of the book is reminiscent of notable works, such as Robert Musil's modernist novel *The Man without Qualities* (1943), which portrays an aimless and directionless protagonist; Herbert Marcuse's *One-dimensional man* (1964), a social critique of the industrial and consumeristic Western society; Giorgio Agamben's *The Man without Content* (1994), which explores key issues of Western aesthetics; and Charles Melman's *L'homme sans gravité: jouir à tout prix. Entretiens avec Jean-Pierre Lebrun* (2002), a work that examines current psychosocial changes from a Lacanian perspective, linking the crisis of the patriarchy with the crisis of the paternal function.

psychoanalytic orientations[15] that have expanded upon Freudian metapsychology in order to account for the emergence of new psychopathological phenomena. Since the new symptoms do not appear as metaphors of the subject's repressed conflicts, that is to say, they are not strictly speaking unconscious compromise formations, Recalcati contends that contemporary psychoanalytic practice must therefore operate in the absence of the unconscious, so to speak. As Recalcati claims:

> Bulimic behaviours or drug addiction, depressive withdrawal, or anorexic petrification are not, in fact, formations of the unconscious in the classic sense of the term; they are not organised as a signifying encryption, or metaphors of the subject. Rather, they present themselves as libidinal practices, as unrestrained practices of enjoyment, as solid identifications that oppose the subject of the unconscious. (Recalcati 2010, pp. 286–287)

Recalcati contends that the new symptoms are manifestations of the real 'in its acephalous dimension as a pure thrust to enjoy, as death drive' (Recalcati 2010, p. 160). He claims that this deadly enjoyment is completely cut off from any dialectic with the symbolic Other and, consequently, dissociated from the experience of desire. For Recalcati, therefore, the new symptoms involve the foreclosure of desire, which is annihilated by libidinal excess, or, simply put, the 'reduction of desire to enjoyment' (2010, p. 277). Ultimately, Recalcati's perspective emphasises that, for Lacan, the subject of the unconscious coincides with the subject of desire. However, Recalcati argues, the subject of the unconscious is not a fixed, 'supra-historical essence immune to social transformation', but rather can 'decline, eclipse, even become extinct'. He thus warns against the idea that the existence of the unconscious is 'guaranteed as an ontological

[15] Recalcati utilises concepts from Green (1986) and Kernberg (1975), such as 'psychotic' and 'borderline' structure, respectively. He references Kestemberg's 'cold' or 'non-delusional psychosis', Bollas' 'normotic personality', and McDougall's 'anti-analysand' (1989) to elucidate the patient's struggle with symbolisation. Although new symptoms are prevalent in contemporary Western society, Recalcati does not suggest that these psychopathologies are 'new' clinical or diagnostic structures. Additionally, Recalcati draws on Melman's Lacanian perspective of the 'new psychic economy', which is no longer centred on the repression of sexual desire but rather on the relentless pursuit of enjoyment by these 'new subjects' (2018). Recalcati's approach demonstrates the pluralistic and inclusive nature of Italian Lacanianism towards non-Lacanian psychoanalysts.

expression of human reality' (2010, p. ix). For Recalcati, this is what the new symptoms reveal. In these new practices of enjoyment, the (subject of the) unconscious is foreclosed and there is the illusion that our constitutive lack can be replaced by gadgets, substances, food, and technological objects. This is why Recalcati calls it a clinic of 'enjoyment without desire' (Recalcati 2010, p. 157). These new forms of the symptom testify that desire faces 'nihilistic obliteration' (Recalcati 2010, p. x) in a contemporary society dominated by the capitalist discourse (see Chap. 4). Desire is no longer the expression of the subject of the unconscious. For Recalcati, this marks the emergence of a new type of subject: the subject without unconscious. Hence, as Sforza Tarabochia aptly claims, for Recalcati such new symptoms are the 'clinical application' (2016, p. 8) of Lacan's discourse of the capitalist and the crisis of the symbolic, which have brought about an 'anti-subjective' and 'anti-psychoanalytic' frame of mind (2016, p. 11).[16]

Moreover, drawing from his experience with anorexic and bulimic patients, Recalcati conceptualises the new symptoms as a holophrase rather than a metaphor, drawing on Lacan's use of the holophrase—originally taken from linguistics, where it denotes a condensed expression, usually a single word or phrase, conveying a complete, fixed meaning—in relation to psychosomatic disorders, cognitive disability, and psychosis. The new symptoms provide an opportunity for the subject to establish a strong identity, one which is rigidly identified with the symptom itself—'I am anorexic', 'I am bulimic', 'I am an addict', for example. The symptom thus functions as an identity marker which strengthens the ego. Recalcati has described this phenomenon as the 'holophrastic inclination' (Recalcati 2010, p. 156) of the new symptoms.[17] The demand from new patients is not a demand in relation to the Other's desire. Rather, it is directed at objects and practices that induce *jouissance*, such as drugs, food, or starvation.

[16] Notably, philosophers familiar with psychoanalysis like Catherine Malabou (2009) and Byung-Chul Han (2015) prioritise the framework of neuronal disorders when discussing the dominant contemporary pathological landscape and tend to dismiss the notion of subjectivity.

[17] This concept underpins Recalcati's clinical notion of the 'security drive', which has been effectively used for sociopolitical criticism, as I will discuss in Chap. 4.

Therefore, the dialectic between alienation in/separation from the Other, which sustains the process of subject constitution, appears to be fractured and polarised. In these new psychopathologies, we can find:

> on the one hand, an individual detached from the wider community, atomised, reduced to a mere social mask, the product of a solid identification, disconnected from all ties due to an excessive alienation from social semblants; and, on the other, the thrust of the drive that rejects symbolic castration and its necessary sublimatory channeling, imposing itself as a Sadian push to consume the object, as an imperative need to obtain enjoyment without any engagement with the Other. (Recalcati 2010, p. xi)

As a result, Recalcati (2010) discerns two main trajectories in the disappearance of the unconscious in the new symptoms. On the one hand, there is a narcissistic strengthening of the ego, which fosters alienation in those social semblants that function as identity markers. This is evident in the rigidified identification of the anorexic, which epitomises an 'Ego without unconscious'. On the other hand, there is the thrust to *jouissance*, as seen in the libidinal compulsion exemplified in addiction, which represents an 'Id without unconscious' and promotes separation from the Other.

Recalcati refrains from offering simple solutions to address the new symptoms in clinical practice. Instead, he underlines that the direction of the cure should focus on rehabilitating the function of the unconscious and ultimately re-subscribe the subject to their unconscious. This process must be initiated from scratch with these patients since the traditional connection between symptom, demand of analysis, and transference that underpins the neurotic treatment has become completely disjointed. Consequently, the preliminary treatment of the demand of these subjects is crucial. To accomplish this, Recalcati claims that what is required is a preliminary treatment of the real of *jouissance* and a 'rectification of the Other', rather than a rectification of the subject (2010, pp. 275–288). This implies that the analyst should embody a new incarnation of the Other, distinct from the one the subject has previously encountered in their history. It must be an Other that can embrace and support the subject. As Recalcati writes, 'In the hypermodern age where there is no Other capable of symbolically supporting the weight of existence, we must try to reintroduce the subject in a liveable dialectic with the Other' (2022b, p. 248).

Recalcati's account of the new symptoms has been particularly influential among the new generation of Italian Lacanians. It has even reached a mainstream audience beyond Lacanian circles, particularly thanks to its sociopolitical significance (see Chap. 4). However, some Italian Lacanians disagree with his perspective. For instance, Antonio Di Ciaccia and Doriano Fasoli (1) acknowledge crucial transformations in contemporary psychopathologies, particularly the increasing fixation with objects of enjoyment. Despite this shift, they nonetheless contend that contemporary symptoms are fundamentally the same as those in the past. For them, even if these new forms of pathologies are more extreme and resistant to the symbolic work of psychoanalysis, they still belong to the order of language. In *Inattualità della psicoanalisi* (2019), Franco Lolli takes a similar stance. He rejects the theory that altered sociocultural conditions modify the process of symptom formation and claims that the new patients are simply people who were previously excluded from psychoanalytic treatments due to the seriousness of their conditions or who could not access such treatments due to their socioeconomic background. He argues that:

> the social, cultural, economic, and historical-religious levels are not what psychoanalysis deems to be key [...] for the constitution of a symptom. The symptom is rooted in the unique and unrepeatable drive-related vicissitudes of the subject; only the forms it takes are influenced by the dominant social discourse. (Lolli 2019, pp. 181–182)

From Lolli's perspective, the new symptoms are simply an up-to-date version of the same old psychic mechanism, adapted to contemporary sociohistorical dynamics. For this reason, Lolli claims that the new symptoms are still based on a conflict between a willingness to enjoy and a renunciation of this enjoyment. He further contends that, rather than dismantling the subject's division, the discourse of the capitalist in fact furthers it as today's capitalist society is still repressive despite its widespread permissiveness. Lolli recognises the need for psychoanalysis to adapt to patients and operate in contexts that are different from those of the past. For these reasons, however, he maintains that it is more important than ever for psychoanalysis to stick to its principles, especially when 'applied' to public or institutional settings. Lolli summarises these principles as the distinction between structure (underlying and unchangeable) and phenomenon (mutable), the existence of the unconscious, the curative power of transference, and the action of the death drive (2019, pp. 181–185).

Moreover, Lolli points out another problematic issue in the use of the term *jouissance* in the clinic of the new symptoms. For Lolli, mainstream Lacanians and public intellectuals, who sometimes generalise when applying Lacanian theory to interpret contemporary society, have contributed to the misconception that these symptoms are mere pathologies of consumerism. This confusion has been fuelled by a misleading equation of *jouissance* with pleasure or hedonism—an oversimplification evident, for instance, in Recalcati's sociopolitical analysis of the Berlusconi era (see Chap. 4). This generalisation has contributed to the accusation of moralism and ideology against Recalcati's Lacanian perspective, particularly his account of *jouissance*, which has been associated with a shallow criticism of consumerism and mistakenly seen as a cautionary plea for moderation against excessive enjoyment (Ronchi 2012; Benvenuto 2020) (see Chap. 4).

This oversimplification of the tension between desire and *jouissance* has led to a polarisation and moral interpretations of the notion of *jouissance* as 'selfish', 'narcissistic', disruptive, and fundamentally evil, as opposed to the positive and generative 'ethical desire' (Di Martino 2016; Verdicchio and Di Martino 2017).[18] As a result, there is also a misleading perception that Recalcati promotes a Lacanian 'religion' of desire in opposition to the dissipative *jouissance* in his account on the new symptoms (Lolli

---

[18] Strong criticisms on a vague and superficial use of the notion of *jouissance* have also been raised in Anglophone Lacanianism. For instance, Darian Leader (2021) criticises the excessive ambiguity surrounding the notion of *jouissance*, debating its validity as a psychoanalytic concept and claiming that the term is often deployed in an overtly simplistic and generic way. Specifically, Leader questions concepts like 'the clinic of jouissance' (p. 4), criticises the personification of the superego frequently associated with the imperative to *jouissance* (Enjoy!), and warns against the conception of *jouissance* as a 'quantity internal to the body' (p. 107), as a bodily energy that needs to be channelled, contained, or managed.

2022). However, these criticisms are unfounded. Recalcati's interpretation of Lacan does not privilege desire over *jouissance* or present a romanticised version of desire as purely generative and beneficial. In his works, he clearly articulates the necessity of integrating, rather than opposing, desire and *jouissance*:

> Psychoanalysis is not a religion of desire. One cannot – and this is the important lesson that neo-Lacanianism has the merit of emphasising – overlook the centrality of the drive in the analytic experience. Desire cannot be seen as a liberation from the drive. This is the Catholic mistake when reading Lacan: conceiving of desire as a place of liberation from the evil enjoyment of the drive. (2020, p. 46)

Instead, Recalcati acknowledges the complexity, and contradiction, inherent in Lacan's account on desire, which is evident, for instance, when Lacan qualifies it as 'paradoxical, deviant, erratic, eccentric, scandalous' (2006, p. 579) or in Seminar VI, when he explicitly highlights these more problematic aspects of desire by stating that 'the more we examine this desire, the less it resembles a pure and simple impulse. […] no desire ever fails to present itself as problematic, dispersed, polymorphous, contradictory, and, in short, far from any oriented coaptation' (2019b, p. 474).

Despite criticisms and conceptual differences among Italian Lacanians, their clinical and theoretical work on the new symptoms has nonetheless significantly enhanced the clinical reputation of Lacanian psychoanalysis in Italy. This recognition has grown among other psychoanalytic orientations, making it particularly relevant in contemporary Italy. Led by Recalcati, this group of Lacanians did more than theorise about the new symptoms while carrying on with their private or institutional practice. Rather, they implemented these theories by establishing a network of Lacanian clinics throughout Italy. They believed that if the (subject of the) unconscious is in danger, action must be taken beyond the confines of their private offices. As we will explore in the next section, the Lacanian clinics founded by Recalcati and his colleagues have integrated Lacanian psychoanalysis deeply into the fabric of Italian society.

Italian Lacanian Clinics

The development of psychoanalysis in Italy has been dominated by the 'primacy of the social dimension' (Benvenuto 1997, para. 3). As discussed in Chap. 2, Italy has a long-standing history of socially committed and politically engaged psychoanalysis. For instance, in the 1940s, Cesare Musatti's pioneering project at the Olivetti typewriter company in Ivrea put psychoanalytic knowledge at the service of Italian industry in order to improve the mental health and working conditions of factory workers (Diazzi 2021). In the 1970s, Elvio Fachinelli's community-based psychoanalytic interventions and Enzo Morpurgo's working-class psychoanalysis were aimed at making psychoanalytic practice accessible to all people, beyond class boundaries (Barbetta 2019). These groundbreaking projects were intended to democratise psychoanalysis, by transforming it from an elitist practice for the wealthy into an inclusive practice for all. In doing so, those Italian psychoanalysts sought to return to the true spirit of Freud's original endeavour, which was profoundly underpinned by social justice.[19] There is, however, a key difference between past practices aimed at proletarianising psychoanalysis and those promoted by Italian Lacanians over the last two decades (no author, 2013).

Lacanians in postmillennial Italy contend that the proliferation of medicalisation, cognitive approaches, and scientific reductionism promoted by neoliberal capitalism threaten the existence of the (subject of the) unconscious. These approaches tend to reduce the subject to an individual suffering from a symptom that must be removed or fixed,

[19] As Danto (2005) points out, Freud advocated for a socially responsible psychoanalysis to grant low-income people access to mental health care and promoted the creation of free-of-charge institutions and outpatient clinics. This inspired the 'activist generation of psychoanalysts' (2005, p. 3) who, from 1918 to 1938, driven by a strong social mission to develop affordable psychoanalytic treatments, succeeded in making psychoanalysis accessible to working-class people and the unemployed by establishing psychoanalytic free clinics in several cities around the world. These pioneering projects were brought to an end abruptly as a result of World War II and the Nazi persecutions. For a groundbreaking discussion of the ethical, sociopolitical, and clinical implications of free and low-cost clinics operating today around the world, see the 2022 special issue *Psychoanalysis for the People: Free Clinics and the Social Mission of Psychoanalysis* published in the journal *Psychoanalysis and History*.

dismissing or entirely overlooking the subject's relation to their symptom, their clinical structure, and their personal history. They promote external and superficial solutions focused on the removal of the symptom and restoring the body-machine rather than engaging in a working-through process. These approaches neglect the possibility that the symptom may carry a meaningful message or even offer an opportunity for the individual. In contrast, Italian Lacanians advocate for taking responsibility for the unconscious, which involves acknowledging the subject's desire and *jouissance*.

Lacan contends that the concept of the unconscious requires that 'it be listened to' (1990, p. 14), and even incorporates the presence of the psychoanalyst into its definition (1998, p. 127). Therefore, Italian Lacanians argue that today, the challenge is not simply to proletarianise psychoanalysis, although this remains a central mission, but to create the necessary conditions for it to continue to exist despite the dominant social discourse that promotes a foreclosure of the (subject of the) unconscious. This can only be achieved by reinserting psychoanalysis into society. Just as psychopathologies do not exist in isolation, psychoanalysis does not occur in a sociopolitical vacuum. Thus, moving beyond the narrow confines of the analytic room to extend the application of psychoanalysis in the social field becomes a necessity not just to promote psychoanalytic practice but also to promote the psychoanalytic way of thinking about subjectivity, human suffering, and mental health. The political core of Italian Lacanianism resides in this social commitment, rooted in their private and institutional clinical practice. As Recalcati puts it:

> How can we establish a programme to defend the subject of the unconscious in an age dominated by cognitive-behavioural psychotherapies that impose a concept of therapeutic effect reduced to the restoration of the so-called normal functions of the subject (appetite, mood, thought, etc.)? How can we safeguard the singular space of freedom that the subject of the unconscious expresses in the face of the mounting scientistic delirium of universal measurement and medicalisation of the notion of health? How can we actively resist the reduction of desire to a repetitive enjoyment of the death drive that underpins the discourse of the capitalist? (2010, pp. 276–277)

In 2003, a small group of Lacanians led by Recalcati established a non-profit psychoanalytic association called *Jonas (Psychoanalytic Clinical Centre for New Symptoms)*,[20] focused mainly on the theoretical and clinical work on the new symptoms and offering psychoanalytically oriented treatment not just to adult patients but also to children and adolescents. The association is distinguished by its strong social mission, its commitment to making psychoanalytic treatment affordable, and its Lacanian theoretical approach (no author, 2013). *Jonas* stands in opposition to the prevalent medicalisation of mental health therapies and the initiatives it carries out extend to a variety of settings including schools, courts, prisons, and hospitals. It also seeks to promote dialogue between psychoanalysts from various schools, rather than exclusively within the Lacanian tradition.

Over the past 20 years, the *Jonas* centres have steadily increased in number and are now spread throughout Italy. They have been actively engaged in community interventions across the country, offering free consultations open to everyone as well as public workshops. They collaborate with schools to involve teachers, students, and families; provide psychotherapeutic support to those who are unemployed and in debt; and organise film screenings, performing arts events, and book launches. These efforts reflect a democratic and progressive approach to psychoanalysis based on a close link between clinical practice and the sociohistorical context in which it operates.

Social engagement is a cornerstone of the Lacanian psychoanalytic approach, which centres on an extroverted and interconnected model of subjectivity. The psychoanalyst's practice does not take place in an ivory tower; rather, it is deeply integrated into the surrounding community

[20] The association is named after the biblical prophet Jonas, who was requested by God to preach in the city of Nineveh but instead fled to another town out of fear, because his story reflects the Lacanian teaching on the importance of not giving up on one's own desire. Today, *Jonas* has expanded to include 35 centres across Italy, which include some specialising in childhood and adolescence (https://www.jonasitalia.it). Recalcati ideated *Jonas* with the vision of creating an institution specialised in researching and treating the new forms of symptoms, viewing it as a crucial strategy for gaining social recognition. By branding themselves as 'subjects supposed to know' in the matter of new symptoms, Recalcati and his colleagues managed to establish psychoanalytic centres that align with, but do not conform to, the dominant social discourse, which favours clinical specialists, particularly in public and institutional settings.

and its inhabitants. As such, it is grounded on an ethical commitment to both the wider community and public institutions. *Jonas* exemplifies a socially progressive psychoanalytic association with close relationships to city councils, local authorities, and other community organisations. In fact, it was one of the first Italian psychoanalytic associations to offer free support to National Health Service workers during the COVID-19 pandemic. Despite facing austerity measures and the pervasive medicalisation of mental illness, *Jonas* has shown remarkable resilience and growth, which has helped ensure its economic, financial, and institutional sustainability and success.

Italian Lacanians identify the subject of the unconscious as the locus of resistance to capitalist discourse, a notion upheld by *Jonas* through its socially engaged and politically committed psychoanalytic approach. The social function of the symptom involves a collective and anonymous identification, providing the subject with a form of identity and social integration. However, this often occurs to the detriment of the subject, reinforcing solid identifications that mask the subject's individuality. The challenge that *Jonas* addresses is how to extract the subject of the unconscious from the endless objects of the market that saturate it. In this respect, the work promoted by monosymptomatic groups epitomises *Jonas*' mission. *Jonas* offers psychoanalytically oriented therapies in monosymptomatic groups that tackle the so-called new symptoms, such as anorexia, bulimia, panic attacks, depression, and addictions. Initially, members identify with the same symptom, which serves to define the group in the societal gaze. The symptom anonymises these individuals, reflecting its alienating social function and obscuring subjective differences. The goal is thus to dismantle this monolithic identity and allow the unique characteristics of each individual subject to emerge. The objective is not to reduce the subject to their symptoms but to foster a subject-centred approach that highlights their particularity against the backdrop of universal conditions.

If the status of the unconscious is fundamentally ethical, as Lacan posits (1998, pp. 29, 33), the unconscious coincides with an ethical commitment, or calling. The responsibility of the subject thus becomes a cornerstone of Italian Lacanianism: from a psychoanalytic standpoint, we are all responsible for our own unconscious (Di Ciaccia and Fasoli 2013,

p. 60). The unconscious is an event which 'implies an encounter with a new and unexpected truth' (Recalcati 2012c, p. 10) and thus involves an 'ethical singularity irreducible to any ontological universal' (Recalcati 2012c, p. 11). Therefore, the ethics of psychoanalysis coincides with the politics of psychoanalysis: 'Psychoanalytic treatment is the continuation of the politics of the unconscious with a means invented by Freud' (Di Ciaccia and Fasoli 2013, p. 22). The political kernel of the Italian Lacanians' approach to the new symptoms is to guarantee and preserve the existence of the subject of the unconscious from being swept away. This is the 'political' praxis of Italian Lacanianism, both on an individual level, as we shall see in the next section, and on a social level, as will be discussed in Chap. 4.

The Italian Way: Subject, Subjectivation, and Sublimation

Three years before his death, while presenting at the 9th Congress of the *École Freudienne de Paris*, Lacan pondered 'how is it that whispering something to the subject who comes to you for analysis has the effect of healing them?' He admitted, surprisingly, that, 'despite everything I once said, I know nothing about it' (2005, p. 15). This question raises a fundamental issue in the Lacanian clinic and metapsychology: how can psychoanalysis, a symbolic practice relying exclusively on speech, effectively address the real? The goal of analysis is not merely to reduce symptoms but to bring about a structural transformation of the subject's real. This transformation involves modifying the subject's libidinal economy, that is to say, changing the relation of the subject with their *jouissance*, (death) drive, and repetition (Di Ciaccia and Recalcati 2000; Cosenza 2003). However, how should the real be handled in analytical practice without taming or domesticating it, thereby avoiding the promotion of a normative and adapting analytic practice? These questions ultimately concern how the relationship between the symbolic and the real is conceptualised, a central issue in Lacanianism to which Italian Lacanians have offered a unique contribution.

In *Lacan al presente*, Alex Pagliardini (2020) contends that the way Lacanians address these questions depends on how they conceptualise the real, which, in turn, informs their understanding and practice of psychoanalysis. For Pagliardini, the first, more mainstream understanding conceives of the real mainly as an irreducible negativity, the impossible that eludes words and images. According to this perspective, clinical practice is primarily oriented at 'treating' the real by means of the symbolic, as Lacan puts it in Seminar XI (1998, p. 6). In this seminar, Lacan interweaves the four fundamental Freudian concepts of psychoanalysis—the unconscious, repetition, transference, and the drive—with his notion of the real. In doing so, Lacan reorients psychoanalysis in light of the 'encounter with the real' (1998, p. 52). Lacan defines this encounter as inherently negative, indeterminate, and insubstantial. Tellingly, here Lacan refers to the real as the 'impossible', that which 'resists symbolisation' and 'eludes us', 'the missed encounter', 'unassimilable', a 'resistance', 'unwelcome', an 'obstacle', or an 'impact' (1998, pp. 53–55, 68–69, 167). Simply put, the real is conceptualised as the disruptive and traumatic interference affecting the symbolic functioning of the subject. In other words, the real is the hard kernel that resists any dialectic with the imaginary and the symbolic. This has led some Italian Lacanians to conceptualise the main goal of clinical work as being to 'modify' (Di Ciaccia and Recalcati 2000, p. 204), 'transform' (Lippi 2020; Terminio 2020), and even 'humanise' the real (Recalcati 2012a, p. 149). Pagliardini points out the danger that this theoretical perspective, which emphasises the symbolic mediation and processing of the traumatic real, could inadvertently lead to a disciplinary and dogmatic conceptualisation of psychoanalytic practice as a 'pedagogical position' (Lacan 2014, p. 288), where the symbolic is deployed to 'cleanse', 'norm', 'regulate', or even 'redeem' the real.

Pagliardini identifies a second perspective which conceives of the real as independent, not mediated by the other two registers, coinciding with the One-all-alone, as Lacan terms it in Seminar XIX. This conceptualisation of the real underpins the understanding of psychoanalysis as 'an apparatus the real of which touches the real' (Lacan 2018, p. 216). For Pagliardini, this perspective has the benefit of highlighting the limitations of the symbolic, which cannot fully grasp the real. Additionally, this perspective considers that a key aspect of clinical work is the possibility of 'touching' the real without necessarily assimilating or subordinating it to the symbolic. As Pagliardini and Ronchi remark, in his late phase of teaching

> Lacan decides [...] to submit psychoanalytic theory and practice to the primacy of the real, and seeks to make it an experience of the real, wherein it is made to speak, not to tame it but rather to encounter it, to the point of producing a singular affirmation, namely the singular affirmation of a subject's real. (2014, pp. 14–15)

In light of this perspective, some Italian Lacanians contend that the aim of a psychoanalytic treatment is to 'affirm the real' (Ronchi 2012; Leoni 2016; Pagliardini 2020) and fully 'experience' the drive (Lolli 2022).

Arguably, this opposition reflects the current polarisation in contemporary Lacanianism, wherein, on the one hand, we find the classical, 'scholastic' Lacanianism—to use Recalcati's expression (2023)—which focuses on the early Lacan and his notions of desire, the subject, Other, and symbolic unconscious; and, on the other hand, neo-Lacanianism—to use Miller's expression (2021)—which mainly draws from the late Lacan, describing *jouissance* as 'idiotic and solitary' (Miller 2019b, p. 76), 'not related to the Other' (Miller 2019b, p. 74), and partaking of 'a body that enjoys itself' (Miller 2021, p. 41) as well as advancing a vitalistic conception of the drive. This divide also led to the binary opposition between desire and *jouissance*, which is now pervasive in contemporary Lacanianism (Braunstein 2003, 2020; Leader 2021) and reflects a tension inherent in Lacan's own teaching, as epitomised by his renowned statement that 'desire comes from the Other, and jouissance is located on the side of the Thing' (2006, p. 724). This issue is also central in Italian Lacanianism, where the new symptoms are seen as the contemporary pathological effects of an excess of *jouissance* and a foreclosure of desire (Fiumanò 2010, Recalcati 2010). Simplified and polarised readings of this perspective have further intensified the opposition between desire and *jouissance*.

Undoubtedly, as representatives of the Slovenian school and Anglophone Lacanianism point out, there is a demotion of desire in

Lacan's teaching (Dolar 2006), involving a change of emphasis from the earlier notion of desire to the later concept of the drive (Fink 1995; Žižek 2014; Zupančič 2014). This shift is particularly clear in Miller's interpretation of Lacan and is reflected in his conception of clinical practice, which increasingly focuses on the notions of *jouissance* and the drive (Miller 2018, 2019a, 2021). This primacy of the real of *jouissance* and the drive in transnational Lacanianism has, however, gradually and subtly reduced the prominence of the symbolic and led to a growing intolerance for notions such as desire and lack among the younger generation of Lacanians (Benvenuto 2020, pp. 53–58). Consequently, the notion of desire appears to have been entirely dismissed in today's emphasis on the drive and *jouissance*, while neglecting the notion of desire (Recalcati 2012a, b). Recalcati argues that these interpretations, which portray the drive as a positive and affirmative force against the negative nature of desire rooted in lack, unintentionally align with the dominant capitalistic ideology. As he contends:

> Does being Lacanian mean endorsing the materialistic cynicism of the drive that the discourse of the capitalist promotes by suppressing the singular experience of desire? Does it imply authorising the monological character of Unian jouissance [godimento uniano][21]? In our time, that of the hyper-hedonism of the discourse of the capitalist, does responding to Lacan not instead mean trying to reconsider his teaching on desire in all its force? The paradox of desire must be preserved against the risk of an involuntary collusion of Lacanianism with the cynical discourse of the capitalist, which endorses enjoyment as the only possible value. (2012b, pp. 189–190)

According to Benvenuto, desire and *jouissance* represent Lacan's most original contribution to psychoanalysis as he redefines Freud's essential insights through the lens of these two key terms (2020, pp. 8 and 54).

Benvenuto and Recalcati, however, urge us to consider desire and *jouissance* as intertwined, rejecting binary formulations that cast desire as

[21] Unian enjoyment [*jouissance Unien*] refers to an absolute, non-relational, self-contained form of *jouissance* that is averse to castration and severs any relation to the Other. It represents a pathological, contemporary deviation of *jouissance*, yet its core structure remains closely linked to the unary trait and the One-all-alone (Lacan 2018), since *jouissance* ultimately tends to be structurally monadic and estranged from the Other.

purely beneficial for the subject and jouissance as purely detrimental (Recalcati 2013a, p. 261) and criticising the idea that 'desiring is sublime' while 'enjoying is shameful' (Benvenuto 2020, p. 59). Conceiving of desire in relation, rather than in opposition, to *jouissance* means that it is not possible to disregard the drive and that this must be considered in conjunction with desire. They emphasise the need to integrate these two facets of Lacan's work. The clinic of anorexia and bulimia, and by extension the new symptoms, has been particularly influential in fostering a deeper understanding of the interplay between desire and *jouissance* in the clinic. This allowed them to develop a reading of Lacan that attempts to combine his earlier phase, where the symbolic and desire are at the forefront, with a later phase of his teaching where the drive, *jouissance*, and the real are predominant. Through the clinical work with patients suffering from anorexia and bulimia, Italian Lacanians explored how these conditions illustrate the complex dynamics between the unrelenting pursuit of jouissance and the indestructible significance of desire, highlighting that these Lacanian concepts are not mutually exclusive but intricately connected. These pathologies show a distorted desire—a desire for death, as in anorexia—and *jouissance*—as a devastation of the drive—that are detrimental for the subject.

This perspective, therefore, focuses on combining the dialectical nature of desire, which is oriented and determined by the Other, with the anti-dialectic, monadic nature of *jouissance*, characterised by the relentless movement of the drive that enjoys itself. The theoretical and clinical challenge for Italian Lacanians is thus to engage with the subject's real while refraining from domesticating or orienting it. This involves simultaneously thinking about the real of *jouissance* and the singular demand of desire. Desire, *jouissance*, the drive, and their relation to the real are at the heart of the Italian Lacanian theoretical perspectives on clinical practice. This relation is addressed and explored through the questions of the subject, subjectivation, and sublimation, which are key notions of Italian Lacanianism.

In his entry on the 'subject' in the *Dictionary of Lacanian Psychoanalysis*, Dylan Evans highlights that the concept of the subject 'is a distinctive feature of Lacan's work, since the term does not constitute part of Freud's theoretical vocabulary, but is more associated with philosophical, legal and linguistic discourses' (1996, p. 197). Lacan's theory of subjectivity is recognised as a groundbreaking aspect of his thought, diverging significantly from the structuralist or poststructuralist notions that famously proclaim the 'death of the subject' (Chiesa 2007, p. 6). In fact, psychoanalysis is not merely a theory of psychic functioning but fundamentally a theory of the subject (Fink 2014). 'The only material of analytic work', Lacan contends, 'is the subject' (2006, p. 53). Rather than aligning with the concept of the individual, however, the Lacanian subject introduces a fundamental dissonance within it. Etymologically, an individual is non-divided, the absence of division.[22] On the contrary, the Lacanian subject is inherently divided and split since it does not coincide with itself and its own being. For Lacan, being a subject implies subjection to the signifier and, consequently, being inherently alienated and subjected to the Other. Lacan's plea to psychoanalysts not to abandon the notion of the subject (2008, p. 89) is central for Italian Lacanians who retain and defend this category against those hegemonic discourses that today tend to abolish it (Recalcati 2012a; Benvenuto 2020).[23] Such discourses include, for instance, the biomedical model and the psychiatric approach (Lolli 2005), cognitive psychology (Tarizzo 2007, 2011), empirical sciences (Cosenza 2003; Benvenuto 2020), and capitalist discourse (Recalcati 2010).

The real can only be conceived of from the perspective of a particular subject and is strictly connected with that subject's singularity, which is uniquely manifested through the (death) drive, repetition, and their individual mode of *jouissance* (Terminio 2009; Di Ciaccia and Fasoli 2013). Inasmuch as the Lacanian real always implies a subject, the category of the real cannot be reduced to a purely speculative, mystical, or metaphysical notion (an idealist version of the real), nor is it merely a factual or empirical reality (a materialist version of the real). In Italian Lacanian clinical thought, the real is homologous to the death drive, repetition, and, ultimately, *jouissance*. These are the essential reiterations of the

[22] The word subject derives from the Latin *subiectus*, meaning subjected or subdued, while individual comes from the Latin *individuus*, meaning undivided, one, and indivisible.

[23] Similarly, the Anglophone and Slovene reception of Lacan place a significant emphasis on the subject. In *Subjects Lessons: Hegel, Lacan and the Future of Materialism* (2020), Russel Sbriglia and Slavoj Žižek focus on the subject of the real to defend the notion of the subject against various strands of new materialism and realisms.

subject's real, or rather of the symptom experienced by the subject, and, as such, constitute the very fabric of any psychoanalytic experience. Italian Lacanianism conceives of the subject first and foremost as the subject of the real, emphasising that the Lacanian real has a 'subjective stance' (Benvenuto 2020, p. 90).

Returning to the opening question of this chapter, however: how can the real of a subject in analysis be handled in a way that avoids the illusion that a correct relationship with their real exists, while also refraining from 'psychological normalization' and 'rationalizing moralization' (Lacan 1992, p. 302)? Or rather, to word this question slightly differently, how can the subject of (symbolic) desire and the subject of (real) *jouissance* be kept together? Psychoanalysis is a symbolic practice that addresses the real of *jouissance*. The drive cannot be fully sublimated; *jouissance* can be deadly when disconnected from desire; and repetition often appears to be endless and meaningless. The symbolic power of the signifier seems to be overshadowed by the untamed, disruptive force of the real qua *jouissance*, the compulsion to repeat through the death drive, and the eclipse of desire and the broken relation with the Other. Thus, the Lacanian subject is both a subject of desire and a subject of jouissance. As Recalcati writes:

> On the one hand, it is evident that the Lacanian subject no longer shares anything with the *subjectum* of classical philosophical reason, both in the sense that they appear to be hollowed out from within by an irrevocable lack (*manque à être*), and in that if there is still a substance to their being, it consists of the excess of the drive in its cogent relationship with the grasping of the signifier (*parlêtre*) and not of any form of personalistic identity of a pre-Freudian nature. Nevertheless, the problem of the subject in Lacan continues to arise precisely at the difficult juncture that connects – in a highly aporetic manner – *manque à être* and *parlêtre*, the unconscious and the drive, desire and enjoyment, the Other and the One, without this unstable relationship ever being definitively resolved in one way or another. (2021, ebook Chapter 3)

In *Vivere la pulsione*, Lolli (2022) argues that desire has been overemphasised in Italian Lacanianism, which has led to the neglect of the subject's intrinsic implication with the drive. Lolli deems the dichotomy of desire—viewed as mainly progressive and propulsive—and the drive—seen almost exclusively as regressive and self-enclosed—unconvincing. For him, the opposition between desire and the drive is unfounded and unreasonable: at the heart of desire, the drive is always at work. He underlines that, according to Lacan, there is an analogy between *jouissance* and the drive but that the two notions do not coincide. As Lolli puts it, one of the objectives of psychoanalysis is to 'allow the analysand, who is at the mercy of their symptom, to establish themselves as a subject where the drive, recruited by the symptom itself, abolished it: to experience the drive and no longer be controlled by the drive' (2022, p. 6). This refers to the end of Seminar XI, where Lacan urges the reader to 'experience the drive' (Lacan 1998, p. 273). Lolli argues that 'the satisfaction that marks the end of analysis is freed from that surplus of symptomatic jouissance' (2022, p. 237).

The real concerns the 'ethical specificity' (Benvenuto 1999) of psychoanalytic treatment, which relates to the impact of the real on the subject and their response to it. It is not just the ethics of psychoanalysis but also the ethics of the analysand. For Lacan, 'One is always responsible for one's position as a subject' (Lacan 2006, p. 729). Recalcati emphasises that the Lacanian subject entails this ethical category of responsibility. In his words, 'The subject is always responsible, in the sense that all the events that affect them acquire their meaning only through the subjective mediation that retroactively signifies them' (Recalcati 2002, p. 286). Recalcati's reading of Lacan is influenced by Jean-Paul Sartre,[24] incorporating a neo-existentialist perspective that includes a critical humanism. It accounts not simply for individualism but also for the social and historical context, emphasising desire, the ethical responsibility, the Other,

[24] Sartre often adopted a critical stance towards psychoanalysis. In *The Transcendence of the Ego* and *Being and Nothingness*, he criticises Freud for excessively emphasising the past, arguing that Freud's conception of the unconscious promotes a deterministic view of human psychic life. Unlike Italian Lacanians, such as Tarizzo (2003) and Benvenuto (2020), who downplay Sartre's influence on Lacan and point out the radical differences in their notions of desire, Recalcati emphasises the connection between Sartre and Lacan. He contrasts contemporary Lacanian trends that overlook desire, lack-of-being, the Other, and, ultimately, the concept of subject. For Recalcati, Sartre serves as a reminder that a subject, albeit subjected to the Other, is never hopelessly determined. 'We are not lumps of clay', says Sartre in *Saint Genet. Actor and Martyr*, 'and what is important is not what people make of us but what we ourselves make of what they have made of us' (2012, p. 49).

inheritance, and subjectivation. It aims to navigate the conundrum between essentialism and structuralism, a critique often directed at Lacan (Frosh 1999). Recalcati argues that Lacan avoids a reductive humanistic interpretation of the subject, contending that connecting the notion of the subject to the theory of the signifier radically empties the subject of any substantiality (2021). This is not based on the existentialist's primacy of existence over essence, but rather on the primacy of the signifier and its action on the subject. Recalcati points out that the peculiarity of Lacan's structuralism uniquely sustains both the singularity of the subject and the universality of the structure.

To be clear, the subject is not responsible for the traumatic events that occur in their life but rather for how they choose to live with them. However, Pagliardini highlights the risks associated with this perspective since overemphasising the category of responsibility could be problematic:

> [...] an existentialist interpretation of the subject's responsibility gravely risks placing an excessive emphasis on this subject, that is, inadvertently reducing it to the Ego, the person, the subject of the intention. [...] It is the logic of the signifier, with its retroactive functioning and its causal discontinuity, that implies and produces an effect, the subject, and it is this one - not a subject suddenly similar to the existentialist one - that is responsible for the effect which it is itself. (Pagliardini 2016, p. 212)

The Lacanian subject is not a predetermined or unchangeable being and is never the product of an immutable and deterministic process. The subject is deterministically shaped neither by the past nor by the Other. For, according to Lacan, human beings always have the possibility to subjectify—namely, to re-signify—and thus modify, what they have inherited from their past or their Other. Even if the subject is always shaped by their past/Other, they are not entirely determined by it. In the analytic work, the analysand reinterprets, by establishing new signifiers, the past based on their ongoing journey towards the future, and it is the prospect of the future that enables them to give new shapes and meanings to past experiences. This aspect is given particular emphasis in Italian Lacanianism, according to which the Lacanian subject thus coincides with an ever-going, never-ending process of subjectivation (Recalcati 2012a; Benvenuto 2020).

As Lolli underlines, 'Being alive and being a subject are not corresponding concepts. The genesis of subjectivity requires further work. We could say that two births are necessary for the subject to be completed: the first as a biologically living being, the second as symbolically determined' (2012, p. 50). Italian Lacanianism regards alienation and separation as significant notions for the process of subjectivation, although the Anglophone reception Lacanian theory has predominantly focused on object a and *jouissance*, paying less attention to alienation and separation (Verhaeghe 2019). Italian Lacanian thinkers explore the status of the Lacanian subject through the conceptualisation of the alienation-separation pair, or rather of that operation which, synchronically, allows the subject to subjectify itself in its being of desire. This process should not be understood as a simple progression from alienation to separation, as from an evolutionary post-Freudian perspective. Instead, alienation and separation are interconnected and do not follow a linear evolutionary path. Separation does not imply alienation as its cause. Rather, separation means a subjectivation of alienation that supposes a singular movement of assuming one's own desire, detached from identification with the signifiers and from the desire of the Other (Recalcati 2012a). The focus is on the subject-and-Other relationship. Despite the emphasis on the real, the subject is always immersed in the symbolic network and cannot escape it. Alienation entails an excessive adherence to the Other, leading to a loss of identity and desire, while separation involves a break from the Other and brings about the subject's own desire. In the new symptoms, the dialectic of alienation and separation is completely altered and polarised; alienation without separation results in homologation and a flattening onto the Other, whereas separation without alienation leads to the rejection of symbolic debts and inheritance. According to Recalcati (2010, p. 154), Lacan defines the subject as being characterised by both alienation and separation, meaning that it is inevitably linked to the signifiers that have determined and identified it and, at the same time, also undergoes a movement away from this initial identification. Thus, for Recalcati, Lacanian subjectivation is primarily a never-ending process of alienation and separation of the subject in relation to the Other. Recalcati deems alienation to be a causative moment, a way of producing the subject, which emphasises the structuring and constitutive role of Lacanian alienation (Tomšič 2015; Di Gregorio 2019).

Lacan employs various analogies to describe the condition of the subject as stemming from, and being shaped by, the Other. Italian Lacanians tend to emphasise the relationship between the subject and Other by referring to some key passages by Lacan: for instance, when he compares the subject to a ripe fruit falling from the signifying chain (Lacan 2008, p. 44), to a messenger-slave who carries the mark impressed by the Other behind their back (Lacan 2006, p. 680), or to a 'poem that is being written' (1998, p. viii), emphasising the subjected and subjugated status of the subject to the Other. Another striking passage often commented on by Italian Lacanians is the following from Seminar XXIII, where Lacan writes:

> In fact, chances push us left and right, and we make of them - because it is we who braid it - our destiny. We make of these chances our destiny, because we speak. We believe that we say what we want, but really, it is what the others wanted, more particularly our family, that speaks to us - take this *us* as a direct object. We are spoken, and because of that, we make, of the chances that push us around, a sort of weave. And indeed, there is a weft - we call that our destiny. (Lacan quoted and translated in Benvenuto 2020, p. 103)

In *Conversations with Lacan*, Benvenuto (2020) argues that Lacan captures the essence of his teaching in the excerpt quoted above and, at the same time, the challenges he faces in articulating the process of subjectivation. On the one hand, there are 'chances' that become a 'destiny', while on the other Lacan states that 'we speak' only to emphasise that, in fact, 'we are spoken'. Benvenuto's reading of this passage underlines Lacan's ambiguity. 'Are we mere readers and interpreters of the wanderings of our life', Benvenuto asks, 'or are we the authors – albeit unaware'? (pp. 103–104). There is undoubtedly a correlation between the two, which is crucial in the clinical context: 'how does the interpretation of our life that we give after the events [...] weave into the way we produce these lives of ours?' (p. 104). Benvenuto underlines that, according to Lacan, the subject's dependence on the Other is not contingent, that is, a result of historical events and evolutionary development, but rather a structural and inherent aspect of every subject. As our desire comes from the Other's desire, and therefore our unconscious too, it may seem as if humans have no choice but to accept this state of subjugation. However, the process of subjectivation provides a way for individuals to continually subjectify—or re-signify—their subjugation to the Other, which is one of the key goals of psychoanalysis that can lead to a modification in the libidinal economy of the subject, and thus to a new relationship between the latter and the real. Lacanian psychoanalysis is not aimed at an ultimate and definitive dis-alienation, which would be utterly impossible given that alienation is structural and inherent in the formation of every subject. At this point, Benvenuto legitimately questions whether Lacanian subjectivation could ultimately be 'a form of resourcefulness that merely attempts to deal with our being slaves to the Other' (p. 82). Benvenuto argues firmly that subjectivation is not about self-determination, emancipation, empowerment, or psychic maturation, nor is it a mere symbolisation of a previously un-symbolised trauma (p. 82). He claims that:

> Even if his approach remains entirely within the dimension of sense, within a theory of subjectivity [...] [Lacan] has nevertheless always insisted on something external to the subjectivity that structures it. He insisted on, bombarded us, with a cause of subjectivity and sense, which he identifies with object a, the object that causes our desire. He calls extimity [sic] that central void implied by subjective interiority. As we saw, every subjectivity, every supposed intimacy, is a going around in a torus, in a lack or void. He would give several names to this extimity [sic]: lack of being, Thing, object a, agalma, central void ... But this externality to subjectivity in Lacan will always be double-faced: on the one hand, the external is what imposes itself as the Real, and on the other, is what is real for a specific subject. (2020, p. 108)

Benvenuto rejects the idea that subjectivation should be reduced to a 'free submission to the Other' (p. 111). Consequently, he also disagrees with the reduction of psychoanalysis to an 'interpretation-based construction' or a 'historical reconstruction' (p. 107). Benvenuto considers these versions of psychoanalysis to be based on superficial conceptions of meaning and causality, respectively. He argues that Lacan attempts to avoid the narrow dichotomy between hermeneutic interpretation, which prioritises the retrieval of meaning, and scientific explanation, which centres on causality (p. 108). For Lacan, what actually links meaning and cause in the analytic practice is, as Benvenuto emphasises, the retroactive temporality (*Nachträglichkeit* in Freud and *après-coup* in Lacan) on which psychoanalysis operates (p. 109). According to Benvenuto, science relies on 'the causal *reconstruction* of processes generated in a supposedly linear temporality' (2020, p. 111), while psychoanalysis operates on a retroactive temporality.

In certain readings of Lacan, there is a significant emphasis on transforming the unknown into the known, and on humanising the impact of trauma. Benvenuto attributes this to 'Lacan's logocentrism' (p. 104), which underscores the primacy of the symbolic. Benvenuto further argues that psychoanalysis functions as a logotherapy, grounded in the belief that working through words can ultimately transform the real. From this perspective, subjectivation is equated with symbolisation of the unconscious and, therefore, the symbolic is regarded as a sort of humanising force. However, this perspective fails to fully account for the real of the drive, reducing the process to a mere symbolic operation aimed at 'taming' or 'signifying' the real. This view also overlooks the fact that the symbolic itself can be traumatic, as the inscription of the subject into the symbolic order inherently involves trauma (Benvenuto 2020; Pagliardini 2016). In fact, as Benvenuto points out, for Lacan the symbolic is the register that negatively affects the subject, stripping away aspects of their being. In Lacan's thought, 'the essential trauma is access to language' (pp. 105–106). As Benvenuto writes:

> The idea that the unconscious depends on using language is the consequence of a very precise philosophical vision: the idea that language tears us away from a sort of natural bliss. Language alienate us from nature, from our very own nature as biological beings, and exiles us from the animal world [...] Language demolishes our biological automatism, not to make us freer, but to subject us further still to the order he calls the symbolic. (p. 57)

Therefore, while the symbolic order humanises individuals by integrating them into the network of signifiers, it simultaneously introduces the dimension of death into life. Benvenuto contends that Lacan's early thought is strongly connected with the romantic tradition that regards humanity as fundamentally deficient, based on a lack of wholeness, and irremediably separated from the immediacy of life. Benvenuto argues that, in his later phase, Lacan's thinking has undergone a shift from a logocentric position underpinned by the primacy of the symbolic to a more 'realist' emphasis on the primacy of the real. As a result, the clinical practice can no longer focus solely on language or words but also needs to take into account the real of the drive.

In *The Telemachus Complex: Parents and Children after the Decline of the Father*, Recalcati (2019b) connects subjectivation with the symbolic process of *ereditare* (to inherit). He discusses the challenges faced by the young Italian generation in a post-economic crisis society, characterised by a lack of future prospects and a widespread 'loss of desire and enslavement to deadly enjoyment' (p. 5). In doing so, Recalcati explores the process of symbolic filiation, focusing on the intergenerational transmission of desire and how the subject nourishes its own desire. In order to exemplify the process of symbolic inheritance, Recalcati juxtaposes Oedipus, the Sophoclean tragic hero, and Telemachus, the mythological character of Homer's *Odyssey*. While the former ends up being stuck in a deadly conflict with his father Laius, the latter welcomes the return of Ulysses. In contrast to the Freudian Oedipus complex, which brings to the fore the dimension of conflict, rivalry, and parricidal violence amongst generations, Recalcati's concept of the Telemachus complex underlines the possibility of establishing a fruitful relation with previous generations, our own past, and ultimately with the Other from which we all originate. Recalcati links the symbolic processes of inheritance with subjectivation because they both require a resignification of the past and of all the traces and marks left on the subject by the Other.[25] He contends that symbolic inheritance:

[25] In *The Son's Secret*, Recalcati (2020b) explores the fictional characters of Oedipus and Hamlet, who were extensively discussed by both Freud and Lacan. While Oedipus lacks a complete knowledge of his past but acts nevertheless, Hamlet is aware of the truth but unable to take action. In Recalcati's view, unlike Oedipus and Hamlet, Telemachus is neither in conflict with his father nor impotent in action. He actually desires his father's return to Ithaca since Ulysses, in Recalcati's reading, embodies the 'Law of the word as the Law of desire' (2019b, p. 6) against the dissipative and deadly enjoyment embodied by Penelope's suitors. Most importantly, Telemachus does not simply wait for Ulysses' return, dwelling in nostalgic and idealised memories of his father; instead, he sets himself in motion by embarking on a journey in search of his father. Surprisingly, this key aspect of Recalcati's interpretation has been overlooked and his account of the Telemachus complex is often

> [...] coincides with existence itself, with a subjectivation of our existence that is never fully complete. We are nothing more than the stratified totality of all the traces, impressions, words and meanings that, coming from the Other, have constituted us. We cannot speak about ourselves without speaking of the Other, of all those Others who have determined, fabricated, produced, marked and fashioned our life. We are our word, but our word would not exist if it were not constituted through the word of others who have spoken to us. (2019b, p. 119)

Subjectivation, much like symbolic inheritance, is not a passive acceptance of what we have received from the Other. Instead, it is a never-ending, never-complete process that entails actively engaging with and integrating the subject's symbolic debt and provenance from the Other. Recalcati argues that subjectivation is 'the effect of a reclamation of that which has been. It is the product of a choice, of a subjective assumption of all our history that is, first and foremost, the history of the Other' (pp. 119–120). This subjective assumption necessarily implies the separation from our symbolic Other (past, origins, family, homeland, traditions) within which we are constitutively alienated:

> This is why it is necessary to be born a second time, to break with kin ('Who is my father? Who is my mother? Who are my siblings?'), to leave one's home, to uproot oneself. To be born is to kill, it is to break the shell, to lean into limitless contingency, to exist in a radical discontinuity with everything that has gone before. Inheritance as reclamation implies, therefore, a time of separation from and forgetting of the past. (p. 125)

Nevertheless, Recalcati does not conceive of subjectivation as a stubborn rejection of the symbolic debt with the Other. Rather, it entails a 'subjective movement of recovery [...] of the past that constitutes us' (p. 117), that is, a reappropriation of those signifiers—such as words and memories—that come from the Other and that moulded our identity in the first place. In simpler words, for Recalcati, subjectivation and symbolic inheritance involve an 'ever-moving reclamation' (p. 119) of

---

misunderstood as a 'nostalgia of the Name-of-the-Father' and a 'turn back toward the past' (Turner 2023, p. 209).

our constitutive 'provenance from the Other' (p. 118). Subjectivation is neither a cancellation nor a passive repetition of the past. It is neither mere 'subjection to the past without invention' nor 'freedom without ties or symbolic debt' (p. 132). In a Sartrean vein, Recalcati contends that the ethical task involved in subjectivising and inheriting the traces and marks left by the Other involves 'doing something with what has been done to us' (2022a, p. 70).[26]

Subjectivation thus implies forging a new relationship with what has determined us, and therefore a new relationship with repetition. However, for true change to occur, mere interpretation and rationalisation are not sufficient. Subjectivation must engage with the real of the drive to alter the libidinal economy of the subject. As Recalcati states, 'the aim of analysis is not to offer the subject the possibility of freeing themselves from the drive, but rather to choose it, to subjectivise it in an unprecedented way' (2016, p. 279). Symbolisation does not necessarily interrupt the circuit of repetition, which binds the subject to the imprints left by the Other. The goal of psychoanalysis is not to eradicate repetition entirely—clearly an impossible task—but rather to facilitate a subjectivised transformation that promotes a fulfilling existence. Complete healing or absolute freedom is just as unattainable as total determinism. What is needed is a variation of this repetition, an 'affirmative twist' on it, as Pagliardini (2020, p. 467) effectively puts it. This transformation involves a retroactive resignification:

> It is not the option for self-affirmation without recognizing the social ties with which our lives have been and are tied. It is never self-generation. Sartre defines it as a "small deviation" (petite décalage), and that "deviation" allows us to subjectivize, to make our own, the starting conditions for our own lives, which we haven't yet chosen. To make, therefore, something

[26] Recalcati (2012a) refers to examples from philosophy, literature, and cinema to exemplify this subject-formation process of inheriting, and relaunching to the future, the debt from the Other. For instance, he cites *The Family Idiot: Gustave Flaubert*, in which Sartre reconstructs Flaubert's biography through two poles, constitution and personalisation. Recalcati sees in these a parallel between determinism and freedom, between destiny and subjectivation. Interestingly, Recalcati also signals an overlapping between his take on Lacan's subjectivation and Malabou's neuronal plasticity, which displays 'The possibility of rewriting what has already been written - of associating traces with other traces in various ways' and this is, Recalcati claims, what 'defines the time of subjectivation' (2019a, pp. 133–134).

> of that which the Other has made of us. This is a clear way of defining the inheritance that makes us human: making our own that which we have received from the Other. If we cannot choose to be free, if we are "condemned to freedom", if we cannot avoid having to make a choice and the irrevocable nature of its obligation, then we are also the continuing possibility for a transformation of the destiny decided for us by others into a new, unexpected adventure. (Recalcati 2022a, pp. 70–71)

Recalcati's perspective here intersects with Elvio Fachinelli's concept of 'reprise'. Fachinelli categorises repetition into three distinct types: replication, which involves a mere duplication of past events; reduction, which results in an impoverished version of ourselves; and reprise, which offers the possibility of opening up to the future (Gutherz 2019). Repetition as reprise can pave the way for new developments beyond repetition (Lippi 2020). Repetition, therefore, is more than just a negative and destructive force; it is based on the potential destinies of the drive.[27] According to Recalcati, the drive can be experienced by the subject both as 'enlargement, expansion, generative enhancement of life' or as 'a restriction, coercion, closure of the possibilities of life' (2019a, p. 58). The dynamics of the drive—fixation and plasticity—are crucial in guaranteeing change.

Italian Lacanians view Lacan's concept of sublimation as the epitome of the transformative potential of the drive, contrasting it with the repetition of the symptom, which represents the subject's mode to enjoy

[27] Lacan remarks that the notion of the death drive, which is 'at the heart of analytic experience' (2007, p. 18), emerged from Freud's clinical experience and deadlocks rather than from abstract speculations (Lacan 1992, p. 28, 2007, p. 16). Unlike other Freudian concepts, such as the unconscious or the Oedipus complex, the death drive is still an 'irreducible, indigestible, unassimilable' notion (Recalcati 2010, p. 291), especially by bio-medical and neoliberal discourses that cannot conceive of a subject inherently against itself. According to Di Ciaccia and Recalcati (2000, p. 197), what is unbearable for these discourses is the idea of a destructive tendency of life-against-itself. They emphasise the radicality of a death drive that cannot be reduced simply to self-destruction or self-sabotaging but that is, rather, rooted and inherent in human life. On this point, Recalcati firmly disagrees with Žižek's reading of the death drive qua undead as this ends up being cleansed of its destructive aspect (Recalcati 2019a, p. 74). Unlike Žižek's vitalistic reading of a death drive that revolves around the 'spectral undead existence' (1999, p. 293)—which seems to refer more to the general survival of the human species than being bound to the singularity of a subject undergoing analysis—Recalcati aims to retrieve the radical Freudian roots of the death drive, what Freud calls a 'daemonic force at work' (Freud 1981, p. 35), linking it more closely to the subject.

(Terminio 2009; Lolli 2022). Lacan's sublimation involves the satisfaction of repetition while simultaneously re-elaborating the lack, leading to innovation rather than mere repetition without novelty. This is an affirmative, that is, beneficial and generative, version of repetition. For Italian Lacanians, sublimation[28] is a key concept in clinical theory as it regards the transformative aspect of the psychoanalytic process in relation to the real: it connects the biography of the analysand, the libidinal economy, and the vicissitudes of the drive. Lacan was instrumental in bringing about a shift away from the Freudian conception of sublimation, which was focused mainly on redirecting and transforming sexual impulses towards non-sexual goals, positing that, rather than being confined to artistic creation, sublimation encompasses a broader dimension. Sublimation is rooted in the relationship between the speaking being and the drive, as well as its integration into the field of language (Mazzotti 2001). In Lacan's sublimation, the drive takes centre stage as it is 'manipulated' and 'transformed'. For Lacan, sublimation is not merely one of the many possible destinies of the drive but rather 'its ultimate structure' (Di Ciaccia and Recalcati 2000, pp. 196–197). Italian Lacanians also insist on Lacan's account of sublimation as neither a defensive mechanism, as in post-Freudian psychoanalysis, nor a repression or idealisation.

[28] According to the classic Freudian definition, *Sublimierung* (sublimation) is a process that consists in diverting and channelling sexual drives towards non-sexual aims (1908, p. 187). The plasticity of the drives, their ability to change targets and objects, enables this diversion. Freudian sublimation could thus relate to artistic creations but also, more broadly, to social and scientific endeavours or religious practices. As a result, sublimation can be misunderstood as sexual abstinence or the avoidance of sex for a higher aim. However, Freud struggled to explain how the sexual drive can be satisfied without reaching its object. This is arguably the reason why he destroyed the manuscript on sublimation rather than including it in his essays on metapsychology (Gay 1988, pp. 372–374). Unlike Freud, Lacan does not link sublimation merely with the creation of an artistic artefact or a scientific discovery. In *Seminar VII* and *Seminar XI*, Lacan claims that sublimation is the 'satisfaction of the drive, without repression' (1992, p. 293, 1998, p. 165), which means that sublimation maintains its relation to the real of the drive and, as such, is not a way of eradicating or taming the drive itself. While in Freud's account, sublimation involves a redirection of the drive to a different (non-sexual) object, in Lacan what changes is not the object but its position in the structure of fantasy. In other words, for Lacan sublimation does not involve directing the drive to a different object, but rather changing the nature of the object to which the drive was already directed, that is, a 'change of object in itself', something which is made possible because the drive is 'already deeply marked by the articulation of the signifier' (Lacan 1992, p. 293).

Echoing Marcuse's concept of repressive desublimation, Recalcati contends that 'the destruction of sublimation' is a recurring aspect of the contemporary clinic of the new symptoms, in which the subject is engulfed by the real of *jouissance* and unable to channel or transform it. Recalcati claims that

> The compulsive nature of the drive-related practices (*pratiche pulsionali*) associated with addictions hinders the possibility of sublimation as a plastic movement of the drive that can surround the void left by the lost object. In the new symptoms, the void is blocked, and the plasticity of the drive is reduced to an inert fixation of enjoyment without any margin of movement. (2019a, p. 140)

In *Family Complexes,* Lacan discusses the 'stagnation of sublimation' being 'the essence of psychosis' (1938, p. 64), identifying it as a symbolic deficiency. Sublimation represents a possibility for the subject to achieve a satisfaction without repression. For instance, a bulimic patient who joins a choir instead of devouring food and vomiting still engages the oral drive, but in a displaced manner. This process is akin to the subjectivation that occurs during analysis. Sublimation is the paradigm, *par excellence*, for dealing with the real and for subjectivation, as it channels the drive and transforms the subject's real (Terminio 2009; Recalcati 2012a). Similarly, Lolli regards sublimation as the convergence of desire and the drive. According to Di Ciaccia and Fasoli, at the end of an analysis there is a new alliance between the subject and the drive (2013, p. 41).

Recalcati conceptualises the drive as an energetic force, while symbolic desire serves as its form. He argues that 'sublimation is not a defensive idealisation or a negation of the drive, but a way of providing a social and symbolic form to the (formless) force of the drive' (2012a, p. 149). This process of subjectivation, reactivated in analysis, is aimed at 'integrating the acephalous thrust of the drive with the singular dimension of desire' (Recalcati 2012a, p. 323). At the core of Lacanian sublimation is the idea that 'the libidinal fixation can be subjectified in the plasticity of the drive' (Recalcati 2012a, p. 323), and that 'making enjoyment converge with desire means subjectively translating the force [of the drive] into a new form' (Recalcati 2012a, p. 323). For Recalcati, sublimation involves giving the force of the drive a new form. In psychosis,

> The force of the drive remains delocalised, invading the subject abusively; it remains formless, not converted into a form. In neurosis, on the other hand, we find form without force. The force of desire is hindered by the crystallised form of the ego. [...] How to reconnect force with form is the problem of psychotic substitution. How to reconnect form – the narcissistic image of the ego – with the force of desire is the problem of neurosis. (Recalcati 2012a, p. 321)

Recalcati emphasises the morphogenetic action of the imaginary and the symbolic towards the real, which he interprets as a 'formalising' component in his reading of Lacan. He argues that this process is not simply about re-signifying the drive but about giving this force a new form. Sublimation, in Recalcati's view, represents the ultimate model of libidinal change and subjective transformation.

In Seminar XII, Lacan addresses the experience of conversion, closely associating desire and drive from an ethical perspective. He states that

> If to be a psychoanalyst is a responsible position, the most responsible of all because he is the one to whom there is entrusted the operation of a radical ethical conversion, the one that introduces the subject to the order of desire, which orders everything that is involved in my teaching as regards historical retrospection, trying to situate the traditional philosophical position, showing you that this order has remained in a way excluded from it. (1964, p. 227)

Recalcati and Benvenuto both view subjectivation and sublimation as the epitome of this conversion of the drive, a concept originally used by Freud (Phillips 2021). They employ the concept of conversion to explain the transformative process that occurs in a successful analysis. This process does not aim to domesticate the real or adapt the analysand to the reality of their surroundings, nor is sublimation merely the channelling of drives into socially acceptable activities. Instead, conversion offers a more effective theoretical framework for understanding the engagement with the subject's real in analysis. Benvenuto refers to this as an 'analytic conversion' (1999), while Recalcati specifically describes it as the 'conversion' of the drive into desire (2020a). This concept unites the two terms, affirming the fundamental importance of the drive alongside the generative power of desire. Touching the real in analysis, Recalcati contends, 'consists in establishing a relationship between desire and the drive' (2020a, p. 41). The aim of analysis is thus to achieve 'an unprecedented desire', a desire 'not subordinate to the demand of the Other and no longer separated from *jouissance*' (2023, p. 196).

Recalcati's perspective does not separate desire from the real. In fact, he emphasises that desire is intrinsically connected to the real. Recalcati argues that advancing Lacan's legacy today requires moving beyond the classical, scholastic Lacanianism, which idealises desire and the symbolic order, without dismissing the drive. He advocates for an approach that integrates both the real and the symbolic, asserting that this conversion is not an escape from the real but an ethical engagement with it. For Recalcati, the ethics of desire must necessarily include the real. As he explains:

> The ethics of psychoanalysis aims to defend the relationship between desire and the real as impossible, without giving in to any rhetoric of liberation. Desire, defined by Freud as "indestructible," is not what needs to be liberated, but rather, that which cannot be bypassed. In this sense, desire is related to the real. The thickness, density, and opacity of desire derive precisely from its inescapability. Moving away from one's own desire sterilises life, crushing it under the weight of a superegoic renunciation. (2007, p. 64)

Sublimation addresses the issue of the singular realisation of desire, which is why the subject's capacity to sublimate can be seen as one of the outcomes of analysis. For sublimation to occur, however, some form of realisation is required. Lacan poses the question: 'What does it mean to realize your desire?' (2019b, p. 412). Recalcati argues that the ethics of desire coincides with an ethics of the act (2020a, p. 162), suggesting that psychoanalysis aims to make desire possible as an active pursuit (2020a, p. 164). Realising one's desire, for Recalcati, means producing something, and thus making desire possible as a creation.

In Seminar VII, Lacan explicitly links sublimation to the real. Lacan claims that two barriers protect and separate human beings from the real: the Good, which is central to ethics, and Beauty, which is key to aesthetics. This is why he affirms that sublimation is 'situated somewhere between a Freudian ethics and a Freudian aesthetics' (1992, p. 159) and must 'be articulated from the point of view of the location of man in relation to the real' (1992, p. 11). For Lacan, both the ethics and aesthetics of psychoanalysis are inseparable from the subject's relationship with the real. By rethinking the ethics of psychoanalysis, Lacan also lays the foundation for an aesthetics of psychoanalysis that revolves around the real (see Chap. 5). The aim is to emancipate the ethics of psychoanalysis from the imaginary dimension of any ideals and to release psychoanalytic practice from potentially harmful 'analytical ideals' (Lacan 1992, p. 8), such as those of love or authenticity. An ethics grounded in the real does not hinge on universally valid rules aimed at achieving a supposed universal happiness, a supreme good, or any other ideal. Rather, it constitutes an 'ethics of the singular' (De Kesel 2009, p. 9) or an 'ethics of the subject'. As Chiesa argues, 'The ethics of psychoanalysis is nothing but an ethic of the real, an ethics of the real desire of the subject who necessarily confronts himself with *jouissance*' (2007, p. 168).

In conclusion, Italian Lacanianism advances an affirmative approach to the real, whether this affirmation demands a confrontation with the subject's singular desire and *jouissance* (Benvenuto 2020; Lippi 2020; Recalcati 2020a; Terminio 2020), experiencing the drive (Lolli 2022), or even the pure affirmation of the real itself (Pagliardini 2020). Italian Lacanians position psychoanalysis as an active and transformative engagement with the subject's real. As Silvia Lippi poignantly argues:

> Psychoanalysis neither valorizes nor devalorizes the suffering of the symptom; instead, it attempts to transform it into the motor of creativity, to convert it into acts, desiring acts: subjective potentiality, power to exist, joy, enjoyment. The decision of desire is an invitation to enjoyment, a certain enjoyment that plays with its impossibility, which is to say with castration. (2020, p. 175)

This encapsulates the core contribution of Italian Lacanianism: the insistence on an active, creative, and affirmative engagement with the real, one that seeks not to deny its challenges but to channel its potential.

In Treatment

As discussed in Chap. 2, postmillennial Italy has witnessed a resurgence of interest in Lacanian psychoanalysis, which has featured prominently in numerous scholarly publications, cultural events, public lectures, as well as newspaper and magazine articles. This increase in cultural and media products has brought talking therapies into the public domain, breaking down the stigma surrounding mental illness. The Italian television series *In Treatment* (Costanzo 2013–2017) provides an example of the popularisation of psychoanalysis in the Italian media. *In Treatment* is the Italian adaptation of the homonymous American series by HBO, originally aired between 2008 and 2010 and relaunched in 2021 (Garcia 2008–2021). The American version, in turn, is a remake of the Israeli series *BeTipul* (Levi 2005–2008), which has been adapted into several other languages.[29] This makes the television series rather peculiar due to its 'complex structure of international origin, adaptation, and subsequent international distribution' (Bainbridge 2014, p. 48).

Overall, the Italian version remains faithful to the American series in terms of its plot, which revolves around Giovanni Mari, a psychotherapist in his fifties who practises in Rome, and the lives of his patients. After many years of clinical practice, Giovanni struggles with his patients due to issues in his own private life, and in order to better cope with these difficulties he seeks the help of his former supervisor, Anna. The series explores the intimate and private relationship between the therapist and his patients, depicting their journey over the course of weeks, months, and sometimes, years. Thus, *In Treatment* offers a twofold 'voyeuristic opportunity' (Bainbridge 2014, p. 56) for viewers to witness a therapy session unfold in the intimate space of the consulting room while also observing the private life of the psychotherapist. The series is structured

[29] The original Israeli television drama *BeTipul* was conceived by Hagai Levi and has been adapted for multiple countries and into multiple languages. The first and most renowned adaptation is the American version but other adaptations of *In Treatment* have also been made in Romania, the Czech Republic, Serbia, Slovenia, the Netherlands, Argentina, Brazil, Portugal, Japan, Croatia, Russia, and Italy. The first season of the Italian adaptation was broadcasted from April to May 2013 on Sky Cinema 1, while the second and third seasons aired, respectively, from November 2015 to January 2016 and from March to May 2017 on Sky Atlantic.

in a modular way, with each season consisting of seven weeks and five episodes per week. Four episodes focus on a therapy session with one of Mari's patients, while the fifth episode shows Giovanni meeting with his supervisor to discuss his work and personal life. The episodes were aired daily at the same time, with the patient sessions broadcasted from Monday to Thursday and the supervisor meetings on Friday. The aim of this format was to reproduce the regularity of therapeutic sessions while making them more digestible for a television audience.

Despite dealing with universal themes of love, sex, death, and the full spectrum of human emotions, *In Treatment* is inherently bounded to the specific language and culture of the country in which it broadcasted. Its characters are deeply rooted in their national contexts and convey the predominant traits of the country being depicted. This is why the series was adapted in several languages since dubbing or subtitling would simply not have sufficed to faithfully convey the inner worlds of the patients and their therapy sessions. As a result, some storylines were modified completely to make them suitable for the local audience. For instance, Dario, a *carabiniere* who fights *'ndrangheta*, the Italian mafia based in the Calabria region, is the counterpart of the Israeli army officer featured in *Be Tipul* and the African-American navy pilot in the HBO show. As a male undercover police officer fighting the mafia, Dario adheres more closely to the Italian context and reiterates the stereotype of Italian masculinity seen in mafia movies. Another case of national adaptation can be found in Irene, who must grapple with the chauvinistic traits of Italian society in which marriage and motherhood are often still viewed as obligations rather than individual choices. The third series features Padre Riccardo, a Catholic priest who is losing his faith in God. Given Italy's Catholic roots, he presents an opportunity to explore the conflict between religious traditions and secularity in contemporary Italy.

It is not surprising that *In Treatment*, which portrays patients dealing with panic attacks, eating disorders, and addictions—ailments that Italian Lacanianism extensively explores in its investigation of the discontent of contemporary society—received significant attention from Italian Lacanian scholars and analysts (Bianchi 2013; Recalcati 2013b). Most importantly, the show effectively portrays how these fictional patients deal with their past traumas, self-sabotaging or compulsive behaviours, and their determination to undermine their own therapy. From a Lacanian perspective, the persistence of certain disruptive or life-threatening behaviours in these patients is manifestations of *jouissance*. A Lacanian reading thus illustrates how *In Treatment* can be seen as an attempt not simply to portray therapy as realistically as possible but to depict the real of a particular patient and their own experience of *jouissance*. For instance, the patient may face an obstacle that prevents them from continuing a romantic relationship, a job, or their daily routine, and which also affects their speech and behaviour in the consulting room. Far from being a deadly encounter with the real as trauma or death, this encounter is instead a disturbing experience with the real of their own *jouissance*. As we have seen in this chapter, the real is the innermost core of the subject, yet it remains beyond their mastery. Since the real is heterogeneous to meaning, irreducible, and resistant to psychoanalytic interpretations, any televisual or cinematic depiction of analysis faces the same challenge: depicting the real of the subject which escapes language and representation. *In Treatment* manages to do this well in part, but it also fails in that it provides a very diluted version of psychoanalysis, which is one of a number of limitations of the Italian TV series.

Pietro Bianchi (1), who has written extensively on Lacan and cinema, ascribes the success of the series particularly to the primacy of dialogue over action. Soundtrack music is usually absent, which heightens the focus on the dialogue, pauses, and silences in the room. The episodes of the show are shot mostly in one take, allowing viewers to experience the dynamics of an entire therapy session without any interruption. This conveys a sense of realism and evolution in the stories beautifully. As Bianchi notes, however, the show misses the most crucial aspect of psychoanalysis, that is, the unconscious. Undoubtedly, the unconscious is the most complex and challenging concept in psychoanalysis to understand and portray, especially in a visual medium like television. The analytic experience emphasises speech over the visual field. As Lacan claims, 'We only grasp the unconscious finally when it is explicated, in that part of it which is articulated by passing into words' (1992, p. 32). Conveying the intricacies of the unconscious in a screen adaptation is a formidable task, which *In Treatment*, despite its best efforts, falls short of accomplishing. Therefore, I can only partially agree with Ankhi Mukherjee's claim that *In Treatment* explores the traditional themes of psychoanalysis (2014, p. 236).

In the series, the analyst and his patients look at each other when they speak, thus portraying a symmetrical relationship between two egos and creating a specular dynamic where the egos of the analyst and patient are reflected back to each other (Bianchi 2013). Psychoanalysis is not a reciprocal conversation but rather an asymmetric relationship between the analyst and the analysand. The psychoanalyst's silence allows the analysand to pay more attention to their own words, as if they were spoken by a stranger, underscoring that the psychoanalytic relationship is not about mere empathy or mutual understanding. In psychoanalysis, words are not used to represent reality, but rather to dig a hole in it (Bianchi 2013, para. 6). *In Treatment*, which centres on the dialogue between therapist and patient in the typical shot-reverse shot cinematographic dialectic that underpins communication, cannot fully capture this asymmetrical dimension of psychoanalysis. Psychoanalytic communication breaks with intersubjectivity and, as a result, the patient lies down on the couch to speak, without anyone nodding to their words (Bianchi 2013, para. 8).[30] Why is the presence of the couch so important for the psychoanalytic process? In *Lacan and Cinema*, Bianchi contends that

> The couch embodies one of the very few rigid rules of psychoanalysis in a field where – especially in the Lacanian community – almost nothing is regulated or planned in advance. The devaluation of the face-to-face relationship between analysand and analyst relies precisely on the pivotal role that language embodies in the formations of the unconscious. Given that in a speech act the other person is not only an addressee of an abstract communication of a content but is first and foremost an instance that joins

[30] *In Treatment* also received criticism from non-Lacanian Italian psychoanalysts. For instance, the Bionian psychoanalysts Antonino Ferro and Giuseppe Civitarese argue that the show depicts 'a therapy of the superficial', which is well explained for those unfamiliar with the world of psychoanalysis, but it lacks any exploration of the 'deeper', unconscious aspects of the patients. In essence, the therapy portrayed in the series deals only with surface-level emotional states, using rationality to reveal the weak or obscure points of the patient' speech (2013, para. 1). Ferro and Civitarese view the show's emphasis on 'confrontation' (2013, para. 3) between the therapist and patient as diverging from the psychoanalytic model, which posits that transformation is attained through the collaborative processing of unconscious thought.

> together an Ego with the signified of his or her own signifiers, the very form of this verbal exchange must be radically put into question. […] the subject of the unconscious is not something that exists in the depth of a human being's soul, it is rather created by a psychoanalytic act. It is nothing more than a supposition, quite far from a substantial entity that could be dissected and analysed by a specific discipline according to the model of the empirical sciences. *The subject of the unconscious is co-extensive with the interrogation regarding it.* (2017, p. 44) [original emphasis]

Instead, the show reduces the practice of psychoanalysis to a mere chit-chat, portraying it as a therapeutic dialogue between two people sitting face to face with one another. Consequently, the essential psychoanalytic experience, which enables the patient to confront the real as a disquieting encounter with their unconscious, is simply eluded. The patients in the show rarely engage in free associations or discuss their dreams. Rather, the focus is on the conscious mind and rational ego of both the therapist and the patients.

Moreover, Giovanni Mari frequently provides articulate explanations for his patients' behaviour, offering an extensive clarification of his views. In this way, however, psychoanalytic interpretations are mistakenly reduced to mere speculations or, at the very best, to rational elucidations. The series thus depicts interpretations in a rather superficial way as a mere decoding of the patient's behaviours and words. Psychoanalytic interpretation differs radically from attempts to uncover the supposed inner truth of a subject. As Lacan contends, interpretation is not a hermeneutics (1998, p. 8). In fact, as Mario Perniola contends, in Lacanian-oriented analytic work, 'the interpretive activity consists, precisely, in making the real come out of its irreducible singularity and placing it within a process' (2004, p. 9). Since the processes of understanding and uncovering meaning partake of the order of the imaginary, this can represent an obstacle to the psychoanalytic process. Mari's interpretations attempt to turn radical Otherness and the unfamiliar into something familiar, which often results in a defensive response by the patient. From a Lacanian perspective, psychoanalytic interpretations should not provide meanings, which could prove reassuring for the analysand and prevent change as a form of rationalisation. Rather, they should push the patient to confront something that is destabilising and still unknown. They should promote a radical reconfiguration of the subject's relationship with the real of their *jouissance*.

As witnessed by the patients depicted in the series, the encounter with the real is always unexpected. As an example, in the first season, the police officer Dario is taken aback by his sudden inability to return to his normal life after undergoing a traumatic experience. He is haunted by a murder he was forced to commit while working undercover in Germany. When he visits Mari's consulting room, he struggles to find the words to describe the traumatic experience and to understand its impact on his personal life. Similarly, Alice, a teenage girl with suicidal tendencies, has a hard time making sense of her self-destructive behaviour, which interferes with her passion for classical dance and her ability to succeed in the field. In the second season, Guido, a successful and confident businessman, is shaken by the unexpected panic attacks that disrupt his life and prevent him from fully committing to his work and family. The attacks make no sense to him, and he cannot fathom why he is experiencing them at this particular point in his life. In line with other new symptoms, they do not appear to be a cyphered message of the unconscious like classic Freudian symptoms. Instead, they manifest themselves as the pure and meaningless real that disrupts the subject, a sort of 'libidinal clogging' (Recalcati 2011, p. 36) which cripples patients and which they struggle to articulate. Psychoanalytic practice, which relies on the symbolic dimension of speech, can modify the way in which the subject enjoys, which refers to their relationship with *jouissance*. Ultimately, the goal of Lacanian psychoanalysis is to help the subject establish a new relationship with their real, one that goes beyond their current state of suffering (Pagliardini 2016, p. 10).

Nevertheless, Recalcati emphasises a significant difference among psychoanalytic approaches when dealing with the real in the clinic. He notes that:

> [...] those who insist on placing the experience of the real as the limit of representation, as something not yet thought, as an internal difficulty of

> symbolic thought in ordering the chaos related to it (the Bionian-Winnicottian strand), and those who instead isolate the real as an experience of malign *jouissance*, bound to the power of repetition (the death drive), which structurally manifests itself as a force that cannot be managed by symbolic power (the Lacanian strand). (2010, p. 149)

There is always a residue of the real, since *jouissance* is not a substance that can be removed and repetition cannot be completely nullified. As previously discussed, Italian Lacanians emphasise instead the need to channel *jouissance* and transform the compulsion to repeat into something generative for the subject. Despite certain limitations, *In Treatment* effectively conveys that the core of psychoanalytic work rests on the unique singularity of the subject (Recalcati 2013b, para. 2), which is not tied to universal ontological properties but is rooted in the specific vicissitudes of the drive. Psychoanalysis is not about fitting the subject into an existing reality or rehabilitating them into the consumerist cycle. Instead, the series provides a glimpse of what happens in a psychoanalytic encounter with the real within the consulting room. It shows the patient's relationship with their symptoms and enjoyment, and how they interact with the psychoanalyst and the setting.

In our society populated by subjects without unconscious, as Recalcati would put it, is not surprising that a TV series turned the unconscious into a show (Recalcati 2013b) and that the traditional psychoanalytic setting, with its iconic couch, has lost its power. The depiction of psychoanalysis in *In Treatment* is aligned with our times, which are marked by a widespread repudiation of the unconscious and a dismissal of its symbolic dynamics, as discussed in this chapter. *In Treatment* seems to draw more from a counselling paradigm than from a psychoanalytic one. It incorporates the psychodynamic components of psychoanalysis but ultimately rejects the pivotal notion of the unconscious. This is a widespread attitude in the contemporary approach to mental health, which often neglects the importance of exploring the subject's experience. Our culture urges individuals to rehabilitate themselves as quickly as possible to re-enter the consumerist cycle by removing or fixing their symptoms. Conversely, psychoanalysis challenges this view and invites individuals to confront themselves, representing an alternative to the prevailing trend.

Under the capitalist discourse, people are intolerant of failure and reliance on others, since the discourse promotes the fantasy of self-sufficient, self-reliant, undivided individuals, emphasising individualism, self-help, self-made success, quick fixes, efficiency, and measurability. Psychoanalysis opposes such a discourse; it does not work instrumentally and represents a resistance of the subject against scientism and capitalism. This is the political core of Italian Lacanianism that I will discuss in the next chapter.

Bibliography

2013. *Jonas. Dieci anni. Psicoanalisi applicata, clinica e legami.* Milan: Et al./Edizioni.

Aguirre, Maria-Cristina. 2011. Bulimia, Anxiety and the Demand of the Other. In *Lacan and Addiction. An Antology*, ed. Yael Goldman Baldwin, Kareen Malone, and Thomas Svolos, 177–185. London: Karnac.

Bainbridge, Caroline. 2014. Psychotherapy on the Couch: Exploring the Fantasies of *In Treatment*. In *Television and Psychoanalysis. Psycho-Cultural Perspectives*, ed. Caroline Bainbridge, Ivan Ward, and Candida Yates, 47–65. London: Karnac.

Barbetta, Pietro. 2019. Psychoanalysis in Milan in the Age of Dis-alienation: The Case of Elvio Fachinelli. In *The Years of Alienation in Italy: Factory and Asylum Between the Economic Miracle and the Years of Lead*, ed. Alessandra Diazzi and Alvise Sforza Tarabochia, 155–172. Basingstoke: Palgrave.

Benvenuto, Sergio. 1997. Italy and Psychoanalysis. *Journal of European Psychoanalysis.* http://www.psychomedia.it/jep/number5/benvenuto.htm. Accessed 18 October 2020.

Benvenuto, Sergio. 1999. "Eyes Wide Shut". Does Psychoanalysis Have Contact with the Real? *Journal of European Psychoanalysis* 8–9:43–66.

Benvenuto, Sergio. 2009. Introduction. In *In Freud's Tracks Conversations from the Journal of European Psychoanalysis*, ed. Sergio Benvenuto and Anthony Molino, 11–24. Plymouth: Jason Aronson.

Benvenuto, Sergio. 2020. *Conversations with Lacan: Seven Lectures for Understanding Lacan*. London: Routledge.

Bianchi, Pietro. 2013. *Psicoanalisi e racconto: In Treatment*. http://www.leparole-elecose.it/?p=9821. Accessed 30 July 2024.

Bianchi, Pietro. 2017. *Jacques Lacan and Cinema: Imaginary, Gaze, Formalisation*. London: Routledge.

Braumstein, Néstor A. 2003. Desire and Jouissance in the Teachings of Lacan. In *The Cambridge Companion to Lacan*, ed. Jean-Michel Rabaté, 102–115. Cambridge: Cambridge University Press.

Braunstein, Néstor. 2020. *Jouissance. A Lacanian Concept*. Translated by Silvia Rosman. Albany: SUNY Press.

Britton, Howard. 2004. Contemporary Symptoms and the Challenge of Psychoanalysis. *Journal for Lacanian Studies* 2 (1): 54–62.

Busiol, Diego, ed. 2022. *Lacanian Psychoanalysis in Practice. Insights from Fourteen Psychoanalysts*. London: Routledge.

Chiesa, Lorenzo. 2007. *Subjectivity and Otherness. A Philosophical Reading of Lacan*. Cambridge, MA: MIT Press.

Cosenza, Domenico. 2003. Appendice. Lacan e il postmoderno. Disincanto, decostruzione e vocazione costruttiva della psicoanalisi. In *L'antifilosofia di Jacques Lacan*, ed. Jorge Alemán, 167–175. Milan: Franco Angeli.

Cosenza, Domenico. 2023. *A Lacanian Reading of Anorexia*. London: Routledge.

Cosenza, Domenico, Massimo Recalcati, and Angelo Villa. 2006. *Civiltà e disagio. Forme contemporanee della psicopatologia*. Milan: Bruno Mondadori.

Cottet, Serge. 1997. Gai savoir et triste vérité. *La Cause Freudienne* 35.

Danto, Elizabeth Ann. 2005. *Freud's Free Clinics: Psychoanalysis and Social Justice, 1918–1938*. New York: Columbia University Press.

De Kesel, Marc. 2009. *Eros and Ethics. Reading Jacques Lacan's Seminar VII*. Albany, NY: SUNY Press.

Dean, Tim. 2000. *Beyond Sexuality*. Chicago: University of Chicago Press.

Di Ciaccia, Antonio, and Massimo Recalcati. 2000. *Jacques Lacan. Un insegnamento sul sapere dell'inconscio*. Milan: Bruno Mondadori.

Di Ciaccia, Antonio, and Domenico Fasoli. 2013. *«Io, la verità, parlo». Lacan clinico. Saggio-conversazione*. Rome: Alpes.

Di Gregorio, Luca. 2019. From the Factory to the Asylum…and Back: A Lacanian Perspective on the Cinematic Representation of Alienation in Elio Petri's *La classe operaia va in paradiso*. In *The Years of Alienation in Italy: Factory and Asylum Between the Economic Miracle and the Years of Lead*, ed. Alessandra Diazzi and Alvise Sforza Tarabochia, 173–190. Basingstoke: Palgrave.

Di Martino, Loredana. 2016. Rebuilding Ethical Desire in the Era of Narcissistic Jouissance: The Reinvention of Fatherhood in Antonio Scurati's *Il padre infedele. Italian Studies.* 71 (1): 128–147.

Diazzi, Alessandra. 2021. Care or Control? Psychology and Psychoanalysis in Italian Factories. In *Italian Industrial Literature and Film: Perspectives on the*

Representation of Postwar Labor, ed. Carlo Baghetti, Jim Carter, and Lorenzo Marmo, 119–135. Oxford: Peter Lang.

Dolar, Mladen. 2006. *A Voice and Nothing More*. Cambridge, MA: MIT Press.

Evans, Dylan. 1996. *An Introductory Dictionary of Lacanian Psychoanalysis*. London: Routledge.

Eyers, Tom. 2012. *Lacan and the Concept of the Real*. London: Palgrave Macmillan.

Feher Gurewich, Judith. 1999. The New Disorders of the Unconscious. In *Lacan and the New Wave in American Psychoanalysis. The Subject and the Self*, ed. Judith Feher Gurewich, Michel Tort, and Susan Fairfield. New York: Other Press.

Ferro, Antonino, and Giuseppe Civitarese. 2013. Commento della prima puntata italiana. http://www.spiweb.it/cinema-serie-tv/592-in-treatment-serie-italiana-marzo-2013/opinioni-a-confronto/3111-primapuntata-italiana-un-primo-commento-da-antonino-ferro. Accessed 22 August 2016.

Fink, Bruce. 1995. *The Lacanian Subject. Between Language and Jouissance*. Princeton: Princeton University Press.

Fink, Bruce. 2013. Translator's Note'. In *On the Names-of-the-Father*, ed. Jacques Lacan, 98–105. Cambridge: Polity.

Fink, Bruce. 2014. *Against Understanding, Volume 1. Commentary and Critique in a Lacanian Key*. London: Routledge.

Fiumanò, Marisa. 2010. *L'inconscio è il sociale. Desiderio e godimento nella contemporaneità*. Milan: Bruno Mondadori.

Focchi, Marco. 2022. Panic as a phenomenon of modernity. In *Lacanian Psychoanalysis in Practice: Insights from Fourteen Psychoanalysts*, ed. Diego Busiol, 155–164. London: Routledge.

Freda, Francisco Hugo. 2001. *Psicoanalisi e tossicomania*. Milan: Bruno Mondadori.

Freud, Sigmund. 1908. "Civilized" Sexual Morality and Modern Nervous Illness. In *The Standard Edition of the Complete Psychological Works of Sigmund Freud*, vol. 9, 177–204. London: Hogarth Press & The Institute of Psycho-Analysis.

Freud, Sigmund. 1981 [1920]. Beyond the Pleasure Principle. In *The Standard Edition of the Complete Psychological Works of Sigmund Freud*, Vol. 18, 1–64. London: Hogarth Press & The Institute of Psycho-Analysis.

Frosh, Stephen. 1999. *The Politics of Psychoanalysis. An Introduction to Freudian and post-Freudian Theory*. Basingstoke: Macmillan.

Gay, Peter. 1988. *Freud. A Life for Our Time*. New York: W.W. Norton & Company.

Gherovici, P. 2011. Bulimia between phobia and addiction. In *Lacan and Addiction. An Antology*, ed. Yael Goldman Baldwin, Kareen Malone, and Thomas Svolos, 93–109. London: Karnac.

Green, André. 1986 [1996]. *On Private Madness*. London: Karnac.

Greenshields, Will. 2021. An Insoluble Enigma? On Lacan's Dissolution. *Angelaki* 26 (6): 111–127.

Gutherz, David. 2019. On Not Getting What You Want: Elvio Fachinelli's Anti-authoritarianism. *Psychoanalysis and History* 21 (3): 267–291.

Han, Byung-Chul. 2015. *The Burnout Society*. Translated by Erik Butler. Stanford: Stanford Briefs.

Kernberg, Otto. 1975 [2000]. *Borderline Conditions and Pathological Narcissism*. New York: Jason Aronson.

Kristeva, Julia. 1995. *New Maladies of the Soul*. New York: Columbia University Press.

Lacan, Jacques. 1938. *The Family Complexes in the Formation of the Individual*. Translated by Cormac Gallagher, Unpublished.

Lacan, Jacques. 1964. *The Seminar of Jacques Lacan, Book XII, 1964–1965 Crucial Problems for Psychoanalysis*. http://www.lacaninireland.com/web/wp-content/uploads/2010/06/12-Crucial-problems-for-psychoanalysis.pdf. Accessed 23 June 2021.

Lacan, Jacques. 1990. *Television: A Challenge to the Psychoanalytic Establishment*. Translated by Joan Copjec and Edited by Denis Hollier, Rosalind Krauss, Annette Michelson, and Jeffrey Mehlmen. London and New York: W. W. Norton.

Lacan, Jacques. 1992. *The Ethics of Psychoanalysis. The Seminar of Jacques Lacan, Book VII, 1959–1960*. Translated by Dennis Porter and Edited by Jacques-Alain Miller. London: Routledge.

Lacan, Jacques. 1997. *The Psychoses. The Seminar of Jacques Lacan, Book III, 1955–1956*. Translated by Russell Grigg. London: W.W. Norton & Co.

Lacan, Jacques. 1998. *The Four Fundamental Concepts of Psychoanalysis. The Seminar of Jacques Lacan, Book XI, 1963–1964*. Translated by Alan Sheridan and Edited by Jacques-Alain Miller. London and New York: W.W. Norton.

Lacan, Jacques. 2005. Intervento al IX congresso dell'EFP 6–9 luglio 1978. *La psicoanalisi* 38.

Lacan, Jacques. 2006. *Écrits. The First Complete Edition in English*. Translated by Bruce Fink in Collaboration with Héloïse Fink and Russell Grigg. London and New York: W.W. Norton.

Lacan, Jacques. 2007. *The Other Side of Psychoanalysis. The Seminar of Jacques Lacan, Book XVII, 1969–1970.* Translated by Russell Grigg and Edited by Jacques-Alain Miller. London and New York: W.W. Norton.

Lacan, Jacques. 2008. *My Teaching.* Translated by David Macey. London: Verso.

Lacan, Jacques. 2013. *The Triumph of Religion.* Translated by Bruce Fink. Cambridge: Polity Press.

Lacan, Jacques. 2014. *Anxiety. The Seminar of Jacques Lacan, Book X, 1962–1963.* Translated by Adrian Price. and ed. Jacques-Alain Miller. Cambridge: Polity Press.

Lacan, Jacques. 2015 [1974]. Freud Forever: An Interview with *Panorama.* Translated by Philip Dravers. Hurly-Burly 12: 13–21.

Lacan, Jacques. 2016. *The Sinthome. The Seminar of Jacques Lacan, Book XXIII, 1975–1976.* Translated by Adrian Price and ed. Jacques-Alain Miller. Cambridge: Polity Press.

Lacan, Jacques. 2018. *…or Worse. The Seminar of Jacques Lacan, Book XIX, 1971–1972.* Translated by Adrian Price and ed. Jacques-Alain Miller. Cambridge: Polity Press.

Lacan, Jacques. 2019a. The Third. Translated by Philip Dravers. *The Lacanian Review* 9: 83–109.

Lacan, Jacques. 2019b. *Desire and Its Interpretation. The Seminar of Jacques Lacan, Book VI, 1958–1959.* Translated by Bruce Fink and Edited by Jacques-Alain Miller. Cambridge: Polity Press.

Lacan, Jacques. 2020. *The Object Relation. The Seminar of Jacques Lacan, Book IV, 1956–1957.* Translated by Adrian Price and Edited by Jacques-Alain Miller. London: Polity Press.

Leader, Darian. 2002. *Stealing the Mona Lisa. What Art Stops Us from Seeing.* New York: Counterpoint.

Leader, Darian. 2021. *Jouissance: Sexuality, Suffering and Satisfaction.* Cambridge: Polity Press.

Lebrun, Jean-Pierre. 1997. *Un monde sans limite. Essai pour une clinique psychanalytique du social.* Toulouse: Erès.

Leoni, Federico. 2016. *Jacques Lacan. L'economia dell'assoluto.* Naples: Orthotes.

Lippi, Silvia. 2020. *The decision of desire.* Translated by Peter Skafish. Minneapolis: University of Minnesota Press.

Lolli, Franco. 2005. *L'ombra della vita. Psicoanalisi della depressione.* Milan: Bruno Mondadori.

Lolli, Franco. 2012. *L'epoca dell'inconshow. Dimensione clinica e scenario sociale del fenomeno borderline.* Milan: Mimesis.

Lolli, Franco. 2019. *Inattualità della psicoanalisi. L'analista e i nuovi domandanti.* Alberobello: Poiesis.

Lolli, Franco. 2022. *Vivere la pulsione. Saggio sulla soddisfazione in psicoanalisi.* Naples: Orthotes.

Malabou, Catherine. 2009. *What Should We Do with Our Brain?* Translated by Sebastian Rand. New York: Fordham University Press.

Maleval, Jean-Claude. 2000. *La Forclusion du nom-du-père: Le Concept et sa clinique.* Paris: Seuil.

Mazzotti, Maurizio. 2001. Introduzione. In *Stili della sublimazione. Usi psicoanalitici dell'arte*, ed. Maurizio Mazzotti, 7–13. Franco Angeli: Milan.

McDougall, Joyce. 1989. *Theatres of the Body. A Psychoanalytic Approach to Psychosomatic Illness.* London: Free Association.

McGowan, Todd. 2004. *The End of Dissatisfaction? Jacques Lacan and the Emerging Society of Enjoyment.* Albany, NY: SUNY Press.

McGowan, Todd. 2013. *Enjoying What We Don't Have. The Political Project of Psychoanalysis.* Lincoln: University of Nebraska Press.

Melman, Charles. 1980. Essay in Clinical Psychoanalysis: The Alcoholic. In *Returning to Freud. Clinical Psychoanalysis in the School of Lacan*, ed. Stuart Schneiderman, 234–246. New Heaven: Yale University Press.

Melman, Charles. 1999. Addiction. *The Letter* 16:1–8.

Melman, Charles. 2002. *L'homme sans gravité: jouir à tout prix. Entretiens avec Jean-Pierre Lebrun.* Paris: Donoël.

Melman, Charles. 2018. A New Psychic Economy. In *The Lacan Tradition: Lines of Development. Evolution of Theory and Practice Over the Decades*, ed. Lionel Bailly, David Lichtenstein, and Sharmini Bailly, 227–234. London: Routledge.

Miller, Jacques-Alain. 1996. Il rovescio dell'interpretazione. *La Psicoanalisi* 19.

Miller, Jacques-Alain, ed. 1997. *La Conversation d'Arcachon.* Paris: Agalma.

Miller, Jacques-Alain. 2000. Biologia Lacaniana ed eventi di corpo. *La Psicoanalisi*28.

Miller, Jacques-Alain. 2018. *L'Uno-Tutto-Solo.* Translated by Antonio Di Ciaccia. Rome: Astrolabio.

Miller, Jacques-Alain. 2019a. A Phantasy. Translated by Thelma Sowley. *Psychoanalytical Notebooks* 34: 139–173.

Miller, Jacques-Alain. 2019b. Six Paradigms of Jouissance. Translated by Janet Haney. *Psychoanalytical Notebooks.* 34: 11–77.

Miller, Jacques-Alain. 2021. The One is the Letter. Translated by Alasdair Duncan. *Psychoanalytical Notebooks* 37–38: 13–44.

Miller, Jacques-Alain, and Éric Laurent. 1997. L'Autre qui n'existe pas et ses comites d'ethique. *La Cause Freudienne* 35:7–20.
Mukherjee, Ankhi. 2014. Primetime Psychoanalysis. In *A Concise Companion to Psychoanalysis, Literature and Culture*, ed. Laura Marcus and Ankhi Mukherjee, 233–249. Chichester: Wiley Blackwell.
Mura, Andrea. 2015. Lacan and Debt: The Discourse of the Capitalist in Times of Austerity. *Philosophy Today* 59 (2): 155–174.
Neil, Calum. 2011. *Lacanian Ethics and the Assumption of Subjectivity*. Basingstoke: Palgrave Macmillan.
Pagliardini, Alex. 2016. *Il sintomo di Lacan. Dieci incontri con il reale*. Rende: Gaaland Edizioni.
Pagliardini, Alex. 2020. *Lacan al presente*. Rende: Gaaland Edizioni.
Pagliardini, Alex, and Rocco Ronchi. 2014. Premessa. Ancora Lacan. In *Attualità di Lacan*, ed. Alex Pagliardini and Rocco Ronchi, 11–16. Villanova di Cepagatti: Textus.
Perniola, Mario. 2004. *Art and Its Shadow*. Translated by Massimo Verdicchio. London: Continuum.
Phillips, Adam. 2021. *On Wanting to Change*. London: Penguin Books.
Porcheret, Bernard. 2000. Hands off my symptom. *Psychoanalytical Notebooks* 4:141–146.
Ramaioli, Isabella, Domenico Cosenza, and Pietro Enrico Bossola, eds. 2003. *Jacques Lacan e la clinica contemporanea*. Milan: Franco Angeli.
Recalcati, Massimo. 2001. On the Analytic Practice of the Group Mechanism in the Treatment of "Eating Disorders". Translated by Veronique Voruz. *Psychoanalytical Notebooks* 7: 107–115.
Recalcati, Massimo. 2002. *Clinica del vuoto: anoressie, dipendenze, psicosi*. Milan: Franco Angeli.
Recalcati, Massimo. 2005a. *Per Lacan. Neoilluminismo, neoesistenzialismo, neostrutturalismo*. Rome: Borla.
Recalcati, Massimo. 2005b. The Empty Subject. Un-Triggered Psychoses in the New Forms of the Symptom. Translated by Jorge Jauregui. *Lacanian Ink* 26: 73–101.
Recalcati, Massimo. 2007. L'eclissi del desiderio. In *Forme contemporanee del totalitarismo*, ed. Massimo Recalcati, 61–79. Bollati Boringhieri: Turni.
Recalcati, Massimo. 2008. *L'ultima cena. Anoressia e bulimia*. Milan: Bruno Mondadori.
Recalcati, Massimo. 2010. *L'uomo senza inconscio. Figure della nuova clinica psicoanalitica*. Milan: Raffaello Cortina.

Recalcati, Massimo. 2011. Hunger, Repletion, and Anxiety. Translated by Wissia Fiorucci. *Angelaki: Journal of the Theoretical Humanities* 16 (3): 33–37.

Recalcati, Massimo. 2012a. *Jacques Lacan. Desiderio, godimento, soggettivazione.* Milan: Raffaello Cortina.

Recalcati, Massimo. 2012b. *Ritratti del desiderio.* Milan: Raffaello Cortina.

Recalcati, Massimo. 2012c. Discorso del capitalista ed evaporazione del padre. In *Il reale del capitalismo*, ed. Alex Pagliardini, 7–17. Milan: et al. Edizioni.

Recalcati, Massimo. 2013a. Intervista a Recalcati. *LETTERa* 3:259–264.

Recalcati, Massimo. 2013b. Il potere del lettino, l'inconscio diventa show. *La Repubblica.* Available from: https://rassegnaflp.wordpress.com/2013/04/05/il-potere-del-lettino-linconscio-diventa-show/ 5 April. Accessed 25 September 2022.

Recalcati, Massimo. 2016. *Jacques Lacan. La clinica psicoanalitica: struttura e soggetto.* Milan: Raffaello Cortina.

Recalcati, Massimo. 2019a. *Le nuove melanconie. Destini del desiderio nel tempo ipermoderno.* Milan: Raffaello Cortina.

Recalcati, Massimo. 2019b. *The Telemachus Complex. Parents and Children after the Decline of the Father.* Translated by Alice Kilgarriff. Cambridge: Polity Press.

Recalcati, Massimo. 2020a. *Convertire la pulsione. Sul processo di soggettivazione nell'esperienza dell'analisi.* Trento: Paginaotto.

Recalcati, Massimo. 2020b. *The Son's Secret. From Oedipus to the Prodigal Son.* Translated by Alice Kilgarriff. Cambridge: Polity Press.

Recalcati, Massimo. 2021. *Ritorno a Jean-Paul Sartre. Esistenza, infanzia e desiderio.* Turin: Einaudi.

Recalcati, Massimo. 2022a. *Temptation of the Wall. Five Short Lessons on Civil Life.* Translated by Alice Kilgarriff. Cambridge: Polity Press.

Recalcati, Massimo. 2022b. Clinic of the void. An Interview with Massimo Recalcati. In *Lacanian Psychoanalysis in Practice. Insights from Fourteen Psychoanalysts*, ed. Diego Busiol, 240–248. London: Routledge.

Recalcati, Massimo. 2023. *Jacques Lacan. Ereditare il reale?* Milan: Feltrinelli.

Recalcati, Massimo, and Uberto Zuccardi Merli. 2006. *Anoressia, bulimia e obesità.* Turin: Bollati Boringhieri.

Ronchi, Rocco. 2012. *Come fare. Per una resistenza filosofica.* Milan: Feltrinelli.

Rousselle, Duane. 2017. *Lacanian Realism. Political and Clinical Psychoanalysis.* London: Bloomsbury.

Sartre, Jean-Paul. 2012. *Saint Genet: Actor and Martyr*. Translated by Bernard Frechtman. Minneapolis: University of Minnesota Press.

Svolos, Thomas. 2011. Introducing the "New Symptoms". In *Yael Goldman Baldwin*, ed. Kareen Malone and Thomas Svolos, 75–88. Karnac: Lacan and Addiction. An Antology. London.

Svolos, Thomas. 2017. *Twenty-first Century Psychoanalysis*. London: Karnac.

Tarizzo, Davide. 2003. *Jacques Lacan*. Laterza: Rome and Bari.

Tarizzo, Davide. 2007. *Giochi di potere. Sulla paranoia politica*. Bari: Laterza.

Tarizzo, Davide. 2011. Biopolitics and the Ideology of 'Mental Health'. Translated by Alvise Sforza Tarabochia. *Filozofski vestnik* 23 (2): 135–149.

Terminio, Nicolò. 2009. *Misurare l'inconscio. Coordinate psicoanalitiche nella ricerca in psicoterapia*. Milan: Bruno Mondadori.

Terminio, Nicolò. 2018. *Introduzione a Massimo Recalcati. Inconscio, eredità, testimonianza*. Genoa: Il melangolo.

Terminio, Nicolò. 2020. *L'intervallo della vita. Il Reale della clinica psicoanalitica e fenomenologica*. Rome: Alpes.

Tomšič, Samo. 2015. *The Capitalist Unconscious: Marx and Lacan*. London: Verso.

Turner, Kirk. 2023. *Lacanian Fantasy. The Image, Language and Uncertainty*. London: Routledge.

Verdicchio, Pasqquale, and Loredana Di Martino, eds. 2017. *Encounters with the Real in Contemporary Italian Literature and Cinema*. Newcastle upon Tyne: Cambridge Scholars Publishing.

Verhaeghe, P. 2008. A Combination That Has to Fail: New Patients, Old Therapists. *Eisteach (Dun Laoghaire)* 8 (4): 4–8.

Verhaeghe, P. 2019. Lacan's Answer to Alienation: Separation. *Crisis and Critique*365–388.

Žižek, Slavoj. 1999. *The Ticklish Subject. The Absent Centre of Political Ontology*. London: Verso.

Žižek, Slavoj. 2006. *The Parallax View*. Cambridge, MA: MIT Press.

Žižek, Slavoj. 2014. From Lacan to Hegel – Interview with Slavoj Žižek. In *ŽiŽek and his Contemporaries: On the Emergence of the Slovenian Lacan*, ed. Jones Irwin and Helena Motoh, 125–146. London: Bloomsbury.

Zupančič, Alenka. 2014. Encountering Lacan in the Next Generation – Interview with Alenka Zupančič. In *ŽiŽek and his Contemporaries: on the Emergence of the Slovenian Lacan*, ed. Jones Irwin and Helena Motoh, 158–178. London: Bloomsbury.

Filmography

Costanzo, Saverio. 2013–2017. *In Treatment* [TV Series]. IT: Sky.
Garcia, Rodrigo. 2008–2021. *In Treatment* [TV Series]. USA: HBO.
Levi, Hagai. 2005–2008. *Be Tipul* [TV Series]. Israel: HOT Cable Network.

4
Politics

Italy on the Couch

In his book *Lacan Politico*, the Italian philosopher Bruno Moroncini openly criticises psychoanalysts for shying away from politics and leaving the political significance of Lacan's theory up to philosophers, who often extrapolate psychoanalytic concepts from their original context to apply them beyond the clinic. Notably, Moroncini states that

> […] analysts are careful not to adopt explicit political positions, and when they do so, there does not seem to be any direct connection with their clinical work and ethical stance. In other words, this does not appear to be a political continuation of the analytical act, which is what distinguishes them when it comes to the social order. Analysts tend to oscillate between indifference toward the choices made by the states in which they operate, sometimes even leaning towards a submissive acceptance of any policies proposed and adopted (only awakening when the state deals with access to the profession and the required curricula for obtaining their qualifications), and public, indignant criticism of culture, often characterised by an inevitably moralistic tone. (2014, pp. 14–15)

L. Di Gregorio, *Lacan in Italy*, The Palgrave Lacan Series,
https://doi.org/10.1007/978-3-031-91528-4_4

Overall, Moroncini's claim is hard to contest considering the moralistic undertone found in some psychoanalysts' critiques of contemporary society and their tendency to avoid any form of political engagement.[1] Yet in highlighting the discontinuity between clinical practice and politics, Moroncini overlooks the case of Italian Lacanianism. As explored in the previous chapters, the clinical practice of Italian Lacanians paves the way for their social commitment and direct engagement with local communities, schools, hospitals, and prisons. It is also important to note that the widespread popularity of Lacanians in Italy derives predominantly, albeit not exclusively, from their political analysis, social criticism, and active engagement in public issues, such as supporting same-sex civil partnerships, addressing immigration challenges, opposing feminicides, and countering the rise of far-right populism. Italian Lacanianism employs a 'clinical approach' (Tarizzo 2021) to society and politics which, rather than pathologising, underscores the interconnectedness and interdependence of the psychic realm with the sociopolitical sphere, linking the private realm of clinical practice with collective discourse (Esposito 2019). This is possible because Lacanian thought is particularly well

[1] Interestingly, Gabriel Tupinambá notes a surge in the 'institutional politicization of Lacanian psychoanalysis in the last years supposedly motivated by the dangers of right-wing populism throughout the globe' (2021, p. 7). In particular, he refers to *La movida Zadig*, an international forum established in 2017 by the World Association of Psychoanalysis (WAP) to examine the political leanings of Lacanian psychoanalysts. However, this sparked controversies within the Lacanian community because it ultimately ended up discouraging any involvement with party politics and leftist political movements (Tupinambá 2021, p. 13). One notable instance involved Massimo Recalcati who, in 2017, established a political school within the Italian Democratic Party named after Pier Paolo Pasolini, the Italian public intellectual and versatile artist. This ignited fierce criticisms which culminated in a petition against profaning Pasolini's name signed by several renowned Italian Lacanians, including Antonio Di Ciaccia, Domenico Cosenza, and Marco Focchi (http://lacaniannet.weebly.com/la-peacutetition-pasolini). In this context, Recalcati also faced public accusations by Jacques-Alain Miller for using psychoanalysis to endorse the political positions of the Democratic Party, of which he was a member, and for his affiliations with Matteo Renzi, the former Italian prime minister (Miller 2017). This sparked heated articles by Miller and other Lacanian figures published in the *Lacan Quotidien* (Fazzi 2017; Focchi 2017; Miller 2017). Beneath the debate about the school's name and his political activism, there was evidently a strong undercurrent of resentment towards Recalcati's popularity and media presence. In his reply to Miller, Recalcati drew parallels between Miller's approach and Armando Verdiglione's practice of 'publicly discrediting analysands who chose to leave him' (Recalcati 2017, online). These events represent a concerning moment in the history of Italian Lacanianism, shedding light on 'the paternalistic and religious roots' of the Lacanian movement (Siciliano 2017, online) and demonstrating that 'pathetic fratricidal wars' (Chiesa 2014, p. 19) and 'provincial quarrels' (Tupinambá 2021, p. 13) are still very much alive among Lacanians.

equipped to address the intersection of the individual and collective domains, adeptly deploying psychoanalytic concepts to shed light on sociocultural dynamics.

The capacity of Italian Lacanianism to extend into political and social spheres beyond the clinic hinges on Lacan's reinterpretation of the Freudian unconscious, as repeatedly emphasised by Miller. In the *Milanese Intuitions*, based on a lecture delivered in Milan in May 2002 at the conference 'Psychoanalysis in the City', held on the occasion of the foundation of the Lacanian School of the Freudian Field in Italy, Jacques-Alain Miller discusses the relationship between the Lacanian unconscious and politics. Miller argues that the renowned aphorism 'the unconscious is politics' (Lacan 1966) is the logical extension of Lacan's conception of the unconscious as transindividual and integral to the discourse of the Other (Lacan 1998). This conceptualisation 'transports the unconscious out of the solipsistic sphere, to introduce it into what is called the City' (Miller 2019a, p. 91). The Lacanian unconscious, Miller goes on to argue, 'is of the order of the social bond' (p. 111), which highlights the interconnectedness of the individual and social domains. Miller's Italian lecture is particularly relevant as it touches upon key themes that Italian Lacanians go on to elaborate further—in particular, the relationship between the decline of the paternal function, the symbolic Law, desire, and *jouissance*—de facto paving the way for the future developments of Italian Lacanianism and its interpretation of Lacan. Interestingly for the Italian context, Miller refers to Silvio Berlusconi and his media power to address the radical changes in the social landscape that form the backdrop against which psychoanalysis exists. While psychoanalysis was born in a disciplinary era dominated by prohibition and repression, today it operates in a radically different context, which Miller calls 'the regime of globalisation' (p. 93). According to Miller, Lacan succeeded in adapting psychoanalysis for the era of globalisation, and thus modernising Freud's theory, because of his emphasis on the notion of *jouissance*, an 'essential term' in the last phase of his teaching and a key concept in the contemporary clinic (p. 97).

Lacan's take on the Freudian unconscious, which he defines as transindividual, historical, and subject to continuous transformations, has had a significant impact on political theory. In the French and Slovene receptions of Lacan, political theory has drawn, in particular, on the notion of the real to develop a 'radical political thought', which could be described as 'interventionist' as it extends to 'the wider political and social movements' (Irwin and Motoh 2014, pp. 39–40). This encompasses themes of antagonism and resistance. For instance, Slavoj Žižek uses the real as a key category to promote radical change in the political sphere, while Alain Badiou considers it to be a 'revolutionary' force and a 'vector of emancipation' (Badiou and Roudinesco 2014, pp. 20 and 21). In the British reception of Lacan, as developed in the early 2000s by the Essex School of Discourse Analysis, the real was instrumental for the development of theories of hegemony and social struggle for scholars such as Ernesto Laclau and Chantal Mouffe (Townshed 2003; Robinson 2004). Subsequently, the use of Lacanian psychoanalysis in political theory has shifted from a critique of ideology and its underlying fantasy structures to an examination of forms of enjoyment and their organisation, mobilisation, and investment by individuals and societies. This focus on the real qua *jouissance*, regarding the libidinal dynamics and economy, 'is primarily grounded in the need to reflect seriously on, and to deal effectively with, the difficulties involved in effecting subjective and social change' (Stavrakakis 2007, pp. 81–82). This perspective considers not only the subject of the signifier but also the subject of *jouissance*—the enjoying (individual and collective) political subject. As Lacan states in Seminar 17, the 'intrusion into the political' by psychoanalysis is rooted in what Lacan terms the 'discourse of jouissance' (2007, p. 78). This discourse extends beyond the individual to encompass broader social frameworks, thus establishing an intersection between the subjective, social, and political realms.

Enjoyment has thus become a key Lacanian category of contemporary political theory. Anglophone and Slovenian Lacanianism have long emphasised the importance of *jouissance* in political and social discourse. This notion has been employed to investigate the constitution of the social bond and thus the connection between individual libidinal economies and social structures, making it particularly adept for social and political analysis (Tomšič 2019). Politics today is effectively a 'politics of jouissance' which concerns 'ways of soliciting, or controlling and regulating' enjoyment (Žižek 2006, p. 309). Enjoyment makes it possible to account for those crucial aspects of contemporary society and politics which appear to be rooted in a mobilisation of *jouissance* and in the capitalist mode of enjoyment (McGowan 2004, 2013, 2016; Tomšič 2015). *Jouissance* has also been recognised as an invaluable and unavoidable concept in psychosocial studies to explore the contemporary issues of consumerism, racism, populism, and nationalism (Hook 2022). The fruitfulness of this notion relates to the possibility it offers to account for the immaterial dimension of affects, which nowadays plays a crucial role in the emotionalisation of politics, post-truth phenomena, and national populism (Mazzarella 2020).

Nevertheless, Italian Lacanianism has not paid much attention to these Anglophone perspectives, most of which have not yet been translated into Italian, except for Žižek's works. Noteworthy, Italian Lacanians make very few references to prominent Anglophone Lacanians who have extensively deployed *jouissance* in their sociopolitical analyses. This omission highlights the limited exchange between Italian and Anglophone Lacanian receptions, but also partly explains the sense of novelty with which the analyses of Italian Lacanians were received in Italy. This sociopolitical application of the Lacanian notion of *jouissance* only gained prominence in Italy fairly recently and was immediately praised for its effectiveness in conceptualising contemporary social and political issues. This is largely thanks to its focus on the libidinal dimension of politics and the social bond (Ronchi 2012a). 'Today's political power', Riccardo Panattoni and Fabio Vighi argue in their *Capitalism and the New Political Unconscious*, 'does not need symbolic or ideological frameworks any longer, but instead relies on its ability to tap into the people's disavowed modes of enjoyment' (2023, p. 1).

Initially, the notion of *jouissance* gained prominence in Italian Lacanianism in relation to the new symptoms and their contextualisation in contemporary society (Chap. 3). This perspective, which focuses on the contemporary imperative of unrestrained enjoyment, inevitably led to discussions about societal and political discourses, which feature prominently in the case of Silvio Berlusconi. As one of Italy's most influential and era-defining politicians, Berlusconi has remained a potent and ever-present signifier over several decades. In Lacanian theory, a signifier is a powerful element that both represents and shapes the history and identity of a subject. Given Berlusconi's profound and multifaceted influence at the social, political, and cultural levels, he is a key figure in the history of Italy. He not only reshaped Italian politics, television, and popular culture, but also spurred a shift towards populism. His impact extends beyond his political actions, epitomising broader and enduring societal transformations. Hence, Italian Lacanians viewed him not only as a political figure but also as a symbol of significant psychosocial transformations in Italy, thus establishing him as an unavoidable point of reference in their sociopolitical analyses. Italian Lacanians consider Berlusconism as a psychosocial trend, which encapsulates the complexities of Italian society. In this context, Berlusconi's iconic persona epitomises the quintessential postmillennial subject and reflects the societal shifts influenced by neoliberal and populist ideologies. Thanks to its focus on notions of desire and *jouissance*, Italian Lacanianism provides a specific analysis of Berlusconism that anticipates the examination of Trumpism in the USA undertaken by Anglophone Lacanian scholars (Mazzarella 2020). Italian Lacanians' critique of Berlusconism extends beyond a mere condemnation of Berlusconi's promotion of a negative model of masculinity, the exploitation of women in his media outlets, his propagation of hedonism, and his legal controversies. Instead, they offer a more substantial analysis that accounts for the irreducible force of *jouissance* in shaping contemporary behaviours, along with the libidinal dimension underpinning postmillennial politics.

In the 2008 article 'Il trionfo della perversione', the Italian philosopher Davide Tarizzo publicly brings Lacanian psychoanalysis into the domain of Italian politics by arguing that, more effectively than political theory and sociology, Lacanian thought provides a particularly effective theoretical framework to investigate the excessive and perverse[2] traits of contemporary politics in postmillennial society. While political theory and sociology lack the appropriate conceptual tools to fully account for

[2] In Lacanian terms, perversion has nothing to do with deviant sexual behaviours. Rather, it designates a particular clinical structure along with neurosis and psychosis. All Lacanian clinical structures are rooted in the subject's Oedipus and the perverse one entails a fundamental disavowal of castration which leads to the subject's peculiar relation to the drive. The perverse subject 'mistakes' lack with deprivation, thus experiencing the Other as incomplete rather than inconsistent, and ultimately confuses the structural and inevitable loss of the primary object of mythic *jouissance* with a contingent deprivation of enjoyment. Hence, the pervert subject attempts to pursue 'jouissance as far as possible' (Lacan 2006, p. 700). This inevitably places the 'ethical dimension' at the forefront (Benvenuto 2016, p. 98).

the perverse logic at play, Lacan's theory is particularly well suited to articulate the dimension of excess and the liminal space it occupies between the individual and social domains. To explain the collapse of the social fabric and the appeal of populist leaders, Tarizzo examines the shift from what he terms a 'politics of desire', focused on public and communal interests, to a 'politics of enjoyment', characterised by extreme individualism and personal gratification (Tarizzo 2008). Tarizzo argues that, more so than any other Italian politician, Berlusconi epitomises the perverse character of contemporary politics, which is defined by three key aspects: spectacularisation, ostentatious enjoyment, and contempt for the law. Italy's so-called *Berlusconisation* goes beyond mere relentless hedonism and the superficial pursuit of pleasure, as some simplistic sociological analyses and moralistic political critiques suggest (Gundle 2015). Instead, it involves an unsettling and excessive compulsion for enjoyment. Lacanian psychoanalysis, Tarizzo contends, is thus crucial for understanding these new political phenomena, which extend far beyond Berlusconi's politics and apply, more broadly, to present-day Italian society as a whole.

These themes are further explored in Recalcati's *L'uomo senza inconscio*, which adopts a Lacanian clinical framework to examine contemporary psychopathology, building upon the dialectic between desire and enjoyment (Chap. 3). The book marks a significant milestone in the Italian reception of Lacan because it combines clinical theory with a sociopolitical analysis of postmillennial Italy, highlighting the political relevance of Lacanian psychoanalysis in an unprecedented way. Published in 2010, during a period of significant challenges in Italy, including the aftermath of the global economic crisis and declining government credibility, the book resonated deeply with Italian readers. Recalcati's exploration of the demise of desire, the pervasive enjoyment promoted by the capitalist discourse and neoliberal society, and his criticism of Berlusconi struck a chord with both academic and lay audiences, sparking debates beyond Lacanian circles and garnering broader attention in the media.[3]

[3] To the best of my knowledge, Recalcati's first appearance on Italian national television was during an interview on political issues, during which he remarked on the interconnection between the psychic and the sociopolitical domains. The interview aired on La7 channel during the political talk-show *L'Infedele* on 14 December 2010 (https://www.la7.it/linfedele/video/o-berlusconi-o-il-nulla-intervista-a-massimo-recalcati-14-12-2010-80271) [accessed 25 November 2021].

Consequently, Lacanian psychoanalysis experienced a surge in popularity in Italy, while Recalcati became a mainstream Lacanian psychoanalyst and a public intellectual.[4]

According to Recalcati, Berlusconi represents the epitome of the contemporary subject devoid of the unconscious emerging from a society that commands enjoyment, which it elevates to the status of an essential right, all while the symbolic Law of castration declines. In Lacanian psychoanalysis, the Law is closely associated with those symbolic rules and prohibitions that structure human experience. In particular, the symbolic Law limits and restrains *jouissance.* On the contrary, according to Recalcati, Berlusconi embodies the perverted contemporary overlap between enjoyment and the Law:

> There is no shame, guilt, or any sense of limit, precisely because there is no separation between the sense of the Law and that of enjoyment, as the place of the Law coincides with that of enjoyment. Everything is openly (perversely) played out, as though castration did not exist. The figure of the head of the government thus rehabilitates the phantoms of the Freudian Father of the horde, the Father who has the right to enjoy all women, the bionic, immortal, invulnerable, obscene, and untouchable Father, not as a limit to enjoyment [...] but as the unlimited exercise of enjoyment. (2010, p. 13)

In this context, perversion signifies the fractured relationship with the Law, where the subject is enslaved to the imperative of *jouissance* and incapable of desire. As such, Berlusconism represents a perverse refusal to accept the inherently human experience of limitation and finitude, instead adhering unwaveringly to the Law of unlimited enjoyment.[5]

---

[4] In 2010, the Censis 44th Report on the Social Situation in Italy (*Censis - 44° Rapporto sulla situazione sociale del paese*), an annual sociological and statistical analysis of Italy, drew extensively from Recalcati's book (Dominijanni 2010a). The report portrayed postmillennial Italians as profoundly affected by unrestrained individualism, hyper-hedonism, ensnared by the media and depicted Italy as, fundamentally, a country 'with neither Law nor Desire' (De Rita 2010), a fragmented society of people subjugated to the fetishist accumulation of commodities and a compulsive pursuit of individualistic enjoyment.

[5] An uncanny parallelism can be drawn between Berlusconi's countryside villa near Milan, where he infamously hosted parties with sex workers (dubbed *bunga bunga* parties), and the villa depicted in Pier Paolo Pasolini's 1975 film *Salò, or the 120 Days of Sodom.* While loosely based on de Sade's

Throughout his teaching, Lacan has repeatedly revisited the paternal function, which explains why Lacanian psychoanalysis has been instrumental in re-establishing the prominence of the father figure in twenty-first-century psychoanalytic discourse (Etchegoyen 2002, p. 26). In the early to middle period of Lacan's work, the paternal function is closely associated with the symbolic Law. While restraining *jouissance*, the paternal function allows the subject to access desire. Hence, Lacan famously claimed that the 'true function of the Father [...] is fundamentally to unite (and not to oppose) a desire to the Law' (2006, p. 698). In this stage of Lacan's work, the paternal function thus embodies castration since it limits enjoyment, thereby enabling the subject to access desire and be integrated into the symbolic order. According to Lacan, 'castration means that jouissance has to be refused in order to be attained on the inverse scale of the Law of desire' (2006, p. 700). Italian Lacanians thus emphasise the twofold nature of the Lacanian father, who not only limits boundless enjoyment but also provides the possibility of structuring a singular desire (Busiol 2022; Lolli 2012; Recalcati 2011). The symbolic Law of castration has a beneficially traumatic impact insofar as it involves the loss of enjoyment, an absolute satisfaction, thus opening up the possibility of desire. Most importantly, the paternal function bears the responsibility—imposed by society—to refrain from enjoyment in exchange for the subject's inclusion in the community (Lolli 2012). Hence, the paternal function holds the pivotal 'socialising function' insofar as it 'contrasts with the human tendency to remain in a condition of undisturbed homeostasis, fosters sociality, and urges one to seek in the world that which was originally prohibited' (Lolli 2012, p. 25). In Lacanian terms, symbolic castration is thus mainly about the subject entering into language and the social order.

novel, the film is set in 1944, in a countryside Renaissance villa in the fascist Italian Social Republic (Republic of Salò). Despite the intertwining of political and sexual dimensions, the underlying concern in this parallelism revolves purely around enjoyment and capitalism. Notably, Pasolini's cinematic endeavour aimed to depict the brutality of the capitalist political ideology, responsible for the widespread exploitation of individuals in consumer society and the objectification of human bodies (Vighi 2006). Similarly, the ideology of Berlusconism, rather than focusing on the erotic dimension of desire, rests on the belief that 'the only eternal thing, the only Thing that counts, the only Law capable of forestalling the inevitability of death, is the "will to enjoyment"' (Recalcati 2019, p. 149).

Miller summarises Lacan's conceptualisation of the paternal function according to three phases. Initially, Lacan unified the Freudian Oedipus complex, castration, and repression through the concepts of the Name of the Father and metaphor and the Freudian libido through desire and metonymy (2019a, pp. 96–97). Subsequently, as the Name of the Father is 'pluralised but also displaced' (p. 97), Lacan overthrew Freud's teaching by attributing repression not to paternal prohibition but to language itself. Language acts as a limitation of enjoyment, imposing on the speaking being the need to renounce the fusional bond with the Thing. In this phase, according to Miller, the concept of desire is displaced into that of *jouissance*: 'rather than lack, [Lacan] emphasises what fills the lack' (p. 97). Finally, in the last phase of Lacan's teaching, 'the essential term is that of jouissance' and 'the signifier itself becomes an operator of jouissance' (p. 97). Hence, for Lacan, the paternal function is not biological since it is equivalent to the symbolic field and thus can be embodied by parents or caregivers regardless of their gender. The paternal function can also manifest itself in non-human forms, such as in the act of writing for James Joyce (Lacan 2016) (Chap. 5).

In light of Lacan's theoretical conceptualisations of the paternal function in relation to symbolic Law and enjoyment, Miller has expanded on the idea that society 'has ceased to live under the reign of the father' (2019a, p. 119), highlighting that the 'decline in effectiveness of the paternal metaphor' (2019a, p. 131) has specific repercussions for individual and social relations. He signals that our civilisation is no longer one of the Freudian superego of prohibition and repression but rather of the Lacanian superego of the imperative to *jouissance* (Miller 2019b). Following in Lacan's and Miller's footsteps, different national Lacanian receptions have also deployed these notions to develop a critical analysis of post-Oedipal society. For example, Slovene and Anglophone Lacanianism have extensively highlighted the connection between the decline of Oedipal paternal Law, in other words the demise of symbolic castration, and the rise of the injunction to enjoy (Žižek 1999, 2000). The traditional symbolic and Oedipal father of desire has now given way to the 'anal father of enjoyment' (Žižek 1992, p. 124; McGowan 2004, pp. 41–57). Unlike the father of prohibition, the anal father embodies a superegoic stance that is to be understood primarily in terms of the drive modality. The contemporary incarnation of paternal authority reflects a society dominated by enjoyment. No longer a figure of restraint, this new father is far more accessible—yet precisely because he encourages enjoyment rather than prohibiting it, he becomes much harder to resist. This 'soft' authority is more difficult to oppose. As McGowan explains, 'Whereas the dead Oedipal father's name presides over a society devoid of enjoyment, the anal father presides over a society crawling with it' (2004, p. 46). Discussing this decline of paternal authority, Anglophone Lacanians refer to the shift from a 'society of prohibition' to a 'society of enjoyment' (McGowan 2004), namely, 'a society that commands jouissance as a "civic" duty' (Copjec 1994, p. 182). From this perspective, the 'post-Oedipal world' appears to be dominated by 'ruinous jouissance' (Weatherill 2017, p. 2).

While the discussion of the transformations of the paternal function and their impact on society remains prominent in all receptions of Lacan, this issue constitutes a distinguishing aspect of Italian Lacanianism (Bollas 2020). Nonetheless, rather than the decline of Oedipus, Italian Lacanians focus, in particular, on the concept of the 'evaporation of the father' (*evaporazione del padre*),[6] bringing this to the forefront of cultural and political debates in postmillennial Italy. Their emphasis on the demise of paternal authority has gained significant traction, which is unsurprising in a country where patriarchal structures remain deeply entrenched in Catholic values and a prevailing chauvinistic culture. In Italy, the signifier 'father' continues to wield considerable influence, underscoring Italy's fundamental status as a patriarchal and heteronormative society. The evaporation of the father underpins the analyses of the clinical and socio-political transformations advanced by Italian Lacanians. Before addressing these contributions, it is thus essential to introduce this notion briefly.

Although Lacan talks about the decline of the paternal imago as early as 1938 in *Family Complexes*, the expression 'evaporation of the father' only appears in passing in his 1968 work *Note to the Father and Universalism*, where he briefly refers to Freud's depiction of paternal roles and their profound implications for various psychic structures. Lacan

[6] It is worth noting that 'decline of the father' is the term most commonly used in English-language Lacanian literature.

suggests that the consequence of what he terms 'the father's disappearance'[7] in contemporary society results in a 'form of segregation that only manages to generate more and more barriers' (2010 p. 11). This appears to contradict the idea that we now live in a globalised world. In *Address on Child Psychoses*, Lacan delves deeper into these societal transformations, observing that we are 'entering a period that has been called "global"', characterised by an unprecedented 'destruction of an old social order' (2012, p. 271), and which has exacerbated segregations, 'the most burning issue of our times' (p. 270). Rather than global uniformity, this segregation fosters further fragmentations. However, unlike the Foucauldian segregation enforced by repressive power targeting individuals deemed abnormal or mentally ill, this contemporary form of segregation assumes the guise of assimilation. This is particularly evident in individual analysis, where 'disorder' becomes an all-encompassing label that defines the analysand's identity, and in monosymptomatic groups, where individuals share the same symptoms. In both cases, the symptom serves as a simple label that reinforces a cohesive identity, uniting individuals through their (alienated) imaginary identification with the symptom and their mode of enjoyment. Hence, working with contemporary patients in private practice as well as monosymptomatic groups in institutions involves facilitating the emergence of each subject's unique individuality, which was previously concealed in an alienated identification with a shared imaginary trait (see Chap. 3).[8]

Italian Lacanian thought deploys the evaporation of the father as a pivotal concept for understanding the radical changes in the

[7] Although Russell Grigg translates *évaporation du père* in English as 'the father's disappearance' (Lacan 2010, p. 11), it is noteworthy that the term *évaporation* evokes the French translation of the famous passage from Marx and Engels' 1848 *The Manifesto of the Communist Party* '*Tout ce qui paraissait solide et fixe s'évapore*' ('all that is solid melts into air') (Mura 2015, p. 161).

[8] In French Lacanianism, Éric Laurent refers to a 'politics of the symptom' in contemporary society (2004) to explain the aggregating role enjoyment plays in shaping the identity of individuals and communities. Similarly, Colette Soler characterises these social groupings as 'segregations that inspire affinities' where individuals freely come together based on shared conditions, essentially becoming 'brothers and sisters in the symptom' (2014, p. 195). These groupings primarily revolve around identifications and provide individuals with a label to sustain their fragile identity. The American Lacanian analyst Thomas Svolos claims that this promotes a 'segregated specialization' in clinicians too (2017, p. 236), who are required by individuals and insurance companies to brand themselves as experts in treating specific disorders and conditions.

psychopathologies and social bonds of today's society. The evaporation of the father, the crumbling of the symbolic, the eclipse of the normative paternal function, and the non-existence of the Other represent diverse conceptualisations of the same phenomenon, which has profoundly disrupted the social bond. This phenomenon is characterised by a stark dissociation between the Law and desire, with deadly enjoyment becoming an imperative that overrides the transcendence of desire. This concept is also linked to the protests against old generations and authority during the student and worker uprising of 1968, which marked a significant moment in the history of Italy (see Chap. 1).

Without making any explicit reference to the evaporation of the father but nonetheless referring to Lacan, Elvio Fachinelli's *Dissident Desire* discusses the issue of the crisis of paternal authority in the context of the 1968 youth dissident movements, claiming that 'the father figure fades out, loses force and autonomy', becoming 'increasingly fragile and impotent' (2019, p. 295 and p. 297). Drawing from the sociological research of the Frankfurt school, Fachinelli locates the 'transformation in the function and significance of the father' (p. 296) as part of a wider transition in modern society. In these youth protests against the 'authoritarian and overpowering father' (p. 295), Fachinelli identifies a significant sociopolitical element, which relates to the attempt to 'call into question the traditional ways of conceptualizing and practising politics' (p. 296). Most importantly, Fachinelli contends that these protests should not be simply reduced to Oedipal conflicts against the father; instead, they are to be understood as a signal of the revolt against the 'renunciation of desire' (p. 297) taking place in 'industrial society' (p. 296). The strong political inflection in Fachinelli's seminal article underscores the role desire plays in the dynamics of individuals and groups. These revolts brought about a politics of dissident desire, novel ways of thinking, and new forms of socialisation. What characterises a desiring group, for Fachinelli, is not a specific object of desire but the 'state of desire' (p. 298). The group needs to abandon the illusion that 'desire could be embodied in a definitive way' (p. 298) and thus avoid a situation in which this is embodied solely—and tyrannically—by a leader.

For Recalcati, the paternal function presides over the possibility of inheriting desire, of passing it onto the next generation. In his analysis, the evaporation of the father encompasses more than just the demise of paternal authority and transcends mere concerns about post-secular society or the challenges of contemporary parenting. Rather, it is associated with a wider sociopolitical and cultural upheaval and indicates the erosion of the traditional guiding role once ascribed to politics, religion, and education, which paved the way for the unrivalled reign of *jouissance*.[9] Recalcati presents a psychoanalytic history of Italian politics revolving around the evaporation of the father, *jouissance*, and desire. Bluntly put, the fascist era (1922–1945) was characterised by a hierarchical power structure with a vertical mass identification with the fascist leader, Benito Mussolini *il Duce*. In this totalitarian regime, the particularity of individual desire is annihilated by the universal Cause, with the masses appealing to the leader as an all-powerful Father (Recalcati 2011). In the First Republic (1946–1994), politicians like Alcide De Gasperi, one of the founding fathers of the Italian Republic, and Enrico Berlinguer, the long-time leader of the Italian Communist Party, exemplified a political commitment to democratic principles and ethical leadership, thus embodying the Oedipal fathers and benevolent patriarchs. Hence, Recalcati regards them as representing 'an ethical tension between the Law and enjoyment, which was still rooted in the Oedipus' (Recalcati 2010, p. 13). On the contrary, during the Berlusconi era (1994–2011), this ethical link between the Law and *jouissance* was significantly undermined. Berlusconi embodies the post-Oedipal father who, instead of limiting enjoyment, promotes a democratic enjoyment for all. This is, however, the 'compulsive and unrestrained enjoyment devoid of desire' that emerges in the post-ideological era (Recalcati 2011, p. 52).

Although Recalcati's brief psychoanalytic history of Italian politics may appear simplistic, his analysis importantly emphasises the structural changes in Italian society. While in twentieth-century totalitarian regimes,

[9] For Recalcati (2011, 2013), two pivotal events epitomise the evaporation of the father in recent Italian history. The first is Berlusconi's sex scandal in 2009, for which he was nicknamed *papi* (sugar-daddy) by the sex workers attending his parties. The second is the resignation of Pope Benedict XVI in 2013, which is fictionalised, and uncannily foreseen, by Nanni Moretti's 2011 film *Habemus Papam*, where the Pope finds himself unable to fulfil the duties of his position as head of the Catholic Church and decides to step down. These events strikingly exemplify the disappearance of the 'foundational, transcendental, normative aspect of the paternal function' (Recalcati 2010, p. 37) in postmillennial Italian society.

the charismatic figure of the leader wielded vertical power over the masses, in the twenty-first century, power is no longer rooted in the ideal Cause embodied by the leader. Instead, there is a 'horizontal totalitarianism of jouissance' (Recalcati 2010, p. 31), in which power centres on the object of enjoyment. In this context, Recalcati claims that

> Berlusconi defines an era, since he raises the issue of what the father figure can become in the time of its evaporation, in the era of the decline of its ideal-orientative function. The answer that Berlusconism provides is in complete harmony with the capitalist discourse: the father, the locus of Law, becomes he who can enjoy without limits. For there is no longer anything truly private about his whim since it takes the form of law, literally becoming law *ad personam*. (2010, p. 10)

For Recalcati, the promise of boundless enjoyment under Berlusconism gave way to the security syndrome that characterised the recent resurgence of nationalism in Italy. Today, with the rise of populism, enjoyment seems to coalesce in the attraction for the border as the object of the libidinal investment (Recalcati 2019, 2022a). This phenomenon has manifested itself in various nationalistic movements worldwide, as exemplified by Brexit and the idea of Trump's wall, which will be discussed later on in this chapter.

Recalcati's analysis of Berlusconism has been criticised for being moralistic and for its equation of *jouissance* with mere hedonism (Lolli 2019; Ronchi 2012a; Moroncini 2014). The Italian philosopher Rocco Ronchi argues that Recalcati's critique of postmillennial Italy reflects a prevailing tendency within Lacanian circles to pathologise enjoyment. Ronchi notes a misuse of the notion of *jouissance* as 'malignant and perverse' in interpreting the degenerative phenomena affecting modern democracies (2012a, p. 75). He cautions against the danger of adopting this perspective since it runs the risk of leading Lacanian psychoanalysts to become 'moralisers concerned with the stability of the social order' (2012a, p. 63). According to Ronchi, 'the Lacanian dyad desire/enjoyment increasingly takes the form of a moral opposition. Psychoanalysis thus tends to present itself, in the social sphere, as a cure for enjoyment' (2012a, p. 81).

Strictly related to this point, another intrinsic issue of Lacanianism affects the prevalent perspective of many contemporary Lacanians worldwide. Lacanian analyses of contemporary society and politics tend to convey the idea that the paternal function orients and limits *jouissance*, establishing a problematic correlation between the symbolic Law, the role of the father, and unrestrained enjoyment, which can easily lead to normative and potentially authoritarian positions. Unsurprisingly, Recalcati's perspective has frequently been criticised either as a yearning for the return of paternal authority or as a nostalgia for the lost authority of the father (Berardi 2021b; Lolli 2019; Moroncini 2014; Righi 2015). International Lacanians such as Žižek also criticise those Lacanians who propose that the decline of the Name of the Father—and so the demise of paternal symbolic authority—might lead to an outbreak of pathological narcissism and the return of the totemic father of the horde (2014). He refers to these views as 'desperate calls for re-Oedipalization' (2006, pp. 296–297). In outlining the main responses in the Lacanian psychoanalytic field concerning the transformations in the father's role (post-Oedipalisation), Žižek presents two predominant possibilities: adapting to current developments to establish 'a new legitimacy', possibly through neurosciences or addressing emerging postmodern psychopathologies, and 'advocat[ing] some kind of return to the symbolic authority of the paternal Law' (2006, p. 297). Similarly, the Brasilian Lacanian analyst Gabriel Tupinambá is particularly sceptical about these comprehensive social analyses, which predominantly revolve around 'changes in the role of the father and of paternal function in modern culture' (2021, p. 26).

This is the case, for instance, for the Italian Lacanian Antonio Di Ciaccia, who contends that there has been a mutation in the paternal figure insofar as, in the past, 'the father was the one who made the symbolic function; he was the one who said no to the incestuous relationship between mother and son or daughter' (Di Ciaccia and Fasoli 2013, p. 18). Di Ciaccia also aligns the symbolic order with the flesh-and-blood father, while at the same time associating the paternal symbolic function exclusively with the male gender. This perspective is a risky one, since it could encourage the reinstatement of a normative father figure in an attempt to revive the lost paternal function—a nostalgic yearning for the authoritative and transcendent power of the Name of the Father. Such a perspective could also yield perilous outcomes, including a correlation between the weakening of the function of the flesh-and-blood father with the potential root cause of homosexuality (Ricci 2013).

Moreover, Franco Lolli (2019) and Silvia Lippi (2020) raise concerns about this approach and the related tendency among Lacanians to speak in mainly pessimistic terms about the decline of the father in contemporary society, labelling these perspectives as declinist. They claim that the 'ideology of the decline of the father' (Lolli 2019, p. 37) is currently pervading Lacanianism, especially in Italy and France. Lippi criticises the declinist approach of the French psychoanalysts Jean-Pierre Lebrun and Charles Melman, who decry the decline of the father in our societies as catastrophic, and argues that their approach epitomises a 'paternalistic psychoanalysis' which 'insists on giving lessons and dictating rules of behaviour based on the Oedipal fiction' (2020, p. 139). Similarly, Lolli contends that it is the current historical-imaginary interpretation of the paternal function in its patriarchal organisation that is in crisis now, not the paternal function itself, which is an indispensable condition for the constitutive process of the subject (2019, p. 16). He claims that:

> The problem raised by theories about the decline of the father lies in the fact that, by correlating contemporary psychopathology with the 'weakened' behaviour of the father, they implicitly support the overlapping of the concept of the third with the actual father. From this perspective, the maternal Thing becomes a sort of black hole that the man (the male) is called upon to 'restrain' through his normative action. (2019, p. 36)

Lolli considers Recalcati to be one of the main representatives of the declinist movement in Italy (2019, p. 38). He reproaches Recalcati's analysis for mistakenly conflating the weakening of paternal authority with the broader crisis of the symbolic, without considering that, on the contrary, this crisis primarily stems from the broader decline of the patriarchy. Moreover, Lolli argues that the decline of the patriarchy does not automatically lead to the erosion of the Law and widespread perversion, 'as if that which lies beyond the father necessarily coincides with the chaos of enjoyment, as if only the paternal figure were responsible for upholding civilisation and culture' (2019, p. 34).

Lolli expresses serious concerns about the potential paternalistic leanings of Italian and French Lacanian psychoanalysis and how these ideas gain traction in public opinion. According to Lolli, the popularity of these declinist theories is driven by analysts who, acting as public intellectuals, blend psychoanalysis with sociological perspectives to attract a broad media audience. In his critique, Lolli refers to Adorno (2014) who, already in the 1950s, underscored the dangers of psychoanalysis morphing into a sociology of human behaviours, reducing it to mere commonsense psychology. He also draws from Lacan, who similarly cautioned against psychosocial approaches, describing them as 'inadequate abstractions in which [the psychoanalyst's] practice gets bogged down and dissolves' (2006 [1955], p. 362).

However, these criticisms overlook the fact that Recalcati does not advocate for a return of the authoritarian father-as-master. In fact, Recalcati (2010, 2011) criticises the 'nostalgic fundamentalism' that mourns the disappearance of the Oedipal father as the ultimate founder and guarantor of the Law and thus of the symbolic order, as exemplified by Melman's approach (2018). He also highlights the risk entailed by certain Lacanian perspectives, such as Miller's, which he believes promote a vitalist materialism that celebrates *jouissance* and the real of the drive as a manifestation of life (Recalcati 2011, pp. 78–79). In *Cosa resta del Padre?* Recalcati provides a clear answer to the question of what happens to the paternal function in the era of the evaporation of the father. He advocates for a path that avoids both the cynicism of enjoyment and the nostalgic longing for an ideal paternal figure. Instead, he proposes a way forward centred on individual testimony of how Law and desire can be held together (p. 81).[10] His response to the evaporation of the father is represented by what he calls the father-as-testimony. This represents an anti-patriarchal version of the father that transcends gender and the human form and that, fundamentally, coincides with the function of

[10] Recalcati (2011) employs the term 'testimony' not in a romanticised, exemplary, or normative way. This would imply an authoritarian and ideological conception of testimony. Instead, the examples of 'testimonies' to which he refers demonstrate that an authentic testimony of paternal function is never exemplary, ideal, normative, or universal. Above all, it can only be appreciated *après-coup*. These examples, taken from North American literature and cinema, include Roth's *Patrimony: A True Story*; Eastwood's *Million Dollar Baby* and *Gran Torino*; and McCarthy's *The Road*.

facilitating the ignition and transmission of desire in conjunction with, rather than in opposition to, *jouissance*.

Lacan hinted at this when he spoke of 'a relationship to a desire that is not anonymous' and described the role of father as 'the vector of the embodiment of the Law in desire' (2012, p. 13). However, according to Recalcati, Lacan did not fully develop the crucial issue of the relationship between the universal function of the Law and the necessity of its embodiment for the effective transmission of desire. In some Lacanian perspectives, the emphasis thus remains on the Name of the Father as a symbolic function, detached from 'the Father as a person, as a living being' (Svolos 2017, p. 32). In contrast, Recalcati's concept of father-as-testimony is not about the symbolic father or the Father of the Name as a signifying function. Rather, it represents a remainder, an embodiment of Law and desire, and a singular act that conveys both the interdiction of enjoyment of the Thing and the gift of desire.

The evaporation of the father can certainly generate the nostalgic return of the father-as-master or even give way to the anarchic power of the object of enjoyment promoted by the capitalist discourse. Therefore, Recalcati argues that a critical issue in today's society is

> avoiding any nostalgic regret for the Oedipal version of the Law [...] without falling into a collusive and uncritical adherence to the promises of salvation cleverly deployed by the capitalist discourse and its emphasis on the most immediate enjoyment of the drive. (2011, p. 80)

The capitalist discourse operates on two fundamental assumptions: that the subject is boundlessly free, motivated solely by the will to enjoy and fuelled by consumption, and that the object of desire can be reduced to tangible commodities. This paves the way for an exploration of how Italian Lacanians critique and engage with the capitalist discourse in the next section.

Capitalism and Its Discontents

In the session dated 19 March 1969 in Seminar 16, Lacan recalls his trip to the Fiat factory in Turin, Italy. During the visit, he notices the unease of Gianni Agnelli, the chairman of the Italian car manufacturer, as they observe assembly-line workers, because Agnelli is unaware of what exactly their tasks are. To mask his embarrassment, Agnelli jokingly suggests to Lacan that these workers are likely happier working at the Italian Fiat factory than they would be at the French Renault one.[11] Lacan uses this anecdote as a starting point to underscore the significant shifts in the power configuration that have recently surfaced, asserting that today 'the power is elsewhere' and 'held in different hands' (2024, p. 206), those of a new and invisible master. This new configuration of power is articulated through what Lacan terms the capitalist discourse. In Seminar 17, Lacan (2007) claims that capitalism is responsible for the 'transmutation' (p. 31) and 'subversion' (p. 32) that invest contemporary society, especially due to the 'curious copulation' (p. 110) between the capitalist and scientific discourses (p. 110), the outcome of which is an 'abundance of the objects designed to be the cause of desire' (p. 162).

On 12 May 1972, in his renowned lecture *On the Psychoanalytic Discourse*, delivered at the University of Milan, Lacan defines the capitalist discourse as 'insanely clever' (Lacan in Contri 1978, p. 196) because it promotes the illusion that lack is not an intrinsic part of the human being but something contingent and amendable. In the discursive regime of the capitalist, every commodity thus appears as a remedy that can fill lack, turning the subject into a mere consumer.[12] Lacan contends that Freud's social theory, according to which human society is built upon the renunciation of the drive and individual sacrifice for the sake of the greater good, is no longer valid (Contri 1978; Lacan 1971). Lacan maintains that it is the discursive regime of the capitalist that permeates society today, fostering the superegoic injuction to *jouissance* and unlimited object consumption. In Lacan's view, social bonds are no longer sustained by the imperative to sacrifice individual enjoyment but are, rather, undermined by a deadly and solipsistic compulsion to enjoy (Lacan, 1990,

[11] Elio Petri's *The Working Class goes to Heaven* (also known as *Lulù the Tool*) (1971) effectively depicts the alienation experienced by Italian factory workers in the capitalist mode of production and the failure of the process of subjectivation of the protagonist, who cannot separate himself from the Other qua factory (Di Gregorio 2019).

[12] In the same years, Pier Paolo Pasolini describes this new power as pervasive, impersonal, totalitarian, and, above all, as capable of turning Italian citizens into mere consumers. For Pasolini, this is an anthropological mutation that affects not only Italy but all Western societies (see Chap. 2).

p. 32). Lacan argues, however, that the capitalist discourse is 'destined to explode'. This is attributed to its being 'unsustainable' because 'it runs as if on wheels, it couldn't go better, but it goes so fast that it wears itself out, it wears out to the point of exhaustion' (Lacan in Contri 1978, p. 196).

What is the role of psychoanalysis in the age of the capitalist discourse? Rather than offering a political reading of Lacan, Italian Lacanians advance a politics of psychoanalysis rooted in their clinical practice, which emphasises ethical and societal stances. Italian Lacanianism regards the foreclosure of the subject of the unconscious as the biggest threat imposed by the capitalist discourse. The latter does not simply dehumanise and exploit workers. Rather, it primarily de-subjectifies individuals (Tarizzo 2011), fosters subjects without an unconscious (Recalcati 2010), and promotes a 'fantasy of mastery' (Busiol 2022, p. 17) by creating the illusion that structural dependence on the Other can be bypassed and the constitutional lack can be filled by a gadget of enjoyment. At its inception, Italian psychoanalysis was hindered by political and religious ideologies, including fascism, communism, and the Catholic church due to its subversive and seemingly dangerous views (Chap. 1). Today, it is the neoliberal ideology—a combination of the capitalist and scientific discourses—that dismisses psychoanalysis as unscientific and ineffective. Italian Lacanians vehemently denounce that the key elements of psychoanalysis—such as the importance of speech and free associations, the significance of time and emotional investment for long-lasting change, the emphasis on personal history, the recognition that subjects are not isolated entities but integral parts of a community, and, most importantly, the notion of unconscious—are simply overlooked and deemed irrelevant.

The critique of capitalist ideology in Italian Lacanian thought stems primarily from clinical practice. Italian Lacanians view the unconscious as the primary point of resistance for the subject and, consequently, as the core of psychoanalytic political engagement. They argue that the capitalist discourse transforms the unconscious subject of desire into a subject driven by demand, a mere consumer, while *jouissance* becomes one commodity amongst others (Pagliardini 2012b). This discourse emphasises the nature of the object that induces dependency and highlights the solipsism of *jouissance*, which connects individuals to objects of libidinal enjoyments rather than to each other (Bonazzi 2012). As a result, the object becomes a solitary means of enjoyment—'one enjoys, alone' (Di Ciaccia and Fasoli 2013, p. 65)—and the capitalist discourse encourages the constant replacement of objects (Recalcati 2016). This relentless pursuit of consumer objects of enjoyment erases the distance between the object of desire and the object of consumption (Bianchi 2010, p. 247), resulting in a 'lack of the lack' (Busiol 2022, p. 16). Consequently, psychoanalysis becomes a political act (Lolli 2018, 2019) by intervening in the libidinal economy of the subject. This has the potential to reconfigure the relationship between the analysand and society by redefining the position of the subject within the big Other, within which the subject was always-already constituted.

Italian Lacanians aim to establish a point of resistance, acknowledging our entrenchment within the capitalist discourse—namely, our inability to break free from it. Yet within this framework, they strive to articulate and comprehend the impact the capitalist discourse has on us, our symptoms, and our modes of enjoyment. This comprehension fosters the exploration of possibilities for resistance stemming from within. Alex Pagliardini believes that investigating the real of capitalism is an ethical duty because capitalism is the first symbolic order capable of laying hands on the real to bend it to its own service: capitalist discourse has a peculiar way of working with and manipulating *jouissance* (Pagliardini 2012a). As Pagliardini notes, to effectively contemplate and determine actions regarding capitalism, we must remain aware of its impacts and the decisions it imposes upon us (2012a, p. 5). As with the analysand in the psychoanalytic treatment, Pagliardini argues that is crucial to question the nature of the real that supports and fuels the discourse of the capitalist. He writes:

> one should aim at its real, question its real core, nor its reality; not its historical variations, however significant, not so much, or rather not primarily, its political and social manifestations, its universal dynamics. Rather, one should strike the target of its real. (2012a, p. 4)

In addressing enjoyment, Lacanian psychoanalysis risks adopting a moralistic or prescriptive approach aimed at managing and regulating it, potentially leading to authoritarian drifts. Since enjoyment is 'going off the track' (Lacan 1990, p. 32) under the capitalist discourse, there may be a temptation to think about putting it back on track. As seen in the clinical context, for Pagliardini, this depends on how the real is conceptualised: that is, whether the real is conceptualised on the basis of the symbolic or considered per se. If the real is understood as the realm of boundless and acephalous drive necessitating the intervention of the symbolic order, which acts as both a barrier and a channel, this approach would inevitably lead to simply promoting the counteraction of the 'absence of limits' and 'unbridled hedonism' (Melman 2018, p. 228 and 234). This reflects the symbolic power exerting its influence onto the real. Hence, reinstating a sense of limit becomes a vital strategy—not necessarily in a reactionary sense—to challenge the capitalist discourse. In this context, the symbolic is seen as a function to restrain and regulate *jouissance*. From this perspective, it is unsurprising that the paternal function becomes one of the main concepts deployed to address the contemporary crisis of the symbolic. The Father is 'tormented, devalued, forbidden, castrated' (Melman 2018, p. 228) and thus no longer capable of restraining enjoyment.

Conversely, if the real is understood as *extimate* to the symbolic order, the capitalist discourse operates within a symbolic framework shaped by this in/exclusion, making it susceptible to the re-emergence of repressed elements. From this perspective, the real remains separate from a specific symbolic structure, such as capitalism, which denies its presence and essentially revolves around this in/exclusion. However, this denial exposes the system to the forceful resurgence of the symptomatic real. Thus, the real emerges as an inherent locus of resistance, resistant to assimilation within the capitalist machinery itself, potentially serving as a focal point for disrupting the totality of the capitalist discourse.

Let us begin by briefly considering Recalcati's perspective, which epitomises the first approach outlined by Pagliardini in Italian Lacanianism. Recalcati discusses contemporary psychopathologies against the backdrop of both the evaporation of the father, the crisis of the big Other, and the capitalist discourse.[13] However, Recalcati is neither conservative nor nostalgic of the authoritarian father. In his view,

> To assert that ours is the era of the collapse of the symbolic and the evaporation of the father means acknowledging the increasing difficulty of maintaining the virtuous character of symbolic interdiction. It means recognising that the promise of (false) salvation offered by the capitalist discourse (incestuously) emphasises the Thing as proximity, envisaging immediate enjoyment as structurally opposed to sublimation, that is, completely focused on the immediate consumption of the object within reach of the hand, mouth, or body. (2011, p. 57)

Recalcati highlights the significance of the paternal function not only in moderating enjoyment but also in facilitating access to desire for the subject—an aspect hindered by the capitalist discourse. For Recalcati, access to desire is what is truly at stake in capitalism. This hindrance results in erratic and unbridled enjoyment, leading to a depletion of desire in neoliberal society. The capitalist discourse rejects lack and the desire it engenders, instead promoting a self-referential, monadic, and sterile form of enjoyment.

Recalcati's analysis of the capitalist discourse draws primarily from Lacan's 1972 lecture *Talking to Brick Walls*, where he identifies the foreclosure (*Verwerfung*) of castration and the neglect of 'matters of love' as central to this discourse.

> What differentiates the discourse of capitalism is *Verwerfung*, the fact of rejecting, outside all the fields of the symbolic. This brings with it the consequence I have already said it has. What does it reject? Well, castration. Any order, any discourse that aligns itself with capitalism, sweeps to one side what we might simply call, my fine friends, matters of love. (Lacan 2017, pp. 90–91)

[13] Some Italian scholars have criticised Recalcati's perspective for overlooking the historical developments of capitalism. For instance, Andrea Righi claims that Recalcati's analysis disregards 'the biopolitical passage from waged work to human capital' (2015, p. 308); Lorenzo Bernini argues that he 'does not seem to pay enough attention to the current phase of capitalism—characterized by post-Fordism, globalization, job flexibility, marked by the global financial and economic crisis' (2017, p. 76); and Fabio Vighi contends that he also neglects the current recurring crises of capitalism (2017, 2019).

Recalcati argues that the capitalist discourse is fundamentally inhumane not simply because of the exploitation of workers, as Marx would suggest, but because of the 'foreclosure of the fundamental principle (symbolic castration) that grants the subject access to the generative potential of desire' (2016, p. 636). This ultimately leads to the dismissal of the unconscious subject, or in other words, the disavowal of the subject of desire. In favouring a superficial pursuit of transient enjoyment, the capitalist discourse suppresses desire, fostering a perverse shift from one object to another. Although there is no genuine desire that can be instantly and fully satisfied by a partial object, the capitalist discourse promotes the illusion that the object that causes desire (object a) can be an actual thing, a gadget, part of a series of objects endlessly available on the market (Recalcati 2010, 2011, 2016).

Moreover, the capitalist discourse upholds 'a bond that is adverse to any forms of bonding' (Recalcati 2016, p. 635), manifesting the destructive and nihilistic power of the death drive. Under capitalism, the social bond relies on a horizontal relationship centred on the compulsive consumption of the object of enjoyment, *jouissance*-as-object, or commodity-*jouissance*. Individuals often prefer inanimate companions (such as drugs, medications, alcohol, social media, gambling, and pornography) over engaging with 'matters of love'. The commodity shields individuals not only from the precarious and unpredictable encounter with the Other but also from life's inherent unevenness. On a societal scale, capitalism's rejection of 'matters of love' results in the commodification of human interactions and the erosion of communities. This commodification affects the social fabric of societies, leading to precarious relationships and ecological neglect.

Ronchi observes that this perspective may risk condemning enjoyment as inherently detrimental to the subject (2012b). Ronchi underscores that enjoyment is not inherently pathological. Drawing from a Deleuzian perspective, he argues against viewing the post-Oedipal and superegoic injunction to enjoy as purely malevolent, something to be constrained and channelled. Instead, he highlights the political essence of enjoyment, which, despite its historical exploitation by fascism and contemporary populist governments, holds 'immense resources, an inexhaustible wealth, forces of attraction different from those already utilised' (Ronchi 2012b, pp. 142–143). The alternative Lacanian approaches outlined below strive to avoid an excessive idealisation of desire and eschew the adoption of a moralistic or patronising tone when discussing contemporary society.

Sergio Benvenuto critiques the tendency of contemporary Italian Lacanianism to idealise desire and stigmatise enjoyment. He argues that Lacanians who view the crisis of desire as the primary effect of capitalist discourse are morally judgemental, fundamentally expressing a fierce condemnation of consumerism. He writes that:

> For decades now, so many have enjoyed repeating the same rants against vulgar 'consumerism', which they see as characteristic of modern capitalism. Desiring is sublime, enjoying is shameful! Except when enjoyment derives from mystical ecstasy, when it is an enjoyment that involves no material objects [...] many are now bored with this imposed anathema against consumerism, an execration that represents the continuation of our metaphysical (ascetic) tradition. (2020, pp. 59–60)

Benvenuto sharply rebukes these perspectives, labelling the condemnation of enjoyment as both 'naïve and hypocritical' (2012, p. 93). He accuses Lacanian psychoanalysts who hold these views of promoting abstinence from consumer goods and the so-called vulgar enjoyment of objects. Instead, they advocate for a desire devoid of a concrete object and romanticise the concept of lack (2012, p. 92). As Benvenuto aptly put it, these Lacanians scornfully condemn 'the enjoyment of goods that would fill the central void of our being' while celebrating 'the lack that cannot be enjoyed' (2012, p. 92). Despite the strong emphasis on *jouissance* amongst Lacanians discussing the capitalist discourse, Lacan has drawn attention to the 'exploitation' and 'industrialisation' of desire under capitalism (Lacan in Contri 1978, p. 94). He contends that the strength of the economy derives from the formidable force inherent in human desires, which influences one's ability, or inability, to satisfy one's own and others' desires.

> The society of today's globalised West can, in many aspects, be defined as the methodical, pervasive, and extensive realisation of the *culture of desire*. Paradoxically, political philosophy, which is opposed to today's commercial society, often appeals to desire as its alternative [...] Many philosophies that aim to radically oppose the capitalist world essentially end up glorifying and

> explicating what lies at the foundation of capitalism itself [...] There is an economy because, fundamentally, we all desire pleasure or happiness, utility, that which Lacanians call enjoyment. Economics does not concern itself with enjoyment and fulfilment, but only with the exchange triggered by dissatisfaction; it emerges from the asymptotic tension of filling a void. (2012, p. 95)

From this perspective, economic growth is intricately tied to the proliferation of desires, which fosters a sense of dissatisfaction. Benvenuto suggests that the volatility of desire, rooted in discontentment, contributes to economic expansion (2012, p. 91). In his argument, Benvenuto appears to utilise the concept of desire somewhat ambiguously, regarding it more as a whim or wish than intrinsically related to lack, rather than objects, as Lacan conceives it. While Benvenuto critiques these perspectives for their polarising stance between idealised desire and condemned enjoyment, he does not propose an alternative approach.

Similarly, Lolli (2019) takes a critical stance against what he calls contemporary Lacanian ideology, which is dominated by a primary focus on boundless and dissipative enjoyment seen as the defining trait of postmodern society, from which the father figure has permanently vanished. Lolli criticises the perspective, which suggests that erratic, totalising, and solipsistic enjoyment is merely an outcome of capitalism, for being overly simplistic. Instead, he underscores that,

> The enjoyment contained within the symptom is not the result of a flaw in the functioning of the symbolic but rather its necessary correlate. Far from completely purifying the real, every intervention of the signifier on the living being stimulates its emergence: therefore, every discourse should be considered as a potential activator of enjoyment. (2019, p. 148)

According to Lolli, the capitalist discourse introduces new mechanisms for relinquishing enjoyment. He posits that symptoms represent a 'personal invention by which the subject of the unconscious (in any historical era and under any economic system) attempts to reclaim a portion of the enjoyment traded for entry into Civilisation' (2019, p. 147).

Lolli claims that the capitalist discourse does not spare individuals from the renunciation of the drives, despite promoting the illusion that perpetual enjoyment through new market commodities can bypass such a relinquishment. On the contrary, echoing Freud's *Civilization and Its Discontent*, Lolli argues that every society, no matter how permissive, must undergo a renunciation of drives to exist (2019, p. 147). Furthermore, any symptom that emerges is rooted in the backdrop of a loss of enjoyment, even if this loss is concealed by its opposite in capitalist societies. Lolli argues that the consumerist system, rather than producing enjoyment, encourages a pursuit of enjoyment and induces a lack-in-enjoying. Lolli is referring here to a passage in *Radiophonie* where Lacan writes that

> surplus value, is the cause of the desire that an economy makes its principle: that of the extensive production, therefore insatiable, of that lack-in-enjoying (*manque-à-jouir*). It is accumulated on the one hand to increase the means of this production on the side of capital. It extends consumption, on the other hand, without which this production would be vain, precisely from its ineptitude in procuring a *jouissance* that would allow it to slow down. (1970, p. 22)

If anything, according to Lolli, the capitalist discourse exacerbates and amplifies the act of desiring, which can never be fulfilled and inevitably leads to dissatisfaction (2019, p. 150).

In a similar vein, Pagliardini argues that the specificity of the real of the capitalist discourse is characterised by a particular form of negation of lack which occurs not by excluding it but by refusing its structuring function (2012b, p. 32). According to Pagliardini, the capitalist discourse does not merely promote enjoyment and the eradication of desire. Rather counterintuitively, he argues that the discourse of capitalism primarily leads to the rejection of enjoyment. Pagliardini contends that the capitalist discourse does not grant full access to total enjoyment—a *jouissance* devoid of any trace of sacrifice or castration, as some Lacanians suggest. Even the complete enjoyment of the real remains inaccessible within the capitalist system: capitalism itself fails to provide access to absolute enjoyment. Something related to enjoyment is sacrificed even within the capitalist discourse. This is the key point for Pagliardini, however: the relationship between enjoyment and the capitalist discourse does not hinge on castration but on the quantification of enjoyment, on rendering it measurable. Pagliardini writes:

> The functioning of capitalism is based on the right to enjoy, but in reality it cannot transform the real of enjoyment—the pulsation of the body and the impossible excess—into a right or norm. It may believe it can, but it cannot. It cannot do so because no discourse or apparatus can accomplish such a thing. Therefore, capitalism is countered—in clinical practice, for psychoanalysis—by asserting real enjoyment, the enjoyment that cannot be grasped by the capitalist apparatus; in other words, by making it explicit that the enjoyment-as-a-right of capitalism is nothing more than a defence and a semblance compared to the real of enjoyment. (2018, online)

Briefly put, Pagliardini argues that, firstly, the evaporation of the paternal function is an amplification of a pre-existing societal trend. Secondly, capitalism has elevated what was once solely a structural, psychical element—namely, the imperative to enjoy—to the level of social discourse. Thirdly, what distinguishes capitalism from previous social systems is its basis in the right to enjoy, making everyone entitled to their own mode of enjoyment. Consequently, capitalism eradicates any process of individuation because individuation necessitates separation, a process that is obstructed by capitalism. Instead of undergoing separation, individuals are confined to the role of entitled consumers, unable to fully develop their distinct ways of enjoying. The political focus on discussions surrounding capitalist society and the influence of capitalist discourse on everyday life inevitably draws Italian Lacanianism into the field of so-called Italian Theory, where biopolitical analysis plays a central role. The following section will explore key intersections between Italian Lacanianism and Italian Theory.

Lacan Meets Italian Theory: The Securitarian Drive, Collective Subjectivation, and the Third Unconscious

Italy has often been seen as a 'privileged laboratory' in the Western world in light of certain significant historical events, such as the social unrest and political struggle of the 1960s and 1970s, the rise of right-wing media populism during the Berlusconi era, and the onset of the Covid-19 pandemic (Hardt and Virno 1996; Chiesa and Toscano 2009; Stimilli 2021). Italian philosophers and political thinkers have proposed distinctive interpretations of these events, which have affected the country in unique ways. As a result, Italian thought is well-positioned to address the complexities of today's globalised and neoliberal world, particularly on account of its eclectic and hybrid nature, its focus on life, politics, and power, and its inclination to combine theory with praxis (Esposito 2012).

Interest in Italian philosophical and political thought has steadily increased within Anglophone academia, nearly reaching the level of fascination once reserved for French Theory (Pasquinelli 2011; Esposito 2012; Lewis 2018).[14] However, until recently, Italian Theory had largely overlooked Lacanian psychoanalysis. Such an omission is somewhat unexpected given the shared inquiries into human nature, politics of life, and the theory of the subject. Despite this close proximity, the longstanding poor reputation of Lacanianism in Italy (Chap. 2), coupled with the strong attachment to the rationality of political thought and its tendency to overlook the individual and collective psychic dimension (Dominijanni 2009, 2012), may help explain why Italian Theory has largely avoided engaging with Lacanian psychoanalysis.

This situation has begun to change over the last decade, with Italian biopolitical thinkers turning to Lacanian psychoanalysis and Italian Lacanians, in turn, engaging with biopolitics (Chiesa 2011; Chiesa et al. 2016; Nedoh 2016; Sforza Tarabochia 2016).[15] The Italian philosopher Ida Dominijanni (2009) points out that feminist thought has been instrumental in this shift. Firstly, it complicates the modern understanding of the individual as 'undivided and one, neutral, sovereign in its ratio-

[14] Over the last decades, a number of edited books (Borradori 1988; Hardt and Virno 1996; Benso and Schroeder 2007; Chiesa and Toscano 2009; Calcagno 2015; Benso and Calcagno 2021) and special issues (*Diacritics* 2009; *Angelaki* 2011; *Annali d'Italianistica* 2011; *Paragraph* 2016; *Italian Studies* 2021) published in English have addressed Italian Theory and helped establish this field in Anglophone academia.

[15] The relationship between Roberto Esposito and Massimo Recalcati epitomises the evolving connection between Italian Lacanianism and Italian Theory. Initially, until Esposito's *Living Thought*, there was an absence of official dialogue, leaving Lacanian theory unexplored in Esposito's work. In contrast, Recalcati had engaged with Esposito's ideas since the 2000s. Over time, this changed, with Esposito recently engaging with Recalcati, and by extension with Lacanian theory. This development underscores the potential for Lacanian psychoanalysis to inform philosophical inquiry and for Italian Theory to fruitfully engage with Lacanian psychoanalysis.

nality, a voluntary actor in the social contract' (p. 140). In contrast, feminist thought articulates the subject of difference as 'an embodied and sexed singularity, born of tensions between reason and drives, aware of his/her vulnerability, marked from and depending on relationships with others' (p. 140).

Secondly, drawing from the activist and scholarly contributions of Italian feminist thinkers of the 1970s, contemporary Italian feminist thought brings to the forefront notions of desire and oppression in relation to life and body. These themes are a common ground between Italian biopolitical thought and Lacanian psychoanalysis. Dominijanni argues that this connection was propelled by Berlusconism, which adeptly tapped into individual desires, collective enjoyment, bodily politics, power structures, and gender roles. Dominijanni asserts that 'Berlusconian biopolitics' garnered support through 'affective *dispositifs*', apparatuses that diverge from the rational political discourse traditionally employed by the Left and that instead involve the media's 'spectralization of the real' (p. 144). Berlusconism epitomises those Foucauldian biopolitical regimes that do not oppose individual freedoms but rather co-opt and reshape them within a neoliberal framework. This dynamic complicates the identification of power structures that are not overtly authoritarian, rendering the development of strategies of resistance even more challenging (p. 143).

Lacanian psychoanalytic theory provides valuable insights into contemporary populism, particularly in terms of how it influences not just the bios but also the individual and collective psyche. The interplay between subjectivity, the body, neoliberal power, and the social bond is central to both Italian Lacanian psychoanalysis and Italian Theory. These concepts resonate strongly with the Lacanian notion of the real, particularly in relation to *jouissance* and the death drive. In the introduction to the *Paragraph* special issue 'Italian Biopolitical Theory and Beyond: Genealogy, Psychoanalysis, and Biology', the editors contend that today there can be

> no viable biopolitical critique without an open assumption of the real of the unconscious and that this real — which is both logical and material, and perhaps suggests that psychoanalysis is a novel kind of philosophical

> anthropology — cannot in turn appropriately be tackled without taking into consideration the current scientific discourse on the human body and life in general. (Chiesa et al. 2016, p. 2)

Italian Theory distinctively develops this idea by linking the Lacanian psychoanalytic concept of the subject of desire with the biopolitical view of the political subject as deeply intertwined with life and power (Chiesa 2011; Chiesa et al. 2016; Nedoh 2016; Sforza Tarabochia 2016).

Recalcati's interpretation of Lacan can be regarded as an essential component of Italian Theory (Sforza Tarabochia 2016). Recalcati's clinical theorisation—and its social ramifications and political implications—have been significantly influenced by Esposito's biopolitical thought and paradigm of immunisation. Drawing on the biological metaphor of the body's immune response, Esposito argues that just as the immune system defends the body by distinguishing between self and other, societies create mechanisms—legal, political, social, medical, and technological—to safeguard their identity and integrity (2008, 2009, 2011). Esposito explores how modern societies protect themselves from perceived threats and claims that the notions of intrusion, alterity, and immunisation are pivotal in today's political and sociological discourses, to the extent that 'immunity constitutes the strategic focus of contemporary societies' (Esposito 2011, p. 153). However, this protective process often involves exclusion, marginalisation, or violence against that which is deemed foreign or dangerous. The paradox of immunisation rests on the fact that preserving life can ultimately be detrimental and harmful, even leading to the death of an individual or societal body. The transplant metaphor further illustrates this dynamic: while a transplant can save a life, it nevertheless requires the body to accept a foreign tissue in order to survive. Similarly, the societal body must navigate the tension between the acceptance and rejection of Otherness (Esposito 2011, pp. 150–153).[16]

[16] Esposito draws inspiration from Jean-Luc Nancy's *The Intruder*. In this autobiographical essay, Nancy (2008) reflects on his personal experience as a heart transplant recipient, touching on key philosophical issues of identity and Otherness that are relevant to both Esposito's biopolitical thought and Recalcati's Lacanian theory. Nancy explains that a successful organ transplant occurs when the body does not reject 'the intruder' by lowering its immune defences, thereby enabling the body to embrace the alterity of the foreign element. As Nancy writes, this process 'lowers the graftee's immunity, so that he can tolerate the stranger. It thereby makes him a stranger to himself,

Recalcati applies this metaphor to the psychoanalytic context: the real Otherness for human subjectivity—the intruder—appears to originate from the external world, yet is primarily an internal presence, or perhaps more accurately, an *extimate* manifestation that we do not recognise as our own and instead project onto others.

While this drive for self-preservation is primordial and inherent in all human beings,[17] to the detriment of life itself, Recalcati identifies in the rejection of the Other the characteristic trait of the new symptoms, which he describes as a securitarian inclination to close off life, as epitomised by the anorexic subject (2019). The foreclosure of desire in the new symptoms manifests itself through a progressive devitalisation of life, coinciding with a securitarian closure. For Recalcati, contemporary psychopathologies and the sociopolitical situation revolve around this libidinal investment in closure. In *The Temptation of the Wall* (2022a), Recalcati addresses what he calls the 'securitarian drive' by elaborating on its sociopolitical implications. According to Recalcati, the limitless freedom to enjoy (as promoted by Berlusconism) coexists in contemporary society with a longing for security, which is currently giving way to the militarisation of the border, with nationalism and racism dominating today's political discourse both in Italy (Matteo Salvini and Giorgia Meloni) and abroad (Brexit, Trumpism). Recalcati calls the former the 'neo-libertine drive' and the latter the 'securitarian drive':

> The neo-libertine degradation caused by hypermodern individualism and the transfiguration of the border into a wall, a stronghold, a fortress, are two sides of the same coin that define our time's lack of civility. In both cases we can identify the markers of new discontents in civilization. On the

to this immunitary identity, which is akin to his physiological signature. An intruder is in me, and I am becoming a stranger to myself' (2008, p. 167). Similarly, the collective body can only be immunised, and thus maintain a healthy life, by accepting, rather than rejecting, the intruder. For Esposito's discussion of the influence of Nancy's *The Intruder* on his own work, see Campbell and Luisetti (2010) and Esposito et al. (2010).

[17] Noteworthily, Recalcati refers to *Beyond the Pleasure Principle*, where Freud asserts that 'protection against stimuli is an almost more important function for the living organism than reception of stimuli' (1981 [1920], p. 27). Freud employs terms centring on defence like 'protection', 'shield', barrier', 'mastering', 'binding', and so forth. In line with the biopolitical immunisation paradigm, Freud argues that healthy psychic life involves an ongoing process of integration, abolishing a rigid confine between normality and madness.

> one hand is a freedom that rejects any limit (the neo-libertine drive), and on the other, we have the loss of the symbolic dimension of the border as a place of transit, and its metamorphosis into a barrier (the securitarian drive). (2022a, p. 1)

The wall epitomises a sovereigntist response to the threat posed by what is perceived as an intruder which, Recalcati contends, is not simply a 'political temptation' but also 'a profound mental inclination' (p. viii). Rather than simply the outcome of nationalist politics, building walls is thus 'a temptation that has always inhabited the human' (p. 11).

Recalcati regards Esposito's paradigm of immunity as a 'metaphor for democracy' (p. 18). He suggests that, just as the immune system of the individual body needs to be lowered in order to welcome and include the real Otherness, the social body must do the same by 'keep[ing] the border porous without turning it into a wall' (p. 19). Not coincidentally, the British psychoanalyst Wilfred Bion identifies 'porosity' as the key attribute of borders—whether mental or physical—as it allows both individual and collective subjects to incorporate Otherness while preserving their own integrity and identity. Recalcati (2005) refers to Bion's notions of 'narcissism' and 'socialism': the ego-centric tendency to strengthen identity through differentiation and the socio-centric tendency towards belonging within a group, respectively (Bion 1992). He draws a parallel between these Bionian tendencies and Lacan's concepts of alienation and separation in the process of subjectivation. Both individual and collective subjects constantly oscillate between alienation, understood as an 'excess of belonging' and closure, and separation, which is an 'excess of wandering' (p. 6) and openness. Recalcati contends, through Bion, that the subject does not arise solely from narcissistic tendencies but also needs to rediscover his/her connection to—or inheritance from—the Other (Chap. 2). Therefore, Recalcati defines psychoanalysis as 'a science of boundaries that values the experience of friendship and hospitality with the internal stranger' (p. 46). The fundamental aim of psychoanalysis, he argues, is to allow the plurality of positions to remain in dialogue with one another, that is, 'not to segregate, not to exclude, not to remove the word but to give it to the person who has been excluded' (p. 46).

This is also the essential function of politics, and Recalcati refers to Christopher Bollas' notion of the 'democratic mind' (2018) to expand upon this idea of healthy community and politics. A democratic mind is to be understood as an apparatus that preserves the plethora of contrasting point of views without reducing them to some rigid alternative, rejecting some whilst preserving the dialogue between them. The democratic mind operates in such a way as to account for all instances or all the different selves by means of the psychic activity that navigates between all the different facets of the mind. Bollas argues that, as humans, we all share the same positive and negative traits in our minds. Regardless of how unpleasant such an idea might be, this aspect unites us to even the most repulsive xenophobe: 'each supporter of Trump or Brexit represents aspects of all selves' (Bollas 2018, p. xii). The current populism, on the contrary, manifests an aversion and repulsion for this 'democratic' approach to the *polis* as it seeks to silence or police, and ultimately erase, certain voices and instances.

The threatening intruder is the Other: the refugee, immigrant, LGBTQ+ person, etc. Porous borders become brick walls with no possibilities for exchange, driven by a fear of contagion, as epitomised in Italy by Matteo Salvini and Giorgia Meloni. Recalcati, however, promptly clarifies that securitarian trends are not simply the result of a nationalistic politics. Instead, he contends, much more radically, that they reside within each of us; they are intrinsic to the human species. This constitutes what he terms, rather provocatively, the 'fascist unconscious'. In this respect, fascism is not merely a traumatic historical period for many nations, but a latent tendency within human nature, 'a tendency', Recalcati claims, 'to prefer obedience to freedom' (p. 3). Freedom can be overwhelming and lead to anxiety; as a result, human beings might choose the comfort of chains over freedom to escape the daunting responsibility of making choices (Recalcati 2022a, p. 55). The fascist unconscious pertains to all humans and is geared at removing, segregating, and erasing the intruder inasmuch as they represent an irreducible Otherness. The aim is to shatter the democratic space of our psychic life in the name of protecting and preserving it.

What happens, though, if the virus is spreading—as with the 2020 pandemic—and the fear of contagion is real? Esposito and Recalcati express similar concerns regarding certain analyses of the measures implemented during the Covid-19 pandemic developed by some Italian philosophers. Recalcati, for instance, defines Giorgio Agamben's stance on the pandemic as an ideological drift (2022b, online), while Esposito disagrees with those who view the state's response as a 'totalitarian grip' (2021, p. 29). Social distancing, Recalcati argues, is not the same as turning the border into a rigid wall. Recalcati contends that what the pandemic showed us, unequivocally, is that freedom is meaningless if it is not coupled with solidarity and charity. The latter accounts for the dimension of 'singularity', which cannot be reduced to the universality/anonymous character of the masses. Freedom is not merely the property of the individual. Rather, ethically speaking, it coincides with the individual's responsibility towards other people and the broader community. The time of the Covid-19 pandemic overturned Thatcher's motto, according to which society does not exist; there are only individuals. Instead, it showed us that society, and community, does exist and, even more importantly, they are the only possibility for the individual to exist. The pandemic revealed the vacuous and ideological nature of freedom as an individual property, teaching us instead that true freedom is not measured by choice or free will, but is to be found in solidarity (Recalcati 2022a, p. x).

This led both Recalcati and Esposito to reflect on the role of institutions today and to denounce the pervasive anti-institutionalism. In Italy, institutions were exploited by Berlusconi and fiercely attacked by populist movements (e.g., the Five Star Movement). According to Lacan, the primary aim of human institutions is the 'reining in of jouissance' (2012, p. 272). An institution does not simply limit or regulate the enjoyment of an individual or group of individuals. Rather, it is concerned with coming together and forging a community by preserving the 'profound bond between freedom and responsibility, between history and future, between individual life and collective life, between Law and desire, between provenance and destination' (Recalcati 2022a, pp. 76–77). During the pandemic, institutions were accused both of exerting excessive control over the population and of hesitation and inaction. Esposito claims that instead of questioning how institutions treated citizens, we should instead consider how communities would have faced the virus without them, and what the consequences would have been without an institutional framework guiding our behaviour (2023, p. 10). In relation to institutions, Esposito defines populism as 'the will to bypass institutions; and before that, the failure to understand their meaning' (p. 13). For Esposito, institutions are 'decisive political subjects' (p. 13) that are responsible for instituting life 'beyond mere biological matter' (p. 19).

The connection between politics and psychoanalysis is also a central issue in the biopolitical work of Davide Tarizzo. Tarizzo argues that the pivotal question underpinning psychology, psychoanalysis, and psychiatry is essentially a Kantian one: What is humanity? These disciplines are concerned with understanding the human psyche, which is ultimately a variation of the broader question of human nature. Addressing this question inevitably leads to inquiries about psychological norms, health, and ailments, all of which are rooted in the fundamental inquiry into humanity itself. Furthermore, since they adopt an approach based on evaluation and assessment, these disciplines are naturally influenced by a specific theoretical perspective, which, being underpinned by cognitive-behavioural concerns, is particularly likely to elicit political controversies concerning the 'delicate issue of the relationship between politics and psychopathology, between political power and psychiatric knowledge' (2007b, p. 32). Defining what is human is an eminently political issue:

> Politics today, but perhaps always, is the battle for the definition of a principle of humanity. The sole and decisive political battle then unfolds, from this perspective, in the departments of neurology and psychiatry, in the waiting rooms of psychotherapists, in the padded rooms of the pharmaceutical industry, and in other similar places. It is there that the game of the human is truly played out, amidst the whispers and cries of those among us who find ourselves on the margins of (our own) humanity. (2007b, p. 37)

In so doing, Tarizzo argues that psychoanalysis is

> the only theoretical model that seems capable today of resisting the gradual biologisation of human nature (which goes hand in hand with the gradual reduction of the political sphere to the biopolitical sphere). And for this

reason, psychoanalysis now represents the key theory on human nature for any serious attempt to delve into the psychopolitical field (as opposed to the biopolitical field). (2007b, p. 51)

According to Tarizzo, the 'deepest vocation' of the biopolitical machine operating in today's society is to radically de-subjectify human beings. The biopolitical order of contemporary society differs from the Foucauldian paradigm based on normalisation. The new biopolitical rationality responds to a logic of optimisation and efficiency. Therefore, the 'techno-rationality of evaluation' (2011, p. 139) can only provide an operational definition of mental health which, according to Tarizzo:

> [...] emerges as measurable, quantifiable, and hence *objectively assessable*, only in behavioural and 'populational' terms. The mind, or the psyche, eventually disappears within the very frame of 'mental health', which becomes a matter of behaviours, rather than mental states, and what is more, it becomes a matter of the populational human being's behaviours, rather than a specific person's, with a forename and a surname. The behavioural-populational-evaluative human being becomes the *subjectum*, the deep anthropological foundation against which one has to measure, compute, and, if necessary, correct the behaviours and the superficial self-evaluations of every single speaking being. The biopolitical machine does not cease to function because this *subjectum* produces a radical de-subjectification of human beings. On the contrary, this is precisely its direction, its deepest vocation. Today's cognitive-behavioural therapies are but one of the many peripheral appendices of this machine, an appendix that has the merit of lucidly showing its intention: to de-subjectify the subject. (2011, p. 139)

In his biopolitics, Tarizzo critically examines the use of the concept of the death drive in political theory, particularly in challenging Slavoj Žižek's perspective. Žižek leverages Lacanian theory to conceptualise a subversive and revolutionary political act, offering a framework for a social and political radical change. However, Tarizzo contends that Žižek's approach, while theoretically provocative, remains overly abstract and leads to what he terms a 'revolution without a program' (2007b, p. 29). According to Tarizzo, Žižek envisions the authentic act—both political and psychoanalytic—as involving a dramatic, radical destruction of all knowledge and the foundational anchors of the subject. This destruction paves the way for a new space, a fresh beginning, which ultimately leads to genuine freedom. This revolutionary act, described by Tarizzo as an 'act of annihilation' (2007b, p. 28) permeated by death drive, is also seen as inherently destructive. Tarizzo argues that Žižek's embrace of the death drive as a path to liberation ultimately leads to what he calls 'the desert of the *Todestrieb*', where the subject is engulfed by pure destruction and nothingness (2007b, p. 29). On the contrary, Tarizzo elevates the notion of desire as the ultimate expression of subjectivity and freedom (2007b, p. 174). He posits that, from a Lacanian perspective, true freedom for the subject lies in obedience to the symbolic order, which intertwines the act of desire with the Other. For Tarizzo, this connection between obedience and freedom, enacted

> in the name of a symbolic power [...] liberates the subject from the deadly and repetitive mechanisms of self-imposed compulsion. This is, at least in my opinion, the truly political dimension of psychoanalysis. (2007b, p. 175)

In *Political Grammars: The Unconscious Foundations of Modern Democracy*, Tarizzo (2021) revisits Lacanian psychoanalysis to explore the political subject and the underlying structure and narratives that define it. He describes this as a clinical approach to political theory which brings together psychoanalysis, quintessentially the discipline that focuses on subjectivity, and political theory, which examines the dynamics of the political sphere. Tarizzo begins his investigation with the following key questions: 'What is the structure of our subjectivity?' and 'What is the real stuff of which our being is composed?' (p. 3). He then turns to Lacanian psychoanalysis, which he defines as 'the most sophisticated science of subjectivity of our time' (p. 28) as it deals with the true fiction that ultimately constitutes the subject. Tarizzo applies Lacan's theory of subjectivity to collective subjectivities, shifting the focus from the *ego*—the individual subjectivity, 'the holder of natural rights' (p. 13), such as peoples and citizens—to *nos*—the collective subjectivity, 'the holder of political sovereignty' (p. 13), such as nations and states. There is a similarity in the process of individual-subject formation, the first-person singular, and the collective-subject formation, the first-person plural. Lacanian psychoanalysis is particularly suited to investigate this symbolic organisation, that is, the individual and collective subjective grammar of the unconscious. For Lacan, the subject is not a substance but rather a continuous process of transformation: 'subjectivity means subjectification' (p. 18). As Tarizzo puts it: 'According to Lacan, the *ego* is merely a hole circumscribed by words and representations that are syntactically organized and distributed around it. There is nothing that prevents us from interpreting the political *nos* along the same lines' (p. 6). Both individual and collective subjectivities are a never-ending process shaped by identifications, traumas, and narratives, that is, a grammatical formation in which 'truth, being and real are knotted together' (pp. 28–29).

Lacan did not develop a specific theory of political subject formation, but Tarizzo's contribution lies in showing how Lacan's distinction between 'subject' and 'identity' can enhance our understanding of modern democratic politics. Tarizzo argues that democracy flourishes when the gap between subjectivity and identity is preserved, suggesting that democracy is a continuous process of navigating the absence of a fixed identity, with its direction shaped by the prevailing political grammar in place. For example, the grammar of fascism rests on the delusion of repressing heterogeneity—getting rid of the intruder qua Other in the biopolitical language of Esposito and Recalcati—and reaching homogeneity. Tarizzo signals the difference between old and new fascism. The old one resulted in the birth of political subjects such as the 'master race', while for the new one 'the result is the birth of an altogether different subject, which is no longer a political actor, properly speaking, but a passive, anonymous entity: the human population' (p. 163). For Tarizzo, the grammar of new fascism, 'unlike the others, fuels the depoliticization and a kind of increasing desubjectification of society. Nowadays, this process usually goes under the name *neoliberalism*' (p. 165). Tarizzo uses medical metaphors to argue that the new form of fascism is more dangerous than the old one. He compares the old fascism to a virus that, while it does not entirely kill off the body politic it parasitises, profoundly disrupts its functioning. In contrast, he likens the new fascism to a cancer, suggesting it is more insidious and potentially lethal for the body politic (p. 177).

Franco 'Bifo' Berardi is another Italian biopolitical thinker who engages extensively with psychoanalytic thought. Berardi's biopolitics examines the impact of contemporary capitalism, which he terms semiocapitalism, on both the individual and the collective psyche. According to Berardi, semiocapitalism is characterised by an economy where the production and exchange of signs, symbols, and information have become central (2009). In this system, the value of goods and services is increasingly determined by their symbolic and cultural meanings rather than their material substance. Berardi highlights the crucial role of the media, communication technologies, and the manipulation of information in shaping economic and social dynamics (2009). Unlike traditional capitalism, which centres on the production of material goods, semiocapitalism relies on info-labour and emphasises the production of psychic stimulation and the control of the mind rather than the body. In this context, Berardi explores the changes in the psychopathologic landscape as society transitions from late industrialism to semiocapitalism, focusing on the transformation of the social psycho-sphere and the mass psychopathologies of current times. To do so, he draws extensively from psychoanalysis, using concepts from Lacanian vocabulary such as the unconscious, desire, and subjectivity. Some of his insights align closely with those of Italian Lacanians, demonstrating the intersection of his work with Lacanian psychoanalytic theory.

In tracing a 'history of the psycho-sphere of a society' (2021a, p. viii), Berardi identifies three main periods the social unconscious has undergone, which he refers to as the ages of the unconscious. In the first age, the social unconscious was explored by Freud, who identified neurosis as the prevailing malaise of bourgeois society. In this psychopathological regime, the repression of sexual drives and the renunciation of desire are the principal cause of psychological suffering. The second age of the unconscious, which coincides with the rise of semiocapitalism and began roughly with the expansion of neoliberal capitalism in the 1980s, sees psychosis replacing neurosis as the 'general mode of psychic suffering' (2021a, p. ix). The rapid expansion of the infosphere, marked by a heightened stimulation of the nervous system from internet communication and the growth of neoliberal globalisation, has paved the way for the collective psychological transformations Berardi describes. This new psychopathological regime is characterised by anxiety, panic, attention disorders, depression, and psychosis (2021a, pp. ix–x). In this post-neurotic psycho-sphere, Berardi contends that 'the intensity of the social and emotional rhythm becomes unbearable and the only way to sever suffering is to sever the link with desire, and, consequently, also the desiring link with reality' (2021a, p. x). This produces a psychopathological response where the unconscious is 'drag[ged] out of itself, externalising it to the point of a psychotic explosion' (2021a, p. x). This mapping of the social unconscious through various stages affecting the collective psycho-sphere reflects the Lacanian periodisation, which underscores the transition from a clinic initially focused on neurosis, as seen with Freud, to a clinic centred on psychosis (see Chap. 3).

According to Berardi, by the end of the twentieth century, repression had receded from the social landscape, and the focus in the new libidinal economy had shifted from repression to the pathologies of desire. Today's dominant pathologies are no longer neurotic and rooted in the repression of libido; instead, they are 'schizo-pathologies, produced by the expressive explosion of the *just do it*' mentality (2009, p. 175). Berardi describes this as 'a psychotic acting out' (2015, p. 56), linking psychosis to 'the dimension of action and an excess of energy and information' (2009, p. 179). He observes that the psychopathologies emerging in 'the first generations of the connective era cannot be understood at all from the standpoint of the repressive and disciplinary paradigm' (2009, p. 180). In this shift, work has moved from being a source of alienation tied to capitalist production to becoming the focal point of psychic and libidinal investment in today's society. This attachment to work often leads to pathologies such as burnout and depression, yet it is frequently perceived as 'the only place providing narcissistic reinforcement to individuals' (2009, p. 80). Berardi argues that repression is no longer the main cause of contemporary psychopathologies. Instead, it is 'the injunction to express' that has become an omnipresent social obligation (2009, pp. 178–179). Desire and simulation are pivotal concepts in Berardi's analysis, particularly in the context of the mediascape. He further explores what he calls the psycho-sphere, where 'reality is replaced by simulation' (2015, p. 24). Berardi argues that the substitution of reality with simulacra is a defining characteristic of semiocapitalism, a contemporary production regime in which capital is valorised through the constant generation of information flows (2015, p. 24). This shift has contributed to widespread psychological conditions such as 'depression, catatonia, and psychotic acting out' (2015, p. 56). His analysis closely aligns with the clinical theories of Italian Lacanians, particularly in their identification of the new symptoms, the imperative of enjoyment, the vanishing of desire, and the psychotic undertones of the contemporary psychopathologies.

Nevertheless, Berardi's analysis considers the impact of technology and the infosphere, areas largely overlooked by Italian Lacanians. He claims that the pervasive integration of technology along with the computerisation of production and social communication impose 'a molecular domination upon the collective nervous network' (2009, p. 188). This domination, which he calls 'thanato-politics', signifies the subjugation of life to inanimate objects, reducing human activity to mere cognitive automatism. According to Berardi, this is the essence of contemporary totalitarianism, where the 'dead object' dominates the living (2009, p. 188). Furthermore, Berardi suggests that the collapse of the global economy can be seen as a re-emergence of the human soul, challenging the neoliberal ideology that sought to reduce human experience to mere rationality. He argues that the neoliberal economic machine is failing because it overlooked the complexity of the human soul, which includes fear, anxiety, panic, and depression—emotions that have surfaced after being suppressed by the promise of the eternal victory of capitalism (2009, p. 207). Berardi critiques neoliberal ideology for its flawed belief that the economy can be understood as 'a balanced system of rational expectations and investments' (2009, p. 208). He asserts that this belief was misguided, failing to account for 'the systemic effects of the social mind' (p. 2010). Consequently, the neoliberal ideal of economic equilibrium has resulted in a 'bipolar economy' that swings 'from euphoria to panic and it is now teetering on the brink of a deep depression' (2009, p. 210).

In the aftermath of the global pandemic, amidst war, economic turmoil, mental health crises, and ecological challenges, Berardi identifies the Covid pandemic as a threshold and a peak, marking 'the erosion of all symbolic and political orders' (2021a, p. vii). He observes the emergence of 'new mental configurations' (2021a, p. 59) within the psycho-sphere, noting that the collapse of a 'universalist representation of subjectivity, based on Western colonialism' is yet to be fully grasped. This disintegration has fuelled a resistance that manifests itself in the forms of racism, nationalism, and fundamentalism witnessed in society (2021a, p. 91). As he writes:

> The intimate foreign land of the unconscious exploded during the age of global connection and hyperexpressivity; then, in the wake of the viral collapse a sort of crepuscular silence followed, a fading of energy, and a game of reciprocal culpabilisation invaded the space of sociality. (2021a, p. 66)

For Berardi, the third age of the unconscious is an era still on the horizon, but we are currently transitioning towards it. This 'open future' will be shaped by our collective consciousness, and the political initiatives, creative vision, and healing practices we develop during this period of change (2021a, p. xi). In this context, Berardi highlights the crucial role of psychoanalysis and philosophy. Instead of panicking or resisting chaos, he suggests that these disciplines should embrace 'chaos and exhaustion as starting points for their reflection' (2021a, p. vii). Berardi challenges psychoanalysis to move beyond its traditional therapeutic role and contribute to the 'collective mental evolution' in the face of apocalyptic scenarios like the one we are experiencing today (2021a, p. 85). This calls for rethinking and reframing the social space of psychoanalysis.

Berardi provides a compelling examination of the concept of sublimation, noting its contentious nature within psychoanalysis. He acknowledges that sublimation is often viewed as repressive and authoritarian when understood merely as the 'postponement and displacement of sexual desire' (2021a, p. 86). Traditionally, in Freudian terms, sublimation served as a mechanism to protect from anxiety, redirecting repressed energies away from immediate libidinal satisfaction and towards more socially acceptable goals (2021a, pp. 86–87). However, Berardi suggests that Lacan's reworking of sublimation transcends this limited view. In a Lacanian sense, sublimation can be seen as a cultural reconfiguration of desire, elevating it to a higher level of creative expression and displacement of libidinal energy (2021a, pp. 87, 93). Berardi, in line with Italian Lacanian thought, argues that 'the neoliberal acceleration and the "just do it" culture' have severely diminished the capacity for sublimation (2021a, p. 87). As society increasingly chases rapid pleasure through standardised experiences and immediate gratification, the space for emotional and psychological elaboration has contracted, leading to a decline in the capacity for sublimation (2021a, p. 87). He contends that, under capitalism, particularly within the fast-paced dynamics of semiocapitalism, desire is perpetually mobilised while genuine pleasure is simultaneously obstructed. This creates an economic and psychological environment where individuals are driven to desire endlessly, yet the opportunity for true pleasure is erased by the relentless demands of competition and accumulation (2021a, p. 126). Berardi's analysis aligns with the perspectives of Italian Lacanians, suggesting that, when disconnected from pleasure, desire becomes a relentless and joyless force—what he calls the 'psychological engine' of capitalism. The enjoyment Berardi describes appears as an enjoyment without pleasure, where the media perpetuate the promise of enjoyment but overload human attention, making actual pleasure unattainable (2021a, p. ix). This perspective underscores the necessity of uniting desire with *jouissance*, as Italian Lacanian thought suggests. When desire is severed from genuine pleasure, it fuels the relentless cycle of capitalist consumption and dissatisfaction (2021a, p. 126). Berardi seems to advocate for reconnecting desire with enjoyment to break free from this cycle and restore a sense of fulfilment and authenticity.

Welcome to the *Unconshow*!

In postmillennial times, a series of pivotal historical, political, and cultural events in the Western world—9/11, the global financial crisis, the rise of populism—set the stage for a resurgence of realism in philosophy and ignited transnational Lacanian debates on the notion of the real. In Italy, the interplay between postmodern relativism, the distortion and virtualisation of reality, and media-driven narratives, particularly under the Berlusconi government, which obscured the severity of the economic crisis facing Italians, brought the concept of realism back into sharp focus as a critical political issue. This return to realism also profoundly influenced Italian philosophy (Di Martino and Verdicchio 2017, pp.

vii–xxxiii) and reshaped its artistic, literary, and cinematic landscape (see Chap. 5). As these discussions evolved, Lacanian theory began to subtly infiltrate the discussions of Italian philosophers, even those not traditionally aligned with Lacanian thought. As a result, a new connection between Italian philosophy and Italian Lacanianism was forged, particularly through Italian new realism's reclaiming of the notion of reality and the Lacanian concept of the real.

In Italy, realism regained prominence largely thanks to the work of philosopher Maurizio Ferraris. In his 2011 text *Manifesto for New Realism* and subsequent work (De Caro and Ferraris 2012; Ferraris 2015a, b), Ferraris develops Italian new realism, aligning it with other realist movements such as speculative realism and object-oriented ontology. He advocates for a return to reality as a response to the constructivist and nihilistic tendencies of hermeneutics. Ferraris posits that new realism represents a broader realist turn (2014, p. xiv) and connects this resurgence with the end of postmodernity. Taking a critical stance on postmodernism, Ferraris challenges its hallmark notions—the erosion of the realist tradition and the derealisation of reality as seen in the works of Fredric Jameson, Jean-François Lyotard, and Jean Baudrillard. These postmodern theorists highlight how reality, reproduced through traditional and digital media, creates hyperreal effects that overshadow and distance us from actual reality. In this view, reality is ultimately replaced by its mediated representation. New realism firmly rejects two core postmodernist claims: that 'all reality is socially constructed and infinitely manipulable' and that 'truth is a useless notion' (Ferraris 2014, pp. xiv–xv).

Ferraris (2014, p. xiii) argues that twentieth-century philosophy primarily embraced anti-realist tendencies (including hermeneutics, postmodernism, and the linguistic turn). The philosophical trends of the twentieth century viewed reality as purely theoretical, social, linguistic, or hermeneutic constructs, neglecting its factual existence. In contrast, twenty-first-century philosophy has witnessed a shift towards realism across various domains, such as ontology, cognitive science, and aesthetics. In reclaiming the notion of reality, Ferraris emphasises the factual essence of reality through the concept of its inherent 'unamendability' (Ferraris 2014), the fundamental impossibility of amending reality. Ferraris asserts that the postmodern derealisation of reality peaked around the turn of the century. In Italy, this derealisation coincided with Berlusconi's entrepreneurial and political rise, where the mediatisation of politics and the media manipulation of reality became defining features of the era. As Ferraris observes:

> The real world has certainly become a tale or, rather—as we shall see—it became a reality show; but the outcome was media populism, namely, a system in which (if one has such power) one can claim to make people believe anything. In news broadcasts and talk shows we did witness the realm of the 'no facts, only interpretations' that—in what unfortunately is a fact and not an interpretation—then showed its true meaning: 'the argument of the strongest is always the best'. (2014, p. 3)

Ferraris coined the term 'realitism' to depict a distinct condition that reached its apex in the postmillennial era, marked by a striking blend of reality and fiction and epitomised by the popularity of reality TV shows in Italy during the 2000s.

Ferraris' new realism ignited a heated debate among Italian philosophers and Lacanians, who argued that the concept of the real, understood as a Lacanian rather than a philosophical concept, challenges the notion of reality but has generally been overlooked in Italian new realism. Non-Lacanian scholars do not account for the category of the real, which could limit their understanding both of the shift that occurred in contemporary society and of the post-2000 return of realism and realist trends. This also prevents them from moving away from a strict dichotomy between reality on the one hand and virtual reality, fake reality, and non-reality on the other. This is particularly apparent when they deal with specific realities broadcasted on television and the Internet, in reality TV shows, on social media, and so forth. On the contrary, since Lacanians distinguish between reality and the real, they offer more appropriate theoretical tools to analyse the new wave of realism in twenty-first-century Italy. Italian Lacanian scholars argue that the crisis of the symbolic, coupled with the dominance of the capitalist discourse, has resulted in a dual outcome: an increase in the imaginary akin to postmodern derealisation on the one hand, and a resurgence of the real on the other (Recalcati 2010; Carmagnola and Bonazzi 2011; Lolli 2012).

Lacan repeatedly critiques the narrow perspective of realists, arguing that their belief in a unified and objective reality is fundamentally flawed (2006 [1957], p. 17, 2013, p. 61). Italian Lacanians emphasise that Lacanian psychoanalysis diverges sharply from conventional psychological theories and other psychoanalytic orientations by rejecting the idea that subjects have direct access to reality. They maintain that new realism overlooks the inherent structural impossibility for human beings to directly interface with reality. For this reason, according to Lacan, reality is always subjectively constructed and fictionalised. In Lacanian terms, reality is not so much an object to be represented as something inherently representational. Lolli, for example, asserts that there is a 'filter' between the subject and the world, a 'veil' that separates them, and a 'medium' that makes the world perceivable and bearable for the subject. Without this filter—the signifier—reality would overwhelm us, reaching us in the form of trauma and shock (2011, p. 55). As Lolli maintains:

> every event of reality is read and interpreted in a certain way by each of us, depending on the relationship the subject has with the signifier [...] We relate to the signifier, not to reality. We always come into contact with the signifier, with a signifying filter that allows us to represent reality. (2011, pp. 55–56)

Pagliardini and Ronchi emphasise the enduring relevance of Lacan's theory and clinical practice today, particularly his ability to define the real without resorting to a realist perspective. They caution against the resurgence of a naive, pre-Kantian realism, which they describe as neo-positivistic and promoted by so-called realist philosophers of the last generation (2014, p. 13). Ronchi specifically warns us against the illusion of objective reality when he writes:

> how can 'there is nothing but language' be reconciled with the assertion of the real 'outside the symbolic', with the notion that 'there is One', without falling back into the naivety of the pre-linguistic? How, in short, can we escape from the claustrophobia of modernity without falling into the trap of realism? There is a strong temptation, among psychoanalysts and philosophers, to resolve the issue by regressing to pre-Kantian ontologies. This is clearly illustrated by many Lacanian analysts' flirtation with neuroscience and the success that proposals for new realistic ontologies enjoy today in

> the philosophical world (the most interesting case in Italy is undoubtedly that of Maurizio Ferraris). However, this is not the path followed by Lacan. (2012a, pp. 69–70)

Similarly, Recalcati (2012) critiques the simplistic understanding of reality advocated by Ferraris and the new realist philosophers, instead championing an anti-realist Lacanian perspective, especially in the clinical context. He acknowledges that the new realism debate centres on the defence of reality by so-called new realists, who push back against the postmodern drift of hermeneutics. Recalcati challenges these polarised perspectives, arguing that the Lacanian notion of the real enables us to step back from the false dichotomy of factual reality versus its interpretation. Both perspectives, he contends, fail to recognise the crucial Lacanian distinction between reality and the real, often using the terms interchangeably. Recalcati explains:

> The impersonal and tautological nature of reality does not involve the subject but rather excludes or forecloses them, as Lacan would say. This means that reality is a 'frame without a subject', it is a function of it; it detaches the subject from their libidinal being, shields them from the possibility of encountering their Real. But if reality is a continuity, the real is the rupture of this continuity, it is a fault line in reality. [...] everything that awakens us from the slumber of reality belongs to the order of the real. (2012, p. 201)

According to Recalcati, 'the real never truly succumbs to being shaped, tamed, or diminished by any interpretation' (p. 201). The real resists any interpretations, emphasising that psychoanalysis is not a hermeneutic practice. This can be appreciated in clinical practice when the death drive—another name for the real—manifests itself as a relentless loop of *jouissance* impervious to reality's demands and beyond the reach of interpretation (p. 204). The aforementioned Italian Lacanians reject the notion of reality conceived of as an independent, factual entity disconnected from subjectivity, insisting that access to reality is inseparable from unconscious fantasy.[18]

[18] This perspective aligns Italian Lacanian thought with that of prominent Anglophone Lacanians, such as Bruce Fink, Slavoj Žižek, and Alenka Zupančič. The Lacanian distinction between reality and the real challenges both philosophical realism and the hermeneutic conception of reality. Žižek

In this debate, Lacan's real emerges as that which disrupts and interferes with our everyday reality. The engagement with Lacan's theory, although often implicit and limited, is primarily filtered through the works of Žižek. One essential reference point when approaching the philosophical debate on the new wave of realism in postmillennial Italy is Žižek's analysis of the 9/11 terrorist attacks, where he explores the clash between the ideology of global liberal capitalism and the real as a traumatic event that forces an abrupt confrontation with the limits of our imaginary and symbolic reality (Žižek 2002).

In his 2015 *Persons and Things*, Esposito acknowledges the 'pressing demand of reality' (Esposito 2015, p. 90) in postmillennial times. Unlike Ferraris, Esposito is among those Italian philosophers who directly refer to Lacan and recognise the crucial distinction between reality and the real. He sees Lacan's theory as a useful theoretical tool to better understand the new wave of realism in postmillennial Italy (see Chap. 5). Esposito maintains that 'after the unrealistic delirium of the postmodern period, the pendulum of thought is now shifting toward a new realism' (p. 90), drawing on Alain Badiou's 'passion for the real' and Jean Baudrillard's indication that 'contemporary hyperrealism is the continuation and counter effect of an identical process of derealization' (p. 91). In line with Italian Lacanian thought, Esposito contends that, in contrast to the postmodern derealisation of reality, an 'excess of the real' (p. 93) is now coming to the forefront:

> the imperative of *jouissance* brings us closer to the heart of the Thing, to its glowing core. No longer covered by protective barriers that shelter us from

---

argues that the key difference between the Lacanian stance and 'naïve realism' lies in the understanding of reality as an imaginary-symbolic representational construct to shield the subject from the real. From this perspective, 'reality itself can function as an escape from encountering the Real' (Tarizzo 2007, p. 222). The real, unlike reality, is not a representation. As Fink points out, Lacan's distinction allows us to identify 'an ideological or ethical difference between certain forms of psychoanalysis and Lacanian psychoanalysis' (1995, p. 25). Moreover, Zupančič highlights that the Lacanian concept of the real problematises our understanding of reality itself (2014a, p. 163). However, Lacan does not endorse an unproblematic ontological realism (Zupančič 2014a, p. 163). As Zupančič states that 'the crucial point of this "psychoanalytic realism" is that the real is not a substance or being, but precisely its limit' (Zupančič 2014b, p. 28). Similarly to Italian Lacanians, Sbriglia and Žižek (2020) insist on preserving the notion of the subject, especially in relation to the real.

> its searing rays, it appears to us in nauseating and violent proximity. When the veil that covers it – the symbolic network that aggregates human experience in the connection of social relationships – is torn away, the terrifying aspect of the real is revealed. It is all that remains of reality once it is deprived of its phantasmal support. When this happens, no longer barred as it was in the infinite deferment of desire, the Thing becomes directly present to us. This de-sublimation of the object causes a collapse of the symbolic space, promoting an immediate relationship with the Other. Trying, in vain, to appropriate the thing, we become caught in a form that both terrorizes and disgusts us. (2015, pp. 95–96)

Esposito refers to this desublimation as the 'excessive aspect' of the real (p. 96) which he regards as the outcome of the shift from postmodernity to hypermodernity. Hence, the turn of the century appears to mark an overlap between derealised reality and reality disrupted by the uncanny return of the real. The real, by means of traumatic events or disturbing images and videos, destructively enters the frame of our everyday reality, which is perceived merely as the product of media representation. In this respect, the real is conceived of as an awakening from the sleep of reality. However, it is also affected by this very derealisation. Drawing from Žižek, Esposito argues that the 9/11 terrorist attacks appear to be the epitome of this oversaturation of the imaginary and the irruption of the real, which are two faces of the same coin, that is to say, the crisis of the symbolic. Esposito agrees with the Lacanians when he defines the real in terms of an awakening: disrupting the familiar frame of our everyday reality, it directly impacts the subject. It is at this point that, 'stripped of any further meaning, crushed into its own immanence, the real shows us its deadly face' (p. 96).

In his eponymous book, Lolli (2012) defines the postmillennial era as the age of the *unonshow*. He is not simply referring here to the shameless and pervasive spectacularisation of private life in the media; rather, he is conceptualising in Lacanian terms the proliferation of the imaginary derived from the deficiency of the symbolic in contemporary society. The primacy, or power, of the imaginary in postmillennial society is the flip side of the weakening of the symbolic, which also goes hand in hand with the disruptive emergence of the real. Lolli agrees with many Lacanian scholars that the crisis of the symbolic order has led to the 'forceful affirmation of the real' (p. 46), which disruptively returns in contemporary psychopathologies and social bonds. According to Lolli, the weakening of the symbolic, the ascendancy of the imaginary, and the irruption of the real have become the new coordinates shaping the emergence of contemporary social and psychic suffering in the age of the *unconshow* (p. 11).

Lolli considers these emerging forms of psychopathologies and social interactions as fundamentally borderline. While the subject without an unconscious was rooted in the clinic of psychosis and perversion (Chap. 3), the subject of the *unconshow* is ultimately a borderline subject:[19] one without limits, floating aimlessly in a world which is equally boundless. He argues that the borderline subject is the inevitable outcome and, at the same time, the epitome of a borderline society. According to Lolli, 'the borderline phenomenon is a symptom of the West, an unsurpassable indicator of the "spirit of the times", a sort of amplifier – through the powerful resonance chamber of psychopathology – of its most distinctive character' (p. 19). The psychic economy of the borderline subject mirrors the dominant discourse of today's sociocultural context, which is marked by the simultaneous presence of two opposing trends: the necessity of limits and libidinal sacrifice (Oedipal statement) and the promotion of disavowing loss and enjoyment (capitalist discourse). In the borderline subject, as in society, one no longer finds the conflict between desire and its interdiction that characterised Freud's era. As Lolli argues,

> A compulsive drive towards the immediate fulfilment of one's needs; an inability to tolerate the slightest frustrations; instability in one's emotional relationships; a rush towards pathological consumption; widespread dependency; uncontrollable hyperactivity; and the denial of any form of narcissistic limitation: these are the elements that define its unique clinical

[19] Although Lolli draws extensively from Otto Kernberg's theorisation about the borderline personality, he nevertheless considers this diagnostic category as evidence of the psychoanalysts' struggle to fully grasp the symptomatic effects of the social transformations occurring from the middle of the twentieth century. More precisely, Lolli regards this diagnostic category as a sign of the limitations of Freudian theory, which is confined to the neurotic/psychotic dichotomy and fails to acknowledge a middle ground between the two. Lolli also acknowledges that the category of the borderline is often overused, particularly due to the complexities of diagnosing contemporary psychopathologies, risking overlooking the underlying personality structure.

> features and which, if we think about it, also characterise contemporary society. (p. 9)

The psychic economy of the borderline subject is marked by pervasive anguish, a constant sense of alarm, ambivalence towards the Other, and a feeling of being overwhelmed by a present that is disconnected from both the past and the future. This emotional precariousness, according to Lolli, reflects the pervasive traits of contemporary society.

In further exploring the age of the *unconshow*, Lolli juxtaposes Lacan's concept of the imaginary with Guy Debord's notion of the spectacle. Although these concepts are distinct, they both reveal the progressive unravelling of the symbolic network, which underpins contemporary processes dominated by the imaginary and the real. Lolli examines the role of television during Berlusconism, emphasising its pervasive influence on social relations and its focus on imagery over mundane reality. Television, particularly reality TV shows, exemplifies the *unconshow* by promoting the illusion that one can become or achieve anything. Lolli's analysis of reality TV highlights the intense competition, the pressure to perform and excel, the obsession with pleasing others for acceptance, self-assertion, and the rejection of genuine relationships. He also addresses how television exposes viewers to the brutality and absurdity of existence and the spectacle of trauma. Lolli argues that the deliberate production of anxiety in citizens appears to be a distinctive feature of the current political-media actions, claiming that

> the viewer, stunned and distressed by the overstimulation of the horrible, becomes a weakened citizen, made fragile by the personal turmoil they experience, absorbed by their desire to find some meaning in what they have witnessed, and therefore less attentive and critical towards the events surrounding them. (p. 129)

The political implications here are significant. Citizens are bombarded with relentless stimuli and messages that foster a perpetual state of concern and anxiety, heightening their perception of threats to their wellbeing. In response, they seek refuge by conforming to the social imperative of consumerism: buying, owning, discarding, and ultimately complying with the system. Despite being overwhelmed by feelings of helplessness and impotence, they remain dutiful consumers, driven by their anxiety to find solace in the objects the market offers. Lolli's analysis suggests a complex interplay between three factors: the relationship between individuals and reality; the intersection of realism and psychoanalysis; and the potential degeneration into media populism.

Videocracy

The documentary *Videocracy—Basta Apparire* (Gandini 2009) portrays the controversial world of postmillennial Italian television, characterised by show business personalities and ruthless wannabes. It sheds light on the process of spectacularisation, which extends from the realm of television into everyday life, placing a significant emphasis on appearance well before the advent of social media. The documentary focuses in particular on Berlusconi's pivotal role in shaping Italian television and, consequently, Italian society. *Videocracy* offers a sharp political critique of Berlusconi's divisive influence as both Italy's prime minister and the owner of its most powerful television empire, depicting how Berlusconism first captivated the public's imagination before infiltrating the political landscape. Predictably, *Videocracy* was labelled an 'anti-Berlusconi documentary' (Gundle 2015, p. 104) and its reception was hindered.[20]

Scholars have observed that, as the title *Videocracy* implies, the documentary critiques the fabricated reality broadcasted on Berlusconi's Italian television networks, with the ancient Greek word *κρατία* (power) emphasising the influence of the media (Rigoletto 2012; Gundle 2015). While the documentary effectively exposes the persistent distortion of reality on Italian television and its profound impact on the public, this perspective risks oversimplifying the documentary's broader significance. To fully appreciate *Videocracy*, it is crucial to ask: What reality does the documentary actually depict? Is it simply a critique of postmillennial

[20] Both RAI and Mediaset refused to broadcast the trailer of the documentary film, claiming, respectively, that the documentary was too political and a sheer attack on commercial television.

Italian television, or does it delve deeper into the social, cultural, and political fabric of twenty-first-century Italy? *Videocracy* transcends a mere portrayal of Berlusconi's Italy; it documents the society of enjoyment, depicting the Italian postmillennial subject as understood by Italian Lacanianism. *Videocracy* documents the real in the Lacanian sense, addressing enjoyment, the driving force behind the hypermodern subject and fuelled by capitalist discourse.

To contextualise the significance of Lacanian theory in this analysis, it is important to consider Federico Luisetti's critical perspective:

> We need not share a Lacanian orthodoxy or worship the 'objet petit à' in order to realize that the democratic dream of constituting an Italian 'people' out of a fragmented landscape of competing local identities and social classes has now been - perversely but also successfully - carried out by the libidinal ties of the naked showgirls and vociferously racist public sphere of Berlusconi's television channels. This dystopian reorganization of political order in Italy is a living testimony of the non-ineluctability of the Western liberal state apparatus. (2011, p. 232)

Luisetti downplays the necessity of a strictly Lacanian interpretation, yet this critique paradoxically highlights the relevance of Lacanian theory in unpacking the libidinal dynamics at play in Berlusconi's Italy. Even as Luisetti questions the need for Lacanian theory, the pervasive influence of libidinal ties in shaping political and social realities underscores why Lacanian analysis remains crucial. Berlusconi's Italy prefigures the rise of politicians like Boris Johnson and Donald Trump, as well as contemporary populist movements (Foot 2016; Kirchgaessner 2016; Mazzarella 2020). Thus, *Videocracy* becomes a key case study, enriching the sociopolitical analysis within contemporary Italian Lacanianism.

Lolli (2012, p. 100) describes *Videocracy* as a remarkable cinematic documentation of Italy during the Berlusconi era. Italian Lacanians view Berlusconism as the distinct Italian manifestation of the Western capitalist command to enjoy.[21] The documentary illustrates the oversaturation

[21] The idea that contemporary society is characterised by a command to 'enjoy!' is a widely accepted idea not only amongst contemporary Italian Lacanians but also amongst contemporary international Lacanians (Fink 2014a, 2014b; McGowan 2004; Salecl 2004; Žižek 1989, 2000). The idea

of the imaginary through the videocratic trend fostered and embodied by television, unveiling the emergence of the real through stories and interviews with real-life characters. Bradshaw's description of the documentary as 'a dreamy, mesmeric and highly disturbing psychogeography of 21st-century Italy' (2010, para. 1) is thus entirely accurate.

In the documentary, *jouissance* is depicted indirectly through the portrayal of the characters and their controversial behaviour, in particular their attempt to pursue unlimited personal enjoyment, to affirm their ego at any cost on the television screen, and to turn their persona into a brand. Saturated in excess, their relentless pursuit of enjoyment is evident in their obsessions to secure a television appearance and quick money. This theme spans from ordinary, unskilled individuals aspiring to fame, to ruthless, well-connected figures, ultimately finding its fullest embodiment in Berlusconi and his insatiable need for adoration. For instance, in a scene at the Mediaset studios, a middle-aged woman undresses without hesitation, incited by a laughing casting director, forcing the audience into discomfort. Other examples include the wealthy neighbour of Berlusconi's villa in Sardinia, who sells pictures of exclusive parties, and a group of young women taking part in castings to become showgirls for Berlusconi's television programmes. Nevertheless, focusing solely on the moral judgement of these characters overlooks the deeper issue at play. The matter extends beyond a simplistic critique of the negative impact of television on society, revealing a fundamental trait of contemporary society. The characters vividly embody the postmillennial subject without an unconscious and belonging to the age of the *unconshow*, earnestly seeking enjoyment and grappling to find their place in society.

Riccardo Carnevali, a factory worker with dreams of becoming a television celebrity, fantasises about joining the Italian version of *Big Brother* as a way to escape his financial and personal problems. Riccardo envisions himself as a hybrid of Ricky Martin and Bruce Lee, combining singing with martial arts. However, his amateurish performance and lack of talent make his aspirations appear somewhat pitiable. What stands out

---

of a shift from a society of prohibition, based on individual renunciation of individual enjoyment for the greater societal good, to a society of enjoyment, which promotes enjoyment as the supreme duty, is shared by transnational Lacanianism.

is his desperate belief in the idea that the world of television can provide everything he needs. For Riccardo, the world of television not only offers him the possibility of being seen, but also serves as a gateway to money, women, success, and a life of endless enjoyment. Lele Mora, a television agent, is portrayed as a key figure in Berlusconi's media empire, being seen as someone who can turn dreams into reality by offering coveted opportunities for fame in Italian show business. Mora has acquired a near-mythical status, adored by many, and lives in an ivory tower where he plays and listens to fascist songs.

One of the most significant characters in *Videocracy* is Fabrizio Corona, a ruthless and money-driven paparazzo who epitomises the superficiality and emptiness of show business. Corona represents the postmillennial subject, undivided and uncastrated, devoid of an unconscious. There is no space for the split subject but only for a solid ego and its performativity. He is indifferent to social bonds and human relationships; instead, he stages his private life for profit. Obsessed with the myth of the self-made person and his own image, Corona is utterly unconcerned with the consequences of his actions, viewing his appearance as a tool for economic gain, and even capitalising on his time in detention. This is the perverted core of what Lolli defines as the age of the *unconshow*: the chimera for 'the restoration of a state of enjoyment uninfected by the virus of castration' (Lolli 2012, p. 102). Contemporary society, according to Lolli, rewards identifications that reject the limitations imposed on the ego, lack, and castration (Lolli 2012, p. 101). The camera follows Corona closely, documenting his everyday life and intimate moments, such as when he stands completely naked in front of a mirror in his bathroom before going to a nightclub as a special guest. Corona's body is young, muscled, tattooed, and apparently strong, invincible, and flawless. He is completely caught up in an ecstatic admiration of his own body and mirror image. Lolli argues that the contemporary dream of changing one's life—whether through a new home, job, body, or lifestyle—is a central theme of many television programmes (2012, p. 90). This dream reflects the capitalist discourse that encourages individuals to seek satisfaction not by questioning their lives but by simply acquiring new objects of enjoyment. This perpetuates the myth of the self-made person and the pursuit of self-realisation. Lacanian psychoanalysis, however, debunks the illusion of a fully self-reliant subject, emphasising the inescapable dependence on the Other.

The documentary explores the perilous interplay between the Lacanian registers of the imaginary and the real. In *Videocracy*, the imaginary takes centre stage, reflecting its overwhelming presence in contemporary society and the social media landscape through a flood of reality television images and programmes. As Mario Perniola emphasises, 'The imaginary is the realm of illusion, specularity, and narcissism. It lacks both the structured and mediated character of the symbolic, and the harsh and inaccessible traumatic character of the real' (2004, p. 10). Lolli distinguishes between Lacan's imaginary and Debord's notion of the spectacle, arguing that these are fundamentally different theoretical constructs that should not be conflated. However, he acknowledges a shared idea: the progressive unravelling of the symbolic in our society activates processes in which elements of the imaginary and the real become increasingly dominant (Lolli 2012, p. 37). In our society, the crisis of the symbolic gives rise to two phenomena: the dominance of the imaginary, which becomes pervasive and overwhelming, and the resurgence of the real, which can be either disruptive (real qua trauma) or excessive (real qua *jouissance*). Therefore, addressing the imaginary is essential to understanding the excess of the real as *jouissance*, as the two are closely interconnected.

In his essay *Applauso: L'impero dell'assenso*, Tarizzo (2007a) contends that contemporary reality is not entirely assimilated by the spectacle; rather, 'everything tends to be transformed into a spectacle' (p. 89). This suggests that reality is not simply obliterated by the artificial reality of television, show business, or, in the last decade, social media, but that there is a pervasive tendency to turn everything into a spectacle. Tarizzo identifies two new central coordinates of the political landscape today. The first is the aesthetic, which is purely spectacular and linked to dissent—a dissent that is ultimately an illusory act destined to be absorbed by consent to the spectacle. Alongside this is the paranoid dimension of the political experience. According to Tarizzo (p. 96), the postmillennial subject experiences a paranoid frenzy where identity is both alienated and hallucinated, only truly becoming one's own when it is appropriated or usurped by others. He asserts that today, we are witnessing a blurring of boundaries between authenticity and inauthenticity, self and others, which underscores the complex and fragmented nature of identity in contemporary world:

> In the case of the current regime, the spectacle emerges as an empty form, which cannot be assimilated to specific contents, like a pure apparatus that grinds, consumes, and sterilises everything, every meaning in the mechanism of pure assent – which literally blinds every experience of consent. If consent entails saying yes to something specific, in the age of the spectacle, there can no longer be an experience of consent but only of approval, which is equivalent to an unconditional yes detached from any act of content. And if consent identifies he/she who says yes with everything to which their consent relates, in the age of the spectacle, there can no longer be an experience of identity because everyone says yes preliminarily. Devoid of any identity, this 'everyone', namely the public, the audience, is the sole possessor of the power of the spectacle. Yet while it does exist, this 'power' belongs to no one; it is faceless, it is of everyone. Hence the repeated and futile attempts to attribute an imaginary face to the spectacle, which is not a face but a gaze, which is not a man but a God: a faceless gaze. (p. 97)

Tarizzo contends that the age of the spectacle coincides with an era of faceless power—a pervasive gaze that eliminates the possibility of genuine dissent. In this context, the realm of meaning is completely subsumed into the sphere of assent, erasing the distinction between the two. Tarizzo posits that the only true resistance to the spectacle comes from the real, which the spectacle continually struggles, yet fails, to fully digest (p. 99). He illustrates this point with the imagery of catastrophic natural events, such as the 2004 tsunami and the 2005 Hurricane Katrina, which expose the spectacle's inability to fully integrate the real. These events leave behind remnants of radical nonsense that the spectacle cannot entirely absorb (p. 101). According to Tarizzo, the task at hand is to continue questioning the world and ourselves, which involves 'making sense of the nonsense' (p. 104) and aligning with the real, as opposed to being co-opted by the spectacle. This critical stance is essential for resisting the all-encompassing nature of the spectacle and reclaiming the space for genuine dissent.

In *Il fantasma della libertà. Inconscio e politica al tempo di Berlusconi*, Fulvio Carmagnola and Matteo Bonazzi (2011) delve into the symbolic significance of Berlusconi, questioning what he truly represents in the context of Italian politics and culture. In *Videocracy*, Berlusconi comes across not simply as the most notorious Italian entrepreneur and politician but rather as 'a signifier and iconic figure' (Carmagnola and Bonazzi 2011, p. 58). As discussed at the beginning of this chapter, Italian Lacanians regards Berlusconism as the epitome of the hypermodern command to enjoy resulting from the evaporation of the Father. Berlusconi and Berlusconism must be considered as distinct. Berlusconism is the Italian attitude in postmillennial society to adhere to the command to enjoy and to do everything to fulfil it. Berlusconi, on the other hand, is the exemplary figure of this new attitude and set of values, completely allied and compliant with the capitalist discourse. According to Carmagnola and Bonazzi, Berlusconi fully embodies the hypermodern political leader since 'his charisma does not directly engage the symbolic and the real, but rather the imaginary and the real' (2011, p. 55). The phenomenon of Berlusconism, like Trumpism, cannot be explained solely through a conventional plea to moral values against hedonism. Berlusconism embodies the allegiance to *jouissance* over desire. What is at stake is the capacity of Berlusconism to sustain the limitlessness of the discourse of the capitalist to promote unrestricted enjoyment. As Carmagnola and Bonazzi aptly point out,

> the hold the figure of Berlusconi has over the citizen/voter/consumer/spectator does not derive (solely) from how impressive his means of communication are but from the fact that we share something with him on the level of drives. (2011, p. 93)

Carmagnola and Bonazzi argue that Berlusconi succeeded in intercepting our fantasy and channelling our desires towards an endless array of objects meant for consumption and enjoyment (2011, p. 62). This manipulation forms the libidinal core of Berlusconi's politics. Recalcati and Raimo (2013, p. 107) further contend that the hypermodern leader's popularity is rooted in this very mechanism, which becomes a focal point for collective emulation and identification within society.[22]

The key issue is to move beyond the fiction/reality dichotomy. Although the argument that Berlusconi's era is dominated by the manipulation of reality is certainly correct, this may not help us fully grasp the peculiarity of postmillennial Italy unless we insist on the Lacanian notion of the real qua *jouissance*. The latter clarifies that Berlusconism is not simply centred on an alteration of reality by the media. This is the ethical challenge of postmillennial times and media populism:

> We will not free ourselves [...] of Berlusconism through a political manoeuvre alone, for the simple reason that Berlusconism is, precisely, an excess from the traditional political syntax to which it does not allow itself to be reduced or returned. [...] What this excess consists of, and how it should be dealt with politically: this is the question we need to answer. (Dominijanni 2010b, p. 10)

As such, Berlusconism could be considered as the paradigm of hypermodern Italy, an antecedent of Matteo Salvini's and Giorgia Meloni's populism. In the documentary, Berlusconi's presence is characterised by a sort of subtle omnipresence and people's desires and behaviour seem to emanate both from him and from the paradigm that his television programmes impose.

Nevertheless, the documentary falls short of offering a deep sociopolitical analysis, instead limiting itself to a surface-level critique of the shallow world of television. As a result, by using Berlusconi as the central figure linking all the various vignettes, *Videocracy* tends to oversimplify the issue, naively attributing all blame for these negative outcomes to Italian television alone. A Lacanian perspective reveals that the core issue is not Berlusconi and his television empire, which have undoubtedly influenced Italy and its people, but rather the broader phenomenon of

[22] Along these lines, referring to Berlusconi, Žižek contends that 'people [...] identify with him as embodying the mythic image of the average Italian: I am one of you, a little bit corrupt, in trouble with the law, in trouble with my wife because I'm attracted to other women' (2009, n.p.). And it is for precisely this reason that Berlusconi 'parades his personal life as if he were taking part in a reality TV show' (2009, n.p.).

Berlusconism—a hypermodern populist trend that extends beyond Italy. The documentary's true focus is not simply on Berlusconi's personal influence, but on the real, embodied in the form of *jouissance*, which underpins and connects all the sequences presented. What *Videocracy* really frames, represents, and documents is the hypermodern command to enjoy. The situations depicted in the film exemplify a societal shift towards prioritising personal enjoyment above all else, including truth, social bonds, and relationships—an imperative that is experienced as irresistible. The real that emerges in this documentary is the unrestrained pursuit of enjoyment, which occurs in place of the symbolic Law, the very structure that should impose limits, and is increasingly detached from desire.

Bibliography

Adorno, Theodor Walter. 2014. Revisionist Psychoanalysis. Translated by Nan-Nan Lee. *Philosophy and Social Criticism* 40 (3): 326–338.

Badiou, Alain, and Elisabeth Roudinesco. 2014. *Jacques Lacan: Past and Present. A Dialogue*. New York: Columbia University Press.

Benso, Silvia, and Antonio Calcagno, eds. 2021. *Open Borders: Encounters Between Italian Philosophy and Continental Thought*. Albany, NY: SUNY Press.

Benso, Silvia, and Brian Schroeder, eds. 2007. *Contemporary Italian Philosophy: Crossing the Borders of Ethics, Politics, and Religion*. Albany, NY: SUNY Press.

Benvenuto, Sergio. 2012. Il disprezzo per il denaro. In *Il reale del capitalismo*, ed. Alex Pagliardini, 87–99. Milan: Edizioni.

Benvenuto, Sergio. 2016. *What Are Perversions? Sexuality, Ethics, Psychoanalysis*. London: Routledge.

Benvenuto, Sergio. 2020. *Conversations with Lacan: Seven Lectures for Understanding Lacan*. London: Routledge.

Berardi, Franco Bifo. 2009. *Soul at Work. From Alienation to Autonomy*. Translated by Francesca Cadel and Giuseppina Mecchia. Los Angeles: Semiotext(e).

Berardi, Franco Bifo. 2015. *Heroes. Mass Murder and Suicide*. London: Verso.

Berardi, Franco Bifo. 2021a. *The Third Unconscious*. London: Verso.

Berardi, Franco Bifo. 2021b. Padri, Figlie e Fratelli (D'Italia). Note sull'autobiografia di Griogia Meloni. https://not.neroeditions.com/padri-figlie-e-fratelli-ditalia/. Accessed 10 December 2023.

Bernini, Lorenzo. 2017. *Queer Apocalypses: Elements of Antisocial Theory.* Translated by Julia Heim. Cham: Palgrave Macmillan.

Bianchi, Pietro. 2010. Marx e Lacan: Il plusvalore come oggetto a. In *L'inconscio dopo Lacan. Il problema del soggetto contemporaneo tra psicoanalisi e filosofia*, ed. Domenico Cosenza and Paolo D'Alessandro, 245–257. Milan: LED.

Bion, Wilfred. 1992. *Cogitations.* London: Karnac.

Bollas, Christopher. 2018. *Meaning and Melancholia. Life in the Age of Bewilderment.* London: Routledge.

Bollas, Christopher. 2020. *Civilization and the Discontented: A Presentation by Christopher Bollas.* https://www.youtube.com/watch?v=7eBWG_DgRAo. Accessed 14 July 2024.

Bonazzi, Matteo. 2012. *Lacan e le politiche dell'inconscio. Clinica dell'immaginario contemporaneo.* Milan: Mimesis.

Borradori, Giovanna. 1988. *Recoding Metaphysics: The New Italian Philosophy.* Evanston, IL: Northwestern University Press.

Bradshaw, Peter. 2010. Videocracy. *The Guardian* [online]. https://www.theguardian.com/film/2010/jun/23/videocracy-review. Accessed 22 May 2016.

Busiol, Diego, ed. 2022. *Lacanian Psychoanalysis in Practice. Insights from Fourteen Psychoanalysts.* London: Routledge.

Calcagno, Antonio, ed. 2015. *Contemporary Italian Political Philosophy.* Albany, NY: SUNY Press.

Carmagnola, Fulvio, and Matteo Bonazzi. 2011. *Il fantasma della libertà. Inconscio e politica al tempo di Berlusconi.* Milan: Mimesis.

Campbell, Timothy, and Federico Luisetti. 2010. On Contemporary French and Italian Political Philosophy: An Interview with Roberto Esposito. *Minnesota Review* 75:109–118.

Carrera, Alessandro. 2011. The Many Challenges of Italian Theory. *Annali d'Italianistica* 29:13–31.

Chiesa, Lorenzo. 2011. Biopolitics in Early Twenty-first-century Italian Theory. *Angelaki: Journal of the Theoretical Humanities* 16 (3): 1–5.

Chiesa, Lorenzo, ed. 2014. *Lacan and Philosophy: the New Generation.* Melbourne: re.press.

Chiesa, Lorenzo, and Alberto Toscano, eds. 2009. *The Italian Difference.* Melbourne: Re.press.

Chiesa, Lorenzo, Boštjan Nedoh, and Marco Piasentier. 2016. Introduction. *Paragraph* 39 (1): 1–9.

Contri, Giacomo, ed. 1978. *Lacan in Italia/En Italie Lacan: 1953–1978.* Milano: La Salamandra.

Copjec, Joan. 1994. *Read My Desire: Lacan Against the Historicists*. Cambridge, MA: MIT Press.

De Caro, Mario, and Maurizio Ferraris, eds. 2012. *Bentornata realtà. Il nuovo realismo in discussione*. Turin: Einaudi.

De Rita, Giuseppe, ed. 2010. *Censis - 44° Rapporto sulla situazione sociale del paese 2010*. Milan: Franco Angeli.

Di Ciaccia, Antonio, and Doriano Fasoli. 2013. *«Io, la verità, parlo». Lacan clinico. Saggio-conversazione*. Rome: Alpes.

Di Gregorio, Luca. 2019. From the Factory to the Asylum...and Back: A Lacanian Perspective on the Cinematic Representation of Alienation in Elio Petri's *La classe operaia va in paradiso*. In *The Years of Alienation in Italy: Factory and Asylum Between the Economic Miracle and the Years of Lead*, ed. Alessandra Diazzi and Alvise Sforza Tarabochia, 173–190. Basingstoke: Palgrave Macmillan.

Di Martino, Loredana, and Pasquale Verdicchio. 2017. Contemporary Iterations of Realism: Italian Perspectives. In *Encounters with the Real in Contemporary Italian Cinema and Literature*, ed. Loredana Di Martino and Pasquale Verdicchio, vii–xxxiii. Newcastle upon Tyne: Cambridge Scholars Publishing.

Dominijanni, Ida. 2009. Wounds of the common. *Diacritics* 39 (4): 135–145.

Dominijanni, Ida. 2010a. Dopo-Berlusconi. Il desiderio del Censis. *Il Manifesto*. 4 December 2010.

Dominijanni, Ida. 2010b. Un nodo simbolico che inchioda la politica. *Il manifesto*, 12 December 2010.

Dominijanni, Ida. 2012. Soggetto dell'inconscio, inconscio della politica. Una traccia. *Filosofia Politica* 23 (1): 25–37.

Esposito, Roberto. 2008. *Bios. Biopolitics and Philosophy*. Translated by Timothy Campbell. Minneapolis, MN: University of Minnesota Press.

Esposito, Roberto. 2009. *Communitas. The Origin and Destiny of Community*. Translated by Timothy Campbell. Standford, CA: Standford University Press.

Esposito, Roberto. 2011. Immunitas. In *The Protection and Negation of Life*, Trans. Zakiya Hanafi. Cambridge: Polity Press.

Esposito, Roberto. 2012. *Living Thought. The Origins and Actuality of Italian Philosophy.* Translated by Zakiya Hanafi. Stanford, CA: Stanford University Press.

Esposito, Roberto. 2015. *Persons and Things, From the Body's Point of View*. Translated by Zakiya Hanafi. Cambridge: Polity Press.

Esposito, Roberto. 2019. Dall'uomo senza inconscio alle nuove melanconie. *La Repubblica.* https://www.repubblica.it/commenti/2019/11/09/news/malinconia_non_sei_piu_quella_di_una_volta-301012239/, 9 November. Accessed 5 November 2023.

Esposito, Roberto. 2021. Cured to the Bitter End. Translated by Emma Catherine Gainsforth. In *Coronavirus, Psychoanalysis, and Philosophy. Conversations on Pandemic, Politics, and Society*, ed. Fernando Castrillón and Thomas Marchevsky, 28–29. London: Routledge.

Esposito, Roberto. 2023. On Institutions. Translated by Francesca Campoli. In *Capitalism and the New Political Unconscious. A Philosophy of Immanence*, ed. Riccardo Panattoni and Fabio Vighi, 9–19. London: Bloomsbury.

Esposito, Roberto, Jean-Luc Nancy, and Timothy Campbell. 2010. Dialogue on the Philosophy to Come. *Minnesota Review* 75:71–88.

Etchegoyen, Alicia. 2002. Psychoanalytic Ideas About Fathers. In *The Importance of Fathers. A Psychoanalytic Re-Evaluation*, ed. Judith Trowel and Alicia Etchegoyen, 18–37. London: Routledge.

Fazzi, Luca. 2017. Profanare Pasolini intitolandogli la scuola di formazione del Partito Democratico. *Lacan Quotidien*, 707.

Ferraris, Maurizio. 2014. *Manifesto of New Realism.* Translated by Sarah De Sanctis. Albany: SUNY press.

Ferraris, Maurizio. 2015a. *Introduction to New Realism.* Translated by Sarah de Sanctis. London: Bloomsbury.

Ferraris, Maurizio. 2015b. *Positive Realism.* Winchester: Zero Books.

Fink, Bruce. 1995. *The Lacanian Subject. Between Language and Jouissance.* Princeton: Princeton University Press.

Fink, Bruce. 2014a. *Against Understanding, Volume 1. Commentary and Critique in a Lacanian Key.* London: Routledge.

Fink, Bruce. 2014b. *Against Understanding, Volume 2. Cases and Commentary in a Lacanian Key.* London: Routledge.

Focchi, Marco 2017. Petition contre la reduction de Pasolini a l'etat de 'intellectual organique'. *Lacan Quotidien*, 710. http://www.lacanquotidien.fr/blog/wp-content/uploads/2017/05/LQ-710-C.pdf. Accessed 5 November 2023.

Foot, John. 2016. We've Seen Donald Trump Before His Name Was Silvio Berlusconi. *The Guardian.* https://www.theguardian.com/commentisfree/2016/oct/20/donald-trump-silvio-berlusconi-italy-prime-minister. Accessed 6 March 2021.

Freud, Sigmund. 1981 [1920]. Beyond the Pleasure Principle. In *The Standard Edition of the Complete Psychological Works of Sigmund Freud*, ed. and trans. James Strachey, vol. 18, 1–64. London: Hogarth.

Gundle, Stephen. 2015. How Berlusconi Will Be Remembered: Notoriety, Collective Memory and the Mediatisation of Posterity. *Modern Italy* 20 (1): 91–109.

Hardt, Michael, and Paolo Virno, eds. 1996. *Radical Thought in Italy: A Potential Politics*. Minneapolis, MN: University of Minnesota Press.

Hook, Derek. 2022. Jouissance as Tool of Psychosocial Analysis. In *The Palgrave Handbook of Psychosocial Studies*, ed. Stephen Frosh et al. Springer Nature.

Irwin, Jones, and Helena Motoh, eds. 2014. *ŽiŽek and His Contemporaries: On the Emergence of the Slovenian Lacan*. London: Bloomsbury.

Kirchgaessner, Stephanie. 2016. Outside Italy, Berlusconi Is Seen as the Original Donald Trump. *The Guardian*. https://www.theguardian.com/world/2018/jan/28/silvio-berlusconi-march-election-matteo-renzi-five-star-movement). Accessed 6 March 2021.

Lacan, Jacques. 1966. *The Seminar of Jacques Lacan, Book XIV, 1966-1967. The Logic of Phantasy*. http://www.lacaninireland.com/web/wp-content/uploads/2010/06/14-Logic-of-Phantasy-Complete.pdf. Accessed 21 December 2020.

Lacan, Jacques. 1970. *Radiophonie*. https://www.lacantokyo.org/img/Radiophonie_tr_en.pdf. Accessed 1 August 2024.

Lacan, Jacques. 1971. *On a Discourse That Might Not Be a Semblance. The Seminar of Jacques Lacan. Book XVIII*. Translated by Cormac Gallagher. Unpublished.

Lacan, Jacques. 1990. *Television/A Chellenge to the Psychoanalytic Establishment (1973)*. Translated by D. Hollier, R. Krauss, and A. Michelson. Edited by Joan Copjec. London: W.W. Norton & Co.

Lacan, Jacques. 1998. *The Four Fundamental Concepts of Psychoanalysis. The Seminar of Jacques Lacan, Book XI, 1963-1964*. Translated by Alan Sheridan and Edited by Jacques-Alain Miller. London and New York: W.W. Norton.

Lacan, Jacques. 2006. *Écrits. The First Complete Edition in English*. Translated by Bruce Fink in collaboration with Héloïse Fink and Russell Grigg. London and New York: W.W. Norton.

Lacan, Jacques. 2007. *The Other Side of Psychoanalysis. The Seminar of Jacques Lacan, Book XVII, 1969-1970*. Translated by Russell Grigg and Edited by Jacques-Alain Miller. London and New York: W.W. Norton.

Lacan, Jacques. 2010. Note to the Father and Universalism. Translated by Russell Grigg. *The Lacanian Review. Hurly-Burly* 3:11.

Lacan, Jacques. 2012. Address on Child Psychosis. Translated by Adrian Price and Beatrice Khiara-Foxton. *The Lacanian Review. Hurly-Burly* 8:269–277.

Lacan, Jacques. 2013. *The Triumph of Religion*. Translated by Bruce Fink. Cambridge: Polity Press.

Lacan, Jacques. 2016. *The Sinthome. The Seminar of Jacques Lacan, Book XXIII, 1975-1976.* Translated by Adrian Price and Edited by Jacques-Alain Miller. Cambridge: Polity Press.

Lacan, Jacques. 2017. *Talking to Brick Walls: A Series of Presentations in the Chapel at Sainte-Anne Hospital*. Translated by Adrian Price. Cambridge: Polity Press.

Lacan, Jacques. 2019. The Third. Translated by Philip Dravers. *The Lacanian Review* 9: 83–108.

Lacan, Jacques. 2024. *From an Other to the other. The Seminar of Jacques Lacan. Book XVI.* 1968–1969. Trans. Bruce Fink and ed. Jacques-Alain Miller. Cambridge: Polity Press.

Laurent, Éric. 2004. Les deux plis du symptôme et de l'institution' *Ornicar?* 224. https://wapol.org/ornicar/articles/224lau.htm Accessed 4 November 2023.

Lewis, Michael. 2018. Editorial. *Journal of Italian Philosophy* 1:i–v.

Lippi, Silvia. 2020. Lacan/Deleuze. Come psicotizzare la psicoanalisi? *aut-aut* 387:128–140.

Lolli, Franco. 2011. Le depressioni contemporanee. In *Il soggetto vuoto. Clinica psicoanalitica delle nuove forme del sintomo*, ed. Massimo Recalcati, 49–71. Trento: Edizioni Centro Studi Erickson.

Lolli, Franco. 2012. *L'epoca dell'inconshow. Dimensione clinica e scenario sociale del fenomeno borderline*. Milan: Mimesis.

Lolli, Franco. 2018. Alcune considerazioni sul rapporto tra politica e psicoanalisi. *Psychiatry Online Italia*. http://www.psychiatryonline.it/node/7699. Accessed 16 January 2022.

Lolli, Franco. 2019. *Inattualità della psicoanalisi. L'analista e i nuovi 'domandanti'*. Bari: Poiesis Editrice.

Luisetti, Federico. 2011. The Italian Anomaly: Populism and the Unpolitical in the New Old World. *Annali d'Italianistica*229–236.

Mazzarella, William. 2020. Brand(ish)ing the Name or Why Trump Is So Enjoyable? In *Sovereignty, Inc. Three Enquiries in Politics and Enjoyment*, ed. William Mazzarella, Eric Santner, and Aaron Shuster, 113–160. Chicago: The University of Chicago Press.

McGowan, Todd. 2004. *The End of Dissatisfaction? Jacques Lacan and the Emerging Society of Enjoyment*. Albany, NY: SUNY Press.
McGowan, Todd. 2013. *Enjoying What We Don't Have. The Political Project of Psychoanalysis*. Lincoln: University of Nebraska Press.
McGowan, Todd. 2016. *Capitalism and Desire. The Psychic Cost of Free Markets*. New York: Columbia University Press.
Melman, Charles. 2018. A New Psychic Economy. In *The Lacan Tradition: Lines of Development. Evolution of Theory and Practice Over the Decades*, ed. Lionel Bailly, David Lichtenstein, and Sharmini Bailly, 227–234. London: Routledge.
Miller, Jacques-Alain. 2017. Candide a Milan. *Lacan Quotidien*, 706. http://www.lacanquotidien.fr/blog/wp-content/uploads/2017/05/LQ-706.pdf. Accessed 1 August 2024.
Miller, Jacques-Alain. 2019a. Milanese Intuitions. Translated by Alasdair Duncan. *Psychoanalytical Notebooks* 34:81–134.
Miller, Jacques-Alain. 2019b. A Phantasy. Translated by Thelma Sowley. *Psychoanalytical Notebooks* 34:139–173.
Moroncini, Bruno. 2014. *Lacan politico*. Naples: Cronopio.
Mura, Andrea. 2015. Lacan and Debt: The Discourse of the Capitalist in Times of Austerity. *Philosophy Today* 59 (2): 155–174.
Nancy, Jean-Luc. 2008. *Corpus*. New York: Fordham University Press.
Nedoh, Boštjan. 2016. Alive or Undead? Biopolitics Between Esposito's Vitalism and Lacanian Psychoanalysis. *Paragraph* 39 (1): 65–81.
Pagliardini, Alex. 2012a. Introduzione. Per il capitalismo. In *Il reale del capitalismo*, ed. Alex Pagliardini, 3–6. Milan: Edizioni et/al.
Pagliardini, Alex. 2012b. Il rifiuto del capitalismo. In *Il reale del capitalismo*, ed. Alex Pagliardini, 18–36. Milan: Edizioni et/al.
Pagliardini, Alex. 2018. *Sulle tracce del reale*. https://operavivamagazine.org/sulle-tracce-del-reale/. Accessed 1 August 2024.
Pagliardini, Alex, and Rocco Ronchi, eds. 2014. *Attualità di Lacan*. Villanova di Cepagatti: Textus.
Panattoni, Riccardo, and Fabio Vighi. 2023. Introduction. In *Capitalism and the New Political Unconscious. A Philosophy of Immanence*, ed. Riccardo Panattoni and Fabio Vighi, 1–6. London: Bloomsbury.
Pasquinelli, Matteo. 2011. L'ascesa in cattedra di un pensiero critico. *Il Manifesto*, 13 Aprile. 11.
Perniola, Mario. 2004. *Art and Its Shadow*. Translated by Massimo Verdicchio. London: Continuum.

Recalcati, Massimo. 2005. *Omogeneo e Rovescio. Per una clinica psicoanalitica del gruppo monosintomatico*. Milan: Franco Angeli.

Recalcati, Massimo. 2010. *L'uomo senza inconscio. Figure della nuova clinica psicoanalitica*. Milan: Raffaello Cortina.

Recalcati, Massimo. 2011. *Cosa resta del padre? La paternità nell'epoca ipermoderna*. Milan: Raffaello Cortina.

Recalcati, Massimo. 2012. Il sonno della realtà e il trauma del reale. In *Bentornata realtà. Il nuovo realismo in discussion*, ed. Mario De Caro and Maurizio Ferraris, 193–206. Turin: Einaudi.

Recalcati, Massimo. 2013. *Patria senza padri. Psicopatologia della politica italiana*. Rome: Minimum Fax.

Recalcati, Massimo. 2016. *Jacques Lacan. La clinica psicoanalitica: struttura e soggetto*. Milan: Raffaello Cortina.

Recalcati, Massimo. 2017. Lettera aperta a JAM 1. *Lacan Quotidien*, 711. http://www.lacanquotidien.fr/blog/wpcontent/uploads/2017/05/LQ-711.pdf. Accessed 5 November 2023.

Recalcati, Massimo. 2019. *The Telemachus Complex. Parents and Children After the Decline of the Father*. Translated by Alice Kilgarriff. Cambridge: Polity Press.

Recalcati, Massimo. 2022a. *The Temptation of the Wall. Five Short Lessons on Civil Life*. Translated by Alice Kilgarriff. Cambridge: Polity Press.

Recalcati, Massimo. 2022b. A Cacciari e Agamben dico: la filosofia può rendere ciechi. https://www.huffingtonpost.it/cultura/2022/01/02/news/recalcati_a_cacciari_e_agamben_dico_la_filosofia_puo_rendere_ciechi_-7397452/. Accessed 3 August 2024.

Recalcati, Massimo, and Christian Raimo. 2013. *Patria senza padri. Psicopatologia della politica italiana*. Rome: Minimum Fax.

Ricci, Giancarlo. 2013. *Il padre dov'era. Le omosessualità nella psicanalisi*. Milan: SugarCo.

Righi, Andrea. 2015. Il figlio e il talamo di Ulisse: la legge del Padre e la crisi neoliberale. In *Differenze Italiane: Politica e Filosofia: Mappe e Sconfinamenti*, ed. Dario Gentili and Elettra Stimilli, 303–319. Rome: Derive Approdi.

Rigoletto, Sergio. 2012. Videocracy. In *Directory of World Cinema: Italy*, ed. Louis Bayman, 250–251. Bristol: Intellect.

Robinson, Andrew. 2004. The Politics of Lack. *The British Journal of Politics and International Relations* 6 (2): 259–269.

Ronchi, Rocco. 2012a. *Come Fare*. Milan: Feltrinelli.

Ronchi, Rocco. 2012b. Il reale del capitalismo. Bataille and Lacan. In *Il reale del capitalismo*, ed. Alex Pagliardini, 126–145. Milan: Edizioni et/al.

Salecl, Renata. 2004. *On Anxiety*. London: Routledge.

Sbriglia, Russell, and Slavoj Žižek, eds. 2020. *Subject lessons. Hegel, Lacan, and the Future of Materialism*. Evanston, IL: Northwestern University Press.

Sforza Tarabochia, Alvise. 2016. From the Obligation of Birth to the Obligation of Care: Esposito's Biophilosophy and Recalcati's 'New Symptoms'. *Culture, Theory and Critique* 58:1–15.

Siciliano, Alessandro. 2017. Lettera aperta di sostegno a Massimo Recalcati. *Lacan Quotidien*, 706. http://www.lacanquotidien.fr/blog/wp-content/uploads/2017/05/LQ-706.pdf. Accessed 1 August 2024.

Soler, Colette. 2014. *Lacan-The Unconscious Reinvented*. Trans. by Esther Faye and Susan Schwartz. London: Karnac.

Stavrakakis, Yannis. 2007. *The Lacanian Left: Psychoanalysis, Theory, Politics*. Edinburgh: Edinburgh University Press.

Stimilli, Elettra. 2021. The Italian Laboratory. Rethinking Debt in Viral Times. In *Coronavirus, Psychoanalysis, and Philosophy. Conversations on Pandemics, Politics, and Society*, ed. Fernando Castrillón and Thomas Marchevsky, 83–86. London: Routledge.

Svolos, Thomas. 2017. *Twenty-first Century Psychoanalysis*. London: Karnac.

Tarizzo, Davide. 2007a. Applauso: L'impero dell'assenso. In *Forme contemporanee del totalitarismo*, ed. Massimo Recalcati, 83–105. Turin: Bollati Boringhieri.

Tarizzo, Davide. 2007b. *Giochi di potere. Sulla paranoia politica*. Bari: Laterza.

Tarizzo, Davide. 2008. *Il trionfo della perversione*. https://www.leftwing.it/2008/06/03/il-trionfo-della-perversione/, 3 June. Accessed 18 September 2021.

Tarizzo, Davide. 2011. Biopolitics and Ideology of Mental Health. Translated by Alvise Sforza Tarabochia. *Filozovski Vestnik*. 23 (2): 135–149.

Tarizzo, Davide. 2021. *Political Grammars. The Unconscious Foundations of Modern Democracy*. Stanford, CA: Stanford University Press.

Tomšič, Samo. 2015. *The Capitalist Unconscious: Marx and Lacan*. London: Verso.

Tomšič, Samo. 2019. *The Labour of Enjoyment. Towards a Critique of Libidinal Economy*. Köln: August Verlag.

Townshed, Jules. 2003. Discourse Theory and Political Analysis: A New Paradigm from the Essex School? *British Journal of Politics and International Relations*. 5 (1): 129–142.

Treiber, Guilel, and Tim Christiaens. 2021. Italian Theory and the Problem of Potentiality. *Italian Studies* 76 (2): 121–127.

Tupinambá, Gabriel. 2021. *The Desire of Psychoanalysis. Exercises in Lacanian Thinking*. Evanston: Northwestern University Press.
Vighi, Fabio. 2006. *Traumatic Encounters in Italian Film. Locating the Cinematic Unconscious*. Bristol: Intellect.
Vighi, Fabio. 2017. Private Conversation – Viva Examination.
Vighi, Fabio. 2019. Genie Out of the Bottle: Lacan and the Loneliness of Global Capitalism. *Crisis and Critique* 6 (1): 390–415.
Weatherill, Rob. 2017. *The Anti-Oedipus Complex: Lacan, Critical Theory and Postmodernism*. London: Routledge.
ŽiŽek, Slavoj. 1989. *The Sublime Object of Ideology*. London: Verso.
Žižek, Slavoj. 1992. *Enjoy Your Symptom! Jacques Lacan in Hollywood and Out*. London: Routledge.
Žižek, Slavoj. 1999. *The Ticklish Subject. The Absent Centre of Political Ontology*. London: Verso.
Žižek, Slavoj. 2000. *The Ticklish Subject. The Absent Centre of Political Ontology*. London: Verso.
Žižek, Slavoj. 2002. *Welcome to the Desert of the Real*. London: Verso.
Žižek, Slavoj. 2006. *The Parallax View*. Cambridge, MA: MIT Press.
ŽiŽek, Slavoj. 2009. Berlusconi in Teheran. http://www.lrb.co.uk/v31/n14/slavoj-zizek/berlusconi-intehran, Accessed 02 February 2016.
Žižek, Slavoj. 2014. *Trouble in Paradise. From the End of History to the End of Capitalism*. London: Penguin Books.
Zupančič, Alenka. 2014a. "Encountering Lacan in the Next Generation" - Interview with Alenka Zupancic. In *ŽiŽek and His Contemporaries: On the Emergence of the Slovenian Lacan*, ed. Jones Irwin and Helena Motoh, 158–178. London: Bloomsbury.
Zupančič, Alenka. 2014b. Realism in Psychoanalysis. In *Lacan and Philosophy: The New Generation*, ed. Lorenzo Chiesa, 21–33. Melbourne: re-press.

Filmography

Gandini, Eric. 2009. *Videocracy. Basta Apparire*. Stockholm: Atmo.
Petri, Elio. 1971. *La classe operaia va in paradiso*. Rome: Euro International Film.

5
Aesthetics

Italian Lacanian Aesthetics

In *Life with Lacan*, Catherine Millot (2018) recalls her frequent trips to Italy with Lacan in the 1970s, vividly describing his unyielding fascination with Italian masterpieces. His passion for art was so intense, she reports, that he consistently managed to gain access to Italian churches and museums, often persuading them to let him in despite their notoriously irregular opening times. Millot also recounts Lacan's profound love for and commitment to art, drawing attention to the hours he spent in Rome meticulously studying Caravaggio's paintings and Bernini's sculptures. To her astonishment, she later realised that the very artworks Lacan had spent hours contemplating had in fact found their way into his seminars.

However, despite his numerous references to visual art, literature, and other creative fields, Lacan never developed a systematic, coherent aesthetic theory. He was also extremely reluctant to apply psychoanalytic theories to artworks. Lacan was particularly sceptical of pathographic and deciphering approaches, which he considered as a flawed extension of

L. Di Gregorio, *Lacan in Italy*, The Palgrave Lacan Series,
https://doi.org/10.1007/978-3-031-91528-4_5

Freudianism.[1] He regarded Freud's aesthetic as a 'tricky matter' (1998, p. 109), which, despite Freud's 'crazy daring', often became 'imprudence' (p. 110) in the hands of his followers. The latter were often less cautious than him when applying psychoanalysis to the arts, frequently attempting to diagnose the artist's psychology and interpreting artworks in dogmatic, and sometime preposterous, ways. Lacan took a different approach, extending his return to Freud into the realm of aesthetics by firmly opposing the direction taken by Freud's disciples. In *The Youth of Gide, or the Letter and Desire*, he states that 'psychoanalysis is applied, strictly speaking, only as a treatment and thus to a subject who speaks and hears' (2006 [1958], p. 630).

Lacan frequently turned to the arts with the intention of gaining useful insights for his clinical practice, guided by Freud's belief that the artist anticipates the psychoanalyst in understanding the unconscious, often grasping intuitively psychological truths that analysts can only reach through extensive clinical work. When Lacan engaged with artworks, his focus was on enhancing clinical theory and practice, rather than speculating about the artist's unconscious complexes (Miller 2022). For example, due to Lacan's emphasis on the linguistic and symbolic dimension of the unconscious—characterised by networks of signifiers and shaped by rhetorical figures—he frequently engaged with literary works, such as Poe's *The Purloined Letter*, Shakespeare's *Hamlet*, Sophocles' *Antigone*, or Plato's *Symposium*. Through the analysis of these literary works, Lacan primarily sought to illustrate the workings of the unconscious as a linguistic system and to demonstrate that psychoanalysts should approach a patient's speech as if it were a literary text (Lacan 1991, p. 153).

In his seminal article 'The Italian Turn: A Certain Tendency in Contemporary Psychoanalytic Aesthetics', Mauro Resmini (2013) examines how Italian Lacanians have engaged with Lacan's legacy in the field of aesthetics, outlining and introducing Italian Lacanian aesthetics to the English-speaking readership for the first time. He maintains that this is

[1] Both Freud and Lacan shared a great passion for the arts, which led them to become art collectors (Gamwell and Wells 1989; Lacan 1992). Unlike Freud, however, Lacan had an appreciation for contemporary art and forged strong relationships with the Surrealists, maintaining a lifelong friendship with Salvador Dalì, for example, whose ideas influenced his conception of psychosis (Berressem 1996).

an emerging and distinct trend in psychoanalytic aesthetics in Italy which, although 'inherently plural and a-systematic' (p. 283), shares a common focus on exploring the broader implications of Lacan's aesthetics insights. Resmini argues that, in line with Jacques-Alain Miller's orientation, the common aspect shared by Italian Lacanian analysts and scholars is their development of a psychoanalytic approach to aesthetics centred around the category of the real.

This approach contrasts with other trends in Lacanian aesthetic theories that, historically, have prioritised one register above the others, often neglecting the real. Such a neglect cannot, however, be solely attributed to the vicissitudes related to the timing of the publication and translation of Lacan's seminars. Rather, it primarily stems from the elusive and non-figurative nature of the real, which conflicts with the conventional focus on representation in aesthetic discourse. As a result, Lacanian psychoanalytic approaches to aesthetics have typically privileged the imaginary and the symbolic, concentrating on concepts that are more directly applicable to visual, cinematic, and literary texts, such as the 'imago' and the 'signifier'.

In *Lacan and Cinema*, the Italian film theorist Pietro Bianchi critiques the pioneering 1970s work of French scholars, particularly Jean-Louis Baudry and Christian Metz (1982), in the field of film theory. Bianchi argues that their interpretation of Lacan was largely misconstrued, resulting in what he describes as a 'reductionist account of Lacan' (2017, p. xxii). These early attempts overemphasise the imaginary and the mirror stage, fostering an inaccurate analogy between the cinematic experience and Lacanian psychoanalytic concepts. One notable example of this is the analogy between the cinematic screen and the mirror, which emphasises the capability of the *imago* to 'cover' and 'reunify' the fragmented body, offering the subject a sense of wholeness and protection against the real. This interpretation primarily regarded the Lacanian specular image, and by extension the cinematic screen, as having a structuring and positive role. However, it overlooked the fact that, for Lacan, the image has not only a formative but also a deformative function. Furthermore, in *Schermi perturbanti*, the Italian film and media scholar Andrea Bellavita (2005) argues that, contrary to Metz's theory of the constructive and constituting mirror—through which the subject supposedly achieves a full sense of the self—Lacan actually theorises a 'broken mirror' which reflects a distorting image, preventing the subject from recognising themselves entirely. Bellavita contends that Metz's interpretation fails to account for the fact that the mirror stage generates a fragmented, rather than a cohesive, subject. The imaginary, according to Lacan, gives rise only to the illusion of unity, not its actual realisation. This is the 'morphogenic action' of the imaginary, the process whereby both filmic and specular images irremediably 'trap' and 'shape' the subject (Lacan 2006 [1946], p. 156), leading to a dual outcome of identification and alienation.

The notion of the gaze is another problematic issue. In the spectatorship theory of the 1970s, the Lacanian gaze was primarily located in the spectator, with the (filmic) gaze considered to be mainly unidirectional: from the spectator/viewing subject towards the cinematic screen/object. The Lacanian theory of vision, however, suggests that the subject is not the active looker but is instead primarily subjected to the gaze, positioned as the recipient being looked at. For Lacan, the act of seeing always presupposes the condition of being seen and, more crucially, a gaze differs from a look in that it represents 'the totality of the *space* where vision occurs', engaging a visual dimension beyond the interaction of active and passive viewpoints (Bianchi 2017, p. 95).

In these early contributions to psychoanalytic film theory, 'the victim was Lacan himself' as these interpretations largely disregarded the real, 'the most destabilising feature of his theoretical edifice' (Vighi 2006, p. 30). During this period, drawing on Lacanian psychoanalysis, film theorists often neglected the intricate connections between the real, the imaginary, and the visual field. Ironically, this emphasis on the imaginary in the 1970s occurred just as Lacan was increasingly delving into the register of the real.

While the imaginary had a significant influence on early psychoanalytic film theory, the symbolic exerted a greater impact on literary theory, especially during the 1980s. This shift can be attributed to Lacan's focus on language and its structures during the 1950s, when he employed linguistics to explore unconscious formations such as symptoms, slips of the tongue, bungled actions, and dreams. Since the laws governing the unconscious parallel those of language, it follows that literary works are also governed by those same rules. Consequently, a Lacanian approach to literature tends to focus on the text's technique and structure, making Lacanian theory particularly relevant for analysing literature and verbal communication. In the 1980s, this focus led to literary studies that drew heavily from Lacan but, similarly to early film theory, they often overlooked the category of the real. Yet again, this omission is understandable considering that during his structuralist phase, Lacan viewed the symbolic as being capable of wholly encompassing and assimilating the realm of the real. The main representative of this trend in Italy is Stefano Agosti, whose 1987 book *Modelli psicanalitici e teoria del testo* explores literary theory from a Lacanian perspective.[2]

The positive outcome of this shift, however, was that by conceptualising the unconscious as rooted in language, it moved the emphasis away from the Freudian stance of the unconscious as the deepest layer of the artist's psyche. This encouraged psychoanalytic aesthetics to pay more attention to the medium as well as the structural and formal aspects of artworks. According to Lacan, spoken words are the gateway to the patient's unconscious and the sole viable means of engaging with it (2006 [1953], p. 248). Hence, Lacan's formulation of the language-like unconscious reshaped psychoanalytic literary criticism, redirecting its focus from probing the psychology of the writer, as exemplified by Marie Bonaparte's works, or the unconscious of literary characters, as seen in Ernst Jones' literary analyses, to an examination of the literary text itself and its interaction with the reader.

In the late 1980s and early 1990s, Lacanian theories of aesthetics increasingly began to shift their focus from the imaginary and the symbolic registers to the realm of the real. This was particularly apparent in the Anglophone reception of Lacan, with academic journals on film study, such as *Screen* in the UK, and art criticism, such as *October* in the USA, beginning to incorporate the notion of the real into film theory and visual studies. Joan Copjec and Slavoj Žižek played a crucial role in popularising this concept, steering the focus away from the subject's experiences of imaginary and symbolic alienations and identifications, and instead employing the real to analyse popular culture and contemporary

[2] In Anglophone academia, key figures in Lacanian psychoanalytic literary criticism include Shoshana Felman, Robert Davis, Elizabeth Wright, John Muller, and William Richardson.

ideology (Žižek and Daly 2004; McGowan 2015). From the 2000s onward, North American Lacanian scholars, such as Todd McGowan and Sheila Kunkle, followed Copjec and Žižek's lead, emphasising the real to explore the political and ideological dimensions of films and how cinema shapes perceptions, beliefs, and subjectivities (McGowan and Kunkle 2004; McGowan 2007).

Italian Lacanian aesthetics departs from the traditional focus on the linguistic and rhetorical dynamics of the unconscious structured like a language, which often treats artworks as a mere externalisation of the artist's unconscious or as texts to be deciphered for hidden meanings. It also diverges from a Marxist-Althusserian analysis of the cinematic apparatus, which seeks to uncover hidden ideologies and hegemonic structures within artworks, analyses art as an expression of its socio-symbolic context, or locates desire, fantasy, or *jouissance* within the cinematic fabric of films. In fact, the cinematic text plays a relatively minor role in Italian Lacanian aesthetics insofar as Italian Lacanians show little interest in exploring the ideological implications of cinema or its power to shape politically engaged subjects.

Instead, Italian Lacanian aesthetics centres on the real—'that which resists symbolization absolutely' (Lacan 1988, p. 66)—underscoring that artworks ultimately resist interpretation and defy definitive meaning. By focusing on the real, Italian Lacanians aesthetics explores the boundaries of representation and representability, recognising the aspects of art that elude interpretation and symbolisation and challenging the assimilation of psychoanalysis into a mere hermeneutic theory of interpretation. Thus, the concept of the real becomes essential in developing a psychoanalytic aesthetics that moves beyond pathographic models and avoids hermeneutic interpretations, but that retains the significance of the formal and technical aspects of an aesthetic object. Moreover, the notion of the real extends to the realms of ethics—what should we do with its traumatic and excessive nature?—and the clinic—how to address it in psychoanalytic practice? Indeed, for Italian Lacanian aesthetics, Lacan's primary insight from artistic practice is an understanding of how a symbolic practice can isolate, encounter, and engage with the extra-symbolic dimension of the real. Thus, the key aesthetic question is: how can the real be included in a representational framework? Although Resmini does not delve into the clinical implications of this issue in his article, he notes that psychoanalysis and art are both symbolic practices that grapple with the real (2013). Italian Lacanians argue that, much like psychoanalysis, artistic practice engages with the non-signifying dimension of the real: that which eludes the realms of the imaginary and the symbolic yet is addressed and framed through these very registers.

In *L'infinito nella voce: su poesia e psicoanalisi*, Franco Lolli (2004) argues that both psychoanalytic and artistic practices are directed at 'the production-revelation of a form of knowledge that tells us something about that which escapes the symbolic order and the imaginary functioning of the world' (p. 15). Lolli claims that art and psychoanalysis face a similar challenge: 'How can one grasp the Real – that which, by definition, escapes the symbolic – if the tool available is symbolic?' (p. 14). The paradox of this question lies in the fact that a symbolic practice, whether art or psychoanalysis, can frame, tackle, and give form to that which does not belong to that register, namely, the real. In the analytic setting, the use of the symbolic practice of psychoanalysis can modify the subject's libidinal economy, demonstrating that the symbolic influences the real and that words can affect *jouissance*. Similarly, art has an effect on the real. While a work of art remains within the symbolic realm, it manages to circumscribe that which exceeds the symbolic domain. Thus, Lolli concludes that both art and psychoanalysis are symbolic practices geared at reaching and encountering the real.

In his article 'Lacan: l'uomo del secolo', Benvenuto (2014) explores further the parallel between artistic practice and Lacanian psychoanalysis. He claims that, much like the twentieth-century art that departed from a realistic and mimetic depiction of reality, Lacanian psychoanalysis attempted to distance itself from the imaginary aspects overemphasised by ego psychology, such as the adaptation to reality or the development of a coherent self-image and a stable ego. Instead, it aimed to enable the subject to symbolically engage with their own real. Benvenuto contends that every subjectivity revolves around a real that remains to be symbolised and imagined yet can never be fully symbolised or verbalised. By emphasising that the Lacanian real exceeds the subject—since it cannot be contained within the mirror image or the speaking body—Benvenuto opens up to the dimension of the drive. The real of the drive does not integrate itself with the image; instead, it is experienced as an excess, a surplus without a place, haunting the subject precisely because it exists beyond the symbolic and the imaginary. Echoing Lacan's critique of ego psychology, Italian Lacanians highlight that the value of art does not lie in its ability to conform to reality or in the notion of the artistic process as a manifestation of a stable ego translating unconscious thoughts into structured artworks. Rather, they regard both psychoanalysis and art as opportunities, imaginary-symbolic practices enabling the subject to engage with the real, facilitating the process of sublimation, rather than as defences of the ego against the unconscious. Art and psychoanalysis reveal that the real, despite its potentially traumatic and excessive nature, emerges within and is inseparable from the realm of language and symbolisation (Bottiroli 2002, 2023).

Therefore, psychoanalysis and art provide avenues for encountering the real in ways that would otherwise be inaccessible. In ordinary circumstances, human beings cannot directly face up to the real due to its traumatic nature (Lacan 1998, p. 55). However, through their imaginary and symbolic frameworks, art and psychoanalysis can accommodate the extra-signifying dimension of the real, allowing the subject to engage with it without catastrophic or lethal consequences. Italian Lacanian aesthetics explores how, within an imaginary and symbolic practice, one could encounter and potentially transform the irreducible dimension of the real. This perspective is rooted in a conception of psychoanalysis as a Borromean clinical practice that relies on an imaginary-symbolic apparatus to access and transform the real. The distinctive nature of Italian Lacanian aesthetics resides in encompassing and integrating all three Lacanian registers. This approach 'retains the importance of the imaginary and the primacy of the symbolic, but only in relation to and in constant negotiation with the register of the real' (Resmini 2013, p. 277).

In Resmini's article, the real in Italian Lacanian aesthetics is presented primarily in negative terms as the impossible, resisting any symbolisation, and ultimately as indomitable, radical, and mortiferous (2013). Consequently, this disrupting real must be tamed, mediated, and symbolised. This framework mirrors the same impasses—risks of moralising and normative drifts—discussed in the previous chapters on the clinical practice and politics (Chaps. 3 and 4). Such challenges are recurring issues within Lacanianism and psychoanalytic thought more broadly, where concepts like repair, containment, harmonisation, and integration appear central. This tension between taming the real and directly confronting its disruptive nature is crucial to both psychoanalysis and aesthetics. How should one deal with the traumatic and ungovernable excess of the real? This question also extends to the field of aesthetics. Are the imaginary and the symbolic tasked merely with channelling and absorbing the untameable real, transforming it into a more palatable, aesthetically pleasing form for consumption and enjoyment? Or do they serve a deeper function in confronting and engaging with the real's inherent traumatic and excessive dimension, beyond simply making it manageable? Resmini writes:

> The task of psychoanalytic aesthetics—and, for that matter, of psychoanalysis in general—today is to provide a different understanding of the 'beyond the Oedipus', one that rejects both the cynicism of global capitalism and the nostalgia of fundamentalism. The Italian turn takes up the challenge and looks at the work of art as the place of an encounter, a convergence between the symbolic nature of form and the real of *jouissance*. […] The artwork becomes then *the testimony of a strictly singular way of holding together the symbolic and the real, Law and jouissance, form and the formless.* (2013, p. 292, original emphasis)

This passage clearly echoes Recalcati's arguments discussed in previous chapters. The emphasis on Recalcati's perspective is not surprising, given the significance of his contributions. He has developed a coherent Lacanian aesthetic, focusing particularly on visual art rather than cinema, and examining how the artistic process—through formal and aesthetic qualities—engages with the real. Recalcati's work centres on visual art as a means of tethering the imaginary and the symbolic to the real within the creation of the aesthetic object. The primary focus of Italian Lacanian aesthetics is thus on highlighting the intersection between artistic and psychoanalytic practice, both of which are imaginary-symbolic practices that engage with the real.

Aesthetics of the Real

In her *Ethics of the Real*,[3] Alenka Zupančič presents a refined approach to ethical theory. She argues that an ethics of the real is not simply an alternative ethical framework but rather an attempt 'to rethink ethics' in its entirety by acknowledging and integrating the impact of the real as it inherently operates within ethical practices (2000, p. 4). I contend that Italian Lacanians attempt something similar in the aesthetic domain. What I refer to as the aesthetics of the real, borrowing Recalcati's term, is their attempt to reconceptualise aesthetic theory by re-examining fundamental concepts such as beauty, sublimation, artwork, and form, while considering their relationship to the real.

Where is the real revealed within the artwork? How can we incorporate into a representational framework that which is inherently beyond it? Most importantly, how can we elucidate art's capacity to transcend the symbolic realm while still operating as a symbolic practice? These questions are paradoxical, given that the real is, by definition, that which lies beyond both the imaginary and the symbolic and thus eludes capture through images and words. The contradiction arises because, as Chiesa notes, the 'crude real of extra-symbolic' (2012, p. 208) can still manifest through the other two Lacanian registers. Therefore, what is at stake in Italian Lacanian aesthetics is the issue of the representability versus non-representability of the real, specifically, achieving what Chiesa describes as the 'representation of the unrepresentable' (2012, p. 208), rather than the 'non-representation *tout-court*' (p. 209). However, the seeming impossibility of representing what is beyond representation is only a superficial dilemma. As Recalcati argues:

> The problem of the real being beyond representation is presented as central in Lacan's discourse, but only within the framework of a practice of figuration. It is through art as a symbolic operation that the real (the unfigurable, the non-figurable, the unrepresentable, the a-specular) can emerge. (2012, p. 613)

[3] Originally published in English in 2000, Zupančič's book was only translated into Italian in 2012. Among other factors, this highlights the issues surrounding what, in Chap. 1, I have called the transnational reception of Lacan. In particular, this delay exemplifies the gap between the reception of Lacan among Italian and Anglophone audiences.

The real is not spiritualised into a mystical, unknowable entity. Instead of dwelling on its 'impossible' status, Italian Lacanians explore the potentialities of the real to be engaged with and transformed through a symbolic praxis. It is not only the 'traumatic kernel' or 'stain' that resists symbolisation—resisting representation through images and words, therefore—but also the real that relents and gives in to the imaginary and the symbolic. As discussed in Chap. 3, the transformation of the real is crucial in the clinical theory of Italian Lacanianism. This marks a fundamental distinction between Italian Lacanians and their Anglophone counterparts, who often view the real primarily as a form of antagonism and resistance to ideology, a perspective prevalent in political and film theory (Stavrakakis 2007; McGowan and Kunkle 2004; McGowan 2007).

Conversely, the central concern within the aesthetics of the real highlights the foundational clinical inquiry of Italian Lacanian thought on an aesthetic level: how can the real be framed and encountered through an imaginary and symbolic praxis such that it becomes not merely a source of trauma for the subject but also a catalyst for transformation—an affirmative possibility that facilitates profound and enduring changes in the subject's libidinal economy? This suggests that in the aesthetic domain, there can be no aesthetic experience without language or without the interplay of the three registers.

Bottiroli argues that the real is not isolated but deeply interwoven with the symbolic and imaginary registers. To effectively 'describe its power and effects', he argues, 'we need a logic of intertwining and connections, a conjunctive logic, not a disjunctive one' (2023, p. 421) (see Chap. 2). Our ability to understand and discuss the real relies on its translation into language; this integration into linguistic frameworks allows us to grasp and articulate its complexities. This necessity for a nuanced interplay among the three registers underpins a comprehensive aesthetic discourse. Thus, the Borromean interplay—a model emphasising the interconnectedness of the real, the symbolic, and the imaginary—emerges as a central concept in Italian Lacanian aesthetics (Bellavita 2005; Recalcati 2007; Resmini 2013; Bottiroli 2023). An aesthetics of the real is legitimate, particularly because it addresses the biases present in approaches that overfocus on a single register. However, Bottiroli contends that merely combining three unilateral aesthetics does not result in a robust aesthetic framework (2023, p. 432). A truly effective Lacanian aesthetics must go beyond simply acknowledging the existence of the other two registers; it must seek to weave the real, the symbolic, and the imaginary into a cohesive and integrated whole.

Building on this foundational understanding of the interplay among the registers, Italian Lacanian aesthetics of the real draws significantly from the French and Spanish receptions of Lacan. In *Conférences d'esthétique lacanienne*, the French philosopher François Regnault views aesthetics as the locus of an imaginary and symbolic articulation of the real, asserting that art 'uses the imaginary to organize the real symbolically' (1997, p. 25). Although Regnault acknowledges that Lacan does not offer a coherent theory of aesthetics, he proposes a categorisation of the arts based on insights from *Seminar VII* and *Seminar XI*, differentiating between the 'arts of the void' and the 'arts of the anamorphosis' (1997, p. 26). Similarly, in *La so(m)bra de lo real: El arte como vomitorio*, the Spanish art historian Miguel Hernández-Navarro (2006) argues that the main Lacanian perspectives on aesthetics are grounded in the concepts of the Thing from *Seminar VII* and of the object a from *Seminar XI*. He notes that the former approach considers that art elevates an object to the status of the Thing, consistent with Lacan's definition of sublimation, while the latter views art as a trap for the gaze, central to Lacan's theory of vision. In these seminars, Lacan raises pivotal aesthetic questions, such as: 'does art imitate what it represents?' (1992, p. 141); 'what is the gaze?' (1998, p. 82); and 'what is painting?' (1998, p. 100)? *Seminar VII* and *Seminar XI*, however, present different aesthetic perspectives: *Seminar VII* delves into the definition of sublimation in relation to the Thing,[4] while *Seminar XI* elaborates on a theory of vision centred on the gaze and the object a, leading to potentially incompatible views on art. This divergence has positioned art historians and psychoanalysts on different fronts. Hernández-Navarro points out that *Seminar VII* and the concept of the

[4] Lacan uses the French word *la Chose* and the German word *das Ding* interchangeably to refer to the Thing. The genesis of this concept is rather peculiar: Lacan extrapolated the word from Freud's *The Project for a Scientific Psychology* [Entwurf], written in 1895. He then reread this through Heidegger's essay, 'Das Ding' (1950), in which the German philosopher had taken the term from Lao Tzu's *Tao Tê Ching*. The Thing becomes the 'essential axis' (Lacan 1992, p. 101) of Seminar VII but then disappears completely in subsequent seminars.

Thing underpin the theories of Lacanians like François Regnault (1997), Gérard Wajcman (1998), and Slavoj Žižek (2000). Conversely, *Seminar XI* and the object have garnered greater interest among art historians such as Rosalind Krauss (1988, 1994) and Hal Foster (1996, 2017).

These two Lacanian seminars, which were among the first to be published and translated into Italian, serve as primary focal points for developing the aesthetics of the real. Italian Lacanians too regard both *das Ding* and object a as the main modalities of the real (Di Ciaccia and Recalcati 2000). Although the Thing and the object a belong to the realm of the real, they are not *stricto* sensu the same concept: the object a is a residual fragment of the Thing, distinct yet derived. Both concepts are the products of a loss and are characterised by an absence—a void that is the object cause of desire. Crucially for aesthetics, the Thing, like the real, transcends the imaginary and symbolic realms. It is the 'beyond-of-the-signified' (Lacan 1992, p. 54). Lacan elaborates that, at the level of representations, 'the Thing is not nothing, but literally is not. It is characterized by its absence, its strangeness' (1992, p. 63). Bellavita describes the Thing as 'the path by which the real stages or expresses its status of excess and of fractures of the practices (imaginary or symbolic-linguistic) of representation' (2005, p. 68). Bottiroli adds that the Thing 'eludes representation and linguistic processing' (2023, p. 421), highlighting that it fundamentally cannot be represented. It is a void within representation itself, a hole in language. Lacan asserts that, 'this Thing is always represented by emptiness, precisely because it cannot be represented by anything else' (1992, p. 129).

Despite eluding representation, the Thing remains the focal point of human beings' entire representational activity. Since it constitutes a lost object that was never actually possessed but imagined as such, its loss leaves an indelible mark in the human psyche. As the ultimate object of desire that is both sought after and fundamentally unattainable, the Thing perpetually drives human representational activities by embodying the void that all symbolic efforts aim, yet ultimately fail, to fill. As Di Ciaccia and Recalcati note, the Thing is a manifestation of the real (2000, p. 191), specifically, 'the real of jouissance' (Di Ciaccia and Recalcati 2000, p. 200). The Thing lays the groundwork for the concept of *jouissance*, which it supports, being fundamentally distinct from the dimension of desire. In *Seminar VII*, Lacan shifts the focus from the big Other to the Thing. This represents a move from the desiring subject, whose unconscious is structured like a language, to the subject of real enjoyment. The linguistic and signifying forces of the symbolic recede, giving rise to the category of the real as *jouissance*. This form of enjoyment is beyond any assigned meaning, embodied by the 'cruel and insistent power' of the Thing (Lacan 1992, p. 163).

After *Seminar VII*, the Thing largely vanishes from Lacan's teaching but is partially replaced by the concept of the object a. Like the Thing, the object a defies visual and verbal representation. It is a remainder that cannot be fully organised or encapsulated by any imaginary-symbolic operation. In the realm of aesthetics, the object a is the stain within the imaginary-symbolic fabric of the artwork, a point of resistance. It is, essentially, 'a symbol of the lack' (Lacan 1998, p. 103). Bellavita explains that 'the object a, in its irreducibility to the dialectic between the Imaginary and the symbolic and the rest of representation, is that which escapes, that which is not the specular image, and that which is not symbolic representation through language' (2005, p. 65).

Recalcati is the theorist who most compellingly and coherently develops these ideas in the aesthetic domain. The main thesis underpinning his work *Il miracolo della forma: Per una estetica psicoanalitica* (2007) is that 'art is a symbolic-imaginary treatment of the real' (p. 3). This is ultimately the miracle of the form alluded to in the title, which echoes Lacan's expression 'the miracle of the picture' (1998, p. 114) from *Seminar XI*. Recalcati's aesthetics of the real explores the connection between art and drive. He interprets the interaction between form (*forma*) and force (*forza*) as the interplay of the three Lacanian registers. *Forma* pertains to the imaginary and the symbolic, while *forza* relates to the real in terms of drive and *jouissance*. According to Recalcati, the aesthetic hold of an artwork lies in its ability to constructively calibrate the relationship between the real of the drive (*forza*) and its plasticity (*forma*). He argues that the key point is that transcending the opposition between form and formlessness—and more broadly, shifting from the binary of form-content to that of force-form—is already embedded in the concept of sublimation (2009,

p. 136).[5] For Recalcati, the registers of the imaginary and the symbolic are not merely defensive barriers against the real; rather, they facilitate a productive encounter with it.

Recalcati identifies three distinct aesthetics of the real in Lacan, each corresponding to a specific rendition of the real: the aesthetics of the void, centred on the Thing/void in *Seminar VII*; the anamorphic aesthetics, focused on the object a in *Seminar XI*; and the aesthetics of the letter/*sinthome*, based on *Lituraterre* and *Seminar XXIII*. These frameworks represent different ways in which the real can manifest itself in the aesthetic domain: as a veiled Thing, as a remainder, and as a letter/*sinthome*. If art is seen as an imaginary-symbolic practice that makes it possible to engage with the real, then these three aesthetics offer three approaches to achieving this engagement, through organisation, encounter, and subjectivation. Rather than comprehensive theories of art, they provide three perspectives on artistic creation that position art in relation to the real. These aesthetics exemplify how the imaginary and the symbolic can intertwine with the real.

The first aesthetics of the real revolves around the void and the Thing. In the section of *Seminar VII* entitled 'The Problem of Sublimation', Lacan defines art through the concepts of the void—or emptiness—the Thing, and sublimation. He begins by stating that sublimation[6] 'raises an

[5] A clear affinity can be seen here with the Frankfurt School, especially with Marcuse's *The Aesthetic Dimension* and Adorno's *Aesthetic Theory*. Much like Marcuse and Adorno, Recalcati explores concepts such as beauty, realism, sublimation/desublimation, form, and content. For these thinkers, art reveals the alienation of everyday life and the dissonance between reality and the ideal, positioning artworks as bearers of a utopian message—an ethics of testimony. Within the context of Italian Lacanian thought, this ethics of testimony is reframed through the aesthetics of the real. The transformative and emancipatory potential of the artwork rests on its capacity to offer an encounter with the real, which can potentially awaken the subject from the illusions of the imaginary and the constraints of the symbolic, positively disrupting the subject's established sense of self and reality.

[6] For Lacan, sublimation 'is a matter of aim and not strictly speaking of object' (1992, p. 110). Unlike Freud, who viewed sublimation as involving a change in the object, according to Lacan sublimation involves a shift in the position of the object within the structure of fantasy. The essence of sublimation, therefore, is not about transforming a forbidden sexual object into a socially acceptable non-sexual substitute, but about transforming the object from its ordinary state into an extraordinary manifestation of the Thing. Lacan staunchly rejects the core idea in Kleinian theory, which considers sublimation as 'an attempt at symbolic repair of the imaginary lesions that have occurred to the fundamental image of the maternal body' (1992, p. 106). To illustrate his definition of sublimation, Lacan offers two examples. The first is a personal anecdote from the Second World War when he visited the country house of his friend Jacques Prévert. Lacan was fascinated by

object [...] to the dignity of the Thing' (p. 112), meaning that sublimation involves repositioning an object from its habitual place to the place of the Thing.[7] Unlike Freud's conception of sublimation, which primarily involves redirecting and transforming sexual impulses, Lacanian sublimation alters the object's position within fantasy, elevating it from the ordinary to an extraordinary manifestation of the Thing. For Lacan, the notion of the Thing intersects with the notion of the void as they both belong to the order of the real (pp. 12, 129). Lacan illustrates the relationship between emptiness and creation using the example of a vase, which 'creates the void and thereby introduces the possibility of filling it' (p. 120). He describes the potter as a mythical creator who shapes the vase by moulding the emptiness with their hands, starting from a hollow space (p. 121). Lacan emphasises that 'emptiness is determinative "in all forms of sublimation"' (p. 130) and further explores the connection between emptiness and the Thing, the object of mythical pleasure always-already lost. In this context, art not only symbolises and elaborates on this loss but also creates a substitute for it. Subsequently, Lacan defines art in relationship to the void: 'art is characterized by a certain mode of organization around this emptiness' (p. 130)[8] which 'designates the place of the Thing' (p. 140). He regards architecture as the epitome of this organisation around emptiness and provides examples from prehistoric and neoclassical architecture, such as the cave walls of Altamira, St Mark's Basilica in Venice, and the Olympic Theatre in Vicenza. Here, Lacan

Prévert's special collection of matchboxes, which he saw as epitomising the elevation of an ordinary object to an aesthetic register (1992, pp. 114 and 118). The second example is the phenomenon of courtly love, which Lacan regarded primarily as an artistic rather than a historical phenomenon. In this context, in the Middle Ages, a woman is transformed from being a mere object of exchange to being idealised as an unattainable object of desire (1992, pp. 128 and 151).

[7] Lacan paraphrases Marcel Duchamp's definition of ready-made as 'an ordinary object elevated to the dignity of a work of art by the mere choice of an artist' (Duchamp quoted in Leader 2002, p. 61). This concept is exemplified by Duchamp's own ready-mades, where everyday manufactured objects, like a bottle drying rack or a porcelain urinal, are elevated to the dignity of art not because of any intrinsic qualities but simply through the artist's decision to remove them from their usual context and place them in an art gallery.

[8] As well as art, Lacan also provides a definition of religion and science based on their relationship with emptiness: religion 'consists of avoiding' and 'respecting' this emptiness (1992, p. 130), whereas science is characterised by a fundamental disbelief in the existence of emptiness. Central to these different modes are the psychological mechanisms of repression [*Verdrängung*], displacement [*Verschiebung*], and foreclosure [*Verwerfung*] (Lacan 1992, p. 131).

refines his definition of art by stating that: 'a work of art always involves encircling the Thing' (p. 141). Finally, given his definition of sublimation as the process of placing the object in the position of the missing Thing, Lacan concludes that art allows for an encounter with the real. He exemplifies this by referencing Cézanne's paintings, where, by painting apples, Cézanne achieves more than a mere reproduction of objects on canvas. In fact, the painting establishes a 'relationship to the real' (p. 141).

Recalcati builds on Lacan's perspective by suggesting that every artistic practice involves an 'encircling' (*bordatura*) (p. 47), 'organisation' (*organizzazione*) (p. 208), or even a 'signifying delimitation' (*circoscrizione significante*) (p. 47) of the void of the Thing. Ultimately, these are all symbolic attempts to approximate the real. From this perspective,

> Art appears as a possible organisation of the unrepresentable void of das Ding, that is, as a form of symbolic delimitation of the void that elevates an image to an enigmatic index of the unrepresentable Real. (Recalcati 2007, p. 52)

It is important to clarify that the void Lacan identifies as central to every artistic process differs from the void associated with the new symptoms discussed in Italian Lacanianism (Chap. 3). For instance, conditions such as melancholia and drug addiction exhibit an excessive proximity to the Thing, which impedes the subject's capacity to desire. The latter void represents *jouissance*, the emptiness that the capitalist discourse perpetuates by constantly promising an illusory and endlessly deferred fulfilment. In the context of the new symptoms, this void is saturated with *jouissance*, rendering it incapable of generating anything meaningful.

On the contrary, the void as the cornerstone of Lacan's definition of sublimation, and by extension of any artistic creation, is not only the precondition for any possibility of creation but also a harbinger of life. This is because it entails the absence of the Thing as a precondition. The proximity to the Thing could be dangerous not only for the subject, as evidenced in the clinical practice, but also for the aesthetic integrity of a work of art. What occurs if the Thing, rather than being veiled, is fully exposed in the aesthetic realm? It is crucial to limit the influence of the

Thing in artistic creation. For Recalcati, without the mediation of the imaginary and symbolic, an unfiltered eruption of the real can lead to pure destruction. The defensive function of the imaginary and the symbolic is not to completely avoid contact with the real and keep it at bay but rather to provide an aesthetic framework for safely encountering and experiencing it (2012, p. 296).[9]

The second aesthetics of the real, the anamorphic aesthetics, centres on the object a. Drawing upon *Seminar XI*, Recalcati expands on the Lacanian idea of the artwork as an encounter with the real—uncanny yet not deadly—understood here as the anamorphic and localised remainder of *jouissance*. The concept of anamorphosis,[10] a distorted image that only becomes visible from a specific point of view, is central to this aesthetics. Lacan focuses on anamorphosis because the anamorphic object high-

[9] Žižek (2000) and Leader (2002) argue that the real of the Thing should always be kept at a distance in artistic production as, for them too, the precondition of any artistic creation is the absence of the Thing. Regarding contemporary art, Žižek contends that the Thing 'is no longer absent, that is, present as a void, as the background of actual events, but threatens to become *directly* present, to actualize itself in reality, and thus to provoke a psychotic collapse of the symbolic space' (2000, p. 39). Similarly, in contemporary artworks, Leader notes a shift towards revealing rather than veiling the human body, exposing everything from genitals to internal organs. Both Žižek and Leader emphasise Lacan's view on beauty as a defence, a veil, or a screen against the disruptive force of the Thing. Leader notes the 'screening function of the visual image' (2002, p. 127) and its relation to the morphogenic power of the *imago*, describing beauty 'as a barrier beyond which is the zone of the Thing, the void that can be imagined in one way as death or destruction' (2002, p. 126). Žižek concurs, suggesting that the gap between beauty and ugliness is 'the very gap that separates reality from the Real: what constitutes reality is the minimum of idealization the subject needs in order to be able to sustain the horror of the Real' ([2009] 1997, p. 66). However, Lacan's stance on beauty is more nuanced and Recalcati contends that beauty, and art more broadly, not only act as a protective screen but also as a gateway to the real. Recalcati refers to Antigone's 'unbearable splendour' and Van Gogh's shoes (Lacan 1992, pp. 247 and 297) to illustrate Lacan's idea that beauty exists at 'the very point of the transition between life and death' (1992, p. 297) and operates 'at the limit' (1992, p. 298). In fact, Lacan suggests that patients' engagement with aesthetics often indicates a proximity to the death drive or the potential emergence of something associated with the real (1992, p. 239).

[10] To illustrate this idea, Lacan refers to Holbein's 1533 *The Ambassadors*, a famous example of anamorphosis. The painting shows two French ambassadors standing and facing the viewer in a highly realistic manner: the perspective is impeccable, the figures are life-sized, and the objects—symbols of power and knowledge—are meticulously rendered. Among these objects is an enigmatic shape at the bottom of the canvas. When viewed from a different angle, it reveals itself as a human skull. Here, the image of death suddenly emerges from an ordinary scene, confronting the viewers directly. Holbein's painting thus makes visible what Lacan describes as the 'triumph of the gaze over the eye' (Lacan 1998, p. 103), that is to say, 'the subject as annihilated' (Lacan 1998, p. 88). This is, according to Bellavita (2005), the gaze of the real.

lights what 'escape[s] from vision' (Lacan 1998, p. 87). Anamorphosis demonstrates that a picture is more than an object for the subject to look at; it also reveals that the subject's position is not simply that of geometric optics. Lacan assigns two functions to anamorphosis: firstly, it shows that a painting is not merely a realistic reproduction of reality and, secondly, it exhibits the captivating power of images (1998, p. 92).

To articulate the encounter with the real, Lacan contrasts two notions borrowed from Aristotle: the *automaton*, or 'the network of signifiers' (Lacan 1998, p. 52); and the *tyche*, 'the encounter with the real' (Lacan 1998, p. 52).[11] The *automaton* is associated with the consistency and familiarity of the imaginary and symbolic network which constitutes reality, while the *tyche* corresponds to the unexpected irruption of the real (Lacan 1998, pp. 53–54). One could argue that the real affects reality in much the same way that anamorphosis alters the painted representation. However, when the real emerges through the imaginary-symbolic device of a work of art, it is not destructive and can be encountered without annihilating or traumatising the subject, albeit with a certain degree of disturbance, and without compromising the aesthetic integrity of the aesthetic object.

Lacan's theory of vision challenges the rigid dichotomy between the viewing subject and the viewed (aesthetic) object, a dichotomy foundational to what he calls 'geometrical' or 'flat optics' (1998, p. 85). Traditional visual aesthetic theories, shaped by this dichotomy, suggest that the subject exerts active control over the act of vision. In this framework, the human mind is likened to an anthropomorphic camera obscura, with the eye serving as the gateway to the external world, where light is filtered through the retina to form a mental image of the observed object. From the Renaissance perspective and Descartes' theory of vision to the modern optical model, the viewer is considered to possess a mastery over the visual object, reducing it to a passive entity for observation.

Lacan's theory of vision, however, subverts this subject/viewer and object/viewed dyad. Instead of treating the subject as an image-capturing

[11] In Book II of *Physics*, while addressing the four causes at the foundation of cosmos, Aristotle introduces the concept of *automaton* [αὐτόματον], which he associates with accidental occurrences (i.e., randomness) concerning inanimate or non-human beings, and *tyche* [τύχη], referring to that which occurs unpredictably (i.e., chance or luck) in relation to human beings.

device, as geometrical optics suggests, Lacan conceives of the image as capturing the human subject. In this model, the subject is no longer the active viewer with mastery over the object; rather, the subject is exposed to the gaze of the world, always being looked at before looking (Lacan 1998, p. 109). The Lacanian subject, therefore, is not the master of their own gaze. Lacan posits that the gaze primarily belongs to the Other, with the subject ensnared within it. This Lacanian perspective differs radically from the Cartesian conception of the subject as the 'artifex of representation' (Recalcati 2007, p. 57).

Recalcati considers anamorphosis as the quintessential encounter with the real in the aesthetic domain. This real emerges as an uncanny object that disrupts the composition of the artwork and subverts the rigid dichotomy between a viewing subject and a viewed (aesthetic) object. The anamorphic aesthetics signals that it is the work of art that enables the real, understood as a scopic (visual) and extimous excess within the artwork, to emerge (Recalcati 2012, p. 613). In Holbein's painting, the anamorphosis cannot be reduced to the linear perspective or geometrical optics. The anamorphic stain in the picture overturns the viewer/object dyad: the viewer is subjected to the uncanny gaze of the stain emerging from the painting, revealing the real of their own existence. The anamorphic skull in Holbein's painting becomes visible only when the viewer looks at the artwork from a specific angle, at which point the viewer realises they are being looked at. This is what Recalcati calls the '*tychic* power' of art (2007), a concept Resmini also refers to as the 'aesthetics of the *tyche*' (2013, p. 283). For Recalcati,

> the central theme of anamorphic aesthetics is in fact that of the work of art as an encounter - through the signifying organisation of the image - with the real, which is irreducible to any principle of organisation. (2012, p. 603)

The anamorphic skull does not represent a specific reality or symbolise death; Lacan seeks to move beyond both realism and symbolism. Instead, it serves as the uncanny manifestation of the real, disrupting conventional modes of representation. According to Recalcati, the true concern in art is not a mimetic representation of the world, but rather a depiction of the non-representable, that which cannot be symbolised. As Lacan asserts repeatedly in both *Seminar VII* and *Seminar XI*, art does not aim merely to imitate or reproduce reality (Lacan 1992, p. 297). Even in seemingly mimetic works of art which offer a realistic portrayal of the object, 'the picture does not compete with the appearance' (Lacan 1998, p. 112).

The third aesthetics of the real is the 'aesthetics of the sinthome', which is Recalcati's most original contribution. In the aesthetics of the void, the irreducible excess of the real is represented by the Thing, which art encircles, providing an imaginary and symbolic organisation of its void. In anamorphic aesthetics, the real appears as the remainder encountered by the viewer as anamorphically present in the aesthetic object. This third approach, more than the other two, establishes a strong connection with the clinical domain that I have highlighted as the hallmark of Italian Lacanianism.[12] Possibly because of its clinical focus, which diverges from traditional aesthetic concerns, Resmini overlooks this particular aesthetic perspective in his seminal article on the topic.

This third aesthetics that Recalcati draws from Lacan seeks to intertwine psychoanalysis and aesthetics, focusing on the real of the subject. Recalcati reconsiders the interplay between the artist's biography, the artwork, and psychoanalytic theory. While psychoanalytic aesthetics has often, perhaps inappropriately, investigated the artist's biography based on the thematic content of the artwork, it typically overlooked its factual elements—its form, structure, and medium. In this third aesthetics, the real of the subject is subjectivised into their *sinthome*. As such, this aesthetics of the real is fundamentally an aesthetics of the subject's singularity. It represents the unique, irreproducible way in which a subject deals with their own enjoyment. The overlap with the clinical experience is evident in how the subject navigates the surplus of the real that resides within them. This surplus can be experienced negatively, as an overwhelming excess that engulfs the subject—the real in its drive-ridden

[12] This perspective has also influenced Italian psychoanalysts from different orientations. For instance, Giuseppe Civitarese (2013) draws directly from Recalcati's Lacanian aesthetics to develop a Bionian aesthetic theory in the book chapter 'The Equation Analysis/Painting and the Aesthetics of the Real'. In particular, Civitarese defines the aesthetic conflict as the 'encounter/collision with the real' (p. 112) where art is seen 'as the preferred device for meeting with and transforming the real' (p. 113). This creates a close connection between artistic and psychoanalytic practices as both disciplines share the 'aim to deconstruct reality in order to approximate the real' (p. 114).

incandescence. Yet it can also be experienced as an overabundance—a surplus of desire that gives shape to the force of the drive.

The main references for this aesthetics are the 1971 text *Lituraterre*, where the materiality of the battery of signifiers and the unconscious is brought to the forefront, and the 1975–1976 *Seminar XXIII*, where Lacan turns to James Joyce to garner insights for his psychoanalytic theory and practice. In the 1970s, Lacan's focus shifts from those symbolic notions of his theory—such as the signifier, speech, language, and the symptom—to more material elements like the letter, discourse, *lalangue*, and the *sinthome*. This transition marks a movement away from the primacy of the symbolic order towards an emphasis on the real and its direct effects on the body, highlighting the materiality of language and the way it leaves marks on the body and the living organism. Whereas in *Seminar XI*, the signifier is seen as mortifying the living body and limiting its *jouissance*, in Lacan's later work in *Lituraterre* and *Seminar XXIII*, the signifier is understood not only to mark the living body but also that which inscribes *jouissance* into it. This shift underscores a more complex relationship between the symbolic and the real, where language is not merely a tool of repression and symbolic mediation but also a means through which the real exerts its influence and inscribes itself on the body.

According to Recalcati, what is at stake in the function of the letter is 'a signifier that, instead of connecting to the chain of other signifiers, acts upon the subject like a unique marker that affects and condenses the enjoyment of the subject and their proper name' (2012, p. 617). Recalcati regards the letter both as a trace which 'separates the singular place of the subject from the universal place of the Other' (2012, p. 619) and as a loose signifier. He proposes that,

> The singular trace of the letter no longer represents the subject for another signifier because it identifies – in a kind of petrification that no longer entails any reference to the Other – the subject's being in their absolute singularity. (2012, pp. 619–620)

The letter functions as a signifier that, instead of connecting to the chain of other signifiers, acts upon the subject as a unique marker that shapes and condenses the *jouissance* of that specific subject. Recalcati associates this with the distinct style of each individual and artist. This is why Lacan (2013a) talks about the shift 'from a *letter* to a *litter*' (Lacan 2013b, p. 327), where the former refers to a structural element in language and the latter represents the waste or leftovers of language that cannot be fully assimilated. Recalcati connects these concepts to the process of subjectivation, which involves the interplay of the signifiers, traces, and residues that reappear in the subject's life, either derailing or reorienting it. Moving away from the earlier focus on the real qua *das Ding* and the object a, prevalent in the receptions of Lacan during the 1990s and early 2000s, Recalcati now emphasises the process of giving form to these traces and remnants, which he ultimately regards as quintessentially the process of subjectivation. As Recalcati writes,

> It is the concept of form that we need to reclaim. When does a life assume a form? Not only the thrust of the drive, but the form of the life itself. When does a life assume a form, a style? Where does such a style come from, the form of a life? From its work? Its way of relating to the Other? Of loving? Of desiring? Of engaging with the world? What gives a life a form? (2020, p. 134)

In *Seminar XXIII*, Lacan (2016) systematically enucleates the conception of the *sinthome* as something that resists psychoanalytic interpretations, rather than fomenting them. Lacan arrives at the definition of the *sinthome* after decades of clinical practice, during which he noticed the deep connection between the symptom and the structure of subjectivity on the one hand, and patients' tendency to refuse to abandon their symptoms on the other. Lacan contends that the end of psychoanalytic treatment should not entail the removal of the *sinthome* of the subject, which could risk subjective collapse. Rather, it should involve a different combination of desire and enjoyment, a new way for the subject to organise their *jouissance*.

In this seminar, Lacan refers to Joyce to illustrate how the *sinthome* serves as the foundation of subjectivity. Rather than focusing on Joyce himself, Lacan's discussion centres on how he uses Joyce's writing to advance his psychoanalytic theory. Lacan does not provide a psychobiography of Joyce; instead, he refers to Joyce's works as a means of advancing his psychoanalytic theory. Through his literary work, Joyce attains consistency and mental stability, affirms his name through a social practice, and reaches a vast audience. Lacan uses Joyce to challenge his traditional notion of the paternal function. From the 1950s to the 1960s, Lacan considered the paternal metaphor as central in limiting and regulating *jouissance*, with the Name of the Father as the pivotal signifier for psychic stability. However, from the 1970s, Lacan expanded this perspective by introducing the concepts of the Father of the Name and *père-version.* As Joyce demonstrates, these are not strictly necessary for achieving psychic stability, as the *sinthome* can fulfil this role. Lacan views Joyce's writing as a compensation for the foreclosure of the Name of the Father, which prevents Joyce from succumbing to psychosis. For Lacan, Joyce represents a singular way of dealing with his *jouissance* through his writing. Thus, Joyce's writing constitutes a form of prosthesis that enables him to achieve self-coherence.

Recalcati regards the *sinthome* and sublimation as homologous since they are two similar possibilities for dealing with the excess, irreducible to the signifier, of the real. The real as *sinthome*, which resists symbolisation and interpretation, contrasts with hermeneutic interpretations. According to Recalcati, the Lacanian notion of the *sinthome* paves the way for a psychoanalytic aesthetics that does not approach art merely as a symptom and in which the biography of the artist is implicated but not as something to be interpreted in the artwork. On this basis, it is a key notion for a psychoanalytic aesthetics that goes beyond hermeneutics and psychobiography. From a clinical standpoint, Recalcati explores how the subject grapples with the real, while from an aesthetic perspective, he examines how the potent force of the real as drive can be harnessed and structured into form through an interplay of imaginary and symbolic processes.

In the aesthetic domain, the outcome of the process of sublimation is an artistic object that is usually recognised and appreciated by the social Other. On the contrary, in the clinical context, there is no strict requirement to create an aesthetic object that gains societal esteem; the focus is instead on the subject's ability to navigate their own relationship with the real while embracing their subjugated—yet not passive—position in relation to the Other. Although a successful analysis often leads to the creation of something—a result of the subjectivation process qua sublimation—this creation does not necessarily need to be an artistic object. This process of sublimation, as it relates to the analysand, and which was linked to subjectivation in Chap. 3, also involves formalisation—the process of giving shape and direction to the surplus of the real that resides within us (Recalcati 2007, 2012).

In conclusion, Recalcati's aesthetics of the real emphasises treating, channelling, and encountering the real through the imaginary and the symbolic, not to eliminate it but to allow for its manifestation without causing excessive disruption. The risk with this perspective is that it might overemphasise the role of the symbolic as a redemptive force for the real. As discussed in Chaps. 3 and 4, this perspective carries the risk of approaching the real merely as something to be tamed by the symbolic—and consequently, *jouissance* as something to be managed, regulated, and limited (Pagliardini 2020). However, this interpretation is not entirely accurate, as the real remains an irreducible, unyielding core. Lacanian thought continues to grapple with how to regulate, channel, and contain *jouissance*. In this section, I have explored the aesthetic paradigms identified by Recalcati in Lacan, focusing on how the imaginary and the symbolic relate to the real. In the following section, I will argue that the real cannot be treated, handled, or interpreted. Even in aesthetics, the real is that which fundamentally resists.

The Unconscious of Art

Italian Lacanians share Theodor Adorno's concerns about the risks of applying psychoanalysis to aesthetics (Bottiroli 2002; Recalcati 2007; Resmini 2013; Bonazzi and Tonazzo 2015). In *Aesthetic Theory*, Adorno notes that

> psychoanalysis considers artworks to be essentially unconscious projections of those who have produced them, and, preoccupied with the hermeneutics of thematic material, it forgets the category of form and, so to speak, transfers the pedantry of sensitive doctors to the most inappropriate objects, such as Leonardo da Vinci or Baudelaire. (2002, p. 8)

According to Adorno, traditional psychoanalytic approaches to art have historically overlooked the 'aesthetic quality' of the artwork, its 'process of production', and its 'idiom and material' (p. 8), almost colluding with an idealist aesthetics that focuses predominantly on the role of abstract ideas and content. He further argues that:

> Only dilettantes reduce everything in art to the unconscious, repeating clichés. In artistic production, unconscious forces are one sort of impulse, material among many others. They enter the work mediated by the law of form; if this were not the case, the actual subject portrayed by a work would be nothing but a copy. Artworks are not *Thematic Apperception Tests* of their makers. (2002, p. 9)

In the psychoanalytic approaches to art criticised by Adorno, one can observe Freud's legacy, as he openly acknowledged prioritising the content of the artwork over its 'formal and technical qualities' (1914, p. 211). For their part, post-Freudians further developed this focus, mainly advancing symptomatic readings of artworks (Glover 2009).

In contrast, Italian Lacanian aesthetics advocates for a psychoanalytic approach to art that neither dismisses a priori the influence and significance of the artist's biography on the artwork nor neglects the formal qualities of the artwork itself. This approach explores the relationship between art and the unconscious, while distinguishing aesthetic objects from unconscious manifestations (Bottiroli 2002, 2023). Unlike symptoms and dreams, artworks are not unconscious compromise formations as they are neither an unmediated outpouring of the artist's unconscious nor the direct products of the artist's personal experiences. Instead, Italian Lacanian aesthetics introduces the idea that the unconscious of an artwork is its untranslatable and irreducible core (Bellavita 2005; Recalcati 2007, 2009; Resmini 2013), emphasising the artwork's resistance to being full assimilated into the imaginary and the symbolic. The notion of the unconscious of art must be distinguished from the idea of the unconscious as an archetypal reservoir of meanings—a perspective rooted in the romantic and pre-Freudian conception of the unconscious as the inner domain of irrational and instinctual forces which Lacan extensively critiqued. Similarly, the unconscious of art differs from the artist's personal unconscious, which pathographic approaches attempt to map onto visual, literary, or cinematic works, treating the artwork as a mere externalisation of the artist's internal world.

The unconscious of art primarily manifests itself as the 'resistance of the artwork to words and as the irreducibility of the real of the artwork to meaning' (Recalcati 2007, p. 155). In other words, this 'kernel of resistance' (Resmini 2013, p. 292) to translation is nothing less than 'a trace, an index, an emergence of the real' (Recalcati 2009, p. 140). This perspective distinguishes Lacanian aesthetics from psychoanalytic aesthetics that merely apply psychoanalysis to art, whether through a pathographic or hermeneutic approach. Italian Lacanian aesthetics conceptualises the unconscious of art not as a release of instinctual forces, but rather as the artwork's resistance to any form of translation—the impossibility of converting its irreducible presence into a formation of meaning. This is akin to the resistance to interpretation encountered in the new symptoms and in psychoanalytic practice more broadly. In this framework, the unconscious related to art does not reflect the artist's unconscious but belongs to the artwork itself, residing in its irreducible kernel which defies interpretation.

Italian Lacanians view artworks as characterised by a dual aesthetic nature: their 'irreducible and inarticulate nature', which represents 'a density that cannot be resolved into knowledge', and their 'linguistic and formally articulated unity' (Recalcati 2007, p. 75). The challenge for Italian Lacanian psychoanalytic aesthetics, therefore, is to maintain an awareness of both these aspects of the aesthetic artefact, without neglecting either one. As Recalcati writes,

> This tension, which animates every work of art, should not be understood as a simple opposition between two rigidly determined regimes of meaning (on the one hand, the inarticulate, the Id, and on the other, the articulate, the ego), but rather as a continuous exchange, overlap, or tension between the two. (2007, p. 75)

The aesthetics of the real challenges pathographic, hermeneutic, and symbolic readings of artworks based either on assumptions about the artist's inner world or on the formal features of the artwork. When adopting the pathographic model, psychoanalysts tend to analyse an artwork solely to uncover the artist's psychology. As a result, the artwork is considered merely as a product of the artist's unconscious complexes, or as a tool for mapping the artist's psychological landscape. Traditionally, applied psychoanalysis adopts a decrypting or deciphering approach to art, treating artworks either a thematic apperception test of the author's psychology or puzzles to be solved. In this approach, psychoanalysis is reduced to a kind of enigma-solver, with the artwork functioning as a Rorschach test, to paraphrase Adorno.

Coinema e icona, Nuova proposta per una psicoanalisi dell'arte epitomises this reductive approach. In this book, Franco Fornari (1978) outlines his psychoanalytic aesthetics based on a hermeneutic and deciphering methodology. While Fornari's psychoanalytic contributions to understanding aspects of war and violence are certainly noteworthy, helping to consolidate the Kleinian school in Italy, his psychoanalytic theory of art is ultimately geared at deciphering and decrypting the text of the artwork, whether literary or visual. Although Fornari maintains that his approach seeks to minimise the interpreter's arbitrariness through specific and rigorous hermeneutical operations, his perspective ultimately reduces the artwork to a mere puzzle to be solved or a thematic apperception test to be interpreted. As he writes:

> Coinemic analysis treats the painting like a dream, yet it reduces the actual dream within the painting to pre-established invariants, making it possible to apply a specific hermeneutic framework. Viewing the artwork as a dream and thus as an enigma, coinemic analysis is not concerned with the formal aspect alone; rather, it takes this as a starting point from which to delve into the processes of affective signification that lie beneath the painting. (1978, p. 194)

Fornari's psychoanalytic aesthetics is heavily influenced by a dualistic vision characteristic of a psychic model based on strict binaries, such as surface and depth, external and internal, manifest and hidden. This dualism is explicitly evident in the terminology Fornari (1978) employs when analysing works of art, including terms like the inner and outer world (*mondo interno* and *esterno*), daytime and night-time order (*ordine diurno* and *notturno*), internal and external referent (*referente esterno* and *interno*), and superficial and deep structure (*struttura superficiale* and *profonda*). Fornari's hermeneutic approach to the psychoanalysis of art relies on a matrix of meaning which allows the interpreter to connect an image with its underlying meaning. Fornari's coinemes thus constitute the pre-established invariants to any interpretation.

The unconscious, however, does not function like a matrix of meaning, as in Fornari's conception of elementary signifiers that form the foundation of an artwork's text. From a Lacanian perspective, psychoanalysis is less a theory of interpretation than a theory and practice of the limits of any interpretation. In this context, the concept of the real represents the Lacanian category that most strongly opposes the hermeneutically delusional tendency in psychoanalysis to decode every signified into a signifier.[13] This hermeneutic approach relies on an imaginary dichotomy between a visible surface—the manifest content of the artwork—and a supposed depth that constitutes the inner meaning of the artwork. In contrast, Italian Lacanian aesthetics regards art not as an experience open to symbolic decryption but as an encounter involving a dynamic resistance against any attempt to decipher the real.

This reductionist approach is also rooted in a mistaken belief in a one-to-one correspondence between the signifier and the signified. Fornari's psychoanalytic perspective on art thus treats the artwork as a mere symbol with a precise and unambiguous meaning, akin to an algebraic equation. On the contrary, Italian Lacanian aesthetics posits that artworks resist the interpretations and meanings imposed upon them. Despite the myriad of words that may be used to interpret or explain the given meaning of an artwork, its essence cannot be encapsulated or fully captured by them; it remains beyond such descriptions. Consequently, a Lacanian psychoanalytic approach centred on the notion of the real should bear

[13] As the American psychoanalyst Thomas Ogden and the psychoanalytic literary scholar Benjamin Ogden note, a common reading of the well-known Freudian phrase, 'Where id was, there ego shall be' (Freud 1933, p. 80), suggests that 'the unconscious seat of forbidden impulses and irrational fears' should be transformed into a 'rational, realistic, adaptive, thinking and feeling' (2013, p. 23). Consequently, the notion of interpretation, in the context of psychoanalytic practice and psychoanalytic aesthetics, could easily be misunderstood as a mere transformation of something that is encrypted or beneath the surface into something readable or on the surface.

witness to the value of art in its radical extraneousness, irreducible to any hermeneutic or symbolic interpretation.

The kernel of the real contained by every artwork consists in the resistance to interpretation and symbolisation. Indeed, more explicitly and straightforwardly than any other psychoanalytic theory, Lacanian psychoanalysis firmly rejects the tendency to decode or unmask the supposed hidden meaning of every 'text', whether it is the psychoanalytic narrative of a patient in the consulting room or the artistic text of a work of art. This 'irreducible presence' (*irriducibile presenza*) of an artwork is what Recalcati calls the 'image-sign' (*immagine-segno*), which is neither the surface or depth of the artwork, nor a symbol that refers to the artist's personal life. In this respect,

> *immagine-segno* does not unite a signifier with a fixed meaning, according to a biunivocal scheme. It cannot be assimilated to a semantic hinge that allows one to trace back, through the code of a language, from the signifier to a specific meaning. Instead, it appears as a kind of indivisible unity that refers only to itself. (Recalcati 2007, p. 98)

As such, the aesthetics of the real aims to disentangle psychoanalytic aesthetics from hermeneutics and symbolism while insisting on the irreducible and untranslatable core of every artwork, which ultimately partakes of the order of the real.

Similarly to the *sinthome*, a work of art does not only imply an unambiguous meaning that leads to a singular interpretation. Bottiroli agrees with Recalcati's perspective and states that 'interpretation is first and foremost articulation' (2006, p. 361), insofar as 'the effective interpreter of a work of art does not "lift" or attempt to separate; rather, they observe the work and try to describe its way of being' (p. 117).

Recalcati's most relevant example is the *arte informale* of Alberto Burri (1915–1995), characterised by non-figurative content and the use of raw, poor materials (Recalcati 2007, 2009, 2012). For instance, Burri's *Combustions* series consists of artworks created by burning materials such as wood, plastic, and paper, exploring themes of destruction, transformation, and the tension between form and decay. The absence of figurative imagery in Burri's work has provoked a proliferation of interpretations, functioning much like a Rorschach test. Some critics, such as Caroli (1979) and Villa (1996), have drawn parallels between Burri's canvases and wounded skin, likening the burns, abrasions, and stitches on the canvas to the skin of an injured body. Many interpret the works as metaphors for bleeding flesh or a wounded body, with Burri, the artist and former doctor, acting as the healer. Critics who favour this interpretation often point to Burri's previous career as a doctor and his experience in a World War II prisoner-of-war camp in Texas as evidence for this interpretation. However, Burri's *Combustions* do not represent, nor can they be reduced to, mere expressions of the artist's personal life or be used as tools to illustrate psychoanalytic theories. Instead, they are *immagini-segno* preserving what Recalcati, in his influential work on Lacanian aesthetics, describes as the miracle of form.

Recalcati employs visual art as a three-dimensional representation of the interplay between force and form—an embodiment of the Borromean knotting of the imaginary, the symbolic, and the real. However, the encounter with the real can also manifest itself through the medium of cinema. As Bellavita contends, cinematic language:

> cannot represent the unrepresentable, but can allude to it. Using the same tools it employs in any form of representation. And it is precisely in this way that it can reveal the weakness of the Symbolic—a weakness that is the impossibility to represent everything and thus the need to leave a remainder. We can define this remainder as the residue of the Symbolic, or as the small object *a*, or as the emergence of the Real. To this remainder, which provokes anxiety and the feeling of the uncanny, the Symbolic can allude, staging its own inability to represent. (2005, p. 246)

The concept of the unconscious of art closely parallels the 'cinematic real' proposed by the Italian Lacanian film theorist Fabio Vighi. In *Traumatic Encounters in Italian Film*, Vighi argues that:

> If on the one hand the unconscious appears inextricably entwined with the Symbolic, on the other hand it is also connected with the Real, the inaccessible domain of what resists symbolisation absolutely. This is why it would be misleading to think the unconscious as a latent narrative waiting to be rescued to signification, temporarily occupying the place of what is repressed. (2006, p. 17)

Vighi emphasises Lacan's shift from the 'linguistic constitution of the unconscious' (p. 17) towards its real foundation. He goes on to state that if 'any symbolic configuration is intrinsically dependent on its hidden relationship with the real, filmmaking is nothing but the distortion it shapes itself into whilst trying to achieve meaning' (p. 18). Thus, the cinematic real can be conceived of as the trace that interferes with a film's imaginary-symbolic framework. In other words, the cinematic real operates as

> a nucleus of traumatic fantasy that operates at the level of the unconscious [...], as an impenetrable hard core of enjoyment that signals the presence of an unconscious desire. (p. 18)

For Vighi, this cinematic real ultimately coincides with the unconscious of a film and 'can only come about as a traumatic encounter with the disavowed core of cinematic representation' (p. 8)—the unconscious kernel of a film that exceeds its imaginary-symbolic construction yet is simultaneously produced by it. Drawing from Pasolini and Lacan, Vighi contends that 'beneath the symbolic order of reality there exists [...] an abyss, in other words that essentially non-symbolic (real) dimension whose legitimacy cinema has the potential to restore' (p. 28). Vighi thus suggests that cinema has the ability to re-establish the generative potential of the real by exposing the void that the symbolic order typically conceals. Cinema, in this sense, offers a confrontation with the real, restoring its presence as a legitimate part of human experience, despite its disavowal in everyday imaginary-symbolic structures.

In this Lacanian approach to film, which places the real at its core, the psychoanalytic interpretation does not merely entail applying psychoanalytic notions and theories to cinema. Rather, it aims to 'identify ways of reaching the cinematic real' (p. 11), namely, that which falls outside of the imaginary-symbolic articulation. Vighi reminds us that Freud perceived a certain incompatibility between psychoanalysis and cinema, revolving around the non-representational nature of the unconscious opposed to the cinema's visual dimension, which is 'ill equipped to render the "invisible presence" of the unconscious' (p. 34). However, Vighi aptly observes:

> Shifting the emphasis on the legibility of the unconscious and on the visibility of the real (with the proviso that the unconscious and the real can be located through the analysis of the effects they have on the visual field), Lacanian theory bridges the Freudian gap between the non-figurative and the figurative, suggesting that it is precisely in the 'too-visual' of cinema, in the redundancy of the image, that one should seek its unacknowledged structuring kernel. (p. 34)

Lacan's theory thus resolves the Freudian conundrum of the non-figurative nature of the unconscious and the figurative (visual) nature of cinema. Vighi contends that 'the cinematic image is always-already destabilised by its own secret liaison with the real, since the real (and this is the Lacanian crux of the matter) not only *sustains*, but also *stains*, what we see' (p. 31) insofar as what we see 'is always-already an effect of the invisible real' (p. 34).

Therefore, Vighi extensively argues that films and reality share a 'common structural constitution' (2012, p. 6), their fictional fabric, as both involve visual-imaginary elements and narrative components. Reality can be regarded as an inherently cinematic form of appearance and comparing reality to cinema highlights the underlying dynamics of sense-making in our everyday lives. Reality is always experienced through its fictional and fictionalised aspects, shaped by the interplay of the symbolic and the imaginary while partially excluding the real. Similarly, films are the artistic expressions of this same interplay. It follows that both cinema and reality reflect 'our constitutive alienation in fiction' (Vighi 2012, p. 7). Reality, Lacan argues, is fundamentally hallucinated, a product of the subject's imagination and symbolisation (Lacan 1997, p. 98). To some extent, reality acts as a protective shield, keeping the subject from encountering the traumatic real. Direct access to reality in its objectivity and factuality is therefore impossible since it is always mediated by the signifier (see Chap. 3). The subject continuously re-creates their own version of reality to screen out the real and maintain a safe distance. Ultimately, 'reality can only be thought of as an intrinsically cinematic form of appearance' (Vighi 2012, p. 8). From Vighi's perspective, the filmmaking process closely resembles how the subject perceives reality as the latter becomes 'the distortion it shapes itself into whilst trying to achieve meaning' (Vighi 2014, p. 280).

At the turn of the century, realism regained prominence in Italian artistic practices and scholarship. This resurgence of interest in realism across various art forms, particularly in literature and cinema, led scholars to advocate for a 'return to reality' and a 'return of the real', making notions of reality and the Lacanian real central to postmillennial Italian cultural discourse. The Lacanian perspective has thus become increasingly relevant in interpreting these artistic trends, providing tools to explore their broader cultural and sociopolitical implications. In the following section, I will briefly explore these new realist trends in postmillennial Italian literature and cinema before focusing on how Italian Lacanians have employed the notion of the real to analyse contemporary art. They speak of an 'emersion' or 'irruption' of the real in contemporary art, which disrupts traditional symbolic frameworks, exceeding the boundaries of representation and meaning. While Italian Lacanian scholars characterise this realism as extreme, traumatic, or psychotic, Lacanian clinicians emphasise that the real becomes synonymous with the abject, trauma, or formless when disjointed from the Borromean knot with the imaginary and symbolic.

The Return of the Real in the Italian Arts

Italian culture has a strong association with realism.[14] Realist trends have regularly resurfaced in various fields—including philosophy, literature, visual art, and cinema—and different sociohistorical contexts in Italian history. Since the unification of Italy, every generation has witnessed the emergence of a new take on realism, which differs from the previous ones due to a variety of factors, such as the specific reality depicted, the mode

[14] The term 'realism' originated in France, with the first attested use of the word *réalisme* dating back to 1826 (Bowlby 2007). However, it quickly became a widespread and much-debated notion 'both in practice and in theory, between painters, novelists, and critics of every kind' (Bowlby 2007, p. XII). Due to its multifaceted nature, realism encompasses various offshoots and has reappeared multiple times, beginning with the movement of French naturalism. Notable exponents of this movement include the writers Émile Zola and Guy de Maupassant, as well as the painter Gustave Courbet, whose famous painting *L'Origine du monde* (1986) was once owned by Lacan (Roudinesco 1997, pp. 183–184). These artists sought to depict reality without filters, bringing aspects of life previously excluded into the representational framework.

of representation, and the medium employed (Hennessey et al. 2017). This inclination towards realist tendencies can be traced back to at least the late nineteenth century, when *verismo* dominated literature, visual art, and opera. Realism then re-emerged in the twentieth century with *realismo magico* in literary and visual artworks and, after World War II, with the internationally renowned *neorealismo* in cinema. Neorealism, in particular, remains the Italian realist trend par excellence. Neorealist films clearly demonstrate how the sociohistorical and cultural milieu can shape the proliferation of realist trends. Emerging in response to the harrowing reality of the Fascist regime and World War II, neorealism became a cinematic retort marked by a strong sociopolitical commitment. The trauma of the war forced a generation of artists to confront reality directly, not only through thematic content but also through specific techniques, such as moving from studio sets to real locations and employing non-professional actors.[15] Although *verismo*, *realismo magico*, and *neorealismo* are the most prominent Italian realist trends, realism did not vanish in the periods between these cycles. From the 1960s, however, realism lost its prominence as the linguistic turn and the focus on theoretical formalism overshadowed it, although Pasolini's cinema represents a notable exception (Vighi 2006).

Realist trends have typically arisen in specific sociohistorical contexts and under exceptional circumstances, such as post-unification Italy, the post-World War II era, and turn-of-the-century Italy, when art and political commitment were closely intertwined. In postmillennial Italy, there has been a resurgence of interest in realism across various disciplines spanning from philosophy (discussed in Chap. 4) to literature and cinema (addressed in this section), growing into an extremely pervasive,

[15] Film scholars have examined neorealism's connection to ideology and counter-hegemonic discourses through the lens of Lacanian psychoanalysis and Marxist theory. Vincent Rocchio, for instance, views neorealism as a period ripe for social change and a challenge to the established order, arguing that 'Lacanian psychoanalysis provides the study of film with the means by which to analyze the ideological functioning of narrative [...] a valuable tool [...] for confronting the hegemonic process' (1999, p. 7). Vighi, on the other hand, posits that 'neorealism was essentially an attempt to translate the encounter with the non-symbolisable real of war and destruction in cinematic terms' (2006, p. 58).

albeit highly debated, academic topic.[16] Particularly noteworthy is the increased prevalence of realist trends across several artistic domains. Literature, films, and documentaries frequently feature themes, characters, and plots about Italian sociopolitical events; the economic crisis and the so-called *precariato*; immigration; mafia culture; and the prosaic reality of everyday life (Di Martino and Verdicchio 2017).

This new wave of realism, which emerged at the beginning of the twenty-first century, is the latest iteration in the cyclic returns of realist trends in Italy (Mazzarella 2011; Serkowska 2011). This phenomenon has, in turn, ignited a renewed scholarly interest in realism within the Italian context, with a proliferation of articles, essays, and books dealing with the topic. The emergence of these new realist tendencies, predominantly in literature and cinema, has led scholars to assert that such trends reflect what Esposito has termed a 'pressing demand for reality' (2015, p. 90) by the contemporary Italian audience. This early twenty-first-century Italian realism is, however, hard to define due to its heterogeneous nature; it lacks uniform features, spans disciplines, and crosses artistic boundaries. Rather than forming a cohesive movement, it reflects the spirit of the times, capturing shifts in the perception of reality and the epochal changes occurring in daily life.

The depiction of reality has become a central focus for most postmillennial Italian literary and cinematic works. The phenomenon of *Gomorra*—spanning Roberto Saviano's book (2006), Matteo Garrone's film adaptation (2008), Mario Gelardi's theatrical version (2007), and the television series (Sollima et al. 2014–2021)—is often considered as the epitome of the return of realist trends in early twenty-first-century Italy, which has led Italian scholarship to call for a return to reality (*ritorno alla realtà*) (Donnarumma et al. 2008). As Italian postmillennial artistic production increasingly focuses on the portrayal of reality, Italian

[16] Numerous unresolved debates surround the definition, boundaries, and themes of Italian realism, making any definitive categorisation challenging. Realism has been described as 'a trans-generic phenomenon that invades other genres' and a flexible 'mode' of aesthetic expression that 'predominates in certain historical and industrial moments and contexts' (O'Rawe 2008, p. 184). The ambiguity of the notion of realism has sparked considerable scholarly debates. In Italian film studies, some scholars caution against overemphasising realism as a value category (O'Leary and O'Rawe 2011, p. 109), while others advocate for moving beyond this paradigm (Marlow-Mann 2010, p. 263).

scholarship has shown a parallel rise in its interest in studying this new wave of realism. This has resulted in a proliferation of studies on the subject, with Italian scholars attempting to identify and understand this very heterogeneous—and as yet undefined—phenomenon. While it is beyond the scope of this book to address this complex, multifaceted, and still ongoing scholarly and artistic trend, it is worth noting that Italian literary and film scholars and critics have rarely engaged with Lacanian theory. Their mention of Lacan is often brief, sporadic, and mediated almost exclusively through the work of Hal Foster and Slavoj Žižek. Broadly speaking, Italian literature and cinema scholars refer ambiguously and interchangeably to reality and to the Lacanian notion of the real (Serkowska 2011). In some cases, reality is regarded as a sociopolitical and cultural construction, while in others, there is a return to a positivistic/empirical understanding of reality. In the latter case, reality is considered mainly in terms of its facticity and knowability, while in the former, it is conceived of as the mere product of theoretical constructions. Here, the Lacanian distinction between reality and the real offers a valuable framework for moving beyond the strict dualism of the debate and deepening our understanding of postmillennial realism in Italy.

While Italian literary and film studies scholarship tends to focus on the notion of reality, Italian Lacanians concentrate on the concept of the real, arguing that this is a return of the real rather that a return to reality. From a Lacanian perspective, reality and the real are opposed. Bluntly put, reality functions to fundamentally prevent the emergence of the traumatic real and shield the subject from it. Yet the two terms are also correlated, as the real can be encountered and to some extent experienced within reality, not outside of it. As Lacan aptly points out, 'In the end, doesn't the feeling of the real reach its high point in the pressing manifestation of an unreal, hallucinatory reality?' (1998, pp. 66–67). From a Lacanian perspective, there is no such thing as an objective reality; reality is not simply what exists 'out there', independently of the observer. Rather, it is always intertwined with the subject's fantasy. For Italian Lacanians, it is the notion of the real, as opposed to reality, that is central to discussions of contemporary art and realism.

The expression 'return of the real' is deliberate for several reasons. First, it emphasises both reality and the Lacanian real. In Italian scholarship, the more the arts—including literature and cinema—focus on realist representations of reality, the more scholars are drawn to examining and framing this resurgence of realism. Similarly, Lacan signals the increasing prominence of the real in contemporary society, which he ascribes to the erosion of the symbolic and the rise of the discourse of the capitalist (Contri 1978; Lacan 1990). Following Lacan's lead, Italian Lacanian scholars and psychoanalysts have observed an emergence of the real in the arts (Bellavita 2006, Lolli 2012), identifying a shift in aesthetic paradigms. Artworks no longer appear as symbolic operations processing the trauma of the real but rather as direct exhibitions of that trauma. The very expression 'irruption of the real' (Perniola 2004) refers precisely to the way in which artworks now provoke a breakdown in the imaginary and symbolic boundaries. The imaginary—Lacan's category for the identification processes that shape self-identity through the morphogenic power of images—and the symbolic—the order of language, culture, and Law—both crumble. Both international and national Lacanian scholars have noted this irruption of the real in contemporary society and its influence on artistic trends. As a result, when Lacanians discuss realism in the arts, they often qualify it with terms such as 'traumatic' (Foster 1996), 'extreme' (Perniola 2004), perverse (Recalcati 2009), and 'psychotic' (Perniola 2004, Recalcati 2007).

Secondly, as previously discussed, the realist tradition has long been influential in Italy, cyclically re-emerging throughout history. Thus, the recent turn to realism in postmillennial Italy should be regarded as a return rather than an entirely new phenomenon. It represents the latest wave of realism in the country. However, rather than offering an exhaustive or definitive explanation, this expression serves as an 'operational term' that allows us to address this complex phenomenon. This term reflects both the ongoing debate surrounding realism in Italian scholarship and the so-called return of the real in Lacanian studies, both nationally and internationally. This framework inevitably presents challenges. The temporal proximity of this recent, ongoing phenomenon makes it difficult to fully grasp or categorise. Moreover, the return of the real is highly multifaceted and heterogeneous, spanning multiple disciplines—including film studies, literary studies, and philosophy—and various media, such as cinema, literature, television, and the Internet. Finally, the phenomenon of the return of the real involves both critics and artists, creating a multi-layered debate that adds to the complexity of the discussion. In this context, Lacan's notion of the real, as received and employed by contemporary Italian Lacanian thought, provides a useful framework for understanding the paradigm shift occurring in postmillennial society and culture as well as in artistic movements.

Italian Lacanians contend that the historical and cultural changes affecting contemporary society and its pathologies are also reflected in artistic productions. This is not simply a result of the commodification of art in modern society, where aesthetic objects are reduced to mere consumer products and artists become traders seeking to maximise profit. Rather, it is because the real increasingly overtakes the symbolic in the realm of art—once considered by Freud as the domain of sublimation *par excellence*, closely tied to the symbolic processes of the unconscious. From this perspective, Italian Lacanian aesthetics asserts that the emerging real is no longer treated, channelled, or mediated *through* and *within* the orders of the imaginary and the symbolic but instead overflows beyond them. In this context, the real manifests traumatically, creating discomfort. It is no longer represented *through* and *within* the imaginary-symbolic framework of art but instead is presented *in spite of* it. This irruption and emergence—the return *of* or *to* the real—does not correspond to an artist's intention to reproduce a raw reality as it would be experienced without filters or to portray everyday life with mimetic accuracy, as in nineteenth- and twentieth-century realism, neorealism, or even hyperrealism. Rather, these artistic expressions emphasise the uncanny and disruptive aspects more aptly encapsulated by the Lacanian notion of the real, understood as trauma, the breakdown of reality, and the death drive.

In *Art and Its Shadow*, the Italian philosopher Mario Perniola argues that Lacan's thought is an indispensable theoretical tool providing 'the possibility of formulating the poetics of extreme realism of the arts today' (2004, p. 6). Specifically, he emphasises the significance of the category of the real in understanding contemporary art's shift away from traditional aesthetic qualities—such as beauty, harmony, and proportion—to those of abjection, formlessness, and degradation. Perniola identifies two prominent and contrasting trends in contemporary Western art. The first involves the derealisation and virtualisation of reality, which transforms it into a virtual spectacle and distances us from it. The second trend moves in the opposite direction, drawing us closer to reality, including its most unsettling and traumatic facets. Discussing the latter trajectory, Perniola notes that

> we have witnessed the manifestation and the spread of an opposite artistic sensibility that has taken shape as a veritable irruption of the real in the rarefied and highly symbolic world of art. The attention of artists has focused on the most violent and most raw aspects of reality and, above all, the themes of death and sex have acquired greater importance. It is not a question, as in the past, of the most naturalistic representation possible of this reality, but of a direct exposure of events, poor in symbolic mediation, that provokes dismay, repulsion, if not outright disgust and horror. The categories of disgust and degradation force themselves arrogantly on aesthetic reflection which now finds itself obliged to abandon the ideal of a pure and disinterested contemplation in favour of a disturbing experience where repulsion and attraction, fear and desire, pain and pleasure, refusal and complicity are mixed and mingled. (2004, pp. 3–4)

Artistic practices of 'extreme realism', characterised by elements of horror and repulsion, are not only strategically designed to shock the audience but are also marked, in Perniola's words, by an inadequate 'symbolic mediation'. In his analysis, Perniola references the art historian Hal Foster who, in his 1996 book *The Return of the Real*, was one of the first scholars to introduce the Lacanian concept of the real into the aesthetic discourse to explore trauma and abjection in contemporary art. As part of a discussion of artistic trends from the 1960s to the 1990s—spanning from pop-art to superrealism—Foster employs the term 'traumatic realism'. His theoretical framework draws directly from Lacan's conceptualisation of 'the real in terms of trauma' (Foster 1996, p. 132), incorporating abjection, repetitions, traumatic effects, and shock as key elements in his analysis. Through the lens of traumatic realism, Foster highlights a fundamental shift in the art world and aesthetics from conceptualising 'reality as an effect of representation to the real as a thing of trauma' (1996, p. 146).

In these artistic trends, the frame of representation is no longer simply a vehicle for naturalistic depictions of reality. Instead, it becomes disrupted in both its imaginary and symbolic components by the violent return of the real. Contemporary artistic movements, especially in their most extreme forms in the late 1980s and 1990s, not only go beyond the register of the imaginary—the realm of the unified and idealised image of the body that conceals the real—but also exceed the order of the symbolic, where the real is articulated through language and cultural laws. Foster contends that 'some contemporary work refuses […] to pacify the gaze, to unite the imaginary and the symbolic against the real' (1996, p. 140). Foster's analysis highlights that the frame of representation functions as a screening to defend against the intrusion of the destabilising real, underscoring the necessity for human beings to shield themselves from it. Through provocative artworks that incorporate elements such as blood, urine, excrement, acts of violence, self-mutilation, and disease, these violated and exhibited bodies engage deeply with the real, displaying its profoundly unsettling, traumatic, and distressing essence.

Perniola concurs with Foster, asserting that the disquieting encounter with the real is precisely what provokes 'anguish and trauma' (2004, p. 6) and introduces these concepts into the Italian aesthetic debate. He contends that these notions are particularly effective in discussions of contemporary art, 'which is characterized, precisely, by a will to confront the viewer with something terrifying and despicable' (p. 6). However, this irruption of the real should not be mistaken with the irruption of the ugly. It has nothing to do with the thematic content of the artwork, but rather with its aesthetic hold, its representational nature, and its underlying imaginary and symbolic dimensions. In fact, Perniola argues that today's extreme realism insists precisely on 'showing the existing without any theoretical and symbolic mediation' (p. 5). In our times, Perniola contends, all symbolic practices, including art, are affected by 'the general process of demystification and secularization' (p. xvi).

Perniola also makes an intriguing observation by drawing a parallel between the inherent, irreducible kernel of any artistic work—its 'radical extraneity', its 'irreducibility to a single identity', its 'essential enigmatic character' (p. 11)—and the Lacanian real. He writes:

> Art can never be dissolved in communication because it contains an incommunicable nucleus which is the source of an infinity of interpretations. Under this aspect, it is similar to the real with which it shares the harsh and rocky inconvenience. (2004, pp. 11–12)

He considers this real alterity as an inherent aspect of every artwork—an unconscious core that resists interpretation, bringing him close to the concepts of the unconscious of art and the cinematic unconscious discussed in the previous section.

Perniola questions what the real in its 'naked existence' would be (p. 6). Like many other Lacanian scholars and psychoanalysts, he conceptualises it as fundamentally ungraspable and disruptive, describing it as 'radically contingent and inaccessible to any theorization', 'extraneous to language and to the symbolic dimension', 'impossible to symbolize and to imagine', and 'alien to any dialectical articulation' (p. 6). He also defines this kind of realism in contemporary art not only as extreme but also as psychotic,[17] borrowing another key category from Lacanian psychoanalysis. In this context, 'psychotic' realism refers to Lacan's clinical theory, in which psychosis is characterised by the non-symbolised return of the real.[18] Drawing from Lacan's clinical remarks, Perniola contends that 'mental illness (the gravest of all, psychosis) is not generated from a refusal of the real but, on the contrary, from a lack, by a hole in the symbolic order' (p. 13). He suggests that the absence of the symbolic function, central to the clinic of psychosis, characterises contemporary artistic trends where 'the traditional structure of separation between art and the real seems collapsed definitively' (p. 21).

Nevertheless, Perniola rejects the idea that art provides direct access to the real due to its inherently imaginary and symbolic nature. He asserts that, from a strictly Lacanian perspective, 'art belongs to the realm of the symbolic and not of the real' (2004, p. 9). Perniola appears to disregard the possibility of engaging with the real through imaginary-symbolic practices, such as art and psychoanalysis, a key tenet of the Italian

[17] It is worth noting that the expression 'psychotic art' is not intended to medicalise or pathologise individual artists, but rather to make sense of contemporary artistic phenomena. In the analysis of Italian Lacanians, clinical terms such as perversion, psychosis, exhibitionism, etc. should by no means be taken as diagnoses of the artists' personalities or any potential psychopathological structure. Rather, they refer solely to artistic language as such. Similarly, Žižek claims that contemporary art is dominated by 'a psychotic collapse of the symbolic space' (2000, p. 39).

[18] In *Seminar III*, Lacan presents his theory of psychosis, explaining that 'what is not symbolized returns in the real' (Lacan 1997, p. 86), and that 'the object of a *Verwerfung* [foreclusion] reappear[s] in the real' (Lacan 1997, p. 190). He describes psychosis as a clinical structure where 'the unconscious is present but not functioning' (Lacan 1997, p. 143), meaning that the subject is directly confronted with the raw, unmediated presence of the real, which intrudes upon their experience.

Lacanian aesthetics discussed in this chapter. He does, however, acknowledge that attempting to access the real directly, without mediation, could pose significant challenges from both aesthetic and clinical perspectives. Attempting to present the real in art without any mediation is, according to Perniola, what constitutes psychotic art.

Perniola is not the only Italian scholar to address the psychotic dimension of contemporary art. For instance, Bellavita finds the concept of psychotic realism particularly pertinent for explaining what he calls the emergence of the real within the symbolic space of representation (2005, p. 84). Bellavita specifically draws on Miller's notion of generalised foreclusion (pp. 84–85) to avoid pathologising art with a psychotic connotation. The issue at hand is, in fact, different. Through Miller, Bellavita argues that the encounter with a real that eludes the symbolic is experienced by all human beings, not only by the psychotic subject. This is because the real is *extimate*—both external and intimate—to the symbolic. Foreclosure, therefore, is no longer merely a process that marks the impossibility for the psychotic subject to access the symbolic order—what Miller refers to as 'restricted foreclosure'—but instead becomes a fundamental condition of human existence: the real, by its very nature, cannot be fully symbolised (pp. 84–85).

Recalcati (2007) builds on Perniola's perspective, arguing that Lacan's theory of psychosis is crucial for understanding contemporary art, much like it is for contemporary psychopathology (see Chap. 3). Recalcati contends that today's artistic landscape is marked by a psychotic fixation on the real, entirely detached from the imaginary and the symbolic. This creates a twofold risk for contemporary art: either reducing artworks to a sterile, self-referential metatheoretical discourse, as seen in some forms of conceptual art, or dismantling the formal configuration of the artwork entirely, as a radical rejection of any aesthetic criteria, as observed in some extreme body art practices (e.g., Schwarzkogler, Acconci, Pane, Franko B, Sterlarc, and Orlan).[19] As Recalcati writes:

[19] In *La so(m)bra de lo real: El arte como vomitorio*, Hernández-Navarro (2006) introduces a similar distinction in contemporary art based on Recalcati's clinical account of anorexia and bulimia. According to Hernández-Navarro, contemporary art is characterised by two main tendencies concerning the visual domain: *scopic anorexia* and *scopic bulimia*. The former dematerialises the object of art, reducing it to a mere conceptual abstraction, leaving the audience's gaze with essentially

> The intrinsic power of a work of art lies in its ability to actualise the trauma of the encounter with the Real, yet this encounter cannot lead to a dissolution of the formal value of the artwork. The Real, which is disjointed – or foreclosed – from the Symbolic, is in fact a definition not so much of art, but, as Lacan posits, of the clinical figure of psychosis. (p. 76)

In Recalcati's view, psychotic realism attempts to subvert the linguistic and formal components of art, undermining the very concept of figuration. He argues that this denotes a psychotic confusion between the real and the symbolic, which is manifested through deliberate provocations aimed at inducing anxiety and capturing the audience's gaze. Recalcati's affirmative perspective on the real asserts that the real is not solely confined to the abject, formless, fragmented, or traumatic aspects (2007, 2012). More precisely, the real can indeed take on such forms, but only when dissociated from the imaginary and the symbolic.

For this reason, Recalcati challenges the perspective developed by the art theorists Yve-Alain Bois and Rosalind Krauss (1997), as well as that of Slavoj Žižek (1997, 2000) in their account of the *informe* (formless) and sublimation. Recalcati's central argument is that their approaches rest on a metapsychological misunderstanding: they wrongly equate sublimation with a form of idealisation or elevation. In *Formless: A User's guide*, Bois and Krauss discuss the 'force of the formless' (1997, p. 9) as a necessary category to understand contemporary practices. They regard form and content as 'useless' categories (Bois and Krauss 1997, p. 9). Furthermore, they associate sublimation with 'the vertical, Gestalt, the law' (p. 244) and, thus, view desublimation as an inevitable 'transgression against the form' (Bois and Krauss 1997, p. 244). Similarly, for Žižek desublimation involves 'the reversal of the sublime object into abject, into an abhorrent, nauseating excremental piece of slime' (2000, p. 37).

---

nothing tangible on which to focus. In contrast, the latter entails an obscene and abject exhibition of the excessive and the extreme, ultimately forcing the audience to avert their gaze. Overall, Hernández-Navarro agrees with the perspective proposed by Lacanian scholars and art critics, in particular Foster, who argues that the notion of the real is essential for the analysing contemporary aesthetics and art in relation to trauma, the obscene, and the abject. In his discussion of body art, Hernández-Navarro affirms that this form of art does not stage or represent the horror but brutally presents it (2006, p. 132), emphasising the contemporary collapse of any imaginary-symbolic configuration in the artistic realm which allows for the irruption of the real.

According to Recalcati, these interpretations establish a false dichotomy between force and form, leading to a fundamental misreading of sublimation, which is regarded simply as a matter of elevation, of high versus low, or drives versus desire.[20] 'The action of the symbolic', Recalcati contends, 'is not accounted for, only the contrast between an imaginary, taken as an ideal, and the excessive obscenity of the real, between the high and the low' (2007, p. 88). Inevitably, for these scholars sublimation consists of 'a process of purifying the subject from contamination with the real' (Recalcati 2007, p. 89). Consequently, desublimation is seen as the exact opposite: a fall from the elevated and idealised form to the base, fragmented, scatological, and abject matter. Thus, Recalcati identifies in these theoretical perspectives the risk of attempting a 'regression toward the real, determined by the tearing of the fetishistic veil of form' (p. 86) in which 'elevation must be replaced by a degradation of the imaginary object to the real of the Thing' (p. 85). After all, Bois and Krauss connotate the real mainly as the 'traumatic' and 'nonsymbolizable', that which 'addresses us with the news of our own death about which there is nothing to say' (1997, p. 191).

According to Recalcati, the aesthetics of the real involves an idea of beauty, sublimation, and the artwork that is connected not to the ideal but to the real, bringing about an awareness and awakening, rather than serving as a screen to protect from it. Burri's works, extensively referenced also by Bois and Krauss (1997), serve once again as the epitome of this

[20] The French Lacanian psychoanalyst Gérard Wajcman makes similar observations in his article 'Desublimation: An Art of What falls' (2007). He argues that 'the Freudian notion of sublimation seems inspired and literally aspired by the chemical and alchemical origins of the term, in which the heavy matter is dissipated into ethereal gas and is purified' (p. 92). While the Lacanian conception of sublimation adds that any object can be elevated to the dignity of the Thing (see Chap. 3), this still maintains a sense of verticality: 'the symbolic ascends, while the real falls' (p. 104). Moreover, Wajcman aptly critiques the use of the notion of sublimation as 'a transcendental concept, eternal, universal and intangible, entirely unconnected in any case from the history of art and of the historicity of works of art' (p. 91). He refers to Seminar VII, where Lacan affirms that 'no correct evaluation of sublimation in art is possible if we overlook the fact that all artistic production, including especially that of the fine arts, is historically situated. You don't paint in Picasso's time as you painted in Velazquez's; you don't write a novel in 1930 as you did in Stendhal's time' (1992, p. 107). Unlike Recalcati, however, Wajcman welcomes Krauss and Bois' perspective and use of the categories of 'desublimation', 'disenchantment', and 'a movement toward the unformed' (p. 110) to discuss contemporary art which, he also acknowledges, is 'directly concerned with the real' (p. 110). Wajcman concludes that 'art shows the malaise in jouissance, the real of the disturbance of subjects' (p. 111).

aesthetic perspective. Recalcati argues that Burri's works, while preserving the 'miracle of form', also facilitate an encounter with the real. A pertinent example is Burri's *Il cretto di Gibellina* (the Crack of Gibellina), a land art sculpture initiated in 1984 and left unfinished in 1989 (eventually completed in 2015). It commemorates the town of Gibellina in Sicily, which was completely destroyed by an earthquake in 1968. While the town was rebuilt in a different location, Burri chose to create a land artwork that incorporated the ruins of the old, abandoned town, retracing the streets and alleyways through walkable blocks, making the memories of the disappeared town almost tangible for the viewers. Viewed from above, the artwork resembles Burri's signature aesthetic of cracks and fractures. Recalcati interprets this work as a way of integrating the traumatic real of the tragedy into an imaginary-symbolic framework. In doing so, however, the real is neither repressed nor idealised but sublimated.

In conclusion, Italian Lacanian aesthetics contends that the order of the symbolic and the symbolic dynamics, on which both the unconscious and sublimation rely, are deeply affected in contemporary society. Italian Lacanians emphasise how contemporary artistic production reflects the transformation of the symbolic landscape. In the age of the *unconshow* (see Chap. 4), aspects of reality previously excluded or banned from the spectator's view are now gaining prominence, with art increasingly centring on an 'exhibition of unbearable visions', and a 'shameless display of everything that is showable' (Lolli 2012, p. 124). Lolli contends that traditional art aimed to organise the void by employing the imaginary and the symbolic to channel the real. In contrast, extreme realism seeks to 'display the void and allow the horror it conveys to freely overflow, without any concern for the effects it might produce' (p. 121). Lolli notes that since the second half of the twentieth century, artistic production has increasingly embraced this mode of creation, reflecting a radical sociocultural shift that has brought previously censored elements into the representable (p. 128).

Italian Lacanian aesthetics contends that this shift in the art world reflects a broader, more radical transformation that affects today's society: the collapse of the symbolic, which goes hand in hand with the domain of the discourse of the capitalist. A shift from an aesthetics of the symbolic to the aesthetics of the real is thus necessary to make sense of contemporary art. This mirrors the shift from the *clinica del simbolico* to the *clinica del reale* to understand contemporary psychopathologies (Chap. 3). In the paradigm of the aesthetic of the symbolic, traditional art operated within an effective symbolic frame, such as a religious one. On the contrary, contemporary art is created in a world where the symbolic is waning. If the crisis of the symbolic causes a proliferation of the imaginary that can, to some extent, be appreciated in the overwhelming presence and domain of virtual and digital reality, reality television, and so on, the return of the real seems to be an antidote, offering an awakening to an otherwise anaesthetised postmillennial subject.

In Italian Lacanianism, the field of aesthetics, clinical practice, and sociopolitical analysis are closely intertwined through an underlying ethical dimension. Lacan engages with aesthetics primarily to address ethical issues that ultimately inform psychoanalytic clinical practice. Building on the trajectory set out in Seminar VII, where Lacan seeks to delve 'more deeply towards the real' to explore ethical concerns, Italian Lacanian thought relates both aesthetics and ethics to the real. From this perspective, aesthetics is connected with ethics because of the 'treatment' of the formless excess of the real in artistic production, which is akin to the psychoanalytic experience. This 'treatment' does not involve repressing, disavowing, or foreclosing the real but rather incorporates it into the Borromean knot with the imaginary and symbolic. It deals with *jouissance*—the paradoxical pleasure in pain that goes beyond the pleasure principle. It is also connected to the discontent of contemporary society, which appears to be permeated by this excess. This is a crucial point in Resmini's discussion of the politics of Italian Lacanian aesthetics. Resmini's reference to art as an act of resistance engages with this 'untamed real' and the 'unmediated *jouissance*' (2013, p. 289). Yet again, art serves as an imaginary and symbolic means of dealing with the real. As Resmini argues, for Italian Lacanians an artwork allows us to rethink the possibility of a 'convergence between the symbolic nature of form and the real of *jouissance*' (2013, p. 292). Thus, the artwork represents

> *the testimony of a strictly singular way of holding together the symbolic and the real, Law and jouissance, form and formless.* Ultimately, the significance of

> the Italian turn resides in its ability to see art as both a question and an answer: a question to psychoanalysis as a discipline, a destabilization of its tenets and foundations, but also as a possible, precarious answer to psychoanalysis's most political question: How can we fasten the power of the drive to the field of the Other? (2013, p. 292, original emphasis)

The ethical commitment of Italian Lacanian aesthetics rests on this mediation between the symbolic and the real, which forms the political core of Italian psychoanalytic aesthetics. The aesthetics of the real offers a means to confront the resistance to meaning inherent in the real, without avoiding it, as religion does, or rationalising it, as science does. In this framework, sublimation transcends the realm of art and becomes an ethical modality for inhabiting the beyond the pleasure principle. As Resmini argues, this ethical and political aspect of aesthetics, developed by Italian Lacanians, revolves around art as an 'experience of limits', a 'collision against boundaries', and a 'struggle with something that resists' (2013, p. 289). Italian Lacanian psychoanalytic aesthetics is rooted in an ethical commitment to addressing the challenges of contemporary society, especially the erosion of the symbolic and the rise of the capitalist discourse, which directly impact postmillennial subjects and their symptoms. For this reason, Italian Lacanian aesthetics remains firmly anchored in the clinical field. In this sense, it might be defined as an ethical aesthetics.

Reality

The film *Reality* partakes in the Italian postmillennial trend known as the 'return to reality' (Di Martino and Verdicchio 2017). Matteo Garrone, the Italian director of the film, is a postmillennial Italian filmmaker influenced by Italian neorealism, which is evident in his depiction of the working class and his use of non-professional actors. The protagonist of *Reality*, Luciano, is in fact played by Aniello Arena, who, despite serving a life sentence in prison, had gained considerable theatrical experience before his involvement in the film. Garrone wrote *Reality* following his international success with *Gomorrah* (2008), a film widely regarded as the epitome of realism in his work, portraying the brutal reality of the Italian mafia. The film *Reality* was immediately followed by *Tale of Tales* (2015), which, in contrast, is a fantasy film based on Giambattista Basile's fairy tales. In *Tale of Tales*, where a world inhabited by fantastical creatures is rendered with striking realism, Garrone explores the interplay between reality and the fantastical, expanding his cinematic exploration into *realismo magico*. Garrone's persistent interest in capturing reality—be it the harsh reality of the *camorra* in *Gomorrah* or the alienated reality of television programmes in *Reality*—establishes his cinema as a profound inquiry into the nature of reality itself.

To which reality does the film's title refer? Initially, the film seems to focus on the dichotomy between everyday reality and the media's portrayal of it, drawing a sharp contrast between the authentic and the fictitious. As Garrone explains, '*Reality* is a film about the perception of reality, the story of a man who departs from reality and enters into the realm of his own imagination' (2012, p. 4). The film tells the story of Luciano, a Neapolitan fishmonger who auditions for *Grande Fratello*, the Italian version of *Big Brother*. Luciano's desire to be selected as a contestant for the TV show soon spirals into a psychotic obsession. The film is set in postmillennial Italy, where television dominates and erodes traditional community bonds, religious practices, and family rituals. Luciano's obsession with gaining visibility on television mirrors Riccardo Carnevali's fixation in *Videocracy*, where media exposure becomes a gateway to popularity and wealth (see Chap. 3). This reflects the broader contemporary obsession with the pervasive portrayal of real lives and experiences through magazines, talk shows, reality series, or social media. Through the medium of reality TV, the film ultimately explores key questions concerning the perception of reality, in terms of both its subjective and social dimensions.

As Lolli's *L'epoca dell'inconschow* (2012) highlights, the media foster a belief in two contrasting realities: the mundane reality of daily life and the glamorous, idealised world depicted on screen. As Lolli argues,

> [...] what television produces, therefore, is not just spectacle but the world of spectacle. In this respect, it differs from cinema. The medium of television, in other words, promulgates the existence of a world that does not actually exist in reality, an artificial world created to enable the citizen, reassured by what they see, to continue their consumerist slumber. (2012, p. 89)

Nevertheless, a Lacanian analysis of *Reality* must move beyond the rigid opposition between the tangible world and the fabricated realm of the media. This dualism, rooted in twentieth-century modernism, is insufficient for grasping the complexities of contemporary society. Viewed through a Lacanian lens, the film becomes an exploration of the fictional nature of reality itself and the emergence of the real within it. Moreover, the film epitomises key themes within Italian Lacanianism: the proliferation of the imaginary, embodied by the pervasive media spectacle; the erosion of the symbolic, marked by the dissolution of social bond, the fragmentation of communities and the disappearance of religious reference points; and the return of the real, which disrupts the subject. In this context, Luciano epitomises the postmillennial subject, living in the age of *unconshow,* who is left without an unconscious and, after giving way to his desire, is compelled to turn to commodities promoted by the capitalist discourse, indulging in a solitary and sterile *jouissance*.

The opening scene of *Reality* epitomises Garrone's blend of realistic and fantastical elements, presenting an airy framing of a countryside landscape that seems at once real and magical. A dreamlike soundtrack contrasts with the modern architecture of the setting, while a fairytale-like carriage drawn by horses and charioteers travels along the road alongside cars and other vehicles. From the beginning of the film, viewers are thus led to doubt what they see and to question the reality depicted on screen. Gradually, it becomes evident that the carriage is transporting a newlywed couple to their opulent wedding reception at a Neapolitan restaurant. The wedding celebration seems to exist in a space where reality and fantasy converge. Lavish and extravagant, the wedding reception features a red carpet for the couple, a boisterous crowd of guests, and traditional Neapolitan songs. This scene establishes a sharp contrast between the authentic Neapolitan atmosphere and the artificiality of television. Throughout the film, Garrone skilfully alternates between realistic and picturesque settings—such as the Neapolitan square where Luciano's fish shop is located, the shopping centre, and the water park—and scenes from *Grande Fratello* as broadcasted on television. This stylistic approach accentuates the tension between (Neapolitan) reality and the artificiality of TV shows, creating a disorienting effect that prompts the audience to reflect on the boundaries between reality and unreality.

At first, Luciano seems to live a fulfilling life, content with his job and surrounded by close friends and family members. His daily routine proceeds without disruption. Beneath the surface, however, his sense of identity seems uncertain and somewhat fragile. Luciano's psychic journey commences just before his initial encounter with Enzo, a former *Grande Fratello* contestant, at the wedding reception. At the gathering, Luciano wishes to perform to entertain the other wedding guests. While Luciano is getting into character in front of a mirror, one of his friends abruptly urges him to stop repeating the same old act and try something different, shouting in Neapolitan dialect 'Do something else. It's not good anymore. Enough, change character!'. Luciano is clearly shocked; he has played that character many times before and does not understand why he must suddenly change it. As he stares at the mirror, he appears utterly lost. In this scene, Luciano confronts the split image of himself in the mirror, and his distress is evident. The reflection in the mirror becomes uncanny, as Luciano can no longer recognise himself. This uncanny mirror image subverts Luciano's gaze, seeming to stare back at him. The scene exemplifies the concept of the 'broken mirror' discussed by Bellavita (2005), a mirror that instead of providing a cohesive sense of identity, reveals the subject's own inconsistency. While Lacan's early theory of the mirror stage suggested that the imaginary could conceal the real by offering a narcissistically coherent self-image, his later work recognised that the imaginary could never entirely fulfil this function, leaving cracks through which the real emerges.

Finally, Luciano is compelled to abandon his habitual character and take on a new role. At this pivotal moment Enzo, a *Big Brother* television star, makes his entrance among the other guests in the dance hall. Delivering a brief speech, Enzo simply reiterates his personal motto: 'Never abandon your dreams! Never give up!' After this short appearance, he leaves the reception in a private helicopter. Luciano, eager to please his daughter who wants a picture with Enzo, follows him. After securing the photograph, Luciano watches in great fascination as the man leaves. Enzo represents Luciano's idealised self-image, the version of himself that was not reflected back in the mirror. This encounter thus leaves a profound, lasting impact on Luciano. Although he continues with his daily life, something within him has been irreparably fractured. This rupture in his sense of self fuels his escalating obsession with appearing on *Big Brother*, like Enzo, ultimately triggering a latent psychosis.

At his first audition for the television show, held in a shopping centre, Luciano encounters Enzo once again. Following the audition, Luciano's desire to be chosen as a contestant for the reality television programme intensifies. He becomes increasingly fixated on being seen by the big (br) Other, seeking validation of his existence through its omnipotent gaze. Garrone's characters often embody societal maladies, and Luciano is no exception. Contemporary Italian Lacanianism addresses the crisis in social bonds, along with the isolation and alienation of the postmillennial subject, who is increasingly devoid of symbolic points of reference. In this context, the world of television, particularly reality shows like *Grande Fratello*, seems to offer the postmillennial subject a way to achieve recognition and secure an identity, as exemplified by Enzo. Through the lenses of the *Big Brother* cameras, television provides an opportunity to attain an identity and to be seen and acknowledged, ultimately compensating for the waning of the symbolic. As Lolli aptly explains

> The one who enjoys, actually, is the Other, in our case, the audience, but perhaps even more so, the 'Big Brother', the one who stands behind the audience, the machinery of the spectacle, and its entrepreneurs who take the true advantage from the entire process. (2012, p. 104)

Although Luciano's condition is pathological and not simply the product of contemporary society, his story reflects the epochal shift identified by Italian Lacanians, particularly Recalcati's concept of the subject without unconscious (see Chap. 2) and Lolli's notion of the *unconshow* (see Chap. 3). Like Luciano, the contemporary subject seems to be shifting from a neurotic structure—where symptoms metaphorically express the unconscious—towards a psychotic one, where symptoms appear to be completely dissociated from the symbolic dynamics of the unconscious.

After Luciano returns to Naples from Rome, following his second round of auditions, his delusion gradually escalates, and a series of unfortunate events trigger a full-blown psychosis. At first, Luciano is confident that he will eventually receive a phone call confirming his participation in

Grande Fratello. To ensure he is completely available for the show, Luciano sells his fish shop and invests the money in modernising his house. As time passes without any contact, Luciano develops the delusion that the casting directors are still deliberating. Eventually, he becomes convinced that a covert team from *Big Brother* is secretly observing him, tracking his every move. To impress the ever-watchful *Big Brother*, Luciano begins performing charitable acts, such as buying food for homeless people and giving away all his furniture to help the less fortunate. Despite his wife's desperate attempts to stop him, shouting at and violently arguing with him, Luciano's belief remains unshaken. Even after the new season *of Grande Fratello* begins without him, Luciano clings on to hope, spending his days mesmerised in front of the television screen. Eventually, he transforms his storage room into a replica of *Big Brother's* diary room. Luciano's increasing isolation causes growing concern among his family and friends.

A strictly Lacanian analysis of the film *Reality* goes beyond the mere juxtaposition of reality and unreality. Interpreting the film solely through the lens of this binary would be reductive. The issue is thus not merely that reality is virtualised or even derealised by the media; rather, it is the encounter with the formless, meaningless real that threatens reality itself. Garrone's film illustrates that external reality is not an objective given but is intricately connected to the subject and their real. Vighi argues that:

> [...] external reality is not simply given in advance, irrespective of the psychic apparatus, but rather *it is posited by the subject through the displacement of its own (the subject's) inherent deadlock*. What we regard as the objective world "out there" is inevitably a by-product, a secondary ontology, as it constitutes itself through a kind of evacuation of that immanent and original antagonism situated at the heart of the human psyche – which Freud, in *Beyond the Pleasure Principle*, branded the death-drive. (2006, p. 20 original emphasis)

Towards the end of the film, Luciano has completely withdrawn from life, fixated only on watching episodes of *Big Brother*. Neither his family, nor his friends, nor the Neapolitan or church communities, can help him in any way. This epitomises the dissolution of social bonds characteristic of hypermodern society and promoted by the discourse of the capitalist, a discourse inherently hostile to communal ties. As these bonds crumble, individuals become trapped in their own peculiar modes of enjoyment, fixated on objects rather than human relationships. In Luciano's case, his object of *jouissance* is television. The act of staring at the screen becomes his only source of fulfilment, pinning him to a solipsistic form of *jouissance* detached from the world around him.

As the film draws to a close, Luciano returns to Rome to attend a religious procession. However, in a sudden, impulsive decision, he slips away from his friends and heads towards the television studios, determined to enter the *Big Brother* house. This moment marks the culmination of Luciano's psychic odyssey and the film's conclusion. Hesitating briefly in front of the red door—the same door Enzo and countless other contestants have passed through to join the reality show watched by millions—Luciano faces a pivotal moment. This scene bears a strong resemblance to the ending of *The Truman Show* (Weir 1998). In *The Truman Show,* the protagonist, Truman Burbank (Jim Carrey), is a creature of habit in his thirties, whose daily life consists of working at a local insurance company and spending his spare time with his wife and best friend. Although Truman has an interest in travelling, he has never left Seahaven Island, his idyllic 1950s-style Californian hometown, due to panic attacks triggered by its proximity to the sea. After a series of strange events, he begins to suspect that his life is a fabricated reality and eventually discovers he is the unwitting star of the world's most popular reality television show. Seahaven Island is, in fact, an enormous television set filled with thousands of hidden cameras tracking his every move, and all the people in his life are actors and extras. Upon learning that his existence is a carefully crafted fiction, Truman longs to escape and experience the 'real' world outside. The film ends with Truman reaching the edge of the enormous television set where he has spent his entire life. He climbs the stairs, opens a door, and steps through, disappearing from view. This ending reflects a distinct twentieth-century dichotomy: reality versus fiction. From a Lacanian perspective, however, this end does not make much sense as reality is itself inherently fictional. There is no distinct 'real' reality waiting to be revealed or uncovered. As Christof, the show's director, tells Truman just before he exits the studio: 'There is no more truth out there than in the world I created for you. The same lies. The same deceit'.

In contrast, Garrone's *Reality* presents Luciano yearning to enter the fictional world of *Big Brother*. As he stands in front of the red door of the reality television studio, brimming with excitement, he opens it and steps inside. This ending is, at the very least, paradoxical: the protagonist, desperate to escape his everyday reality through the media, ultimately orchestrates his own 'imprisonment' within the confines of the *Big Brother* house. Unlike Truman, who seeks to escape the fabricated world of the television studio, Luciano longs to be 'inside' the reality TV studio, leaving his reality 'outside'.

He beams with joy as he observes the hidden cameras filming the participants behind the glass wall. In the final scene, Luciano is shown lying on a sunbed in the courtyard of the *Big Brother* house, exactly where he wanted to be, even at the cost of becoming invisible—or perhaps even dead. Now that he is inside, no one acknowledges his presence: *Big Brother* is not watching. Unlike Truman, who comes to view his reality as fictitious and strives to break free, Luciano does not question the authenticity of his reality and has no desire to escape. Truman belongs to the era of postmodernity, while Luciano embodies the spirit of hypermodernity. Reality is inherently fictional, a construction, much like our identities. As Recalcati convincingly puts it,

> [...] what one finds is not a lost identity but the very impossibility of identity itself. Not an identity but an extimacy. An otherness that is excavated, without being absorbed by identity, deep down within the subject. An outside that manifests itself from within. An intimacy, a proximity that reveals itself as an indomitable, foreign exteriority, unassimilable into the identity of the ego. So, what is the extimacy of the subject if not the death drive? (1996, p. 69)

These closing scenes, one at the extreme border that separates the fictitious space of the *Truman Show*'s colossal television set from the outside world and the other within the Italian studio of *Big Brother*, encapsulate the contrast between a conventional view of reality and subjectivity, rooted in Euclidean geometry, and one grounded in Lacanian topology. The former adheres to a realist framework that distinguishes between the interior and exterior, while the latter embraces the *extimacy* of the real.

There is no hidden reality behind the veneer of reality television. Luciano's deepest desire is not to unmask his true self but to fully embrace the mask itself. In contrast to Pirandellian characters, who recoil from the fictitious aspects of their personas and strive to erase them, Luciano embraces absolute appearance. Unlike Truman, Luciano does not believe in the existence of an authentic reality beyond the realm of appearances, and unlike Neo, the protagonist of *The Matrix* (Wachowski and Wachowski 1999), he does not want to be awakened and would prefer to swallow the blue pill and return to his slumber.

Bibliography

Adorno, Theodor W. 2002. *Aesthetic Theory*. Translated by Robert Hullot-Kentor. London: Continuum.

Bellavita, Andrea. 2005. *Schermi perturbanti*. Milan: Vita e Pensiero.

Bellavita, Andrea. 2006. L'emersione del Reale: perché una psicoanalisi del cinema contemporaneo? In *Cinema e psicoanalisi*, ed. Lucilla Albano and Veronica Pravadelli, 203–224. Quodlibet: Macerata.

Benvenuto, Sergio. 2014. Lacan: l'uomo del secolo. In *Attualità di Lacan*, ed. Alex Pagliardini and Rocco Ronchi, 247–271. Textus Edizioni: L'Aquila.

Berressem, Hanjo. 1996. Dalì and Lacan: Painting the Imaginary Landscapes. In *Lacan, Politics, Aesthetics*, ed. Willy Apollon and Richard Feldstein, 263–293. Albany, NY: State University of New York.

Bianchi, Pietro. 2017. *Jacques Lacan and Cinema: Imaginary, Gaze, Formalisation*. London: Routledge.

Bois, Yve-Alain, and Rosalind Krauss. 1997. *Formless: A User's Guide*. New York: Zone Books.

Bonazzi, Matteo, and Daniele Tonazzo. 2015. *Lacan e l'estetica. Lemmi*. Milan: Mimesis.

Bottiroli, Giovanni. 2002. *Jacques Lacan. Arte, linguaggio, desiderio*. Bergamo: Bergamo University Press.

Bottiroli, Giovanni. 2006. *Che cos'è la teoria della letteratura?* Turin: Einaudi.

Bottiroli, Giovanni. 2023. *Jacques Lacan. Oltre la scolastica*. Verona: Ombre Corte.

Bowlby, Rachel. 2007. Foreword. In *Adventures in Realism*, ed. Matthew Beaumont, xi–xviii. Oxford: Blackwell Publishing.

Caroli, Flavio. 1979. *Burri: la forma e l'informe*. Milan: Mazzotta.

Chiesa, Lorenzo. 2012. Of Bastard Man and Evil Woman, or, the Horror of Sex. *Film-Philosophy* 16 (1): 199–212.

Civitarese, Giuseppe. 2013. *The Violence of Emotions. Bion and Post-Bionian Psychoanalysis*. Translated by Ian Harvey. London: Routledge.

Contri, Giacomo, ed. 1978. *Lacan in Italia/En Italie Lacan: 1953–1978*. Milan: La Salamandra.

Di Ciaccia, Antonio, and Massimo Recalcati. 2000. *Jacques Lacan. Un insegnamento sul sapere dell'inconscio*. Milan: Bruno Mondadori.

Di Martino, Loredana, and Pasquale Verdicchio, eds. 2017. *Encounters with the Real in Contemporary Italian Literature and Cinema*. Newcastle upon Tyne: Cambridge Scholars Publishing.

Donnarumma, Raffaele, Gilda Policastro, and Giovanna Taviani, ed. 2008. Ritorno alla realtà? Narrativa e cinema alla fine del postmoderno. *Allegoria* 57.

Esposito, Roberto. 2015. *Persons and Things. From the Body's Point of View*. Translated by Zakiya Hanafi. Cambridge: Polity Press.

Fornari, Franco. 1978. *Coinema e icona, Nuova proposta per una psicoanalisi dell'arte*. Milan: Il saggiatore.

Foster, Hal. 1996. *The Return of the Real: the Avant-garde at the End of the Century*. Cambridge, MA: MIT Press.

Foster, Hal. 2017. *Bad New Days: Art, Criticism, Emergency*. London: Verso.

Freud, Sigmund. 1914. The Moses of Michelangelo. In *The Standard Edition of the Complete Psychological Works of Sigmund Freud, Volume XIII (1913–1914): Totem and Taboo and Other Works*, 209–238.

Freud, Sigmund. 1933. New Introductory Lectures on Psycho-Analysis. In *The Standard Edition of the Complete Psychological Works of Sigmund Freud*, vol. 22, 3–250. London: Hogarth Press & The Institute of Psycho-Analysis.

Gamwell, Lynn, and Richard Wells, eds. 1989. *Sigmund Freud and Art. His Personal Collection of Antiquities*. New York: Harry N. Abrams.

Glover, Nicky. 2009. *Psychoanalytic Aesthetics: An Introduction to the British School*. London: Karnac.

Hennessey, Brendan, Laurence Hooper, and Charles Leavitt. 2017. Realisms and Idealisms in Italian Culture, 1300–2017. *The Italianist* 37 (3): 281–288.

Hernández-Navarro, Miguel. 2006. *La so(m)bra de lo real: El arte como vomitorio*. Valencia: Institución Alfonso el Magnánimo.

Krauss, Rosalind. 1988. In *The Im/pulse to see*, ed. Hal Foster, 51–78. Seattle: Vision and Visuality, Bay Press.

Krauss, Rosalind. 1994. *The Optical Unconscious*. Cambridge, MA: MIT Press.

Lacan, Jacques. 1988. *Freud's Papers on Technique. The Seminar of Jacques Lacan, Book I, 1953–1954*. Translated by John Forrester and Edited by Jacques-Alain Miller. London: W.W. Norton.

Lacan, Jacques. 1990. *Television/A Challenge to the Psychoanalytic Establishment (1973)*. Translated by D. Hollier, R. Krauss and A. Michelson and Edited by Joan Copjec. London: W.W. Norton & Co.

Lacan, Jacques. 1991. *The Ego in Freud's Theory and in the Technique of Psychoanalysis. The Seminar of Jacques Lacan, Book II, 1954–1955*. Translated by Sylvana Tommaselli and ed. Jacques-Alain Miller. London: W.W. Norton.

Lacan, Jacques. 1992. *The Ethics of Psychoanalysis. The Seminar of Jacques Lacan, Book VII, 1959–1960*. Translated by Dennis Porter and Edited by Jacques-Alain Miller. London: Routledge.

Lacan, Jacques. 1997. *The Psychoses. The Seminar of Jacques Lacan, Book III, 1955–1956*. Translated by Russell Grigg and Edited by Jacques-Alain Miller. London: W.W. Norton.

Lacan, Jacques. 1998. *The Four Fundamental Concepts of Psychoanalysis. The Seminar of Jacques Lacan, Book XI, 1963–1964*. Translated by Alan Sheridan and Edited by Jacques-Alain Miller. London/New York: W.W. Norton.

Lacan, Jacques. 2006. *Écrits. The First Complete Edition in English*. Translated by Bruce Fink in Collaboration with Héloïse Fink and Russell Grigg. London and New York: W.W. Norton.

Lacan, Jacques. 2013a. Lituraterre. Translated by Dany Nobus. *Continental Philosophy Review*, 327–334.

Lacan, Jacques. 2013b. *The Triumph of Religion*. Translated by Bruce Fink. Cambridge: Polity Press.

Lacan, Jacques. 2016. *The Sinthome. The Seminar of Jacques Lacan, Book XXIII*. Translated by Adrian Price. Cambridge: Polity Press.

Leader, Darian. 2002. *Stealing the Mona Lisa. What Art Stops Us from Seeing*. New York: Counterpoint.

Lolli, Franco. 2004. Introduzione. In *L'infinito nella voce. Su poesia e psicoanalisi*, ed. Franco Lolli and Lucilio Santoni, 13–16. Milan: Franco Angeli.

Lolli, Franco. 2012. *L'epoca dell'inconshow. Dimensione clinica e scenario sociale del fenomeno borderline*. Milan: Mimesis.

Marlow-Mann, Alex. 2010. Beyond (Post-) Realism: A Response to Millicent Marcus. *The Italianist* 30 (2): 263–268.

Mazzarella, Arturo. 2011. *Politiche dell'irrealtà. Scritture e visioni tra Gomorra e Abu Ghraib*. Turin: Bollati Boringhieri.

McGowan, Todd. 2007. *The Real Gaze: Film Theory After Lacan*. Albany, NY: State University of New York Press.

McGowan, Todd. 2015. *Psychoanalytic Film Theory and the Rules of the Game*. London: Bloomsbury.
McGowan, Todd, and Sheila Kunkle, eds. 2004. *Lacan and Contemporary Film*. New York: Other Press.
Metz, Christian. 1982. *Psychoanalysis and Cinema. The Imaginary Signifier*. London: MacMillan.
Miller, Jacques-Alain. 2022 [1984]. Lacan Clinician. Translated by Anthony Stavrianakis. *The Lacanian Review* 12: 100–137.
Millot, Catherine. 2018. *Life with Lacan*. Translated by Andrew Brown. Cambridge: Polity Press.
O'Leary, Alan, and Cathrine O'Rawe. 2011. Against realism: on a "certain tendency" in Italian film criticism. *Journal of Modern Italian Studies* 15 (1): 107–128.
O'Rawe, Cathrine. 2008. "I padri e i maestri": Genre, Auteurs, and Absences in Italian Film Studies. *Italian Studies* 63 (2): 173–194.
Ogden, Benjamin H., and Thomas H. Ogden. 2013. *The Analyst's Ear and the Critic's Eye. Rethinking Psychoanalysis and Literature*. London: Routledge.
Pagliardini, Alex. 2020. *Lacan al presente. Per una clinica del reale*. Rende: Gaaland Edizioni.
Perniola, Mario. 2004. *Art and Its Shadow*. Translated by Massimo Verdicchio. London: Continuum.
Recalcati, Massimo. 1996. *L'universale e il singolare. Lacan e l'al di là del principio di piacere*. Milan: Marcos y Marcos.
Recalcati. 2007. *Il miracolo della forma. Per una estetica psicoanalitica*. Bruno Milan: Mondadori.
Recalcati. 2009. *Melanconia e creazione in Vincent Van Gogh*. Turin: Bollati Boringhieri.
Recalcati. 2012. *Jacques Lacan. Desiderio, godimento, soggettivazione*. Milan: Raffaello Cortina.
Recalcati. 2020. *Convertire la pulsione. Sul processo di soggettivazione nell'esperienza dell'analisi*. Trento: Paginaotto.
Regnault, François. 1997. *Conférences d'esthétique lacanienne*. Paris: Agalma.
Resmini, Mauro. 2013. The Italian Turn: A Certain Tendency in Contemporary Psychoanalytic Aesthetics. *American Imago* 68 (2): 271–297.
Rocchio, Vincent. 1999. *Cinema of Anxiety. A Psychoanalysis of Italian Neorealism*. Austin: University of Texas Press.
Roudinesco, Élisabeth. 1997. *Jacques Lacan: Outline of a Life, History of a System of Thought*. Translated by Barbara Bray. Cambridge, UK: Polity Press.

Serkowska, Hanna, ed. 2011. *Finzione, Cronaca, Realtà. Scambi, intrecci e prospettive nella narrative italiana contemporanea*. Milan: Transeuropa.
Stavrakakis, Yannis. 2007. *The Lacanian Left: Psychoanalysis, Theory, Politics*. Edinburgh: Edinburgh University Press.
Vighi, Fabio. 2006. *Traumatic Encounters in Italian Film. Locating the Cinematic Unconscious*. Bristol: intellect.
Vighi, Fabio. 2012. *Critical Theory and Film. Rethinking Ideology through Film Noir*. London: Continuum.
Vighi, Fabio. 2014. The Unwanted Guest. Some Remarks on Italian Cinema's Love Affair with Psychoanalysis. In *The Italian Cinema Book*, ed. Peter Bondanella, 311–317. London: British Film Institute.
Villa, Emilio. 1996. *Scrittura dell'ultimo giorno: scritti per Alberto Burri*. Florence: Le Lettere.
Wajcman, Gérard. 1998. *L'object du siècle*. Lagrasse: Verdier.
Wajcman, Gérard. 2007. Desublimation: An Art of What Falls. Translated by Barbara P. Fulks. *Lacanian Ink* 29: 86–111.
Žižek, Slavoj. 2000. *The Fragile Absolute Or, Why Is the Christian Legacy Worth Fighting For?* London: Verso.
Žižek, Slavoj. 2009 [1997]. *The Plague of Phantasies*. London: Verso.
Žižek, Slavoj, and Glyn Daly. 2004. *Conversations with Žižek*. Cambridge: Polity Press.
Zupančič, Alenka. 2000. *Ethics of the Real: Kant, Lacan*. London: Verso.

Filmography

Garrone, Matteo. 2008. *Gomorra*. Rome: 01 Distribution.
Garrone, Matteo. 2012. *Reality*. Rome: 01 Distribution.
Garrone, Matteo. 2015. *Il racconto dei racconti*. Rome: 01 Distribution.
Sollima, Stefano, Francesca Comencini, and Claudio Cupellini. 2014–2021. *Gomorra - La serie*. Rome: Fandango.
Wachowski, Larry, and Andy Wachowski. 1999 *The Matrix*. US: Warner Bros. Pictures.
Weir, Peter. 1998. *The Truman Show*. US: Paramount Pictures.

6

Conclusion: Towards an Affirmative Real

In this book, I have outlined the reception and legacy of Lacan in Italy by introducing, contextualising, and discussing Italian Lacanianism to an English-speaking audience, providing the first comprehensive account of the relevance and contributions of Italian Lacanians. My aim has been twofold: firstly, to firmly place Italian Lacanianism on the map, highlighting its significance and uniqueness; and secondly, to build a bridge to allow for dialogue and connection with Lacanian traditions and receptions across different countries and languages.

In Chap. 2, I traced the history of Italian Lacanianism, from its marginal status in the late 1950s to its hegemonic position in postmillennial Italy. Through this historical and critical account, I highlighted that issues surrounding the ethics of psychoanalysis were particularly prominent in Italy, especially due to the case of Armando Verdiglione, whose criminal actions exposed the risks of authoritarian, normative, and dogmatic tendencies within psychoanalysis. I also argued that Italian Lacanianism is characterised by the primacy of the real—a fundamental category for the survival of psychoanalysis (Lacan 1970, p. 20).

In Chap. 3, I argued that Italian Lacanianism employs the notion of the real to make sense of the so-called new symptoms. In these

L. Di Gregorio, *Lacan in Italy*, The Palgrave Lacan Series,
https://doi.org/10.1007/978-3-031-91528-4_6

contemporary psychopathologies, the real of *jouissance* comes to the forefront, while the dimension of desire, originating from lack, fades away. This allows Italian Lacanianism to explore the interplay between psychopathology and social discourse, placing a strong emphasis on social commitment. Clinical work involves addressing a subject's real, namely, their unique mode of *jouissance*, repetition, and death drive. The real is understood here as 'something that at once exceeds and produces' the subject (Benvenuto 2020, p. 108). The psychoanalytic experience thus becomes an opportunity to re-engage with the random traces from the Other that have constituted the subject, and with the inheritance of this real, of which the subject is the result, *après-coup*. A new articulation of desire with *jouissance* underpins Italian Lacanians' take on subjectivation and sublimation.

In Chap. 4, I claimed that Italian Lacanians' sociopolitical analyses of neoliberalism, nationalism, and populism are underpinned by a focus on unbridled *jouissance*, the absence of desire, the evaporation of the Father, the erosion of the symbolic, and the discourse of the capitalist. Italian Lacanianism promotes a politics of psychoanalysis, rooted in the clinic, which integrates the force of the drive—the thrust of *jouissance*—with the opening up of desire to the field of the Other. This involves the establishment of communal and institutional bonds that reject the totalitarian utopia of the One, instead embracing the not-all, absolute difference, and separation. The real, in fact, is not singular or the One, but relational: 'the real is actually two' (Lacan 2020, p. 31). However, several political themes remain largely unexplored by Italian Lacanians, such as issues surrounding trans people, reproductive technologies, racism, and ecology. This contrasts with the extensive literature on these topics in Anglophone Lacanianism. Cultural factors, including Italy's limited colonial history, patriarchal and heteronormative society, and the influence of the Church, may explain such an omission. This reflects a blind spot within Italian Lacanianism and suggests some regressive positions among certain Lacanians.[1]

[1] For instance, Sergio Benvenuto's claim that 'After all, homosexual inclination is partially narcissistic, because in this case one desires a sexual "double" of oneself' (2020, p. 131) is highly problematic, to say the least, and may reflect broader systemic issues worth addressing.

In Chap. 5, I contended that Italian Lacanianism views psychoanalysis and art as two imaginary and symbolic practices directed at encountering and engaging with the real. The aesthetic domain serves as a way to articulate this interaction between the real and the other two registers. The real of art resists interpretation and symbolisation, standing as an index for a core, irreducible kernel—the radical alterity of the real. Sublimation, far from being a process of purification or idealisation of the obscene or abject real, transcends the aesthetic domain and becomes an ethical modality, a possibility to transform the real. Italian Lacanian aesthetics is thus closely linked to ethics: it deals with the formless excess of the real. However, this is not a question of repressing, disavowing, or foreclosing the real but rather of weaving it into the Borromean knot, alongside the other two registers.

In this book, I have argued that, while acknowledging the fundamental destabilising and unsettling aspects associated with *jouissance*, the death drive, and repetition, Italian Lacanianism does not conceptualise the real in exclusively negative terms—as that which is impossible, unrepresentable, unsymbolisable, traumatic, dissipative, disruptive, and deadly. Rather, it also underscores the 'affirmative modalities' that emphasise its generative, life-affirming possibilities (Lippi 2020; Pagliardini 2020; Recalcati 2023; Terminio 2020). This affirmative conceptualisation of the real emerges, I have contended, within a broader transnational context. On the one hand, it follows on from central notions put forward by key representatives of French Lacanianism, such as Jacques-Alain Miller's and Colette Soler's the 'real unconscious', whose focus on the late Lacan has amplified the prominence of the real in various national receptions of Lacan outside France. On the other hand, it can also be situated alongside those developments of Lacan's negative ontology, both in political thought—radical politics, social antagonism, and the construction of everyday social reality—and in the psychosocial domain, particularly in Anglophone Lacanianism and in the Slovenian Lacanian orientation (Hook 2022; Rousselle 2024; Stavrakakis 2007).

Italian Lacanianism nonetheless questions and problematises these perspectives. While Miller emphasises *jouissance* over desire—'there is nothing but jouissance, to the detriment of truth and meaning' (Miller 2019 p. 133)—and prioritises the *One-all-alone* at the expense of the

Other—that 'the Other does not exist means exactly that the One exists' (Miller 2021, p. 14)—political and psychosocial Anglophone applications of Lacanian theory tend to promote a declinicised approach to Lacan. This results in an emphasis on the real as trauma, excess, and the 'undead': a post-human vitalism that seems to dispense with the notion of the subject; not the abstract philosophical subject, but the subject in analysis—the analysand—with their personal and unique history.

In contrast, I have claimed that Italian Lacanianism largely seeks to integrate, rather than oppose, the classic Lacan of the symbolic (desire) with the late Lacan of the real (*jouissance*). Aside from individual differences, Italian Lacanians rethink and reframe the primacy of the real in light of the prominence of desire, which 'must not be sacrificed, neither to the law nor to the drive' (Bottiroli 2023, p. 175). Desire, however, is not 'a pure and simple vital impulse' (Lacan 2019, p. 474) but, like the real of *jouissance*, it unsettles the subject. Italian Lacanians, therefore, move beyond the false dichotomy of Oedipal desire and narcissistic *jouissance* to reconcile the dialectical nature of the former with the anti-dialectical nature of the latter. This also involves accounting for both the transferal/semiotic unconscious—as the discourse of the Other, structured like a language, and inhabited by desire—and the real unconscious, as the effect of *lalangue* on the body, described as 'cut in action' (Lacan 2006, p. 712), 'projectiles riddling a surface' (Lacan 2020, p. 37). As Nicolò Terminio writes:

> When we consider the symbolic dimension, what the unconscious reveals to us pertains to a narrative that runs throughout our lives, constructed over the years. In this sense, the symbolic points to the unconscious as a form of knowledge of which we are unaware but that nonetheless shapes our lives, like a script we repeat across different moments and contexts. When, on the other hand, we stress the level of the real, we are referring to the unconscious as a form of knowledge that *is yet to be realised*. The real is a trauma within the symbolic narrative; it disrupts the repetitive flow of signifiers and compels each individual to symbolise something that has not yet been written, something that remains outside of meaning. *The real persists in life as the possibility for a new way of existing, beyond what has already been solidified and established*. The work of analysis involves uncovering the unconscious narrative built in the past that tends to repeat itself. At the

same time, analysis must introduce the experience of the real as a stumbling block, a trauma of meaning, such that the analytic process becomes an opportunity to reconfigure the narrative and allow the unconscious to emerge as a form of knowledge yet to emerge. Psychoanalysis has the task of bringing the unconscious into existence, *not by colonising the real with the symbolic*, but by making the symbolic permeable to the existence of the real. The real is what keeps the symbolic from becoming saturated, and for this reason, it prefigures the generative and creative possibilities of the symbolic. (2020, pp. 85–86, emphasis added)

According to this affirmative stance, the symbolic is no longer a defence against the real—the libidinal excess clogging a drive-ridden body—and psychoanalytic practice does not seek to simply treat the real. From Alex Pagliardini (2020), I have drawn the argument that psychoanalysis is not merely about knowing, unveiling, treating, or mastering the real. Instead, he contends, it is about an assent to the real: an affirmation of the specific, *extimate* real of the subject. As Silvia Lippi further notes, 'the real changes connotation: it stops being only trauma, an unhappy and missed encounter', and instead emerges as 'an alternative network of associations/dissociations' (Lippi 2020, p. 173). What is at stake is thus an encounter with the real that brings about an 'unactualised potentiality', to borrow from Roberto Esposito's affirmative biopolitical thought (2021, p. 133)—a generative potential.[2]

[2] Interestingly, this Lacanian perspective overlaps with psychoanalysts from other orientations who advocate for a psychoanalysis that does not merely 'colonise', 'domesticate', or 'contain' the patient's unconscious. Instead, they envision it as a risky, lively, open exploration—a space where patients can re-signify themselves and embrace possibilities once unthinkable for both analyst and patient. This conception of psychoanalysis shifts the focus from understanding and meaning to a practice that enables transformative, unexpected, and enduring effects in patients. For instance, the post-Bionian Thomas Ogden (2022) distinguishes between epistemological and ontological psychoanalysis: the former emphasises understanding, where both the analyst and the patient engage in apprehending the interplay of the patient's unconscious with interpersonal dynamics and the external world, while the latter focuses on the experience, wherein the patient is concerned less with self-understanding and more with the process of *becoming* their true self. Similarly, Avgi Saketopoulou (2023), drawing extensively from Jean Laplanche, views the analytic space not as a place to dissect experiences and dreams in search of meaning or hidden truths—thereby 'killing off their vitality'—but rather as a space to 'follow their intensity' (p. 55). In her approach, the notion of 'overwhelm', explored in aesthetic and sexual realms, plays a central role in challenging, shattering, or unbinding the ego—not as something to be merely tamed, but as a valuable resource for subjective transformation and new, more generative, avenues of repetition. She thus proposes a

Ultimately, this affirmative approach is by no means a positivisation or downplay of the negative; it does not stigmatise or suppress the fundamental tragic condition of human life. Nor does it represent a superficial 'positive' twist that aligns with the (naïvely) optimistic orientation of the mainstream psychotherapeutic and wellbeing culture. Rather, it reflects the fundamental ethical responsibility of the subject. Throughout this book, I have argued that what unites the clinical approach, sociopolitical analysis, and aesthetic thought in Italian Lacanianism is an ethical responsibility to confront and transform the traumatic, excessive, and untamed real, both individually and societally, into a generative possibility.

Bibliography

Benvenuto, Sergio. 2020. *Conversations with Lacan: Seven Lectures for Understanding Lacan*. London: Routledge.

Bottiroli, Giovanni. 2023. *Jacques Lacan. Oltre la scolastica*. Verona: Ombre Corte.

Esposito, Roberto. 2021. Unfinished Italy. *Italian Studies* 76 (2): 128–134.

Hook, Derek. 2022. Jouissance as Tool of Psychosocial Analysis. In *The Palgrave Handbook of Psychosocial Studies*, ed. Stephen Frosh et al. Springer Nature.

Lacan, Jacques. 1970. *Radiophonie*. https://www.lacantokyo.org/img/Radiophonie_tr_en.pdf. Accessed 1 August 2024.

Lacan, Jacques. 2006. *Écrits. The First Complete Edition in English*. Trans. Bruce Fink in collaboration with Héloïse Fink and Russell Grigg. London/New York: W.W. Norton.

Lacan, Jacques. 2019. *Desire and Its Interpretation. The Seminar of Jacques Lacan, Book VI, 1958–1959*. Translted by Bruce Fink and Edited by Jacques-Alain Miller. Cambridge: Polity Press.

Lacan, Jacques. 2020. The Lacanian Phenomenon. Trans. Dan Collins. *The Lacanian Review* 9: 16–43.

Lippi, Silvia. 2020. *The decision of desire*. Translated by Peter Skafish. Minneapolis: University of Minnesota Press.

Miller, Jacques-Alain. 2019. Milanese Intuitions. Translated by Alasdair Duncan. *Psychoanalytical Notebooks* 34: 81–134.

'traumatofilic' perspective, viewing trauma not simply as a form of deterministic, life-defining, and indelible damage but as a source of potential transformation.

Miller, Jacques-Alain. 2021. The One is the Letter. Translated by Alasdair Duncan. *Psychoanalytical Notebooks* 37–38: 13–44.

Ogden, Thomas. 2022. *Coming to Life in the Consulting Room: Toward a New Analytic Sensibility*. London: Routledge.

Pagliardini, Alex. 2020. *Lacan al presente*. Rende: Gaaland Edizioni.

Recalcati, Massimo. 2023. *Jacques Lacan. Ereditare il reale?* Milan: Feltrinelli.

Rousselle, Duane. 2024. Introduction. In *Negativity in Psychoanalysis. Theory and Clinic*, ed. Duane Rousselle and Mark Gerard Murphy, xiv–xv. London: Routledge.

Saketopoulou, Avgi. 2023. *Sexuality Beyond Consent: Risk, Race, Traumatophilia*. New York: New York University Press.

Stavrakakis, Yannis. 2007. *The Lacanian Left: Psychoanalysis, Theory, Politics*. Edinburgh: Edinburgh University Press.

Terminio, Nicolò. 2020. *L'intervallo della vita. Il Reale della clinica psicoanalitica e fenomenologica*. Rome: Alpes.

Further Reading

Selected Writings in Italian

Bellavita, Andrea. 2005. *Schermi perturbanti*. Milan: Vita e Pensiero.
Benvenuto, Sergio. 2015. *La psicoanalisi e il reale*. Naples: Orthotes.
Bottiroli, Giovanni. 2002. *Jacques Lacan. Arte, linguaggio, desiderio*. Bergamo: Bergamo University Press.
Bottiroli, Giovanni. 2023. *Jacques Lacan. Oltre la scolastica*. Verona: Ombre Corte.
Contri, Giacomo, ed. 1978. *Lacan in Italia/En Italie Lacan: 1953–1978*. Milano: La Salamandra.
Cosenza, Domenico. 2003. *Jacques Lacan e il problema della tecnica in psicoanalisi*. Rome: Astrolabio.
Cosenza, Domenico, and Paolo D'Alessandro, eds. 2010. *L'inconscio dopo Lacan. Il problema del soggetto contemporaneo tra psicoanalisi e filosofia*. Milan: LED Edizioni Universitarie di Lettere, Economia, Diritto.
Cosenza, Domenico, Massimo Recalcati, and Angelo Villa. 2006. *Civiltà e disagio. Forme contemporanee della psicopatologia*. Milan: Bruno Mondadori.
Di Ciaccia, Antonio, and Doriano Fasoli. 2013. *«Io, la verità, parlo». Lacan clinico. Saggio-conversazione*. Rome: Alpes.
Di Ciaccia, Antonio, and Massimo Recalcati. 2000. *Jacques Lacan. Un insegnamento sul sapere dell'inconscio*. Milan: Bruno Mondadori.

L. Di Gregorio, *Lacan in Italy*, The Palgrave Lacan Series,
https://doi.org/10.1007/978-3-031-91528-4

Fiumanò, Marisa. *L'inconscio e' il sociale. Desiderio e godimento nella contemporaneita'*. Milan: Bruno Mondadori.
Focchi, Marco. 2020. *La clinica psicoanalitica di Jacques Lacan*. Naples: Orthotes.
Lolli, Franco. 2012. *L'epoca dell'inconshow. Dimensione clinica e scenario sociale del fenomeno borderline*. Milan: Mimesis.
Lolli, Franco. 2019. *Inattualità della psicoanalisi. L'analista e i nuovi domandanti*. Alberobello: Poiesis.
Lolli, Franco. 2022. *Vivere la pulsione. Saggio sulla soddisfazione in psicoanalisi*. Naples: Orthotes.
Moroncini, Bruno. 2014. *Lacan politico*. Naples: Cronopio.
Moroncini, Bruno, and Rosanna Petrillo. 2007. *L'etica del desiderio. Un commentario del seminario sull'etica di Jacques Lacan*. Naples: Cronopio.
Pagliardini, Alex. 2011. *Jacques Lacan e il trauma del linguaggio*. Rende: Galaad edizioni.
Pagliardini, Alex, ed. 2012. *Il reale del capitalismo*. Milan: Edizioni et/al.
Pagliardini, Alex. 2016. *Il sintomo di Lacan. Dieci incontri con il reale*. Rende: Gaaland Edizioni.
Pagliardini, Alex. 2020. *Lacan al presente. Per una clinica del reale*. Rende: Gaaland Edizioni.
Pagliardini, Alex, and Rocco Ronchi, eds. 2014. *Attualità di Lacan*. Villanova di Cepagatti: Textus.
Ramaioli, Isabella, Domenico Cosenza, and Pietro Enrico Bossola, eds. 2003. *Jacques Lacan e la clinica contemporanea*. Milan: Franco Angeli.
Recalcati, Massimo. 1996. *L'universale e il singolare. Lacan e l'al di là del principio di piacere*. Milan: Marcos y Marcos.
Recalcati, Massimo. 1997. *L'ultima cena*. Milan: Bruno Mondadori.
Recalcati, Massimo. 2001. *Il vuoto e il resto. Il problema del reale in Lacan*. Milan: CUEM.
Recalcati, Massimo. 2002. *Clinica del vuoto: anoressie, dipendenze, psicosi*. Milan: Franco Angeli.
Recalcati, Massimo. 2007. *Il miracolo della forma. Per una estetica psicoanalitica*. Milan: Bruno Mondadori.
Recalcati, Massimo, ed. 2007. *Forme contemporanee del totalitarismo*. Turin: Bollati Boringhieri.
Recalcati, Massimo. 2010. *L'uomo senza inconscio. Figure della nuova clinica psicoanalitica*. Milan: Raffaello Cortina.
Recalcati, Massimo. 2011. *Che cosa resta del padre? La paternità nell'epoca ipermoderna*. Milan: Raffaello Cortina.

Recalcati, Massimo, ed. 2011. *Il soggetto vuoto. Clinica psicoanalitica delle nuove forme del sintomo*. Trento: Edizioni Centro Studi Erickson.

Recalcati, Massimo. 2012. *Jacques Lacan. Desiderio, godimento, soggettivazione*. Milan: Raffaello Cortina.

Recalcati, Massimo. 2016. *Jacques Lacan. La clinica psicoanalitica: struttura e soggetto*. Milan: Raffaello Cortina.

Recalcati, Massimo. 2020. *Convertire la pulsione. Sul processo di soggettivazione nell'esperienza dell'analisi*. Trento: Paginaotto.

Recalcati, Massimo. 2023. *Jacques Lacan. Ereditare il reale?* Milan: Feltrinelli.

Recalcati, Massimo, and Uberto Zuccardi Merli. 2006. *Anoressia, bulimia e obesità*. Turin: Bollati Boringhieri.

Recalcati, Massimo, Domenico Cosenza, and Angelo Villa. 2006. *Civiltà e disagio. Forme contemporanee della psicopatologia*. Milan: Bruno Mondadori.

Tarizzo, Davide. 2003. *Introduzione a Lacan*. Bari: Laterza.

Terminio, Nicolò. 2009. *Misurare l'inconscio? Coordinate psicoanalitiche nella ricerca in psicoterapia*. Milan: Bruno Mondadori.

Vighi, Fabio. 2018. *Crisi di valore. Lacan, Marx e il crepuscolo della società del lavoro*. Milan: Mimesis.

Selected Writings in English

Benvenuto, Sergio. 2016. *What Are Perversions? Sexuality, Ethics, Psychoanalysis*. London: Karnac.

Benvenuto, Sergio. 2020. *Conversations with Lacan. Seven Lectures for Understanding Lacan*. London: Routledge.

Benvenuto, Sergio. 2024. *Lacan, Kris and the Psychoanalytic Legacy: The Brain Eater*. London: Routledge.

Benvenuto, Sergio. 2024. On Sigmund Freud's "Negation". In *Negativity in Psychoanalysis: Theory and Clinic*, ed. Duane Rousselle and Mark Gerard Murphy, 61–87. London: Routledge.

Benvenuto, Sergio. 2024. My Transference with Lacan as a Thinker. In *Philosophy After Lacan: Politics, Science, and Art*, ed. Alireza Taheri, Chris Vanderwees, and Reza Naderi, 27–44. London: Routledge.

Benvenuto, Sergio, and Anthony Molino, eds. 2009. *In Freud's Tracks Conversations from the Journal of European Psychoanalysis*. Plymouth: Jason Aronson.

Bianchi, Pietro. 2017. *Jacques Lacan and Cinema: Imaginary, Gaze, Formalisation.* London: Karnac.

Busiol, Diego. 2022. *Lacanian psychoanalysis in practice. Insights from Fourteen Psychoanalysts.* London: Routledge.

Castrillón, Fernando, and Thomas Marchevsky, ed. *Coronavirus, Psychoanalysis, and Philosophy. Conversations on Pandemic, Politics, and Society.* London: Routledge.

Cosenza, Domenico. 2023. *A Lacanian Reading of Anorexia.* London: Routledge.

Di Ciaccia, Antonio. 1999. The Love of God and of the Neighbour. Translated by Richard Klein. *Psychoanalytical Notebook* (3): 41–54.

Di Ciaccia, Antonio. 2015. The Queer Brother. Translated by Richard Klein. *Psychoanalytical Notebook* (29): 61–64.

Fachinelli, Elvio. 2019 [1968]. Dissident Desire. Translated by David Gutherz *Psychoanalysis and History* 21 (3): 293–300.

Focchi, Marco. 2005. The Indiscrete Language and the Unrepeatable. *The Symptom* 6. https://www.lacan.com/symptom6_articles/focchi1.html. Accessed 30 July 2024.

Focchi, Marco. 2008. A Spectacular Health. Translated by Gianmaria Senia. *Lacanian Ink* 31: 63–83.

Lewis, Michael, and David Edward Rose, eds. 2022. *The Bloomsbury Italian Philosophy Reader.* London: Bloomsbury.

Lippi, Silvia. 2020. *The Decision of Desire.* Translated by Peter Skafish. Minneapolis, MN: University of Minnesota Press.

Recalcati, Massimo. 2001. On the Analytic Practice of the Group Mechanism in the Treatment of "Eating Disorders". Translated by Veronique Voruz *Psychoanalytical Notebooks* 7: 107–115.

Recalcati, Massimo. 2005. The Anorexic Passion for the Mirror. Translated by Jorge Jauregui. *Lacanian Ink* 24 (25): 74–91.

Recalcati, Massimo. 2005. The Empty Subject: Un-Triggered Psychoses in the New Forms of the Symptom. Translated by Jorge Jauregui. *Lacanian Ink* 26: 73–101.

Recalcati, Massimo. 2007. Triggering Determinants in Anorexia. Translated by Jorge Jauregui. *Lacanian Ink* 30: 100–115.

Recalcati, Massimo. 2008. Madness and Structure in Jacques Lacan. Translated by Jorge Jauregui. *Lacanian Ink* 32: 97–121.

Recalcati, Massimo. 2011. Hunger, Repletion, and Anxiety. Translated by Wissia Fiorucci. *Angelaki: Journal of the Theoretical Humanities* 16 (3): 33–37.

Recalcati, Massimo. 2012. Hate as a Passion of Being. Translated by Ramsey McGlazer. *Qui Parle* 20 (2): 151–182.

Recalcati, Massimo. 2014. Separation And Refusal: Some Considerations On The Anorexic Choice. Translated by Anna Milleri. *The Journal Lacunae* 3 (2): 98–118.

Recalcati, Massimo. 2019. *The Telemachus Complex. Parents and Children after the Decline of the Father.* Translated by Alice Kilgarriff. Cambridge: Polity Press.

Recalcati, Massimo. 2019. *The Mother's Hands. Desire, Fantasy and the Inheritance of the Maternal.* Translated by Alice Kilgarriff. Cambridge: Polity Press.

Recalcati, Massimo. 2020. *The Son's Secret. From Oedipus to the Prodigal Son.* Translated by Alice Kilgarriff. Cambridge: Polity Press.

Recalcati, Massimo. 2020. *In Praise of Forgiveness.* Translated by Alice Kilgarriff. Cambridge: Polity Press.

Recalcati, Massimo. 2020. *The Night in Gethsemane.* Translated by Ann Goldstein. London: Europa Compass.

Recalcati, Massimo. 2021. *The Enduring Kiss. Seven Short Lessons on Love.* Translated by Alice Kilgarriff. Cambridge: Polity Press.

Recalcati, Massimo. 2022. *Cain's Act.* Translated by Will Shutt. London: Europa Compass.

Recalcati, Massimo. 2022. *The Temptation of the Wall. Five Short Lessons on Civil Life.* Translated by Alice Kilgarriff. Cambridge: Polity Press.

Recalcati, Massimo. 2022. Extinction of the Unconscious? A Recent Anthropological Mutation. Translated by Katherine Langley and Michael Lewis. In Michael Lewis and David Edward Rose, ed. *The Bloomsbury Italian Philosophy Reader*, 257–263. London: Bloomsbury.

Recalcati, Massimo. 2023. For a Clinical Theory of the Institution. In *Capitalism and the New Political Unconscious: a Philosophy of Immanence*, ed. Riccardo Panattoni and Fabio Vighi, 21–33. London: Bloomsbury.

Resmini, Mauro. 2013. The Italian Turn: A Certain Tendency in Contemporary Psychoanalytic Aesthetics. *American Imago* 68 (2): 271–297.

Riccardo, Panattoni, and Vighi Fabio, eds. 2023. *Capitalism and the New Political Unconscious: a Philosophy of Immanence.* London: Bloomsbury.

Ripa di Meana, Gabriella. 1997. *Figures of Lightness. Anorexia, Bulimia, and Psychoanalysis.* Translated by Sara McVane. London: Jessica Kingsley Publishers.

Tarizzo, Davide. 2020. *Political grammars. The Unconscious Foundations of Modern Democracy.* Stanford: Stanford University Press.

Selected Websites

Associazione Lacaniana Internazionale. https://www.ali-to.it/it-IT/homepage.
Associazione Lacaniana Italiana di Psicoanalisi (AliPsi). https://www.alidipsicoanalisi.it/.
European Journal of Psychoanalysis. https://www.journal-psychoanalysis.eu/.
Istituto di Ricerca di Psicoanalisi Applicata (IRPA). https://www.istitutoirpa.it/.
Istituto Freudiano. http://www.istitutofreudiano.com/.
Jonas Italia. Centri di clinica psicoanalitica. https://www.jonasitalia.it/.
La Psicoanalisi. Studi Internazionali del Campo Freudiano. http://www.lapsicoanalisi.it/.
Massimo Recalcati's official website. https://www.massimorecalcati.it/.
Scuola Lacaniana di Psicoanalisi del Campo Freudiano. https://www.slp-cf.it/.
Sergio Benvenuto's official website. https://www.sergiobenvenuto.it.
Società cittadine di psicoanalisi. https://www.lesocietadipsicoanalisi.it/.

Index[1]

[1] Note: Page numbers followed by 'n' refer to notes.

L. Di Gregorio, *Lacan in Italy*, The Palgrave Lacan Series,
https://doi.org/10.1007/978-3-031-91528-4

The manufacturer's authorised representative in the EU is Springer Nature Customer Service Centre GmbH, Europaplatz 3, 69115 Heidelberg, Germany. If you have any concerns regarding our products, please contact ProductSafety@springernature.com

Printed and bound by CPI Group (UK) Ltd, Croydon, CR0 4YY

30/09/2026

02225583-0011